The Irish Conservative Party, 1852–68

Land, Politics and Religion

ANDREW SHIELDS

IRISH ACADEMIC PRESS
DUBLIN • PORTLAND, OR

For my parents

First published in 2007 by
IRISH ACADEMIC PRESS
44, Northumberland Road, Dublin 4, Ireland

and in the United States of America by
IRISH ACADEMIC PRESS
ISBS, Suite 300, 920 NE 58th Avenue
Portland, Oregon 97213-3786

www.iap.ie

British Library Cataloguing in Publication Data
An entry can be found on request

ISBN 978 0 7165 2773 2 (cloth)
ISBN 978 0 7165 2882 1 (paper)

Library of Congress Cataloging-in-Publication Data
An entry can be found on request

Typeset in 11/12pt Bembo by FiSH Books, Enfield, Middx.
Printed by Biddles Ltd., King's Lynn, Norfolk

Contents

List of illustrations

Acknowledgements

THIS BOOK has been a long time in the making and as a result, I have accumulated many debts along the way. My principal debt is to Professor Trevor Lloyd, who not only supervised the thesis on which this book is based, but also read and commented on the manuscript of the book itself. I would like to thank him for his encouragement, his consistently helpful advice, and his exemplary patience. I would also like to thank Professor Sidney Aster, Professor Richard Rempel, Dr David Wilson and Dr Lori Loeb, the other members of my thesis committee, for their constructive criticisms and suggestions for improvements. I am also grateful to Sidney Aster for his support and helpfulness, often beyond the call of duty, over the years. I am greatly indebted to Philip Bull, who read and commented on the entire manuscript and, in doing so, greatly improved it.

A great many other people have helped me in various ways over the years. Among them I am particularly grateful to Roy Foster, who offered extremely helpful advice at an early stage of the research and to Daire Hogan who gave me the benefit of his unrivalled knowledge of nineteenth-century Irish legal history. I am also grateful to Mr David Holland and to Mr Jeffrey Lefroy, who generously gave me access to the papers in their possession. The late Isabel Napier kindly drew my attention to the unpublished family history written by her late husband, Sir Joseph Napier. I would also like to thank Professor Mel Wiebe and Ms Ellen Hawman of the Disraeli Project, Queen's University, Kingston, Canada, for their generosity in providing me with transcripts of many of Disraeli's letters relating to Ireland. My interest in nineteenth-century Irish history owes a great deal to the teaching of Gearoid O'Tuathaigh at University College Galway (as it was then). Gearoid also proved to be a model supervisor when I undertook my first forays into postgraduate research there.

I am especially grateful to my friends, Fergus Campbell and Stephen Ball, for reading drafts of sections of the book and I have benefited greatly from their comments on it. I have also learnt a great deal about Irish history (and much else besides) through conversations with them both. I have also profited over the years from conversations on various aspects of Irish history with Tom Crean, Paul Dillon and David Wilson among others. Here in Australia I am grateful to John Gascoigne of the University of New South Wales, for his help and support, and to Judith Keene of the

University of Sydney, for her hospitality in providing the ideal location in which to finish this manuscript.

The staffs of the following libraries and archives were extremely helpful while I was working on this book and I am deeply indebted to those that gave me permission to quote from the manuscripts in their care: the Public Record Office of Northern Ireland, Belfast; the Dublin Diocesan Archives, Dublin; the Gilbert Library, Dublin; the National Archives of Ireland, Dublin; the National Library of Ireland, Dublin; Trinity College Archives Department, Dublin; the Scottish Record Office, Edinburgh; the Hertfordshire Record Office, Hertford; Liverpool Record Office, Liverpool; the British Library and the Public Record Office, London; the Bodleian Library and Rhodes House Library, Oxford; the Fisher Library, University of Sydney and the Somerset Record Office, Taunton. I must also thank Noel Kissane of the National Library of Ireland for permission to examine the uncatalogued section of the Mayo papers held there and Stephen Ball for bringing these to my attention. I am also grateful to Steve (again) and to Michael Kelly for their hospitality, which made several research trips to London and its environs possible.

My family – my sisters, Maura and her late husband, Tom Glynn, Dottie and her husband, Brian McLoughlin, and Hattie and her husband, David Rogerson, my brothers, Vincent and his partner, Majella, Stephen and his wife, Anne, Tommy and his wife, Ger, and Dan and his wife, Meg – has also been a constant source of support and encouragement over the years. In particular, my sisters, Hattie and Dottie provided hospitality and encouragement well beyond the call of duty while I was working on this book. Brian also rescued at least one chapter from disappearing into cyberspace. My nephew, Danny Shields, provided valuable technical assistance and computer wizardry. My brother, Dan, also provided valuable support to the project on a number of occasions. I am also grateful to him for reading the proofs. The knowledge of and enthusiasm for all aspects of Irish culture of my late father-in-law, Seaghan Ua Conchubhair, were an inspiration and I can only hope that he would have forgiven any grammatical heresies that appear in the pages that follow. Without the love, support and encouragement of my wife, Fiona (not to mention her eagle-eyed proof-reading), this book would not exist.

The book is dedicated to my parents, Dan and Kitty Shields. Without their patience, forbearance and support it could not have been completed.

Andrew Shields
Bulli
January 2007

Foreword

The relationship between Ireland and Britain in the last quarter of the nineteenth century was dominated by three apparently intractable and interconnected issues – connected in particular by the centrality of each to the identity of the old ascendancy society of Ireland. These were the issues of land, the church and education, linked together symbolically by William Ewart Gladstone in the metaphor of the Upas Tree. While under Gladstone's leadership the British Liberal Party attempted to resolve the conflicts surrounding these issues, its ultimate incapacity to do so satisfactorily led to increasing demands for Irish political autonomy, initially in the development of a Home Rule movement. Between the Famine and the onset of this Liberal 'mission to pacify Ireland', however, these issues were a constant concern to Irish politicians, not least to the Irish Conservative Party, then still a force of some significance in Irish politics, accounting at times during this period for a majority of the Irish seats in the House of Commons. Despite the vast body of literature now existing on the political history of Ireland in the nineteenth century, including monographs on virtually every political party that achieved any strength, there is no comprehensive study of this important party in the heyday of its influence. Why is this so? Partially at least because of the dominance of a nationalist historiography, often structured around a sense of the inexorable progress towards Irish independence, in which Conservatism has been seen as irrelevant, except in a negative sense, to that grand narrative.

Andrew Shields has now done something about that gap in our knowledge of nineteenth-century Irish politics with this very important study of the Irish Conservative Party between 1852 and 1868. The dates are important: the study is framed by the initial recovery from the trauma of the Great Famine and the onset of Gladstone's famous 'mission to pacify'. It is an era in which the traditional elite of Irish society found themselves put to the test in an unprecedented way, challenged to use their role as the dominant group within Irish society to rectify the now manifest defects of the social and political order. This book is a chronicle of how they went about attempting that, and an analysis of why they failed. But it is a lot more than that. It is a study of the party to which they were attached, in terms of its strengths and weaknesses, its leaders and membership, the ethos underpinning its actions and, perhaps most importantly, the tensions that inhibited it from responding appropriately to the issues with which it had to grapple. The relationship of the party to its British Conservative allies is also a constant focus of analysis in the book, demonstrating in this particular case the abiding difficulty for Irish politicians negotiating Irish strategies in a political context in which those issues were neither fully understood nor considered sufficiently important to distract attention away from British and imperial concerns.

The author uses the methods of the political historian as they should be used. The reader is never allowed to lose sight of the wider society within which politicians operate, but we are also introduced to their more private world of political negotiation and discussion. In all this Dr Shields demonstrates a great mastery of his sources; he has explored comprehensively all the relevant private collections of correspondence, the newspapers of the period, and other contemporary publications. He places his work confidently within the context of the previous literature, and develops his interpretation and argument consistently towards his conclusions about the party's demise. Based on too exclusive a social and religious base, the more prescient amongst its members frustrated by the more rigid attitudes and immediate vested interests of their colleagues, not having open to them the opportunities available to their British counterparts of alliances with newer urban wealth, the Irish Conservative Party could not weather the storms endemic in Irish politics at that time. This is not, however, a chronicle of the party's history. Dr Shields adroitly weaves the story of the Irish Conservative Party in this period into detailed and comprehensive analyses of the three issues dominating the politics of the period. He shows how Irish Conservatives were divided over how much could be conceded to tenant farmers on their claim for more secure tenure of the land, to what extent the position of the Church of Ireland was fundamental to the constitution which bound Ireland to England, and how Protestant principles of religious education could be preserved while providing an educational system acceptable to a Roman Catholic majority.

This is a scholarly book of great quality, but it is also timely. The issues dealt with may seem remote from the contemporary world, but in an Ireland coming to terms with the complexities of its history this book, with its dispassionate but not unsympathetic portrayal of the aspirations of a largely forgotten elite, provides a reminder that those who may lose out in the tide of history do nonetheless tell us something valuable about how a society and its values evolved.

Philip Bull,
La Trobe University,
Melbourne

Introduction

THIS BOOK is a study of the political opinions and attitudes of the leaders of the Irish Conservative Party between the years 1852 and 1868. It was in these years that the party achieved its greatest electoral success. In 1859, when it won 55 seats out of the 105 Irish seats at Westminster, it even accounted for the majority of the Irish representation there. It had also achieved a degree of success in attracting Irish Catholic support, although the base of its support remained the Irish Protestant, particularly the Church of Ireland, community. The party's relative success in this period owed much to the ability of its leaders, who were a group of shrewd politicians with a lengthy experience of Irish politics. Throughout this book, the focus is on the national elite of the party in Ireland, rather than on the party at the local level. While this leading group exercised a major influence on Irish politics in this period, it has not yet been the subject of detailed scrutiny. In order to redress this neglect, this book examines closely the relationship between the leaders of the Conservative Party in Ireland and their counterparts at Westminster. It also explores the complex ways in which they interacted with the principal forces opposed to them in Irish society, in particular, the Roman Catholic Church. The ambivalent relationship that existed between the leaders of the Irish Conservative Party and their counterparts in the Independent Irish Party from 1852 onwards is also analysed.

Through a series of detailed analyses of Conservative Party attitudes and policies on the land question (Chapters 2 and 3), on the national education system (Chapters 5 and 6) and on Church questions (Chapters 4 and 7), the book examines whether an 'indigenous' Irish Conservatism existed, different both in tone and content from its English counterpart. Chapters 2 and 3 reveal the divisions which existed even *within* the Irish Conservative Party on the issue of the 'rights' of property, while Chapters 4 and 7 demonstrate the difficulties which the Evangelical sympathies of many Irish Conservatives created for the more pragmatic members of the party leadership.

The chapters on the education question and those on the position of the Church of Ireland reveal the central importance that Irish Conservatives attached to religious issues. Chapter 4 examines the relationship between the Irish Conservative Party and the Roman Catholic Church during and in the aftermath of the controversy over the Ecclesiastical Titles Bill. It precedes the two chapters on the education question, as an understanding of the effects of the controversy over the bill is important for a comprehension of the course of Irish politics, particularly with regard to religious questions, in the later 1850s and early 1860s. The controversy over the national system of education in Ireland also brought into stark relief the problems inherent in the Church of Ireland's claim to be the 'national' Church there. Chapter 7 deals with Irish Conservative attempts to defend its position as the Established Church in Ireland in the years leading up to disestablishment. The disestablishment crisis marked a turning point in the history of Irish Conservatism, which changed its character after 1869. In general, then, the book is structured thematically, although the various sections within it are organised in a chronological fashion.

More generally speaking, the book is concerned with the obstacles faced by Irish Conservatives in attempting to have their priorities reflected in the policies pursued by the leaders of the party in Britain. It also delineates Irish Conservative attitudes towards the Union with Britain and their attempts to ensure that the post-Union political dispensation in Ireland would not see their position there undermined. The conflicting pressures on the Conservative Party leadership at Westminster, whose concerns were not always necessarily those of Irish Conservatives, will also be considered. In addition, the book examines the way in which British cabinets reached decisions on Irish policy and the extent to which Irish politicians influenced this process. It may be useful, at this point, to indicate what this book is *not*: it is not a general political history of the mid-Victorian period in Ireland, although such a work is much needed, nor is it a general history of the Irish Conservative Party or a history of popular Conservatism in Ireland during this period.[1]

Until recently, the history of the Irish Conservative Party has been a neglected topic among Irish historians. This was largely due to the fact that the focus of modern Irish historiography has been on Nationalist political organisations and movements. As a result, both the Irish Conservative Party and the Irish Liberal Party have received insufficient attention. Indeed, the first discussion of both parties to be based on extensive primary research was that by K.T. Hoppen in his study of electoral politics and society in nineteenth-century Ireland.[2] It remains the most useful account yet published. The detailed account of mid-nineteenth-century Irish society in Hoppen's work means that it is an essential starting point for any student of the period. His book also provides an immensely detailed and closely researched account of the way in which the Irish electoral system worked in the years between 1832 and 1885. However, Hoppen's emphasis on the localist nature of Irish politics in this period means that he devotes comparatively little attention to the intellectual and ideological currents which shaped Irish Conservatism. Moreover, it could be argued that any work that focuses as closely on electioneering, as Hoppen's book does, is likely to overemphasise the importance of localism in political life. In this respect, Hoppen's work is admirably complemented by Joseph Spence's ground-breaking PhD thesis on Irish Conservative thought from the passing of the Reform Act in 1832 to the Famine.[3]

Spence's thesis is particularly concerned with the *mentalité* of a small but influential circle of Irish Conservatives, centred on such figures as Isaac Butt[4] and Sheridan Le Fanu. This circle was closely associated with the *Dublin University Magazine*, which had been established in Dublin in 1833. It was the most influential and intellectually challenging journal associated with the Irish Conservative Party.[5] Spence argues that this group was motivated by a Protestant nationalism, expressed in its criticisms of Irish Catholicism for being unduly influenced by Rome and its simultaneous willingness to criticise the British government for its neglect of Irish economic interests.[6] Indeed, one of the key texts produced by this group, Isaac Butt's *The Famine in the Land*, was a comprehensive onslaught on the failures of the Irish policies of the Whig-Liberal government during the Famine. Butt was particularly critical of the Whig government's failure to treat the relief of distress in Ireland during the Famine years as an imperial responsibility. In his view, this was the approach that the logic of the Union had implied.[7]

A central bulwark of the intellectual position of these Conservative thinkers was their contention that the Act of Union had been a compact between two sovereign nations. As a result of this, they believed, Ireland was an equal partner in the United Kingdom and had a right to have its national interests protected by the British parliament. The primary duty of Irish Conservatives was, therefore, to ensure that Irish interests received due attention there. In their view, the 'national interests' of Ireland were closely tied up with the maintenance of the Union with Britain. From the Irish Conservative perspective, Irish economic interests were better served by remaining part of the British Empire than they would be by the Repeal of the Union. According to James Whiteside, the most likely results of such an Irish separation from Britain would be 'social confusion, intestine [sic] war, [and] political anarchy'.[8] Irish Conservatives also believed that the Union could only be maintained if the predominant position of Irish Protestants, the only group there whose loyalty to the British connection was undoubted, was preserved intact.[9] In their view, Irish Nationalism posed a direct threat to the pursuit of Ireland's best interests, both in economic and in political terms.

Spence's thesis covers the period up to 1852, which is where this book commences. While his thesis concentrates on the intellectual under-pinnings of Irish Conservatism, by contrast, this book is largely concerned with the ways in which Irish Conservatives translated, or attempted to translate, their ideas into practice in the world of practical politics. The book also explores the extent to which Irish Conservatism was an indigenous phenomenon. Although Irish Conservatives shared many of the prejudices and assumptions of their colleagues in England, Scotland and Wales, the very fact of their being Irish gave their Conservatism a different flavour from that found elsewhere. The fact that Protestants were a minority population within Ireland meant that religious questions and questions of national identity had to be confronted more directly there than they did elsewhere in Britain.[10]

It was their minority position in Ireland, and the insecurity they felt about the maintenance of their dominant position there, which bred the defensiveness that was such a marked characteristic of Irish Conservatism.[11] While for many Conservatives elsewhere in Britain, opposition to concessions to Roman Catholics might be viewed as a question of principle, for Irish Conservatives such opposition could be viewed, as was the case with Catholic Emancipation, as a 'question of political life and death'.[12] As we shall see in the course of the book, this defensiveness made it extremely difficult for more moderate Conservatives to pursue conciliatory policies towards Irish Roman Catholics.

At the heart of Spence's thesis is his treatment of the galvanising effect which the introduction of Catholic Emancipation had on Irish Conservatives. The proliferation of the strongly anti-Catholic Brunswick Clubs in the period 1828–29 brought a new layer of middle- and working-class activists into the ranks of Irish Conservatism.[13] While these clubs were a transitory phenomenon, the foundation of the Dublin-based Protestant Conservative Society in 1832 was of more lasting significance. The Reverend Charles Boyton, the founder of the society, laid special emphasis on its role in uniting Protestants across class lines. He viewed this as being especially necessary to counteract O'Connell's success in mobilising Catholics behind the campaign for the Repeal of the Union. While the society had several large landowners as patrons, its most active members were a group of Dublin lawyers, lesser gentry and clergymen. For many of these men, membership of the society was their introduction to political life.[14] A number of these individuals, including such notable figures as Lord Naas,[15] George Alexander Hamilton[16] and Joseph Napier,[17] were to be leading figures in the Conservative Party in the ensuing decades. The rhetoric used by the leaders of the society combined strident anti-Catholicism with Protestant populism. This combination was to be a consistent feature of a series of such organisations in Dublin from the time of the society, through the Irish Metropolitan Conservative Society, to the heyday of the Dublin Protestant Association in the 1850s and 1860s. These groups played a key role in the revitalisation of Irish Conservatism in the period. The Conservative share of the vote, for example, increased by some 15 per cent between 1832 and 1852 from 32 to 47 per cent.[18] The Protestant Conservative Society also laid the groundwork for future innovations by the close attention which it paid to electoral matters.

Throughout the period covered by this book, the Conservative Party as a whole was in a minority in the House of Commons. The split within the party, which had resulted from Peel's decision to repeal the Corn Laws in 1846, had seriously weakened its position. As a result, its three terms in government in this period, in 1852, 1858–59, and 1866–68, all resulted from divisions within the Liberal Party. In all three cases, its survival in office was dependent on securing support across partisan lines. Consequently, throughout this period Conservative freedom of action was limited. Furthermore, Irish MPs as a body were a minority within the British parliament. The total Irish representation amounted to 105 MPs in a House of Commons consisting of over 650 MPs. Even in 1859, at the height of Conservative Party electoral success in Ireland, Irish Conservatives made up only 55 MPs, or 18 per cent, of the party's total representation of 306 MPs at Westminster. On a number of occasions between 1829 and 1852, the introduction of Catholic Emancipation and the increase of the grant to Maynooth in 1845 being notable examples, the leaders of the Conservative Party in Britain had proved themselves capable of carrying important legislation in the face of widespread opposition from Irish Conservatives.

It was obvious, therefore, that even on issues which they saw as critical, they could not hope to impose their priorities on the central party leadership. Reflecting this, Irish Conservatives made frequent, if sometimes unavailing, efforts to ensure concerted action and discipline among their ranks. At a meeting of Irish Conservative MPs held at the Carlton Club in February 1852 it was decided to hold regular conferences in order to achieve 'a general unanimity on all matters connected with Ireland'. The number of MPs involved was estimated at 'between thirty and forty', but the envisaged conferences do not seem to have occurred on a regular basis.[19] In June 1853, Joseph Napier, a prominent Irish Conservative, wrote to Lord Naas, the *de facto* leader of the party in Ireland, stressing that he 'was more than ever impressed with the importance of having our Irish party kept together'. He urged Naas to keep in regular communication 'with each...[and] every [one] of them...[and to] endeavour to arrange a united action...[and] regular conference[s] on Irish matters.' 'Without political influence...[and] power', he continued, 'any class is treated as a cypher – & hence the Protestants of Ireland are regarded as living on sufferance'. As a result, Ireland was treated 'as a mere political convenience', a 'treatment' which Napier would not submit to 'without exposure...[and] remonstrance'.[20] Unfortunately for Irish Conservatives, however, their most potent threat against the party leadership, voting against it or abstaining on critical divisions, was one that they were generally reluctant to use. In the circumstances of the 1850s and 1860s such a course of action would only have benefited the Liberal Party, an outcome they were unwilling to risk. Throughout the period covered by this book, therefore, Irish Conservative MPs generally remained loyal to the party leadership at Westminster, although at times this appeared to be in default of anything better.

This marginalised position has led Alvin Jackson to describe the Irish branch of the Conservative Party, at least up to 1886, as being merely a regional wing of the British Conservative Party. Jackson contended that, lacking a 'permanent Irish caucus', Irish Conservatives 'were little more independent than any other group of Tories possessing a geographically distinct basis'.[21] While there is some truth in this verdict this book nonetheless argues that Irish Conservatives had a greater influence within the party than this statement would suggest. This influence was strengthened because of the existence of a separate administrative structure in Ireland. In all three of the Conservative administrations that held office in the period covered by this book, Irish Conservatives generally filled the senior positions in the Irish administration and had a key influence on the development of Irish policy.

To date, the period between the Famine and the disestablishment of the Church of Ireland has been a neglected one in Irish historiography. As Roy Foster has pointed out, however, it was during this period that a number of themes were established that dominated 'Irish life and politics for the rest of the century'.[22] It is these central themes in Irish politics that are addressed in this book. These themes are first, the land question, second, the question of how to construct an education system in Ireland, at primary and at university level, which would satisfy the demands of both Irish Catholics and Irish Protestants, and, third, the related but distinct question of the future status of the Church of Ireland, the Established Church there.[23]

The history of the Irish Conservative Party deserves more attention than it has received to date for a number of reasons. These include its own intrinsic interest as the predominant political organisation representing Irish landowners, at a time when they retained their dominant social and economic position in Ireland. Irish Conservatives also played an important role within the Conservative Party itself, particularly in shaping the Irish policies adopted by the leaders of the party in Britain. Irish Conservatism was also an important influence on later political movements in Ireland. These included the Ulster Unionist Party, and, as Alvin Jackson has recently demonstrated, the early Home Rule movement in Ireland.[24] The central aim of this book, therefore, is to restore to its proper significance the vital role played by the Irish Conservative Party in Irish political life in this period.

NOTES

1   For a discussion of popular Conservatism in Ireland in this period, see K.T. Hoppen, *Elections, Politics and Society in Ireland, 1832–1885* (Oxford, 1984), pp. 286–91 and pp. 309-32. See also Jacqueline Hill, 'The Protestant response to Repeal: the case of the Dublin working class', in F.S.L. Lyons and R.A.J. Hawkins (eds), *Ireland Under the Union, Varieties of Tension: Essays in Honour of T.W. Moody* (Oxford, 1980), pp. 35–68 and Martin Maguire, 'The organisation and activism of Dublin's Protestant working class, 1883-1935', *Irish Historical Studies*, 29 (1994), pp. 65-87.

2   Hoppen, *Elections, Politics and Society*. There is also an excellent short account of the history of the Irish Conservative Party in Alvin Jackson, *Ireland, 1798–1998: Politics and War* (Oxford, 1999), pp. 58–68. For a discussion of the careers of a later generation of Irish Conservatives see 'To the Northern counties station: Lord Randolph Churchill and the Orange card', in R.F. Foster, *Paddy and Mr Punch: Connections in Irish and English History* (London, 1993), pp. 233–61. See also the same author's, *Lord Randolph Churchill: A Political Life* (Oxford, 1981), pp. 40–2, A.B. Cooke, 'Introduction: Lord Ashbourne's political career', in A.B. Cooke and A.W. Malcolmson, *The Ashbourne Papers, 1869–1913: A Calendar of the Papers of Edward Gibson, 1st Lord Ashbourne* (Belfast, 1974), pp. ix–xvi, and Alvin Jackson, *The Ulster Party: Irish Unionists in the House of Commons, 1884–1911* (Oxford, 1989). While R.V. Comerford's *The Fenians in Context: Irish Politics and Society, 1848–82* (Dublin, 1985) concentrates on the history of the Fenian movement, it is also extremely useful for the 'high' politics of this period. See also the same author's chapters on Irish political history from 1850 to 1870 in W.E. Vaughan (ed.), *A New History of Ireland, Vol 5: Ireland Under the Union, 1801–1870* (Oxford, 1980), pp. 396–450.

3   Joseph Spence, 'The philosophy of Irish Toryism 1833-52: a study of reactions to liberal reformism in Ireland in the generation between the First Reform Act and the Famine, with especial reference to expressions of national feeling among the Protestant ascendancy', unpublished PhD thesis, Birkbeck College, University of London, 1990.

4   Isaac Butt (1813–79): born County Donegal: educated Trinity College, Dublin: one of the founders of the *Dublin University Magazine*: called to the Irish bar, 1838, QC 1844: MP for Harwich, 1852, for Youghal 1852–65 and for Limerick 1871-79: president of the Amnesty Association, 1869: founded Home Government Association, 1870: leader of the Home Rule party in parliament, 1871–79: seen by other Irish Conservatives as having defected to the Palmerstonian camp from as early as 1856 onwards.

5   For Sheridan Le Fanu's political and literary career see W.J. McCormack, *Sheridan Le Fanu and Victorian Ireland* (Dublin, 1991 edn).

6   See Spence, 'The philosophy of Irish Toryism' pp. 10–15, pp. 249–50. See also D.G. Boyce, '"Trembling solicitude": Irish Conservatism, nationality and public opinion', in D.G. Boyce, Robert Eccleshall and Vincent Geoghegan (eds), *Political Thought in Ireland Since the Seventeenth Century* (London, 1993), pp. 124–41 and Alvin Jackson, *Home Rule: An Irish History, 1800–2000* (Oxford, 2003), pp. 21–4.

7   Isaac Butt, *A Voice for Ireland: The Famine in the Land: What has been Done and What is to be Done* (Dublin, 1847)

8   James Whiteside, *Essays and Lectures, Historical and Literary* [ed. by W.D. Ferguson] (Dublin, 1868), p. 202.

9   For a discussion of the contradictions and tensions inherent in this position, see D.G. Boyce, *Nationalism in Ireland* (London, 1982 ed), pp. 104–7.

10   This is not, of course, to discount the problems which the divisions *between* the various Protestant churches in Britain caused for the Conservative Party in the years

covered by this book. For the problems these divisions created for the party in Scotland and in Wales, see I.G.C. Hutchinson, *A Political History of Scotland, 1832–1914* (Edinburgh, 1986), pp. 15–17, pp. 20–25 and pp. 84–5 and John Davies, *A History of Wales* (London, 1994 edn), pp. 428–34.

11   See A.P.W. Malcolmson, *John Foster: The Politics of the Anglo-Irish Ascendancy* (Oxford, 1978), p. xvii and Spence, *The Philosophy of Irish Toryism*, p. 10.

12   See Malcolmson, *John Foster*, p. xxiv.

13   For a discussion of the composition and activities of the Brunswick Clubs, see Fergus O'Ferrall, *Catholic Emancipation: Daniel O'Connell and the Birth of Irish Democracy* (Dublin, 1985), pp. 207–9.

14   See Spence, 'The philosophy of Irish Toryism', pp. 70–4. See also Jacqueline Hill, *From Patriots to Unionists: Dublin Civil Politics and Irish Protestant Patriotism, 1660–1840* (Oxford, 1997) and the same author's, 'Artisans, sectarianism and politics in Dublin, 1829–48', *Saothar: Journal of the Irish Labour History Society*, 7 (1981), pp. 12–27

15   Richard Southwell Bourke (1822–72): born in County Kildare: son of the fifth Lord Mayo: his mother, Anne Jocelyn, was a granddaughter of the first Earl Roden: known by the courtesy title of Lord Naas until he succeeded his father as sixth Lord Mayo in 1868: educated at Trinity College, Dublin: MP for Kildare, 1847–52, for Coleraine, 1852–57 and for Cockermouth, 1857–68: Irish Chief Secretary, 1852, 1858–59 and 1866–68: Viceroy of India, 1868–72: assassinated on a visit to the Andaman Islands, February 1872.

16   George Alexander Hamilton (1802–71): born in County Down: educated Rugby and Trinity College, Oxford: prominent member of the Protestant Conservative Society in the 1830s: appointed Honorary Secretary of the Lay Association for the Protection of Church Property, 1834: MP for Dublin city, 1835–37 and for Dublin University, 1842–59: Financial Secretary to the Treasury, 1852 and 1858–59: appointed Permanent Secretary to the Treasury, a civil service position, in 1859: Commissioner of Church Temporalities in Ireland, 1868–71.

17   Joseph Napier (1804–82): born in Belfast: educated Belfast Academical Institution and Trinity College, Dublin: called to the Irish bar, 1831, QC 1844: prominent member of the Protestant Conservative Society in the 1830s: MP for Dublin University, 1848–58: Irish Attorney General, 1852, Lord Chancellor, 1858–59: Baronet, 1867: appointed to the Judicial Committee of the Privy Council 1868: one of three Commissioners of the Great Seal of Ireland, appointed, in place of the Irish Lord Chancellor, in 1874: resigned on the death of his son, William, February 1875: Vice-President of Trinity College, Dublin, 1867–82.

18   Spence, 'The philosophy of Irish Toryism', p. 13.

19   *Daily Express*, 3 February 1852.

20   Napier to Naas, n.d. [but June 1853], Mayo papers, National Library of Ireland, Dublin, Ms. 11,017 (6).

21   Jackson, *Ulster Party*, p. 23.

22   R. F. Foster, *Modern Ireland, 1600–1972* (London, 1989 edn), p. 373.

23   See Jackson, *Ireland, 1798–1998: Politics and War*, p. 92.

24   See Jackson, *Home Rule*, pp. 22–4.

ONE

The social composition of the Irish Conservative Parliamentary Party, 1852–68

THIS CHAPTER examines the social composition of the Irish Conservative Party, in the belief that this will shed new light on the general character of the party and on the reserves of strength on which it could draw. The general view of the party, as evidenced by writers on this period,[1] has been that it was pre-eminently the party of the Irish landed interest. In order to test the validity of this verdict, a detailed prosopographical analysis was undertaken of the 119 Conservative MPs elected between 1852 and 1868. As can be seen from Table 1.1, 66 or 55.4 per cent of these MPs were landowners with estates valued over £1,000. If those MPs closely related to landowning families with estates valued at over £1,000 are included in this group, this figure rises to eighty-eight MPs, or 73 per cent of the total. Some twenty-eight MPs, or 23.5 per cent of the total, were landowners with estates valued at over £10,000. This group included landowners such as Sir Charles Coote, an MP for Queen's County who owned 49,686 acres valued at £19,255 and Charles Powell Leslie, an MP for Antrim County from 1842 to 1879, who owned 49,968 acres valued at £21,500. Viscount Hamilton, the Conservative MP for Donegal between 1860 and 1880, inherited lands valued at over £50,000 on the death of his father, Lord Abercorn, in 1880. In general, the eldest sons of peers sat in parliament only until they inherited their estates.

As Table 1.2 below shows, thirteen MPs were small landowners, with estates valued at under £1,000. These MPs generally combined land-ownership with other careers. As landowners, Irish Conservative MPs, like their English counterparts, were prominent in local government. As can be seen from Table 1.3, they were well represented as magistrates on the Grand Juries, which played a key role both in local government and in the administration of justice at the local level. These positions also enhanced their influence in their localities. More senior appointments, such as those of High Sheriff and Deputy Lieutenants and Lord Lieutenants of counties, had a higher status and usually were reserved for larger landowners. Lord Lieutenants, in particular, had considerable say in the distribution of local patronage, particularly in the appointment of magistrates.[2] To secure appointment as Lord Lieutenant was a clear sign of government favour, a fact that may account for the relatively low number of Conservative MPs appointed to this position during the years covered by this book. Throughout this period, Irish landowners retained a strong presence in Irish local government, the real decline in their influence coming only after the electoral reforms of 1884–85.[3]

Table 1.1 Occupations of Irish Conservative MPs elected
between 1852 and 1868

	Number	*Percentage*
Landowners over £1,000 valuation	66	55.4
Eldest son of landowners with lands over £1,000 valuation	9	7.6
Younger sons of landowners with lands over £1,000 valuation	14	11.8
Land agents	2	1.7
Legal profession	15	12.6
Merchants/industrialists/members of the higher professions	7	5.9
Civil servants	2	1.7
Military	3	2.5
Uncertain profession	1	0.8

Sources: This table is based on data from a variety of sources including John Bateman, *The Great Landowners of Great Britain and Ireland* (New York, 1973 edn); U.H. De Burgh, *The Landowners of Ireland: An Alphabetical List of the Owners of Estates of 500 acres or £500 Valuation and Upwards in Ireland* (Dublin, 1878) and the *Return of Owners of Land in Ireland, Showing with Respect to each County, the Number of Owners Below an Acre and in Classes up to 100,000 Acres and Upwards, with the Aggregate Acreage and Valuation of Each Class* K.C. 1876 (422), 59. The list of landowners in *Thom's Almanac and Official Directory* for 1880 (Dublin, 1880 edn) was also consulted. The figures contained in this table can be usefully compared with those in Jackson, *Ulster Party*, pp. 62–77 and those in Fergus Campbell, 'Elites, power and society in Ireland, 1979–1914' (unpublished paper delivered to the American Conference of Irish Studies, New York, June 2001). For a comparison with the social composition of the party as a whole, see Paul Smith, *Disraelian Conservatism and Social Reform* (London, 1967), pp. 126–7 and pp. 315–16. According to Smith, 73 per cent of the total number of Conservative MPs elected at the 1874 general election were landowners. See also the tables contained in J.A. Thomas, *The House of Commons, 1832–1901: A Study of its Economic and Functional Character* (Cardiff, 1939), pp. 4–5.

Table 1.2 Land holdings of landed Irish Conservative MPs elected
between 1852 and 1868

	Number	*Percentage*
Landowners under £1,000 valuation	13	10.9
Landowners over £1,000 valuation	22	18.5
Landowners over £5,000 valuation	16	13.4
Landowners over £10,000 valuation	28	23.5

Sources: See sources given in Table 1.1. The figures contained in this table can be usefully compared with those contained in the tables of the landed element among Irish MPs in Hoppen, *Elections, Politics and Society*, p. 338.

Table 1.3 Conservative MPs in local government positions 1852–68

	Number	*Percentage*
Lord Lieutenants of counties	13	10.9
Deputy Lieutenants	54	45.3
High Sheriffs	34	28.6
Justices of the Peace/Magistrates	77	64.8

Sources: These figures are derived from a variety of sources including Michael Stenton and Stephen Lees (eds), *Who's Who of British Members of Parliament*, 4 vols (Hassocks, 1976–81); U.H. De Burgh, *The Landowners of Ireland* (Dublin, 1878) and *Thom's Directory* for the years between 1852 and 1868. Some Lord Lieutenants of counties were not eligible to sit in the House of Commons, as they held seats in the House of Lords.

A simple enumeration of the number of Irish Conservative MPs who were landowners seriously underestimates the role that the landed class played within the party. A group of Irish Conservative peers, most of whom sat in the House of Lords, were more influential than most MPs. This group included Evangelical landowners such as Lord Roden[47] in Down and Lord Farnham in Cavan.[5] It also included more moderate politicians such as Lord Donoughmore,[6] the dominant figure in Conservative electoral politics in the South of Ireland, and smaller landowners like the fifth Lord Mayo and Lord Glengall, who became prominently involved in Conservative politics through their opposition to the repeal of the Corn Laws in 1845.[7]

While many Irish Conservative MPs had residences in England, most lived in Ireland for at least part of the year. Indeed, Irish Conservatives were frequently critical of their Liberal opponents for being absentees. By contrast, there were seventy-three Irish Conservative MPs who owned land

1. 'Lord Mayo': engraving from A.C. Ewald, *The Right Hon. Benjamin Disraeli, and His Times* (London, 1884)

in the constituencies for which they were elected, while ninety-three, or 78 per cent, had a residence either in or near the constituency they represented. However, many of them did have close family ties with English landowners; some, such as William Ormsby Gore, a Conservative MP for Leitrim, owned land in England themselves. Many had married into English landowning families; for example, Lord Naas was married to a daughter of Lord Leconfield, who was a major landowner in both England and Ireland.

Like their counterparts in Britain, Irish landowners also frequently served in the British army. Indeed, thirty-six of the landowning group of MPs had served either in the army or in the navy. No fewer than nine Irish Conservative MPs had fought in the Crimean war. This military group within the party included Edward Pakenham, a relative of the Earls of Longford, who was killed at Inkerman, and Sir William Verner, the long-time MP for Armagh, who had fought at Waterloo.

Irish Conservative MPs were also integrated into the British establishment by attending public schools there, which no fewer than fifty-four MPs out of the 119 had done.[31] Over half of these, twenty-eight MPs in total, were pupils at Eton. There were thirty-eight MPs who studied at either Oxford or Cambridge, a combined total greater than the thirty-five MPs who attended Trinity College, Dublin. As Terence Dooley has pointed out, the nature of their education, combined with their marriage patterns and their involvement in the British military, meant that Irish landlords made up 'an integral part of the much broader British landowning class'.[9] However, the majority of the Irish Conservatives appointed to positions in the Irish administration, particularly those holding legal offices, were educated at Trinity. All of the Irish Attorneys General appointed by Conservative governments between 1852 and 1868, for example, were Trinity educated. As Alvin Jackson has pointed out, for 'aspirant [Irish] lawyers, Trinity brooked no equal'. The college's importance to the Irish Conservative Party as a seedbed for young talent and a bastion of Conservative values within Ireland was indisputable.[10]

The next largest occupational group after the landowners were the fifteen MPs, or 12.6 per cent of the party, who came from the legal profession. For many barristers and solicitors, politics provided opportunities for advancement in their profession, which they could not otherwise have secured. For example, only practising or former barristers could hold three of the most senior appointments within the Irish administration, Lord Chancellor, Attorney General and Solicitor General. Those MPs with legal backgrounds could also hope to benefit, in time, from other forms of government patronage. Of the fifteen MPs with a legal background, ten ended their careers as judges in one or other of the Irish courts, while the most successful of them, Lord Cairns,[11] served twice as Lord Chancellor of England, and was, for a short period, leader of the Conservative Party in the House of Lords. At a time when oratorical talent was in short supply on the Conservative benches, barristers with a reputation for eloquence such as Cairns and James Whiteside[12] were a welcome addition to the party's ranks in the House of Commons. While Irish Conservative MPs were principally valued by the party leadership for their knowledge of Irish affairs, the more eloquent among them, such as Whiteside and Cairns, frequently spoke on other issues in parliament. After Whiteside's speech on the fall of Kars in

April 1856, for example, Lord Malmesbury, a senior English Conservative, noted in his diary that he believed him to be 'decidedly a greater orator than Disraeli,[13] although his Irish accent, which is very strong when he gets animated, spoils the effect on English ears'.[14] As well as this, the practical legal knowledge of men such as Cairns and Joseph Napier proved invaluable to Conservative governments of this period when considering measures on such complex issues as the Irish land question.

Table 1.4 Educational background of Conservative MPs elected between 1852 and 1868

	Number	Percentage of total
English public school	54	45.3
Irish public school	16	13.4
Oxford/Cambridge	38	31.9
Trinity College, Dublin	35	29.4
Military academies (Sandhurst, Woolwich, etc.)	9	7.6

Sources: It did not prove possible to trace the educational background of all the Irish Conservative MPs elected during this period. It is likely, however, that some of these were privately educated. The statistics for the educational background of the other Irish Conservative MPs are derived from a variety of sources including Michael Stenton and Stephen Lees (eds), *Who's Who of British Members of Parliament*; F.E. Ball, *The Judges of Ireland*, Vol. 2, 1221–1921 (London, 1926); Joseph Foster, *Alumni Oxonienses: The Members of the University of Oxford, 1715–1886: Their Parentage, Birthplace, and Years of Birth, with a Record of their Degrees*, 4 vols (London, 1888); J.A. Venn, *Alumni Cantabrigienses: A Biographical List of all Known Students, Graduates and Holders of Office at the University of Cambridge, From the Earliest Times to 1900*, Part 2, Vols 1–6 (Cambridge, 1927–54); and G.D. Burtchaell and T.V. Sadlier, *Alumni Dublinenses: A Register of the Students, Graduates, Professors and Provosts of Trinity College, in the University of Dublin* (London, 1929). For a comparison with the broader educational patterns among Irish landowners, see Terence Dooley, *The Decline of the Big House in Ireland: a Study of Irish Landed Families, 1860–1960* (Dublin, 2001), pp. 71–3.

A third group, of merchants, industrialists and professional men, accounted for seven of the Conservative MPs elected in this period. This group included such individuals as John Vance, a prominent Dublin merchant, and Jonathan Richardson, a leading linen trader in Ulster. There was also a small group of Conservative MPs with close Irish connections, who sat for constituencies in England. The most notable of these included William Beresford, the Conservative Chief Whip between 1846 and 1852 and Seymour Fitzgerald, who was Under-Secretary for Foreign Affairs in the short-lived Conservative government of 1858–59. This group, however, had only a limited influence within the party and did not, other than in exceptional circumstances, appear to take a particularly keen interest in Irish affairs.

Gentlemen's clubs (see Table 1.5) were an important meeting place for Irish Conservatives, with the vast majority of MPs being members of at least one. These clubs provided an ideal opportunity for cementing social ties built on similar educational backgrounds and political ideas. They also gave ambitious young politicians the chance to develop contacts with party leaders. The most popular club among the party's Irish MPs was the Carlton, the leading Conservative club in London. It was essentially a political rather than a social club, designed 'to be a point of union and the centre of organization for the whole party'.[15] To join it was a statement of political intent and a clear expression of identification with the Conservative cause.

Table 1.5 Club membership among Irish Conservative MPs elected between 1852 and 1868

	Number	*Percentage of total*
Carlton/Junior Carlton	90	75.6
Kildare Street Club	31	26.1
Sackville Street Club	28	23.5
National	16	13.4
United Services	15	12.6
White's	14	11.8
University [Dublin]	9	7.6
Army & Navy	9	7.6
Travellers	8	6.7
Guards	5	4.2
Conservative [London]	4	3.4
Boodles	3	2.5
Arthur's	4	3.4
Ulster	4	3.4

Sources: See the sources given for Tables 1.1 and 1.4.

Second in popularity to the Carlton was the Kildare Street Club, a cross-party club in Dublin which included Liberal landowners among its members. Membership of the Kildare Street Club was a sign of belonging to the Irish political and social elite, rather than an indication of political allegiance.[16] The premier Irish Conservative club was the Sackville Street Club, which counted many of the more prominent party men among its members. It served as the party's headquarters for electioneering purposes, especially after 1853 when the newly formed Central Conservative Society of Ireland acquired offices on the same street. The fact that the club was in Dublin, however, meant that its membership was biased towards those MPs representing southern constituencies. Northern MPs were more likely to join the Carlton Club, as they were liable to be in London for at least part of the parliamentary session. The Ulster Club in Belfast had only a small Conservative Party membership, although this changed dramatically after 1885.[17] Some sixteen MPs were members of the 'high Tory... [and] Evangelical' National Club, which was based in London.[18] Irish Conservative MPs also frequented non-political clubs such as the Traveller's Club and, reflecting the fact that so many MPs had military experience, the United Services Club and the Army and Navy Club.

The vast majority of Irish Conservative MPs elected during these years were members of the Church of Ireland. Indeed, fourteen of the 119 MPs elected between 1852 and 1868 were the sons of Church of Ireland clergymen. For example, James Whiteside's father, William Whiteside, was the Anglican curate at Delgany in County Wicklow at the time of his birth. On his father's death, Whiteside and his brother, John William, were taken under the guardianship of Reverend James Whitelaw, author of a well-known census of St Catherine's parish, Dublin. John William Whiteside later followed his father and his guardian into a career as a clergyman, serving as vicar of Scarborough between 1848 and 1864.

The dominance of the Church of Ireland within the Irish Conservative Party was shown by the fact that only two Roman Catholics, two Presbyterians and one Quaker were elected as Conservative MPs between 1852 and 1868. The longest serving of these MPs was John Pope Hennessey, the Roman Catholic MP for King's County[19] between 1859 and 1865.[20] As a whole, the party represented an alliance of three of the central pillars of the Irish establishment in this period, the land, the law and the military. The other pillar, the Church of Ireland, had its own representation in parliament through the presence of Irish bishops in the House of Lords.

The importance of the Evangelical strain within the Irish Conservative Party has generally been underestimated by writers on this period. Evangelicalism played a crucial role in uniting Irish Protestants across class and sectarian lines.[21] Such prominent figures as Joseph Napier, George Alexander Hamilton and Hugh Cairns came from this wing of the party. Of this group, Napier and Hamilton were particularly close to the Evangelical section of the Irish clergy. Joseph Napier's father, William, had been a member of a Presbyterian congregation in Belfast, and it was from this background that Napier, though a staunch Church of Ireland man in later life, acquired that 'Evangelical Protestantism' which his biographer argues 'was the great animating spirit of his life'.[22] In his early years at Trinity College, Napier's tutor had been Joseph Singer, the acknowledged leader of the Evangelical party in the Irish Church.[23] By the early 1830s, Napier's closeness to the Evangelical wing of the Church had earned him the nickname of 'Holy Joe'.

These Evangelical Irish Conservative MPs were heavily involved in the vast array of proselytising societies, which sprang up in Ireland from the late eighteenth century onwards. These included societies such as the Irish Church Missions and the Irish Society and charitable organisations such as the Association for the Relief of Distressed Protestants and the Orphan Refuge Society.[24] Irish Conservative MPs were also prominent in the Church Education Society, a largely Church of Ireland body founded in opposition to the national system of education.

When selecting candidates to fight elections, local connections and the ability to sustain the expense of a contest were predominant concerns. It was generally expected that prospective candidates would have some 'interest' in the constituency they wished to represent. In 1852, for example, John Bates, the Conservative Party agent in Belfast, identified 'local influence' as essential to the return of a Conservative candidate there. At election times, Conservative candidates frequently laid stress on their status as resident landlords. Nominating Robert Burrowes, the Conservative candidate for Cavan at the 1855 by-election, the local Church of Ireland minister, Reverend Francis Saunderson, praised him as a member of 'a family of vast possessions in the county' and of 'equally extensive reputation'.[25] In 1859, a Conservative agent in Cork, warned Lord Donoughmore that a 'stranger' could not be elected for the county seat there, while 'a popular and resident county man' stood a good chance of success.[26] The selection of candidates was frequently made at meetings of local landowners. Generally, these meetings reaffirmed support for sitting MPs. Occasionally, however, they adjudicated on disputes between rival candidates or selected new candidates to fight vacant seats. These were often stage-managed affairs, the selection of candidates having previously been decided on between the more prominent local families and the national party leadership.[27] Unless the candidate was supported by party funds or by an influential patron, it was essential that he had the resources to fund his election campaign, particularly if the seat were contested. Election expenses in such cases could be very high: in 1868, for example, Sir Arthur Guinness spent £15,000 to secure his return for Dublin city.[28] Although, given Guinness's wealth and the particular nature of the Dublin city constituency, this sum was exceptional, it does give some indication of the demands which electioneering could place on a candidate's finances. In March 1852, John Boyd, the Conservative MP for Coleraine, complained to Lord Naas that his two contests for the borough had cost him 'above £3,000' and had forced him to retire from his position as manager of the Northern Bank.[29] In practice, candidates could expect to pay substantial sums to secure election and this, in part, explains the landed domination of the Irish Conservative representation during this period.

The province of Ulster was a particular stronghold of the party with fifty-eight of the 119 Irish Conservative MPs elected between 1852 and 1868 holding seats there.[30] In total, fifty-eight MPs were elected for constituencies outside Ulster. Of these MPs, three were elected for constituencies both within Ulster and outside the province. These three were Lord Naas, who sat for Kildare and later for Coleraine, James Whiteside, who sat for Enniskillen and subsequently for Trinity College, and John Vance, who was elected for Armagh in 1867 after losing his Dublin city seat. Next to Ulster, Irish Conservatives were most successful electorally in Leinster, with thirty-one MPs being returned for the province. They were less popular in Munster and Connaught, returning only twenty-six MPs between both provinces in the period covered by this book. On occasion, however, as with James Spaight in 1857 and Michael Morris in 1866, Conservative candidates could win unexpected victories in largely Roman Catholic constituencies such as Limerick city and Galway city respectively.[31]

Landlord influence played a critical role in these Conservative electoral successes in this period, particularly in the North of Ireland. A small group of land-owning families controlled several of the county seats there. These were generally, although not always, more susceptible to landlord influence than were the borough constituencies. An example of this landlord influence was Fermanagh County, which was represented by a member of the Archdall family from 1730 to 1885. A member of the Abercorn family held a Tyrone County seat for a period of close to forty years, from 1835 to 1874. Other northern counties such as Cavan and Derry were similarly dominated by members of the Annesley and Bateson families, albeit not for such long periods.[32] Outside Ulster, three members of the Bernard family were successively MPs for Bandon between 1842 and 1863, while the Cooper and O'Hara families exercised a similar electoral dominance in Sligo.

In the mid-nineteenth century the total number of voters in Ireland represented only a small proportion of the population there. K.T. Hoppen has estimated that after the Franchise Act of 1850 the total Irish electorate amounted to 163,546, approximately one-sixth of the adult male population of the country.[33] Despite local variations, the electorate in county constituencies was also biased towards large farmers, who were more likely to vote Conservative than were small farmers.[34] Throughout this period, landlords usually instructed their tenants on how they wished them to vote at elections. While notices to quit were sometimes issued in order to ensure that tenants voted in the desired fashion and were a potent reminder of the power that the landlord held over the tenant, the implied threat was rarely acted upon. Landlords were, however, likely to insist on the early payment of arrears by those who voted against their instructions.

This exertion of landlord influence was made easier by the fact that, before the introduction of the Secret Ballot Act in 1872, voting was held in public. As a result, landlords knew how each of their tenants had voted.[35] It was one of the central tenets of Irish Conservatism that the exertion of landlord influence at election times was one of the legitimate rights of property. On those occasions when the landowner's candidate was defeated, blame was usually attached to the illegitimate influence exercised by the priests or by outside agitators who had disrupted what was, in the words of the Dublin Conservative newspaper, the *Daily Express*, the 'naturally harmonious' relationship between landlord and tenant.[36]

The backbone of the Irish Conservative Party's electoral organisation was the Central Conservative Society of Ireland, formed in February 1853.[37] As with similar bodies previously, the society had several aristocratic patrons. However, with the exception of individuals like Naas and Donoughmore, the bulk of its work was done by a group of Dublin legal men and their counterparts in other parts of the country. Although its annual meeting held in January each year after 1853 was a useful meeting point for the most prominent Irish Conservatives, the real focus of the society was on the conduct of elections. It was especially concerned with the registration of voters.[38] Given the small size of some Irish constituencies,[39] the addition of a few extra Conservative voters, or indeed the removal of some of their opponents' supporters from the register, could make the difference between the Conservatives winning or losing a seat.

The Central Society in Dublin provided local Conservative registration societies with legal expertise and information on existing electoral law. It also sought to establish such societies in areas where they did not already exist. The society frequently sent agents to the revision sessions, where new voters were registered and objections to the names on the existing register were considered. These courts were of considerable importance as, if one party or another established a sufficient majority, a contest was unlikely to be held. One example from the society's 1859 report shows the potential benefits, which this type of attention to the electoral register could bring. In the Louth County constituency, for example, the local Conservative agent reported that some 127 'Radical' voters had been struck off the electoral lists. While twenty-nine Conservatives had been removed from the register, this loss had been made up by the addition of another thirty-nine new Conservative voters. In total, the revision session saw a Conservative gain of 131 votes, an increase which guaranteed their retention of the seat. As a general election was imminent at the time the 1859 report was issued, the revision courts had taken on an added significance.[40]

The society generally operated through local agents, usually legal men, who maintained close contact with the central society in Dublin. Their funding came principally from local landowners, while the leaders of the party in Ireland received funds for election purposes from the central party organisation in England. In April 1856, for example, Lord Donoughmore attempted to found a local Registration Society for Tipperary. He estimated that a 'fund of from £60 to £80' would be sufficient to secure the services of 'professional men' to overlook the registration process. For this purpose, he, Lord Glengall, Lord Hawarden and other local proprietors had agreed to subscribe '£5 a year a piece'. At the same time, Donoughmore was also pressing landlords in Cork to set up a similar body in that county.[41]

The importance of the society in the resurgence of the party after 1852 is indisputable, but there were other, equally important, reasons for its revival. Chief among these was the decline of the Independent Irish Party, which at the general election of 1852 had appeared to pose a significant threat to landlord electoral dominance. At that election the Independent Party won forty-eight seats, although many of the MPs elected under its banner were really Liberals who had taken the 'Independent' pledge in order to be elected. The party's original stance was that it would remain independent of both the main British political parties. This position was based on an explicit rejection of Daniel O'Connell's policy of pursuing an alliance with the Whig–Liberal Party, a position that had been discredited in the course of the Famine years.[42] The leaders of the Independent Party believed that this policy had failed, in the final analysis, to achieve its professed objective of securing material improvements for the majority of the Irish population. They also believed that it was only by maintaining its independence from the two main British political parties, the Liberal party and the Conservative Party that the new party could hope to gain concessions from either of them. Like their counterparts in the later Home Rule Party, the leaders of the Independent party believed that their best hope of securing their objectives lay in holding 'the balance of power' at Westminster.[43] They also hoped that, by maintaining an independent stance, they would increase the pressure on the leaders of both of the main parties in Britain to make concessions to their demands. In their belief, it was essential that the leaders of the Liberal Party in Britain should not be allowed to take Independent Party support for granted, but rather, that it should be clear to them that they would have to earn it. However, the party's policy of remaining independent from both of the major British parties was always a difficult one to maintain and it was fatally compromised in 1853, when William Keogh and John Sadleir, two of its leading members, accepted office in the coalition government led by Lord Aberdeen.

The defection of Sadleir and Keogh from the Independent Party increased the fissiparous tendencies within it. As a result, many of those MPs who had previously taken the 'Independent' pledge reverted back to their traditional support of the Liberals. Of the MPs elected in 1852, only twenty-six remained loyal to the 'Independent' principle by 1853. The divisions between its northern and southern wings and among its leaders in parliament further exacerbated the party's difficulties. At the 1857 general election, only thirteen Independent Party MPs were elected. The party's threat to landlord influence, which in 1852 had appeared so formidable, by this time, had largely evaporated. Its effectiveness was further diminished in 1859, when its remaining MPs split on the Conservative government's Reform Bill. Although a number of Irish Catholic MPs continued to vote with the Conservative Party between 1859 and 1865, this was as isolated individuals rather than as a coherent group.[44] However, it was not until Palmerstonian inactivity gave way to Gladstonian reform, that the idea of a tactical alliance between the remaining Independent Party MPs and Conservative MPs finally lost its appeal for both sides. Such a tactical alliance would, however, only have been a temporary one and would have been based on grounds of expediency on both sides. Ultimately, the leaders of the Independent Party believed that it should not owe any long-term allegiance to either of the two main British political parties.

The decline of the Independent Party coincided with a revival of the fortunes of the Irish Liberal Party, the most consistent, if not necessarily the most potent, threat to the Conservative Party between 1852 and 1868. One of the difficulties in assessing the party's strength in this period is that the term 'Liberal', in contemporary usage, was often applied to all the non-Conservative MPs returned for Irish constituencies.[45] Thus, for example, an Independent Party MP like John Francis Maguire,[46] who in the late 1850s and early 1860s regularly voted with the Conservatives, was usually identified as a 'Liberal' by contemporary observers.

Like the Irish Conservative Party, the Irish Liberal Party had a considerable landed element. Even at the 1868 general election, for example, close to 44 per cent of the Liberal MPs elected came from a landed background.[47] Some of the largest landowners in Ireland, including the Duke of Devonshire, Earl Fitzwilliam and Lord Lansdowne were members of Whig families.[48] Like its British counterpart, the Irish Liberal Party can best be seen as a coalition of various factions, often with widely varying political objectives.[49] The leading members of the party, like their Conservative counterparts, were wealthy landowners. This 'Whig' group formed the elite of the Irish Liberal Party. While they were a minority among Irish landowners as a whole, they exercised a considerable influence within the broader Liberal Party itself. Indeed, John Vincent has estimated that, in the 1860s, no fewer than forty-six out of the total number of 184 Whig–Liberal peers owned land in Ireland.[50] The larger landowners within the party tended to be members of the Church of Ireland and, in general, were staunch Unionists and strong defenders of the rights of the Irish landed class.

Unlike the Conservatives, however, the Liberals had a strong Catholic presence within the parliamentary party. This presence included members of the Catholic gentry in Ireland, who supported the party in comparatively large numbers.[51] The party also had a strong Catholic professional element, which included journalists and barristers. Unlike their Conservative counterparts, Liberal governments regularly appointed Roman Catholics to the offices in their gift throughout this period. Most of the Irish Attorney Generals appointed by Liberal governments, including William Keogh, John D. Fitzgerald and Thomas O'Hagan, were Roman Catholics. All three men ended their careers on the bench. This 'Catholic' group of Liberal MPs was itself divided between 'moderate' Liberals who generally supported the party leadership in Britain and a more independent-minded group of Liberal MPs, some of whom broke away from the party to form the Independent Irish party in 1851.

O'Connell's tactical alliance with the Whig–Liberal Party had also given it a residual support base among Irish Catholics. Furthermore, it had more appeal to Irish middle-class opinion, particularly in the North of Ireland, than had the Conservative Party. As the party of 'Free Trade' it appealed particularly to the manufacturing interest there. It also had greater general appeal to Northern Presbyterians than had the Irish Conservative Party, with its close links to the Church of Ireland. In many respects, popular Liberalism in the North of Ireland bore a greater similarity to its counterparts in the North of England and Scotland than it did to Liberalism elsewhere in Ireland.

The history of the Irish Liberal Party has been neglected: both contemporaries and more recent historians have ascribed most of its strength during this period to the party's stranglehold over official patronage. Its relative success in Ireland has often been ascribed to its ability, often through the judicious use of such patronage, to gradually absorb other 'anti-Tory' elements there.[52] With Liberal governments holding office for the bulk of the period from 1852 to 1868, this argument undoubtedly has some validity. However, the diversity of the political views that existed within the Irish Liberal Party in this period means that it would repay further scrutiny. In this respect, there is a need for a detailed study of the party to supplement K. T. Hoppen's pioneering account.[53]

At each of the general elections held between 1852 and 1859, the Irish Conservative Party achieved significant electoral gains (see Table 1.6 below). The party achieved its greatest electoral success at the 1859 general election. In that year it won fifty-five out of the 105 Irish seats, a clear majority and an improvement of fourteen seats on its performance in 1852. The party was particularly successful in Ulster, winning all of the seats there. It also made a clean sweep of the six Dublin seats, two each for the Dublin City, County and University constituencies. This result was an improvement by eight seats on the party's performance at the 1857 election. In that election, the party had won forty-seven seats, although James Whiteside claimed that 'with more time... [and] a wiser selection of candidates'[54] it might have won three or four additional seats.

Table 1.6 election results, 1852–68

	Conservative	Liberals	Independent Party
1852	41	16	48
1857	47	45	13
1859	55	43	7
1865	47	58	11
1868	39	66	–

Sources: See B.M. Walker, *Parliamentary Election Results in Ireland*. See also the tables in Hoppen, *Elections, Politics and Society*, p. 264 and p. 289 and the table in the same author's, 'Tories, Catholics and the general election of 1859', p. 56. The estimates given for Irish Conservative electoral strength differ between the two latter sources. The figures given here are based on an analysis of the estimates of party strength given in Irish Conservative politicians' own correspondence and in contemporary newspaper accounts. However, see endnote 5 for some of the problems involved in estimating party strength in this period. See also Whyte, *Independent Irish Party*, p. 143 for a discussion of the voting strength of that party in parliament between 1852 and 1859. The figure for the number of Independent Party MPs elected at the 1865 election is taken from R.V. Comerford, *The Fenians in Context: Irish Politics and Society, 1848–82* (Dublin, 1998 edn), p. 139.

The 1859 general election was marked by the close co-operation between the Independent Irish Party and the Conservative Party on electoral matters.[55] A number of factors were responsible for this: these included Palmerston's lack of a positive Irish programme in government, which meant that the Conservatives could hope to win Independent Party support with comparatively minor concessions. The Conservative Party's prospects in Ireland had also been enhanced by events in Italy, where moves towards unification threatened Papal control over its dominions. Palmerston's anti-Papal views and his support for the unification of Italy were well known. On the other hand, Lord Derby, the leader of the Conservative Party, was perceived by Irish Catholic opinion as being supportive of the Austrian presence in Italy, which was one of the bulwarks of the papacy's position. These considerations impelled some Roman Catholics, notably Cardinal Wiseman, the Archbishop of Westminster, to support the Conservatives at the election. The government's decision to remunerate Catholic chaplains in prisons and to recognise the position of their counterparts in the military had also been designed to win Catholic support. Its award of a transatlantic packet station to Galway had also proved popular with Irish MPs, regardless of party.[56]

There was some disagreement among both contemporaries and writers on this period regarding the exact number of Conservative MPs returned at the general elections of this period. In July 1852 the *Daily Express* admitted that it was 'not very easy in some cases to fix the political opinions of the newly elected MPs'.[57] These discrepancies primarily arose from the fluctuating allegiances shown by some MPs in these years.[58] For example, four MPs previously elected as Conservatives supported the Liberal government's Conspiracy to Murder Bill in 1858. Indeed, one of these MPs, Henry Herbert had been appointed Irish Chief Secretary by Palmerston in 1857. Herbert was one of the few Irish Peelites and the vagaries of his career reflected this. Other MPs whose allegiance to the Conservative Party was equivocal at best included Sir Richard Levinge, the MP for Westmeath between 1857 and 1865, and Francis Dunne, who was successively MP for Portarlington and Queen's County.[59] These shifts in allegiances owed a great deal to the Conservative Party splits of the 1840s and to Palmerston's success in attracting Irish Conservative support. As an Irish landowner himself, Palmerston was popular with Irish Conservatives. As early as August 1853, Napier had looked to an arrangement between Palmerston and Derby as being essential for the formation of 'a really good... [and] efficient [Conservative] party'.[60] After Palmerston's death in 1865, a movement in the opposite direction, from the Liberal Party to the Conservatives, was briefly discernible. The most notable of these Liberal defectors were Michael Morris, appointed Irish Attorney General by the Conservatives in 1866, John Thomas Ball, who was appointed to the same office for a brief period in 1868 and Abraham Brewster, the Irish Lord Chancellor from 1867 to 1868.

Although, as we have seen, the majority of Irish Conservative MPs came from landowning families, these men were not necessarily the most influential members of the party. Many of them, in fact, fit H.J. Hanham's description of English county members; 'The typical county member was a solid county gentleman or the son of one of the lesser peers... He was not a politician in the ordinary sense, rarely spoke in the House [of Commons] and spent a great deal of the [parliamentary] session in the country.'[61] The diary of Henry Bruen, a Conservative MP for Carlow for twenty-three years, closely fits this description. It is only at election times that his diaries become political, and then, usually merely describe his canvassing in Carlow. National politics are rarely touched on.[62] The poor attendance at Westminster by Irish Conservative MPs was frequently criticised by the Irish Conservative press. For example, one MP, Sir William Verner, did not attend a single vote in the House of Commons in the session of 1853–54.[63] When Thomas Connolly, the Conservative MP for Donegal County, voted in a division in February 1853, the *Daily Express* observed sarcastically that the 'rarity of this occurrence' meant that it deserved special notice.[64] This problem of slack attendance by Irish Conservative MPs was particularly acute at times when the party was in opposition and seemed to have little chance of attaining office. While these county gentlemen were the backbone of the party in terms of its parliamentary strength, the intellectual leadership of the party lay elsewhere.

Throughout the years 1852–66 this elite of the Irish Conservative Party remained remarkably consistent. This leading group had a lengthy experience of Irish Conservative politics, all having been involved from the 1830s onwards. They were also drawn from a small self-contained circle. Along with Lord Naas, three times Irish Chief Secretary between 1852 and 1868, other members of this group were Joseph Napier and his brother-in-law, James Whiteside. Whiteside was married to Napier's sister, Rosetta and the two men maintained an extremely close political alliance throughout their parliamentary careers. Both men had grown up in Evangelical Protestant households and had gone on to study at Trinity College, Dublin. They were both highly intelligent, articulate and well-read men. Temperamentally, they were polar opposites: while Napier was extremely cautious and diplomatic, Whiteside was far more impetuous and volatile in nature. One contemporary described the two men in the following terms: 'While Whiteside was all effervescence, reminding one of a mountain torrent after rain, foaming, seething, boiling, overrunning with power and impetuosity, Mr Napier was cool as an icicle, quiet, smooth, calm, unruffled.'[88] Napier's suave and rather 'unctuous'[66] manner led some contemporaries to doubt the sincerity of his religious convictions. Indeed, one contemporary account claimed that he was 'generally regarded as a lying, deceitful, double faced hypocrite with a profession of religion that was altogether false'.[67] From a reading of Napier's correspondence with other party leaders, this appears a notably unfair assessment of his character, although he did display the Victorian tendency to equate worldly success with divine favour.[68]

Unlike Napier, Whiteside was personally popular with the majority of his backbench colleagues. However, his impetuosity and reputation for

2. '*James Whiteside*': sketch from the *Dublin University Magazine*,
March 1849

indiscretion meant that some of the leaders of the Conservative Party were
wary of him. In a letter in which he praised Napier's 'clear sense and habits
of business', Lord Derby,[69] the leader of the Conservative Party, worried that
Whiteside carried 'more sail than ballast'.[70] These temperamental differences
meant, however, that the two men's gifts were essentially complementary. It

was claimed by one contemporary observer that the two men 'co-operate[d] on all occasions and so tenfold increase[d] their strength'.[71] Whiteside's principal gift was as a parliamentary speaker, while Napier played a much more active role in the formulation of Irish policy and in the drafting of legislation.

Lord Naas was a more stolid figure than Whiteside and he was less intellectually inclined than Napier. Indeed, one Nationalist newspaper described him as a 'fat, steady country gentleman'.[72] Although he was hardly noteworthy as a parliamentary debater[73] or as an original thinker Naas combined the talents of a shrewd party manager with those of an efficient administrator. He was also an excellent electoral strategist, a role in which he was ably assisted by Thomas Edward Taylor, the Irish-born Chief Whip of the Conservative Party between 1859 and 1868.[74] Like Napier and Whiteside, Naas grew up in a strongly Evangelical household. Unlike them, however, he proved notably moderate in his religious opinions. He was close to Disraeli, who respected his judgement, a 'quality' he believed to be 'rare, in any degree in an Irishman'. In 1866 Disraeli argued that this combination of 'eminent judgement' with 'a complete knowledge of Ireland' made Naas an ideal Irish Chief Secretary.[75] In the Conservative governments of 1852 and 1858–59 this group of senior Irish Conservatives, along with Lord Eglinton,[76] the Scottish-born Lord Lieutenant, played a key role in formulating Irish policy. Together with other prominent Irish Conservatives like Taylor and George Alexander Hamilton, these three men were given a good deal of freedom in doing so by the leaders of the party in England.[77]

After the abolition of the Irish parliament as a result of the Act of Union of 1800, Irish MPs attended the Westminster parliament rather than the Irish parliament at College Green, Dublin, as they had previously done. With the abolition of the Irish parliament, the framing of Irish legislation became the direct responsibility of the British government. Despite the Act of Union, however, the administrative structures in Ireland remained markedly different from those that existed in the rest of Britain.[78] The nominal head of the Irish administration remained the Lord Lieutenant, who resided for the greater part of the year at the Vice-Regal lodge in Dublin. As the representative of the British Monarch in Ireland, the Lord Lieutenant played an important ceremonial role there. As a result, in Gearoid O'Tuathaigh's words, a wealthy 'nobleman who had already attained distinction in politics or diplomacy'[79] usually filled the office. The position, in theory at any rate, was an extremely powerful one. The Lord Lieutenant had a considerable say in the distribution of government patronage in Ireland, in the management of the armed forces stationed there and in the running of the Irish financial departments. The extent of the Lord Lieutenant's contribution to the actual framing of Irish policy, however, depended largely on the character and the political ability of the incumbent and on his relationship with the Chief Secretary of the day. During his two terms as Lord Lieutenant in 1852 and 1858–59, for example, Lord Eglinton played a much more direct role in the formulation of Irish policy than did Lord Abercorn, who held the position between 1866 and 1868 and from 1874 to 1876.

Unlike the Lord Lieutenant, the Chief Secretary was generally an MP and had the responsibility for defending the Irish policies of the government in which he served in the House of Commons. In general, he was more involved in the day-to-day administration of Irish affairs than was the Lord Lieutenant. The responsibilities of the Chief Secretary were exceptionally varied and this fact has led Norman Gash to describe the position as the equivalent of 'Prime Minister, Home Secretary, First Lord of the Treasury, President of the Board of Trade, and Secretary for War rolled into one'.[80] The post was often given to promising young politicians, a notable example being Sir Robert Peel who served as Chief Secretary between 1812 and 1818. In this respect, it proved a testing ground for the administrative abilities of a number of young MPs like Peel, Lord Melbourne and Arthur Balfour, who later achieved political prominence. Naas' case was slightly different, however: despite his administrative ability, he had neither the political ability nor the personal inclination to aspire to be a front-rank politician. He was also unusual in being Irish-born, as most of the Conservative Chief Secretaries appointed before him were English. It is probable that his appointment stemmed from the absence of men of proven administrative ability on the Conservative Party front bench. It may also have been due to the recognition, on the part of the leaders of the party in Britain, of the need to be sensitive to Irish Conservative opinion after the damaging split that had occurred within the party over Peel's decision to repeal the Corn Laws.

In carrying out the duties of his position, the Chief Secretary relied heavily on the advice he received from the Under-Secretary, the senior official in Dublin Castle and from the Irish law officers. While the position of the Under-Secretary was, in theory at least, a non-political one, the senior law officers, that is the Attorney General and the Solicitor General, were usually political appointees. As this book clearly demonstrates, they exerted a considerable influence in shaping the policies pursued by the Irish administration. More often that not, they held seats at the Westminster parliament and stood in for the Chief Secretary there, when he was absent in Ireland.

As a result of Naas' political inexperience in his first period as Chief Secretary in 1852, the Lord Lieutenant, Lord Eglinton and the Irish law officers, and in particular, the Attorney General, Joseph Napier, played an unusually prominent role in determining the policies pursued by the Irish administration. Along with the law officers, the Irish Lord Chancellor, the senior judge in the Irish judicial system, also played an important role as an adviser to the government on both legal issues and the general administration of the country. Irish Lord Chancellors tended to be former barristers, who had gone on to make a reputation in parliament. Given its seniority, the appointment was an especially prized one and it was this fact that accounted for James Whiteside's bitterness on being passed over for the office in 1866.

The framing of policy by the Irish administration was complicated by the fact that all of the major decisions it reached had first to be approved by the British cabinet before they could be implemented. In consequence, the Lord Lieutenant and the Chief Secretary had to keep in regular contact with both the Prime Minister and the Home Secretary, who was the member of the cabinet with theoretical responsibility for Irish affairs. In the later sections of this book, particularly in the chapters on the education question, we will see some of the difficulties, which this complicated system of administration posed for politicians on both sides of the Irish Sea.

The detailed examination of the social composition of the Irish Conservative Party in this chapter has largely borne out the traditional portrayal of it as a landlord-dominated institution. There is no doubt that Irish landowners were the bulwark of the party's parliamentary strength, while their influence played a critical role in its electoral successes in this period. In return, they looked to the party at Westminster to protect their privileged position within Irish society. However, as a group, they tended to take little direct involvement in the initiation or formulation of Conservative Party policy. As a result, the legal element within the Irish Conservative Party, which largely took on that role, had an influence within it out of all proportion to its numbers. However, their perspectives on such questions as the land question were not necessarily identical to those of Irish landowners. In Chapter 2, we will turn to a consideration of the way in which such differences affected Irish Conservative attitudes and policy on the land question: the question which, above all others, directly affected the material interests of Irish landlords.

NOTES

1   See, for example, J.H. Whyte, *The Independent Irish Party, 1850–9* (Oxford, 1958), p. 15 and pp. 55 6.

2   For a detailed discussion of the role played by the Lord Lieutenants of counties, see Virginia Crossman, *Politics, Law and Order in Nineteenth-century Ireland* (Dublin, 1996), pp. 57–8.

3   See W.L. Feingold, *The Revolt of the Tenantry: The Transformation of Local Government in Ireland* (Boston, MA, 1984).

4   Robert Jocelyn (1788–1870): educated Harrow: MP for Dundalk, 1810–20:

succeeded as third Earl Roden, 1820: a grand master of the Orange Order: dismissed as a commissioner of the peace in 1849, as a result of his involvement in an affray between Orangemen and Roman Catholics at Dolly's Brae, County Down: the leading Evangelical among the Irish peers.

5   See Hoppen, *Elections, Politics and Society*, pp. 123–4.

6   Richard John Hely Hutchinson (1823–66): educated Harrow: succeeded his father as fourth Lord Donoughmore, 1851: entered the House of Lords, 1851 and quickly became the Conservative Party's chief spokesman on Irish affairs there: President of the Board of Trade 1858–59: senior grand warden of the Freemasons of Ireland: leading Irish Conservative spokesman in the House of Lords.

7   The fifth Lord Mayo, Lord Glengall and Lord Donoughmore were prominently involved in the great Protectionist meeting held at the Rotunda in Dublin in February 1850. See 'Free Trade and the Poor Law incompatible', *Dublin University Magazine*, February 1850, pp. 270–3.

8   For a discussion of the general pattern of education among Irish landowners, see Terence Dooley, *The Decline of the Big House in Ireland* (Dublin, 2001), pp. 70–3.

9   See Dooley, *Decline of the Big House*, p. 74.

10 For a discussion of the role of Trinity College in Irish intellectual life, see R.F. Foster, *The Irish Story: Telling Tales and Making it Up in Ireland* (London, 2001), pp. 49–50. See also Jackson, *Ulster Party*, p. 63.

11 Hugh McCalmont Cairns (1819–85): educated Belfast Academical Institution and Trinity College, Dublin: called to the English bar, 1841, QC, 1856: MP for Belfast, 1852–66: English Lord Justice of Appeal 1866–68, Lord Chancellor, 1868 and 1874–80: led the Conservative Party in the House of Lords 1868–69: a stern Evangelical and the most successful Irish Conservative politician of his generation.

12 James Whiteside (1806–76): born County Wicklow: educated Trinity College, Dublin: called to the Irish bar, 1830, Q.C. 1841: came to prominence through his defence of Daniel O'Connell and William Smith O'Brien at their state trials in 1843 and 1848 respectively: regarded along with Isaac Butt as the leading orator at the Irish bar: MP for Enniskillen, 1851–59 and for Dublin University, 1859–66: Irish Solicitor General 1852, Attorney General, 1858–59, Lord Chief Justice, 1866–76.

13 Benjamin Disraeli (1804–81): born London: educated Higham Hall: MP for Maidstone, 1837–41, for Shrewsbury, 1841–47 and for Buckinghamshire, 1847–76: entered the House of Lords as the Earl of Beaconsfield, 1876: Chancellor of the Exchequer, 1852, 1858–59 and 1866–68: Prime Minister, 1868 and 1874–80: leader of the Conservative Party, 1868–81.

14 Earl of Malmesbury, *Memoirs of an Ex-minister*, 2 vols (London, 1884), Vol. 2, p. 46. Opinions about Whiteside's abilities as a parliamentary speaker tended to divide along partisan lines. Thus, for example, Sir William Fraser described him as the best 'natural orator' that he had ever heard, while E.M. Whitty claimed that his 'failure... in the House of Commons was most overwhelming' as a result of his bringing the 'contentions of... [his] native arena' into the House of Commons. See Sir William Fraser, *Disraeli and his Day* (London, 1891), pp. 390–1 and E.M. Whitty, *St Stephens in the Fifties: The Session, 1852–53, a Parliamentary Retrospect with an Introduction by Justin McCarthy and Notes by H.M.W.* (London, 1906), p. 43.

15 Norman Gash, *Politics in the Age of Peel: A Study in the Technique of Parliamentary Representation, 1830–1850* (Hassocks, 1977 edn), p. 398.

16 See R.B. McDowell, *Land and Learning: Two Irish Clubs* (Dublin, 1993). See also Dooley, *Decline of the Big House*, p. 62.

17 See Jackson, *Ulster Party*, p. 73.

18 John Wolffe, *The Protestant Crusade in Great Britain, 1829–1860* (Oxford, 1991), p. 215.

19 King's County was the name used by contemporaries for present-day County Offaly.

20   John Pope Hennessey (1834–91): born Cork city: educated Queen's College, Cork: clerk in the Privy Council Office, 1855–59: MP for King's County, 1859–65, Home Rule MP for North Kilkenny, 1890–91: called to the English bar, 1861: Governor of Labuan, 1867–71, Administrator of West African settlements, 1872–73, Governor of the Bahamas, 1873–74, Governor of Windward Islands, 1875–77, Governor of Hong Kong, 1876–81, Governor of Mauritius, 1882–87, knighted 1880.

21   See Jackson, *Ireland, 1798–1998*, pp. 66–7.

22   Alexander Charles Ewald, *The Life and Letters of the Right Hon[oura]ble Sir Joseph Napier bar[one]t* (2nd edn, London, 1892), p. 47.

23   Singer's son, Paulus, later married Napier's daughter, Cherry. For an account of Singer's career see Desmond Bowen, *The Protestant Crusade in Ireland, 1800–70: A Study of Protestant–Catholic Relations Between the Act of Union and Disestablishment* (Dublin, 1978), pp. 67–8.

24   For a discussion of the Evangelical strain within the Church of Ireland see Bowen, *Protestant Crusade in Ireland* and David Hempton and Myrtle Hill, *Evangelical Protestantism in Ulster Society, 1740–1890* (London, 1992).

25   *Daily Express*, 9 April 1855.

26   Fitzsimons to Donoughmore, 13 April 1859, Donoughmore papers, Trinity College Dublin, Manuscripts Department, H/19/1/489.

27   See, for example, Alymer to Naas, n.d., Mayo papers, National Library of Ireland, Dublin, 11,018 (1), Davison to Naas, 31 August 1853, Mayo papers 11,017 (5), the diary of Henry Bruen for 11 April 1859, Bruen Diary, National Archives of Ireland, Dublin, 1175/1, and Brownlow to Naas, 18 April 1859, Mayo papers, 11,025 (15).

28   See Hoppen, *Elections, Politics and Society*, p. 84.

29   Boyd to Naas, 27 March 1852, Mayo papers, 11,018 (3).

30   See B.M. Walker (ed.), *Parliamentary Election Results in Ireland, 1801–1922* (Dublin, 1978). Throughout this book, Ulster refers to the nine counties of the province of Ulster rather than the six counties of present day Northern Ireland.

31   For a discussion of the reasons for these victories, see Hoppen, *Elections, Politics and Society*, p. 59 and pp. 446–7. However, Hoppen's portrayal of Morris downplays his acute legal and political intelligence. See Maud Wynne, *An Irishman and his Family: Lord Morris and Killanin* (London, 1937). See also Foster, *Lord Randolph Churchill*, p. 42.

32   For a discussion of landlord influence see B.M. Walker, *Ulster Politics: The Formative Years, 1868–86* (Belfast, 1989), pp. 2–5. See also Peter Gibbon, *The Origins of Ulster Unionism: The Formation of Popular Protestant Politics and Ideology in Nineteenth Century Ireland* (Manchester, 1975), pp. 114–15.

33   K.T. Hoppen, *Ireland Since 1800: Conflict and Conformity* (Harlow, 1989 edn), p. 114.

34   See Hoppen, *Elections, politics and society*, pp. 17–18. See also Liam McNiffe, 'The politicisation of Leitrim, Sligo and Mayo in the general election of 1852' (unpublished MA thesis, St Patrick's College, Maynooth, 1979), pp. 96–8.

35   The nineteenth-century Irish electoral system is examined in detail in Hoppen, *Elections, Politics and Society*, see in particular pp. 1–73. See also J.H. Whyte, 'Landlord influence at elections in Ireland, 1760–1885', *English Historical Review*, 80, (1965), pp. 740–60.

36   *Daily Express*, 13 June 1853. See also Hoppen, *Elections, Politics and Society*, pp. 145–51.

37   See the report of the first meeting in the *Daily Express*, 1 March 1853. There is an excellent discussion of the parliamentary and electoral organisation of the Conservative Party in England just prior to this period in Norman Gash, 'The organisation of the Conservative Party, 1832–46: part 1: The Parliamentary Organization' in *Parliamentary History*, 1 (1982), pp. 137–81. The second part of this article, 'The organisation of the Conservative Party, 1832–46: part 2: the electoral organization' is in *Parliamentary History*, 2 (1983), pp. 131–52.

38 The annual reports of the society laid special stress on its role in this area. See, for example, the *Daily Express*, 28 January 1854, the *Daily Express*, 26 January 1856 and the *Dublin Evening Mail*, 30 January 1857. See also the *Report of the Sub-Committee to the Central Conservative Society of Ireland* (Dublin, 1859), pp. 1–3.

39 For example, there were only seventy-one voters in the Portarlington constituency in 1851. See Clarke to Donoughmore, 22 May 1851, Donoughmore papers, H/11/1/22.

40 See the *Report of the Sub-Committee*, pp. 3–6. The *Report* details the society's activities throughout the country, and concludes that, with one exception, wherever a 'Conservative Registration Society exist[ed], or where the Registry... [was] attended to by competent agents, an improved registration has invariably been the result.' *Report of the Sub-Committee*, p. 1. For a discussion of the activities of election agents and registration societies see B.M. Walker, 'Party organisation in Ulster, 1865–92: registration agents and their activities', in Peter Roebuck (ed.), *Plantation to Partition: Essays in Ulster History in Honour of J.C.L. McCracken* (Belfast, 1981), pp. 191–209. For Donoughmore's attempts to found registration societies in Tipperary and Cork, see Donoughmore to Derby, 1 April 1856, Derby papers, Liverpool Record Office, 158/6. See also Naas to Derby, 29 June 1855, Derby papers, 155/9 and Hamilton to Derby, 26 June 1855, Derby papers, 150/9, both of which claim that with financial support from the party in England, the Central Conservative Society could ensure that 'several seats' would be gained by the party at the next general election.

41 See Whyte, *Independent Irish Party*. See also S.R. Knowlton, *Popular Politics and the Irish Catholic Church: The Rise and Fall of the Independent Irish Party, 1850–1859* (Stanford, CA, 1991).

42 See Donnelly, *The Great Irish Potato Famine* (Stroud, 2002), pp. 194–9.

43 There is an interesting discussion of the principle of 'independent opposition' as it was understood by Charles Stewart Parnell in Frank Callanan, *The Parnell Split, 1890–91* (Cork, 1992), pp. 204–18.

44 See Whyte, *Independent Irish Party*, p. 154. For the brief revival of the Independent Party in 1865–66, see Comerford, *Fenians in Context*, pp. 139–42.

45 This practice is, indeed, still followed by some recent reference works, which include all of the Independent Party MPs elected between 1852 and 1859 in the Liberal Party ranks. See, for example, Chris Cook and John Stevenson, *The Longman Handbook of Modern British History, 1714–1987* (Harlow, 1983) and Robert Blake, *The Conservative Party from Peel to Thatcher* (London, 1985).

46 John Francis Maguire (1815–72): born Cork city: called to the Irish bar, 1843: founder and editor of the *Cork Examiner*. MP for Dungarvan, 1852–65, for Cork city, 1868–72: Mayor of Cork, 1853, 1862, 1863 and 1864: awarded a Papal knighthood, 1856.

47 See Hoppen, *Elections, Politics and Society*, p. 338.

48 See Vincent, *Formation of the British Liberal Party* (Hassocks, 1976 edn), pp. 6–7.

49 See J.P. Parry, *The Rise and Fall of Liberal Government in Victorian Britain* (New Haven, CT, and London, 1993), pp. 6–7.

50 See Vincent, *Formation of the British Liberal Party*, p. 6.

51 See Hoppen, *Elections, Politics and Society*, p. 127.

52 For a discussion of the role that the exercise of patronage by Liberal governments played in the decline of the Independent Irish party, see Whyte, *Independent Irish Party*, p. 147.

53 See Hoppen, *Elections, Politics and Society*, pp. 258–78. See also Paul Bew and Frank Wright, 'The agrarian opposition in Ulster politics, 1847–87', in Samuel Clark and J.S. Donnelly (eds), *Irish Peasants: Violence and Political Unrest, 1780–1914* (Manchester, 1983), pp. 192–229, G. Greenlee, 'Land, religion and community: the Liberal Party in

Ulster, 1868–85', in Eugenio Biagini (ed.), *Citizenship and Community: Liberals, Radicals and Collective Identity in the British Isles, 1865–1931* (Cambridge, 1996), pp. 253–75, and G.L. Bernstein, 'British Liberal politics and Irish Liberalism after O'Connell', in S.J. Brown and D.W. Miller (eds), *Piety and Power in Ireland: Essays in Honour of Emmet Larkin* (Belfast and Notre Dame, 2000), pp. 43–64.

54 Whiteside to Jolliffe, 18 April 1857, Jolliffe papers, Somerset Records Office, Taunton, DD/HY/24/11.

55 K.T. Hoppen, 'Tories, Catholics and the general election of 1859', *Historical Journal*, 13 (1970), 48–76.

56 See Hoppen, 'Tories, Catholics and the general election of 1859', p. 53.

57 *Daily Express*, 26 July 1852.

58 See J.B. Conacher, *The Peelites and the Party System, 1846–52* (Newton Abbot, 1972), p. 115. See also the same author's, *The Aberdeen Coalition, 1852–1855: A Study in Mid-Nineteenth-Century Party Politics* (Cambridge, 1968), pp. 556–8.

59 The difficulty of ascribing political labels to such MPs is exemplified by the case of Sir Robert Ferguson, described by J.B. Conacher as 'a Whig' in *Aberdeen Coalition*, p. 557 and as 'largely apolitical' by K.T. Hoppen in *Elections, Politics and Society*, p. 269. Ferguson's vote oscillated between the two main parties throughout the 1850s, although in May 1859 he promised Taylor that he would give the Conservatives 'a general support'. See Taylor to Donoughmore, 15 May 1859, Donoughmore papers, H/19/1/1604.

60 Napier to Naas, n.d. [but probably August 1853], Mayo papers, 11,017 (14). In a letter to Disraeli in late 1853, Whiteside referred to the Irish Conservative 'admiration for his [Palmerston's] abilities, eloquence and statesmanship'. Whiteside to Disraeli, 27 December 1853, Disraeli papers, B/XXI/W/294.

61 H.J. Hanham, *Elections and Party Management: Politics in the Time of Disraeli and Gladstone* (London, 1959), p. 4.

62 Diary of Henry Bruen, National Archives, Dublin, 1175/1–5.

63 See the *Daily Express*, 16 September 1853.

64 *Daily Express*, 19 April 1853.

65 J.R. O'Flanagan, *The Irish Bar: Comprising Anecdotes, Bon-Mots, and Biographical Sketches of the Bench and Bar of Ireland* (London, 1879), p. 405.

66 Daire Hogan, '"Vacancies for their Friends": judicial appointments in Ireland 1866–67' in Daire Hogan and W.N. Osborough (eds), *Brehons, Serjeants and Attorneys* (Dublin, 1990), p. 217.

67 J.G. Swift MacNeill, *What I Have Seen and Heard* (London, 1925), pp. 47–8.

68 On his appointment as Lord Chancellor of Ireland in 1858, Napier wrote to his wife claiming that he 'had sought it not: the Lord in his wonderful goodness has heaped upon me these great honours, so that I feel almost sinking under the load of favor'. He suggested that he needed 'many, many prayers that I may be kept faithful and humble'. Napier to his wife, n.d., quoted in Ewald, *The Life of Sir Joseph Napier, Bart, ex-Lord Chancellor of Ireland from his Private Correspondence* (London, 1887 edn), p. 166.

69 Edward George Geoffrey Smith Stanley (1800–69): born Lancashire: son of the thirteenth Earl of Derby: educated Eton and Christ Church, Oxford: MP for Stockbridge, 1820 26, for Preston, 1826–30, for Windsor, 1831-32, and for Lancashire North, 1832–44: entered the House of Lords as Lord Stanley, 1844: succeeded his father as fourteenth Earl of Derby, 1851: Irish Chief Secretary, 1830–33, Secretary of State for the Colonies, 1833–34 and 1841–45: Prime Minister, 1852, 1858–59 and 1866–68: leader of the Conservative Party, c. 1846–68.

70 Derby to Eglinton, 1 June 1852, Eglinton papers, GD3/5/53. At the time I examined the Eglinton papers, they were in the process of being re-catalogued. As a result, the manuscript numbers used here may have been changed since that time.

71   Barton to Donoughmore, 12 December 1861, Donoughmore papers, H/21/1/51.

72   *The Nation* quoted in *The Times*, 1 March 1852.

73   When applying for the Presidency of Madras in 1858 Naas himself told Lord Derby that he believed that he was better 'at administration' than 'in Parliament'. See Naas to Derby, 31 October 1858, Derby papers, 155/1A. In a letter to Spencer Walpole, written in 1867, Whiteside argued that although Naas might be considered an able 'manager' he 'never was a debater or a logician'. Whiteside to Walpole, 3 March 1867, Holland papers, 1399n.

74   Thomas Edward Taylor (1811–83): his father was the fourth son of the Earl of Bective while his brother became the first Marquis of Headfort: educated Eton: Captain in Dragoon Guards, retired 1846: MP for Dublin County, 1841–83: Conservative Whip, 1855–59, Chief Whip, 1859–68 and 1873–74: Lord of the Treasury, 1858–59, Secretary to the Treasury, 1866–68, Chancellor of the Duchy of Lancaster, 1868 and 1874–80: a party manager *par excellence*.

75   Quoted in W.F. Monypenny and G.E. Buckle, *The Life of Benjamin Disraeli, Earl of Beaconsfield*, 6 vols (London, 1910–20), Vol. 4, p. 444. In his autobiography, Sir William Gregory described Naas as 'clear-headed, able and singularly liberal in his views.' Lady Augusta Gregory (ed.), *Sir William Gregory, K.C.M.G, formerly Member of Parliament and Sometime Governor of Ceylon: An Autobiography* (London, 1894), p. 245.

76   Archibald William Montgomerie (1812–61): born in Palermo: educated Eton: succeeded his grandfather to become thirteenth Lord Eglinton, 1819: entered the House of Lords, 1834: organised mock medieval 'Eglinton tournament', 1839: Protectionist whip, 1846: Lord Lieutenant of Ireland, 1852 and 1858–59.

77   See Hoppen, *Elections, Politics and Society*, pp. 293–98.

78   For a detailed discussion of the way in which the Irish administrative system operated, see R.B. McDowell, *The Irish Administration, 1801–1914* (London, 1964). See also Gearoid O'Tuathaigh, *Ireland before the Famine, 1798–1848* (Dublin, 1972), pp. 80–97.

79   O'Tuathaigh, *Ireland before the Famine*, p. 81.

80   Norman Gash, *Peel* (London, 1976 edn), p. 22.

TWO

The Irish Conservative Party and the land question

The introduction of the Irish land bills, 1852

A S WE saw in Chapter 1, landlord dominance of the parliamentary representation in Ireland, as in the rest of Britain, was out of all proportion to their numbers.[1] Irish landlords were a relatively small group, with some 6,461 landowners with estates valued at over £500 owning over 87 per cent of all the land in Ireland. The larger landowners were an even smaller group, with 303 proprietors of estates over 10,000 acres owning over one-third of all Irish land, both rural and urban.[2] According to the 1851 census, there were 570,338 tenant farmers in Ireland, but this number underestimated those dependent on the land for their livelihood.[3] Together with their families and those of the labourers who worked on their farms, this group constituted the majority of the Irish population. Of these holdings, just under 48 per cent were fifteen acres or over in 1851, an increase of close to 17 per cent from the comparable figure in 1845.[4] This consolidation of Irish landholdings was one of the long-term effects of the Famine. The process of consolidation was further accelerated by the widespread evictions that took place during the Famine years.[5] For some contemporary thinkers, these changes had opened up an opportunity for a more efficient and profitable use of Irish farm land.

Even after the Famine, Irish tenants generally held their land from year to year. Under these yearly tenancies, landlords had, in theory at any rate, the power to increase rents annually and to evict tenants with only six months' notice. They were also under no legal obligation to reimburse tenants for improvements they had made at their own expense.[6] The critics of this system believed that the insecurity generated by such tenancies militated against tenants undertaking improvements to their land. Unlike their English counterparts, Irish landlords spent relatively little on improvements to their estates. While there was a widespread variation in the sums spent on improvements on different estates, the total landlord expenditure on improvements was no more than £7 or £8 million in the years between 1850 and 1875.[7] In consequence, many contemporary commentators were extremely critical of Irish landlords for what they saw as their failure to fulfil their social responsibilities. In particular, they criticised their tendency to invest too much of their incomes on what Peter Gray has described as 'prestigious but largely unproductive projects such as houses, demesnes and urban development'.[8] This type of expenditure was seen as being particularly wasteful at a time when many Irish tenants were living in abject poverty.[9] It was also argued that this wastefulness on the part of Irish landlords had left many of their estates heavily encumbered with debts. As a result, it was argued, this accumulated debt prevented their successors from improving their estates, as they should have done.

As a consequence of this low level of expenditure by Irish landowners, it was Irish tenants, rather than their landlords, who were generally responsible for agricultural improvements. Such improvements included drainage, the reclamation of waste land, the construction of farm buildings, manuring and so on. Despite this, if tenants were evicted, they had no legal right to receive compensation for any improvements they might have made to their holdings. As a result, the attempt to win a legal right to such compensation was to be a key component of the various campaigns for Irish land reform from the mid-1830s onwards.

The four Irish land bills devised by Joseph Napier, the Irish Attorney General in the Conservative government of 1852, were framed within this context. Napier intended that the bills would form a complete code of Irish landlord and tenant law. His objective was to preserve both the rights of the Irish landowners as he saw them and to protect the interests of those tenants who had invested in improvements to their holdings. Taken as a whole, the bills represented the most ambitious attempt at a settlement of the Irish land question made by any British government in the period between the end of the Famine and the introduction of Gladstone's Land Act of 1870. Despite this, to date, they have not received the attention from historians that they deserve.

The true significance of Napier's bills can only be understood in the context of the contemporary debates both on the reasons for and on the solutions to the problem of Irish agricultural backwardness.[10] This debate had concentrated on a number of interlinked areas. Before the Famine, much attention had been focused on what was seen as the chronic problem of Irish over-population and the related prevalence of smallholdings there. It was widely believed that these factors combined had acted as a brake on agricultural improvements in the country. Furthermore, many contemporary observers believed that the system of smallholdings in Ireland made it impossible for Irish tenants to accumulate enough capital to invest in their holdings. It was also claimed that the practice of subdividing Irish farms made it impossible for landowners there to run their estates efficiently and profitably.[11]

The success of the British 'agricultural revolution' of the late eighteenth and early nineteenth centuries, persuaded many leading political economists there, like Nassau Senior, that it was only by replicating the conditions which had formed the basis for that 'revolution' that Irish agriculture could be modernised successfully. Only then, they believed, could the chronic problems of Irish poverty and underdevelopment be addressed effectively. Essentially, their solution to the problems of the Irish land system lay in the extension to Ireland of the class structure of rural England. This system was based, in Peter Gray's words, 'on the tripartite division of labour between landlord, capitalist tenant farmer and landless wage-labourer'.[12] To secure this end, they believed that it was imperative that the small farmer and cottier class in Ireland should lose the little amount of land they possessed. This would facilitate the consolidation of their holdings into larger farms and would allow for the emergence of a class of substantial farmers in Ireland.

In the long term, they believed that this would encourage the development of a capitalist farming system in Ireland, in which the relationship between landlords and tenants would become a purely contractual one. Under this system, rents would be set by the free play of the market, that is, purely by the forces of supply and demand, rather than being based on tenants' ability to pay. It was believed that the emergence of a new class of 'yeoman' farmers in Ireland would increase capital investment in agriculture there. Such farmers would also, it was argued, be in a position to pay higher wages to the agricultural labourers who worked on their holdings than their predecessors had been.

Ironically, however, one of the long-term effects of the Famine was that it facilitated the consolidation of Irish landholdings which had been recommended by such thinkers. This was because, through death and through emigration, it had disproportionately affected the smallholders and agricultural labourers, who, as the poorest groups in Irish society, had been those most dependent on the potato. The effects of this process can be seen from the fact that while in 1845 some 35 per cent of Irish landholdings were less than five acres, by 1851 these accounted for only 20.7 per cent. By contrast, while landholdings of above fifteen acres accounted for 30.6 per cent of landholdings in 1845, by 1851 they accounted for 47.8 per cent of all of the holdings in Ireland.[13]

Some contemporary thinkers believed that this removal of the poorest section of the Irish population from the land had opened up an opportunity for its more efficient and profitable use. In a parliamentary debate in July 1849, for example, Joseph Napier described the Famine as a 'great and remedial visitation', which offered the prospect of raising Ireland 'to a state of real and permanent prosperity'.[14] As a deeply religious man, strongly influenced by Evangelical Protestantism, Napier believed that the Famine had had 'remedial purposes which in the course of trial and of judgement from above' would be 'disclosed to the observing mind and heart'.[15] As Peter Gray has shown recently, this 'providentialist' interpretation of the Famine was not restricted to Napier alone: rather, it had an important influence on the response to the potato blight by senior British politicians and administrators, like Sir Charles Trevelyan.[16] According to this interpretation of events, the Famine had been designed by providence to eliminate the social evils caused by over-population in Ireland. Ultimately, its effect would be to bring an end to the chronic poverty there caused by the Irish people's improvident over-dependence on the potato. The logical implication of this view was that it was essential that this opportunity to re-shape Irish rural society should be grasped and Napier's bills could be interpreted as an attempt to achieve this end.

Of the four bills that Napier introduced, three were designed to encourage Irish landowners to emulate their British counterparts and to invest in their estates. They were also designed to give Irish tenants access to the capital which they needed to improve their holdings. In essence, the bills were intended to facilitate efficient and profitable estate management. As such, they fell within that phase of Irish land reform that lasted from the 1840s through to the 1880s when, in Philip Bull's words, parliament attempted 'to help landlords [to] assert themselves more strongly as the providers of capital and the promoters of prosperity and order in the countryside'.[17] The most controversial of the bills, the Tenants' Compensation Bill, which was designed to give tenants compensation for improvements made at their own expense, had a different objective. It was aimed at countering the threat posed to Conservative strength in the North of Ireland by the Tenant League.

The national Tenant League was formed at a conference in Dublin in August 1850, but the organisation had its roots in the Tenant Associations founded across the country in the late 1840s. This agrarian agitation had arisen as a result of the increased insecurity felt by tenants in the years immediately after the Famine. This insecurity had been accentuated by the large-scale evictions of the Famine years. In 1849 alone, for example, over 72,000 persons were permanently evicted from their holdings. It has been estimated that, in total, close to a quarter of a million persons were evicted between 1849 and 1854.[18] Tenants were also badly affected by the poor wheat harvests of 1849 and 1850. As a result of this agricultural depression and the insecurity generated by their experiences during the Famine years, they began to organise to seek an improvement in their conditions. In 1849, a Tenant Protection League was established for this purpose in Callan in County Kilkenny. Between October 1849 and June 1850, twenty-eight similar societies were established across the provinces of Munster, Leinster and Connaught. In general, these Tenant Associations campaigned for the lowering of rents and the introduction of 'fixity of tenure' which essentially meant that tenants should not be evicted so long as they paid their rents.[19] They were strongest in the province of Leinster, which traditionally had been one of the most prosperous regions of the country. The larger farmers there had been seriously affected by the rapid fall in wheat prices, which had declined by up to 35 per cent between 1847 and 1849. Broadly speaking, the Tenant League was a movement of relatively prosperous tenant farmers, who had a long experience of production for the Dublin market and the export market to Britain.[20]

At the same time as this agitation was taking place, there was a largely separate tenant agitation taking place in Ulster. Relations between landlords and tenants in Ulster had traditionally been better than those elsewhere in Ireland. However, in the late 1840s, Ulster tenants had begun to face the same insecurities as tenants elsewhere in the country. In particular, they were afraid that landlords there would use the agricultural depression, which had followed the Famine, to attack the operation of the Ulster Custom. As well as providing for fixity of tenure, the Custom also involved incoming tenants making payments to outgoing tenants when they left their holdings. These payments generally covered both the costs of any improvements that tenants had made to their holdings and also of their 'interest' or 'goodwill' in them. This was a tacit recognition that, over time, a tenant had acquired a kind of 'property' in his holding. As K.T. Hoppen has pointed out, the chief peculiarity of the Ulster Custom was its implication 'that tenants somehow possessed property rights in land they did not own'.[21] Unlike the southern agitation, the tenant agitation in Ulster was principally directed at achieving legal recognition for the Custom there. It was strongest among Presbyterian tenants in the province and had the support of a large number of Presbyterian ministers.[22]

The problem for Ulster tenants lay in the fact that the Custom had no legal standing there and its operation was dependent on the landlords consenting to it. Many landlords were, in fact, prepared to sanction it in practice, as it meant that outgoing tenants could use the payments they received to clear off any arrears of rent they might have owed. However, Ulster landlords were generally opposed to the Custom being converted from a customary into a legal right. Many of those who favoured the modernisation of Irish agriculture, including Napier himself, were ambivalent in their attitudes towards the Custom. It was frequently argued that it drained the financial resources of incoming tenants and prevented them from undertaking necessary improvements.[23]

These two largely separate southern and northern tenant agitations were brought together at a conference held in Dublin in August 1850. The conference was attended by 200 delegates from both the south and the north of Ireland. It was also attended by a number of Liberal MPs, who were supportive of the tenants' campaign. This meeting led to the establishment of the Tenant League, which was designed to co-ordinate the activities of the various Tenant Associations across the country. The league also drew up a programme of demands, which included the introduction of fixity of tenure, the lowering of rents and the legalisation of the 'Ulster Custom' in those areas where it existed.

Unusually for an agrarian agitation, however, the conference also decided on the creation of a parliamentary party to agitate for the tenants' demands. The main proponents of the creation of a parliamentary party were Charles Gavan Duffy, a leading Young Irelander who edited *The Nation* newspaper and Frederick Lucas, an English-born convert to Catholicism who edited the Catholic newspaper, *The Tablet*. Both men believed that the new party had the potential to become a national political organisation, which might succeed, where O'Connell had failed, in uniting Irishmen across religious lines. They also believed that the extension of the Irish electorate by the 1850 Franchise Act, which had given the vote to the larger farmers there, gave the new party the opportunity to achieve considerable electoral success.[24] The league's programme, as defined in 1850, went further than a mere legalisation of the existing Custom. It demanded that rents be based on a compulsory and independent valuation of land (fair rent), that tenants should be left undisturbed in the possession of their holdings so long as they paid their rent (fixity of tenure) and that tenants should have the right to sell their 'interest' in their holding to an incoming tenant (free sale).

In the British parliament, however, Tenant League spokesmen tended to narrow down the focus of its demands. There, they generally stressed the provision of compensation for improvements as being their central demand. This was done for a number of reasons; first, as Philip Bull has pointed out, because compensation for improvements could more easily be fitted into the broad framework of British political economy than could the other demands of the league. It could be claimed that it was only natural justice that tenants should be recompensed for the outlay they had made on their holdings.[25] This argument also coincided with the view held by many contemporary British political economists that the land was essentially an economic resource like any other, which should be managed as efficiently as possible. If landlords were not prepared to invest in their holdings, tenants should not be penalised for doing so on their own initiative. Napier described this as a 'just principle, that [the] outlay of capital or labour to convert land into a farm, and to give it suitable and valuable adjuncts necessary for its beneficial occupation'[26] should be recompensed, regardless of whether it was undertaken by the landlord or the tenant.

Rather than strengthening landowners' control over their estates, the Tenant League's proposals would have clearly restricted their right to do as they pleased with them. Its proposals would have set clear limits both on their rights to raise rents and to evict tenants. In this respect, they were at variance with the proposals for Irish land reform being put forward by those British political economists which we discussed earlier. Indeed, the proposals put forward by the Tenant League suggested that a tenant acquired an interest in his holding simply through his occupancy of it, a right that had no counterpart in contemporary English law. In general, they implied a less absolutist view of the rights of property than that being put forward by contemporary British political economists. In Ireland, however, the exercise of property rights in such an absolutist fashion would have raised particular problems. As Philip Bull has pointed out, the relations between landlords and tenants in Ireland 'were historically complicated and confused'.[27] Many landlords in Ireland ultimately owed the titles to their land to the dispossession of the original owners and this fact had left many Irish tenants, even those who were not descended from those who originally owned the land, with a strong sense of grievance. There was also a general belief in Ireland that long-term occupancy gave tenants some rights over their holdings.[28]

From the 1830s onwards, a number of Irish thinkers began to question the assumptions on which the British political economists' recommendations for Irish land reform were based. Unlike their British counterparts, these men were not professional economists, but instead were practically involved in the Irish land question themselves as farmers, land agents and even as landowners. The ideas of these thinkers were to have a considerable influence on the programme put forward by the Tenant League. Among the most notable of them were William Conner and William Blacker. Both men believed that Irish circumstances were essentially different to those existing in England. Consequently, they believed that models derived from the English experience did not necessarily provide the best solutions for Irish agricultural problems. Unlike England, which had gone through an 'Industrial Revolution' in the late eighteenth and early nineteenth centuries, most of Ireland, with the partial exception of Ulster, went through a process of de-industrialisation in the same period. While England was gradually moving away from being a predominantly agricultural country, the Irish population was becoming more rather than less dependent on agriculture. As a result of this, many English landlords were able to increase their incomes through involvement in these new industrial enterprises, such as coal-mining for example, which facilitated their investing capital on improving their estates. However, this was not an option for most Irish landowners. This meant that there were few alternative sources of employment apart from agriculture for Irish cottiers and smallholders.[29]

Unlike their British counterparts, both Conner and Blacker believed that the peculiarities of Irish agriculture meant that the rights of tenants had to be taken into account in any proposed reforms of the system of landholding there. Rather than allowing rents to be set by the laws of supply and demand, Conner believed that they should be set on the basis of an independent valuation of the worth of a tenant's holding. He proposed this as a solution to the problem of exorbitant rents in Ireland, which he believed were a product of the rapid rise in the population there in the late eighteenth century. Once rents had been fixed in this manner, Conner believed that tenants should be secure in the possession of their holdings, so long as this rent was paid. Conner's proposals for a 'valuation and a perpetuity', as they came to be known, obviously implied a restriction on the landlord's rights over their property.[30] Although the ideas developed during the Famine by the radical Irish land reformer, James Fintan Lalor, tended in this direction, very few other thinkers at the time were suggesting the outright transfer of land from the landlord to the tenant. In general, there was little popular support at this time for the creation of a 'peasant proprietary' as it later came to be known.

The rise of the Tenant League coincided with an increase in the levels of agrarian crime in Ireland. Between 1846 and 1849, for example, there were 5,595 agrarian outrages in Ireland, and this number included seventy-two homicides.[134] By 1849, however, this wave of agrarian crime had begun to subside, although there was a smaller, more concentrated increase in the North of Ireland which lasted from 1849 through to 1852. This was particularly acute in parts of south Armagh, south Down, Monaghan and Louth.[32] This regional upsurge in agrarian crime included a number of attacks on both landlords and their agents. The most notorious of these murders was the killing of Thomas Douglas Bateson near Castleblayney in County Monaghan in December 1851.[33] Bateson was a member of a well-known landed family in the North of Ireland and an agent on the Templeton estate there. His murder and the general increase in agrarian crime in Ireland drew the attention of British and Irish politicians to the grievances of tenants there. It also increased the pressure on the incoming Conservative government to introduce some measure of Irish land reform.

After the Devon Commission's report, issued in 1845, which had recommended compensation for improvements, numerous failed Irish land bills had been introduced into the House of Commons. In his early years in parliament, Napier had taken a close interest in the progress of these bills. In April 1848, speaking on Sharman Crawford's Outgoing Tenants Bill, he had recommended the appointment of a committee to simplify and codify the existing body of landlord and tenant law in Ireland.[34] Later in the same year he had served on a select committee on the abortive Irish land bills introduced by the Chief Secretary, Sir William Somerville. Somerville's bills had included a provision for compensation in cases where the landlord had consented to the improvement being made. In August of the following year, Lord Monteagle, one of the leading Whig experts on Irish affairs, moved for a commission of the House of Lords to inquire into the state of landlord and tenant law both in Britain and Ireland.[35] This motion was defeated, however, and Napier was extremely critical of this failure to move towards a settlement of the question.[36]

The Conservative government that attained office in February 1852 was a minority one led by Lord Derby. It owed its position primarily to divisions within the Whig leadership and to Independent Party disillusionment with Lord John Russell's conduct over the Ecclesiastical Titles Bill.[37] It was widely believed that its term in office would be a short one. Napier was appointed as Irish Attorney General in the government while his brother-in-law, James Whiteside, was given the post of Solicitor General. Lord Eglinton and Lord Naas were appointed as Lord Lieutenant and Chief Secretary respectively. Napier's first act as Attorney General was to move for the appointment of a select committee to inquire into the state of districts in counties Armagh, Monaghan and Louth. As we have seen, this area was a regional centre of agrarian disturbances in this period. At the same time, Napier also declared his intention of bringing in an Irish Landlord and Tenant Bill in the near future. He also implied that Tenant League agitation had contributed 'largely though no doubt inadvertently and unconsciously'[38] to agrarian crimes in these districts. This was a theme which both Napier and Whiteside pursued consistently in their questioning of witnesses before the select committee. They attempted to fit these particular incidences of agrarian crime into a wider pattern of Ribbon conspiracy. Indeed, Whiteside claimed that a systematic campaign 'of intimidation and terror' was taking place, which was designed to drive landowners from their properties or to 'compel them to submit to such terms as were demanded'.[39]

The select committee sat between March and May 1852, and examined a wide range of witnesses including several resident magistrates and local clergymen for the counties involved. Its report, issued in May 1852, recommended a series of coercive measures, such as giving the superior courts the power to change the venue of murder trials where there was a suspicion of involvement by agrarian secret societies like the Ribbonmen. It was also suggested that such cases should be moved to counties better 'adapted to secure a fair and impartial trial'. This alteration in the law was obviously intended to make it easier for the government to secure convictions in them. Other resolutions dealt with raising the level of the poor law qualification for jurors and with withholding licenses from publicans who allowed secret societies to meet on their premises. The ninth resolution, however, adopted a different tone. It suggested that the government should introduce a measure to consolidate the land laws in Ireland. Furthermore, the committee recommended that it should consider the practicality of introducing legislation which would provide 'adequate security to tenants for permanent improvements, and otherwise place the relation [between landlords and tenants] on a more satisfactory footing'.[40]

Following their appointments, all three leading members of the Irish administration with seats in parliament, Naas, the Chief Secretary, Napier, the Attorney General and Whiteside, the Solicitor General, were obliged to stand for re-election. In their election campaigns, all three pledged themselves to the introduction of an Irish land measure including a provision for tenants' compensation. Speaking in Coleraine, Naas promised that if the government remained six months in office, it would bring in a measure 'preventing landlords from taking advantage of money laid out upon land by tenants'. He argued that tenants should 'be secured in the enjoyment' of their holdings, providing they improved them as they 'ought to do'.[41] This suggestion went beyond anything that had yet been suggested by Napier. In Enniskillen, Whiteside made a similar pledge on improvements, while again stressing his opposition to fixity of tenure.[42] All of the leading members of the Irish administration had, thus, declared their intention to introduce a comprehensive landlord and tenant code well before Napier introduced his bills in November.

In March 1852, in a debate on Sharman Crawford's Tenant Right Bill, both Napier and Whiteside made clear their opposition to the leading tenets of the Tenant League. Whiteside condemned the three central planks of its original programme – fixity of tenure, compulsory valuation, and free sale – as being opposed to 'the rights of property'.[43] Napier claimed that it was impossible to legalise Tenant Right as it existed in Ulster, as even there it varied from estate to estate and was based on local custom.[44] In a later debate on the bill, Lord Naas argued that its principles were 'as dangerous and as communistic as were ever broached in the wildest time of revolution'. It would, he claimed, convert the landlord into 'a mere rent-charger on his estate'.[45] Naas' comments reflected the general opposition felt by Irish landowners to any attempts to interfere with their ability to run their estates as they saw fit. The tone of these debates also revealed clearly the limitations within which Napier's bills would be drafted. It was now obvious that a government bill would deal principally with the narrower question of compensation for improvements rather than with the wider programme espoused by the league.

During the 1852 election campaign, many Irish Conservatives, particularly in northern constituencies, made support for Napier's proposed measures a central plank in their election addresses. A typical example was Henry Corry in Tyrone who declared his support for any measure, which 'without infringing on the just rights of property' would secure compensation to tenants for unexhausted improvements.[46] In contemporary usage, 'unexhausted' improvements were understood as improvements which continued to increase either the productivity or the monetary value of the tenant's holding. The logic behind this was that certain types of improvement lost their value over time. The Conservative candidates for

3. '*Joseph Napier*': sketch from the *Dublin University Magazine*, March 1853

the county seats of Antrim, Monaghan, Londonderry, Armagh and for the borough seat of Downpatrick also gave similar pledges of support for the principle of compensation for improvements.[47] In Belfast, Richard Davison argued that the principle was 'tangible in character, substantive in form, and honest and equitable in its object'.[48] While stressing their support for compensation for improvements, these candidates were at pains to distance themselves from the wider proposals of the Tenant League. In Downpatrick, the Conservative candidate, C.S. Hardinge, made clear his opposition to 'all measures of compulsory valuation and other such obnoxious measures'.[49] These promises seem to have had some effect in Ulster, where William Kirk was the only candidate sympathetic to the Tenant League to be elected. In a major blow to the league, its most prominent candidate in Ulster, William Sharman Crawford, was defeated in County Down. This Conservative strength in the North of Ireland was based on a number of factors. Landlord influence there was stronger than it was elsewhere in the country. The practise of Tenant Right on some Ulster estates may also have made for better relations between landowners and their tenants than existed outside the province. It was also the case that landowners in the North could threaten to withdraw their consent to the Custom if their nominees were not elected.[50]

Writing to Spencer Walpole,[51] the Home Secretary, soon after the elections, Napier claimed that it was 'a happy circumstance' that he had 'predetermined so long ago to deal with this question, for otherwise we might have lost some of the Northern counties'. He believed that it was probable that, without the promise of a government measure on the land question, the Conservatives might have lost support from Presbyterian tenant farmers in Ulster.[52] In the rest of the country, however, the Independent Party had a far greater degree of success. This was partly due to the proclamation against Roman Catholic processions issued by the government in June 1852. Many Irish Catholics viewed this proclamation as being directly responsible for the subsequent sectarian riots in Stockport.[53] This belief deepened the sectarian flavour of the 1852 election in the South of Ireland and, as a result, damaged the Conservative Party's prospects there.

The combination of religious and agrarian issues raised by Independent Party candidates meant that they attracted a good deal of support from the new electorate enfranchised under the 1850 Franchise Act.[54] In total, forty-eight Independent Party MPs were returned at the election. In September 1852, at a conference in Dublin, forty of these MPs pledged to keep themselves 'independent of, and in opposition to' any government which did not make it a 'cabinet question' to introduce a bill embodying the principles of Sharman Crawford's bill.[55] This was a reference to the bill Sharman Crawford had introduced in 1851, which had allowed compensation both for improvements and for dispossession. It was clear by this point, however, that Napier's bills would be restricted to providing compensation solely for improvements.

By the end of August, Napier had submitted an outline of his bills to Lord Eglinton, the Irish Lord Lieutenant. At this stage, however he had prepared only three measures, a Compensation for Improvements Bill, a Leasing Powers Bill, and a consolidation bill dealing with the law of landlord and tenant. Eglinton's summary of the bills in a letter to Walpole on 30 August shows that these were essentially the same as those introduced by Napier in November.[56] By late September, Walpole was stressing his anxiety to see the draft bills. He believed the success of the Irish administration would 'greatly depend or at least be advanced by a judicious settlement of that important question'. Walpole hoped the bills would promote a settlement of the question, in order to prevent an 'incessant agitation' which would 'enlist on its side all the idle and useless tenants who wish[ed] to "improve" the landlords only [out] of their estates'.[57] The tone of this letter revealed the difficulties that Napier would face in drafting a bill which could be supported both by Conservatives, with similar views to Walpole's on the 'rights' of property, and Independent Party MPs pledged to the principles of Sharman Crawford's bill.

In general, both Liberal and Conservative landlords were agreed that the solution to Ireland's agricultural backwardness lay in the strengthening of their control over their property. They regularly argued that the modernisation of Irish agriculture was dependent on increasing their powers to evict smallholders, to consolidate the holdings on their estates and to set rents at market levels. They were also opposed to any state interference with their administration of their estates and were insistent on their right to run them as they saw fit.[58] From their perspective, landowners were the best judges of the types of improvements which should be carried out on their estates. There were two contradictory pressures being brought to bear on Napier when he was preparing his land bills. From the landlord side, he was being pressured to recognise the 'absolute' rights of landowners over their property, while the Tenant League was demanding the introduction of legislation which would recognise the rights of Irish tenants.

Between drawing up the bills in July and forwarding them to Walpole in September, Napier sent them for approval to some of the leading political and legal figures in the Conservative Party in Ireland. These included John Wynne, the Under-Secretary at Dublin Castle, and George Alexander Hamilton, a prominent Irish Conservative MP, who was then Financial Secretary to the Treasury. Both men were well acquainted with the technical aspects of the Irish land question, as they had been members of the Devon Commission. Napier also submitted the bills to the two leading Irish judges, Francis Blackburne, the Irish Lord Chancellor, and Thomas Lefroy, the Irish Lord Chief Justice, and to two prominent Irish Conservative landowners, Lord Clancarty and Lord Donoughmore. They all agreed to the main provisions of the bills at the time, although some of them later expressed reservations about aspects of them.[59] The drafting of the bills was, however, done largely by Napier himself, with the assistance of William Dwyer Ferguson. From Napier's surviving correspondence, it appears that they were drafted with very little involvement on the part of senior members of the cabinet. Writing to Sir James Emerson Tennent, the Conservative MP for Lisburn and a close personal friend, Napier admitted that he expected some opposition to his bills from other members of the government. He hoped, however, that Lord Derby 'would not allow Lord St Leonards,[60] or any of the Monkbarns[61] school to mar a generous arrangement founded on sound policy... [and] justice'. He warned that 'old stale notions refusing a just arrangement will not do'. Tenants should be 'treated equitably' and this would, Napier believed, 'result in great advantages to the proprietors themselves'.[62]

After receiving the bills, Walpole wrote to Eglinton expressing his reservations about aspects of the Tenants' Compensation Bill. He maintained that unless it included a provision that the landlord be notified of any prospective improvement 'neither the government nor our friends would be likely to support it'.[63] Walpole's letter was the first clear signal of the potential opposition to Napier's bill which existed within the Conservative Party. Eglinton's response was to insist that the bill Walpole had seen had been merely a draft, and that Napier did not intend that improvements should be made without the landlord's consent.[64] However, this assurance did not stifle the growing criticisms of the bills within the cabinet. These divisions within the Conservative Party led Naas to summon Napier to London for a cabinet discussion of his bills.[65]

After receiving this summons, Napier advised Naas that 'on principle of policy' it would be 'the most suicidal course' for the cabinet to reject the Tenants' Compensation Bill. The support given by Irish Conservative candidates to the principle of compensation for improvements had, in Napier's opinion, pledged the government to introduce a bill. Would it not 'be dishonourable & treacherous as well as impolitic' for him 'to say that there was now to be no bill' on the subject.[66]

Writing to Naas on 5 November 1852, Whiteside reiterated Napier's warning of the damaging effect that a failure to introduce the Compensation Bill would have on the government. He warned that its abandonment at that stage would be 'destructive' to the Irish Conservative Party.[67] In a letter to Disraeli, he pointed out that the ninth resolution of the Crime and Outrage committee had pledged both him and Napier as 'parties to that recommendation' to introduce a Tenants' Compensation Bill. The resolution had, he argued, been 'proclaimed throughout Ulster where our [the Irish Conservative Party] strength lies, and if not fully carried out, will set that province in a flame'. The measure would, he asserted, affect only improving tenants, and as there 'were none such in Connaught and Munster', its effects would be felt almost exclusively by the Protestant tenantry in Ulster. If the government alienated their support, he warned, 'our party in Ireland is gone'.[68] Both Napier and Whiteside made it clear on a number of occasions that their main concern when introducing the bills was to secure the position of the Presbyterian tenantry in Ulster. The two men had close family ties with the North of Ireland. As we have seen, Napier's father was a Presbyterian tenant farmer, who had later founded a brewery in Belfast, while Whiteside's father had been born in County Derry. It is probable that their close ties with the North of Ireland increased both men's sensitivity to the demands being made by the Tenant League.

In early November, Napier and Naas attended the cabinet, and, in Napier's words, 'with the aid of ... [his] dull ear, and such response as readily occurred to threadbare objections', they secured the consent of the cabinet to the introduction of the bills in late November. According to Napier, Lord Derby's support had been essential to their acceptance by the cabinet.[69] The chief opposition to Napier's bills from within the cabinet came from Lord St Leonards, the Lord Chancellor of England, who described the Montgomery Act, a Scottish act on which Napier had modelled his Land Improvement Bill, as 'one of the most mischievous [acts] ever passed'.[70] Derby's support for Napier's bill may have been based on his own experiences in Ireland. He had a good knowledge of Irish conditions, having been Chief Secretary there, as Lord Stanley, from 1830 to 1833. As Chief Secretary, Derby had adopted a 'two-pronged' approach, on the one hand, 'rigorously putting down political agitation' and on the other, initiating reforms such as the Irish Church Temporalities Act of 1833 and the creation of the Irish national education system. In 1845 he had introduced his own Tenants' Compensation Bill, based on the Devon Commission's report.[71] Furthermore, Derby was an Irish landlord himself and took an active interest in the management of his estates in Tipperary and Limerick.[72] As we shall see later in the book, however, his experiences in Ireland had also made him more sensitive to the susceptibilities of Irish Conservatives than was Disraeli.

Napier's statement introducing the land bills in the House of Commons in November 1852 gave a comprehensive, if partisan, account of the history of the Irish land question. In the speech he ascribed the evils of the Irish land system to the prevalence of yearly tenancies there. In his view, these militated against capital being expended on improvements. He also outlined the three main purposes of his bills; first, they were designed to 'give facility for the employment of capital' and to remove restrictions on its use, second, to facilitate the granting of leases and to ensure their observance, and, third, to deal with the cases of 'those parties' who had not entered 'into express agreements'.[73]

The first of Napier's bills was the Land Improvement Bill. This was largely based on a similar Scottish act introduced in 1847, but expanded its provisions to cover the case of tenants with limited interest in the land, such as tenants for life. The bill enabled them to borrow money to make improvements and to charge the expense of this on the estate for a limited period. It also authorised the type of improvements, such as the drainage, enclosure or fencing of land, which could be made. According to Napier, the encouragement of improvements would increase the employment available to agricultural labourers in Ireland. In consequence, the money advanced under the bill would be employed for 'the material good and general benefit of the country'.[74]

The second bill, the Leasing Powers Bill, was designed to give limited owners, such as those holding under trusts or settlements or those who held land for a fixed term (forty years for example), the right to lease land for certain designated purposes.[75] It also facilitated the making of agreements between limited owners and their tenants on the scale of compensation to be paid for specified types of improvements. These included drainage, the cultivation of waste land, and the erection of fences. This provision was designed to ensure that any improvements that were made would be 'productive' ones. The bill also made it easier for such landowners to lease lands and designated the length of time for which such leases could be granted. This provision was designed to make long-term leases a more usual feature of Irish agriculture than they had been up to that point. Napier also proposed what he described as 'compensation periods'; if tenants remained in possession for a specified length of time, they would have no claim to compensation for the improvements they had made. If, however, they were evicted before the compensation period elapsed, they would be entitled to a sliding scale of compensation. There was to be no right to compensation in cases where tenants were in arrears with their rent or where they had left their holding voluntarily.[76] This second condition meant that Napier's bill would have operated in a more limited way than did Tenant Right as generally practised.

Napier's third bill, the Landlord and Tenant Bill, formed the basis for Deasy's Act of 1860. Its central provision has been described as 'revolutionary' in its implications, if not in its practical application, by a leading legal expert on Irish landlord and tenant law.[77] This was that, henceforward, the relations between landlord and tenant should rest on contract rather than on the feudal notion of tenure. In this respect, the bill could be seen as part of the wider British movement away from the protection of customary rights and towards a more contractual idea of the relationship between landlord and tenant.[78] The placing of the relations between them on a contractual basis was likely, 'given the prevailing views of contract', to prove more beneficial to the landlord than to the tenant.[79] To presume that they entered such a relationship on an equal basis or by free choice was hardly consonant with the realities of Irish life in the mid-nineteenth century. Essentially, the bill implied that landowners' rights over their property were only limited by the conditions contained in the leases that they granted their tenants. It clearly did not recognise any rights based either on custom or on the long-term occupancy of land.

The bill also contained provisions against sub-letting and the 'wasting' or burning of land. It also simplified the law relating to evictions.[80] This provision made it simpler for landlords to evict smallholders from their estates. In the eyes of many contemporaries, this was an essential first step towards the creation of a class of 'yeoman' farmers in Ireland. According to Napier, the bill was designed to consolidate and simplify the existing code of Irish landlord and tenant law, 'so as to enable those who had made contracts to secure their enforcement'. Napier later described this bill as 'being favourable to the landlord' in 'simplifying and sharpening his remedies in several respects'.[81] Given these types of provisions, Napier's first three bills have been described with justice as 'landlords' bills'.[82] The fourth, and the most controversial, of his bills, however, was the Tenants' Compensation Bill. This was designed to deal with the cases of tenants who had made improvements without express contracts for compensation. In particular, it was meant to cover the cases of 'improving' tenants who held their land on a yearly basis. However, Napier stressed the fact that the bill 'would not interfere with' or 'prejudice' the practise of Tenant Right on those estates where it existed.[83] Under the terms of the bill, tenants were given the right to undertake certain specified improvements which, as in the Land Improvement Bill, would entitle them to either a money compensation or to a compensatory period of occupancy. Once this period had elapsed, the improvement was taken to be 'exhausted' and they would no longer be entitled to compensation. If the landlord so wished he could undertake the proposed improvement himself and charge the tenant a higher rent after it was completed. Furthermore, the tenants' claim arose only in cases where they were evicted for reasons other than non-payment of rent or other breaches of a lease.[84]

The bill's most controversial aspect was its retrospective operation. Essentially, this meant that it allowed for compensation for past as well as prospective improvements made by tenants. The inclusion of the 'retrospective' clause distinguished Napier's bill from previous Tenants' Compensation bills, introduced by earlier British governments from the early 1840s onwards.[85] Napier justified this on the grounds that, as Irish tenants generally paid for any improvements made to their holdings, it was only fair that they should receive adequate compensation for doing so. Whiteside defended this provision in a letter to Disraeli on 4 November. He argued that the fact that Irish tenants undertook improvements, which in England would have been the responsibility of their landlords, justified its introduction.[86] The bill did not, however, interfere with the setting of rents between landlord and tenant, which Napier believed should be left to 'mutual contract'.[87] Indeed, Napier's bills did not explicitly touch on any of the 'Three F's' that had been the basis of the Tenants League original programme, nor on the 'Two F's', fair rent and free sale, which had been embodied in Sharman Crawford's bill of 1851.

Nevertheless, the response of the Independent Party to Napier's bills was not wholly negative. In his memoirs, Gavan Duffy described them as 'being better' than the Independent Party had expected, 'the vital principle of compensation for past improvements being distinctly recognised'.[88] In the Commons, William Shee,[89] the MP for Kilkenny County, gave a cautious welcome to the first three of Napier's bills. He criticised them, however, for not giving any legal sanction to the 'Ulster Custom'. Without this, he suggested, landlords there could simply refuse to be bound by it.[90] The response to the bills, however, seems to have been generally favourable; the *Dublin Evening Mail* reporting that they were received 'even by the [Irish] Brigade,[91] in a better spirit than expected'. It argued, however, that the Tenants' Compensation Bill verged 'in its purview on the territory of Mr Sharman Crawford and the Tenant League'.[92]

On 7 December, Shee introduced his own Tenants' Compensation Bill, based largely on Sharman Crawford's earlier measure in the House of Commons. He condemned Napier as a 'tardy convert' to the principle of compensation for improvements. However, his principal objection to Napier's bills was for their failure to deal with the question of rents. In general, the sums paid for the outgoing tenants' 'interest' in their holdings varied with the level of the rent that they had paid. The higher the rent that was paid, the lower was the value of the Tenant Right. Through Napier's failure to deal with this issue, Shee believed that his bills would allow landlords in the province to use rent increases to subvert the practise of Tenant Right on their estates. Furthermore, Shee suggested that landlords could also use rent increases in order to nullify the compensatory periods intended by Napier's bills. By raising rents to a punitively high level, landlords could ensure that they received the benefits of their tenants' improvements or, in extreme cases, even force them off their holdings. In light of these criticisms of Napier's bills, Shee asked that his own bill be referred along with them to a select committee for consideration.[93] In reply, Ross Moore, the Conservative MP for Armagh City, said that as the bills 'contained conflicting principles' it would not be appropriate to send them together to a select committee.[94] At the close of the debate, however, Walpole made the unexpected suggestion that, considering 'the great interest taken in the subject', both Napier's bills and Shee's bill, should, as Shee had suggested, be referred to a committee.[95]

The committal of the bills to a select committee proved immediately controversial with Irish Conservative MPs. Writing to Eglinton on 1

December, Naas described the background to the debate. He told Eglinton
of a meeting that he and Napier had had with Walpole on the morning of
the debate. They had found 'him frightened by a vague rumour which
rested only on [Lord] H[enry] Lennox's[96] authority' that the Whigs and the
Peelites were going to vote together in favour of the reference of both
Napier's bills and Shee's bill to a committee. Naas discovered afterwards
that there were 'no grounds whatever for this report'. To counter this
perceived threat, Walpole suggested that the government should agree to
Napier's three bills alone being submitted to the committee.

Both Naas and Napier were opposed even to this concession but
eventually they agreed that 'if the House looked threatening' and it looked
as if 'the main body of the Whigs and Peelites seemed inclined to oppose
us we should then concede so far as to consent to refer the Tenants'
Compensation Bill and the Landlord and Tenant [Bill]...to a select
committee'. Naas stressed that he had emphasised his objection to any
'tampering with Shee's bill or admitting...[its] principle in any way'.
During the debate, he reported, 'neither Whigs nor Peelites appeared' and
there had been no 'apprehension of any danger' of a government defeat.
Consequently, Walpole's agreement to the committal of the bills had an
'electric' effect on the government's supporters.[97] It is clear from Naas'
account that their committal to the select committee had come as a shock
to the members of the Irish administration.

From what happened subsequently, however, it seems likely that Walpole
and Disraeli had agreed on this course of action before the debate. Disraeli
later told John Delane, the editor of *The Times*, that, before the debate on
the budget had commenced, a member of the Independent Party[98] had
called on him and offered to support it, on the condition that Shee's bill
would be submitted to a select committee along with Napier's bills.[99] This
offer makes Walpole's actions on the night of the debate more under-
standable. The government was facing defeat in the house on Disraeli's
budget, introduced on 3 December, and needed support from whatever
quarter it could gain it. At this point, Disraeli and Walpole had agreed solely
to the committal of the bills to the select committee. They had not decided,
as Robert Stewart has suggested, that 'the government would accept a
recommendation from the select committee then sitting in favour of
Sharman Crawford's bill'. In fact, the select committee was not appointed
until after the Conservative government had lost office.[100]

After the debate Walpole met with Shee and asked him to specify the
conditions on which the Independent Party would support the
government. Along with Frederick Lucas and Charles Gavan Duffy, Shee
drew up a list of concessions, which would lead the party to follow that
course. The chief of these was that a measure providing retrospective
compensation for improvements should be made one 'on which the

government would stake its existence'. Other lesser conditions, reflecting
the influence of the Catholic Defence Association, were the granting of a
Charter to the Catholic University in Dublin and the appointment of
Catholic chaplains in the army and navy and in prisons and workhouses.
Duffy later maintained that although some of these conditions were
rejected or postponed for future consideration, enough was conceded 'on
the main point' to allow them advise other Independent Party MPs to
support the government on the budget.[101]

Meanwhile, however, the Irish Conservative backlash against the referral
of the bills was growing stronger. After the debate on Shee's bill, one Irish
Conservative MP threatened to vote against the budget, as he considered
the land question to be safer 'in Lord John's [Russell] hands' than in the
government's.[102] The Dublin Conservative paper, the *Daily Express*,
suggested on 11 December that a number of Irish Conservative MPs
intended to pursue this course.[103] Naas felt 'betrayed'; he complained that a
decision had been come to 'on a most important question' in direct
opposition to the wishes of the Irish administration. Indeed, he claimed
that his first reaction had been to resign from his office unless Irish affairs
were 'more entrusted to my and Napier's guidance'.[104] Eglinton also advised
Derby that the committal of Shee's bill to the select committee had
'disgusted some' of the Conservative Party's 'best Irish supporters' to a
'degree' he feared 'to contemplate'. Like Naas, he was concerned at the
'awkward position' in which the Irish administration had been placed.[105]

The opposition to the committal of Shee's bill was further displayed on
9 December when a deputation of Irish Conservative MPs, largely from
northern constituencies, called on Derby to protest against the move. The
deputation included Sir Arthur Brooke, the MP for Fermanagh County,
Lord Claud Hamilton, the MP for Tyrone County, and Thomas Connolly,
the MP for Donegal County. All three men were representatives of the
landlord class in the North of Ireland.[106] This discontent within the party
led to the holding of a meeting of Irish MPs at Derby's house in London
later that day. At this meeting, Richard Davison 'expressed his regret' that
the Irish administration's advice with regard to Shee's bill had not been
followed. Derby defended Walpole's actions, while regretting 'the mode' in
which the committal of the bills had taken place. According to Naas,
Walpole spoke in 'a rather Jesuitical strain' claiming that his only objective
had been to facilitate the progress of Napier's bills. In Naas's own view,
Walpole had committed the 'devil of a blunder', and he was worried that
its effect would be to 'kindle up the [Tenant Right] agitation again'.[107]

On the following day, Lord Roden, a leading Irish Conservative
landowner, asked Derby in the House of Lords whether the government
would be prepared to carry Shee's bill into law if the committee approved
it. Roden claimed that the bill contained 'propositions of so communist a

character' that it had twice before been rejected by the House of Commons.[108] In response, Derby insisted that its second reading had been merely 'pro forma' in order to have it sent with Napier's bills to the select committee. The principle of the bill was, he believed, 'entirely subversive of the rights of property' and, as such, he maintained 'no House of Commons committee would ever sanction ... [its] adoption'.[109] Even if the committee approved the bill, the government would not endorse it. This reply, of course, altered the complexion of the question; if the government had predetermined to oppose Shee's bill even before the appointment of the select committee, then the Independent Party could hardly continue to support it, without losing its political credibility.

In a debate in the House of Commons on 15 December, Frederick Lucas asked if the select committee could be a 'fair and impartial' one after the speech delivered by Derby in the Lords.[110] Lord Naas responded that as Shee's bill had previously been defeated in the House, it was extremely unlikely that the committee would adopt it. His own objections to the principles and details of the bill 'remained perfectly unchanged'.[111] The acrimonious tone of this debate can be explained by the fact that the Independent Party had already decided to oppose the government on the budget at a meeting held on the previous day. At that meeting, Frederick Lucas had urged that the party should either vote with the Conservatives or abstain on the vote. He maintained that there was no reason to believe that a Liberal government would introduce a measure more favourable to Irish tenants than Napier's bill had been. However, the majority at the meeting voted in favour of opposing Disraeli's budget, and Lucas voted in accordance with this decision in the House of Commons.[112] The decision made by the Independent Party meant, in effect, that there was no longer any necessity for Irish Conservative MPs to make conciliatory statements towards it.

In his study of the Independent Party, J.H. Whyte has argued that had Derby given an 'evasive' answer to Roden's question in the House of Lords, twenty or so Independent Party MPs might have voted for Disraeli's budget.[113] It is clear from his correspondence, however, that Derby's main concern was to prevent a split among his own supporters, especially among Irish Conservatives. Writing to Disraeli, Derby advised him to be cautious 'in dealing with the party of the S. Crauford [*sic*] school, however plausible and gentlemanlike may be the individuals whom they put forward as their agents'. If the Conservative Party lost the support of the Irish landed gentry, 'especially of the North', he warned, 'we are gone'.[114] The tone of this letter bears out Robert Blake's contention that Derby was 'at times irritated' by what he saw as Disraeli's attempts to secure 'implausible alliances and fantastic reshuffles of the political pack'.[115] In the short term, however, Derby's reply to Roden's question had effectively ensured that the

Independent Party would not support the budget, and on 22 December the government was defeated in the House of Commons by 305 votes to 286.

In an account of the history of the Tenant League written in 1886, Sir Charles Gavan Duffy accused the Derby government of having introduced Napier's bills merely in order to 'dangle' them before 'the eyes of Irish members, but not to press any of them to a division' until its own future was secured. From this viewpoint, the bills were designed purely to win Independent Party support and could be jettisoned once this objective was secured.[116] However, this assertion does not hold up under detailed scrutiny. Napier's bills represented a carefully framed code for Irish landlord and tenant law, built on a coherent, if not necessarily complete, analysis of the problems affecting Irish agriculture. While the landowners' 'rights' over their property were secured and, in some instances, extended, the bills encouraged them to invest in their estates and to take a more active role in estate management. They would have been expected to fulfil a more socially responsible role than they had done up to that point. Along with many of his contemporaries Napier believed that one of the main factors restricting Irish agricultural growth was its under-capitalisation and his bills were, therefore, intended to extend credit facilities for both landlords and tenants.[117] From the landlord's point of view, the originality of Napier's scheme lay in his acceptance, in the Tenants' Compensation Bill, that, through the expenditure of their capital and labour, tenants had acquired a degree of 'property' in their holdings.[118] It was this aspect of the bill that explained the landlord hostility to it and which was responsible for the divisions that it caused within the Irish Conservative Party itself.

Another significant feature of the bills was that they were designed to facilitate the emergence of a substantial tenant farmer class in Ireland, similar to that which existed in England. Napier hoped that such tenants would provide a bulwark against radical agrarianism and, perhaps, a stabilising force in Irish society generally. His Tenants' Compensation Bill had the further aim of counteracting the Tenant League's appeal to the Northern tenantry. The Conservative fear of this potential threat to their position was reflected in the willingness of party candidates to support Napier's proposed bills at the 1852 general election.

This is not to suggest, however, that the Conservative Party leaders at Westminster felt the same commitment to Napier's bills as he and other members of the Irish administration did. Their willingness to support the introduction of the bills was based on the particular political circumstances existing in late 1852. If the bills secured the support necessary for the government's survival, then they would have served their purpose. It is also probable that, in the immediate aftermath of the Famine, both British and Irish politicians were prepared to accept a more radical settlement of the

Irish land question than they would have been in other circumstances. The fall of the Conservative government, however, had altered the political situation and many members of the party had become anxious to distance themselves from the bills. There was also little enthusiasm for them among leading members of the Liberal Party, both in Britain and in Ireland. In the next chapter, we will turn to an examination of the consequences that this had for the future progress of the bills.

NOTES

1   See D.G. Boyce, *Nineteenth Century Ireland: The Search for Stability* (Dublin, 1990), p. 131 and Foster, *Modern Ireland*, p. 377.

2   See W.E. Vaughan, *Landlords and Tenants in Mid-Victorian Ireland* (Oxford, 1997), p. 6 and Hoppen, *Elections, Politics and Society*, pp. 106–9. Both authors derived these figures from the parliamentary return, *Return of Owners of Land in Ireland, Showing with Respect to Each County, the Number of Owners Below an Acre, and in Classes up to 100,000 Acres and Upwards, with the Aggregate Acreage and Valuation of Each Class*, H.C., 1876 (422), lix.

3   Boyce, *Nineteenth Century Ireland*, p. 122.

4   See James S. Donnelly, *The Great Irish Potato Famine* (Stroud, 2002), p. 161.

5   Hoppen, *Election, Politics and Society*, p. 91.

6   Vaughan, *Landlords and Tenants in Mid-Victorian Ireland*, p. 7.

7   See Paul Bew, *Land and the National Question in Ireland, 1858–82* (Dublin 1978), p. 22.

8   Peter Gray, *Famine, Land and Politics: British Government and Irish Society, 1843–50* (Dublin, 1999), p. 4.

9   See Bew, *Land and the National Question*, p. 22.

10   There is an excellent discussion of intellectual attitudes towards the Irish land question in both Britain and Ireland in the mid-nineteenth century in Gray, *Famine, Land and Politics*; see in particular pp. 1–40.

11   Gray, *Famine, Land and Politics*, pp. 3–7.

12   Gray, *Famine, Land and Politics*, p. 9.

13   See Donnelly, *Great Irish Potato Famine*, p. 161.

14   *Hansard*, 3rd series, CVII, 330.

15   Joseph Napier, *Address Delivered at the Dublin Oratorical and Literary Institute on the 5th of July 1847 by Joseph Napier, Esq., Q.C., President of the Society* (Dublin, 1847), pp. 7–8. See also R.D. Collison Black, *Economic Thought and the Irish Question, 1817–1870* (Cambridge, 1960), p. 28.

16   See Gray, *Famine, Land and Politics*, pp. 252–5. See also Donnelly, *Great Irish Potato Famine*, pp. 30–2 and pp. 233–6.

17   Philip Bull, *Land, Politics and Nationalism: A Study of the Irish Land Question* (Dublin, 1996), p. 2.

18   Donnelly, *Great Irish Potato Famine*, p. 140.

19   There is a good short account of the early history of the Tenant League in Joseph Lee, *The Modernization of Irish Society, 1848–1918* (Dublin, 1973), pp. 39–41. See also J.H. Whyte, *The Tenant League and Irish Politics in the Eighteen-Fifties* (Dundalk, 1966), pp. 6–8.

20   See Lee, *Modernization of Irish Society*, p. 39.

21   Hoppen, *Ireland since 1800*, p. 89.

22   For a discussion of the origins of the tenant agitation in Ulster, see Bew and Wright, 'Agrarian Opposition in Ulster politics', pp. 194–200. See also Frank Wright, *Two*

Lands on One Soil: Ulster Politics before Home Rule (Dublin, 1996), pp. 165–207.

23 In a letter to Lord Donoughmore in 1854, Napier agreed with his description of the Custom as an 'unmixed evil'. Napier argued that the Custom hindered agricultural improvements by draining the capital of incoming tenants. However, he went on, the 'evil' existed, and it could only 'be cautiously undermined by indirect agencies and gradual extinction'. See Napier to Donoughmore, n.d., Donoughmore papers, H/13/1/267.

24 See Whyte, *Tenant League and Irish Politics*, pp. 8–9.

25 Bull, *Land, Politics and Nationalism*, p. 37.

26 Napier to Newcastle, n.d., quoted in Ewald, *Life and Letters of Sir Joseph Napier* (2nd edn, London, 1892), p. 73.

27 Bull, *Land, Politics and Nationalism*, p. 9.

28 For a discussion of the nature of this belief and the reasons that lay behind it, see Oliver MacDonagh, *States of Mind: A Study of Anglo-Irish Conflict* (London, 1983), pp. 45–7.

29 See Bull, *Land, Politics and Nationalism*, pp. 28–35.

30 For a discussion of William Conner's ideas, see Bull, *Land, Politics and Nationalism*, pp. 28–30. See also Gray, *Famine, Land and Politics*, p. 47. For Blacker's ideas, see Oliver MacDonagh, *Ireland: the Union and its Aftermath* (London, 1979), pp. 46–7 and the same author's *States of Mind*, pp. 46–7.

31 See Vaughan, *Landlords and Tenants in Mid-Victorian Ireland*, p. 279.

32 See Vaughan, *Landlords and Tenants in Mid-Victorian Ireland*, p. 238.

33 For an account of Bateson's murder, see *The Times*, 10 December 1851.

34 *Hansard*, XCVII, 1322.

35 *Hansard*, CXIII, 612.

36 *Hansard*, CXIII, 706. After the failure of Monteagle's motion, Napier commissioned two Dublin solicitors, William Dwyer Ferguson and Andrew Vance, to undertake a study of the subject and the result was a book published in 1851. Napier supplied Ferguson and Vance with 'many valuable notes and public papers' and his bills, with one exception, were, to a large degree, modelled on their recommendations. Even before he became Irish Attorney General in February 1852, Napier had already acquired an in-depth knowledge of the Irish land question. See W.D. Ferguson and Andrew Vance, *The Tenure and Improvement of Land in Ireland Considered with Reference to the Relation Between Landlord and Tenant and Tenant-right* (Dublin, 1851). See also W.D. Ferguson, *Literary Appropriations and the Irish Land Bills of the Late Government* (Dublin, 1853).

37 For a discussion of the controversy over the introduction of the Ecclesiastical Titles Bill, see Chapter 4 below.

38 *Hansard*, CXIX, 1184.

39 *Report from the Select Committee of Outrages (Ireland): Together with the Proceedings of the Committee, Minutes of Evidence, Appendix, and Index* (London, 1852), p. 541.

40 *Report from the Select Committee of Outrages*, pp. iii–iv.

41 *Dublin Evening Mail*, 24 March 1852.

42 *Dublin Evening Mail*, 8 March 1852.

43 *Hansard*, CXX, 474.

44 *Hansard*, CXX, 448.

45 *Hansard*, CXXI, 276.

46 *Dublin Evening Mail*, 2 July 1852. For 'unexhausted' improvements see T.C. Mossom Meekins, *Report to the Attorney General for Ireland (the Right Hon. Joseph Napier) on Compensation to the Tenants for Improvements* (London, 1852), p. 5. In their work on landlord and tenant relations, Ferguson and Vance differentiated between improvements such as the building of farmhouses and roads, the drainage of lands,

and the chalking or claying of the soil, which added long-term value to the tenant's holding and more 'transient' improvements like the manuring or liming of land and the house-feeding of cattle. The latter class of improvements were more speedily 'exhausted' than the first. See Ferguson and Vance, *The Tenure and Improvement of Land in Ireland*, p. 399.

47 See the election addresses or reports of speeches of George Macartney for Antrim County, of Sir George Forster for Monaghan County, of Theobald Jones for Londonderry County, of Ross Moore for Armagh County, and of C.S.Hardinge for Downpatrick in the *Daily Express*, 5 July, 12 July, 19 July and 27 July 1852.

48 *Daily Express*, 12 July 1852.

49 *Daily Express*, 12 July 1852.

50 Jonathan Bardon, *A History of Ulster* (Belfast, 1992), p. 316. See also B.M Walker, *Ulster Politics: The Formative Years*, pp. 2–5 for a discussion of landlord influence in the north of Ireland.

51 Spencer Horatio Walpole (1806–98): educated Eton and Trinity College, Cambridge: called to the English bar, 1831, Q.C. 1846: MP for Midhurst, 1846–56 and for Cambridge University, 1865–82: Home Secretary, 1852, 1858–59, and 1866–67. As a leading English Evangelical and prominent member of the National Club, Walpole was close to Irish Conservative MPs, and, in particular, to Napier and Whiteside.

52 Napier to Walpole, n.d., Holland papers, in the possession of Mr David Holland, 928g.

53 For a fuller discussion of the Stockport riots, see Chapter 4.

54 For a discussion of the effects of the 1850 Act, see Hoppen, *Elections, Politics and Society*, pp. 17–18.

55 Quoted in Whyte, *Independent Irish Party*, p. 88.

56 Eglinton to Walpole, 30 August 1852, Holland papers, 894C. There is a copy of this letter in the Eglinton papers, GD3/5/51/4429a.

57 Walpole to Eglinton, 22 September 1852, Eglinton papers, GD3/5/52/4428.

58 For a discussion of the landlord attitude to the land question in this period, see Gray, *Famine, Land and Politics*, pp. 4–6.

59 See Napier to Donoughmore, n.d., Donoughmore papers, H/13/1/266, Whiteside to Naas, 5 November 1852, Mayo papers, 11020 (39), and Napier to Naas, 3 August [1853], Mayo papers, 11017(14).

60 Sir Edward Sugden (1781–1875): born London: called to the English bar, 1807, KC 1822: MP for Weymouth, 1828-30, for St Mawes, 1830–31, for Cambridge, 1831–37, and for Ripon, 1837–41: Solicitor General of England, 1829–30, Lord Chancellor of Ireland, 1834–35, 1841–46: Lord Chancellor of England, 1852: entered the House of Lords as Lord St Leonards, 1852.

61 Jonathan Olbuck, the laird of Monkbarns, was the antiquarian hero of Sir Walter Scott's novel, *The Antiquary*.

62 Napier to Tennent, n.d., Tennent papers, Public Record Office of Northern Ireland, Belfast, D922/B/27/9.

63 Walpole to Eglinton, 16 October 1852, Eglinton papers, GD3/5/52/4428. There is a copy of this letter in the Holland papers, 894c.

64 Eglinton to Walpole, 23 October 1852, Eglinton papers, GD3/5/52/4428.

65 This letter has not survived, but see Napier to Naas, n.d., Mayo papers, 11020 (15).

66 Napier to Naas, n.d., Mayo papers, 11020 (15). There are some problems in determining the extent of the influence that senior members of the cabinet had over the provisions of his land bills. Napier's papers have not survived and his biography gives away little on this point. Their correspondence shows that Derby knew of Napier's interest in the land question before his appointment as Attorney General. See Napier to Derby, 22 February 1850, quoted in Grace Gardiner (ed.), *The Lectures, Essays and Letters of the Right Hon. Sir Joseph Napier, Bart* (Dublin and London, 1882),

p. 78. Given Napier's prior involvement with the issue, it was presumably understood that he would introduce a Landlord and Tenant Bill, the details of which would be left up to him. Monypenny and Buckle give Disraeli credit for 'encouraging' Napier and Whiteside to introduce the bills but do not give any source for this. See Monypenny and Buckle, *Life of Benjamin Disraeli*, Vol. 3, p. 401. Disraeli himself made a similar claim in a speech on Gladstone's Land Act of 1870. See *Hansard*, CXCIX, 1810–11. There is, then, some evidence to suggest that the bills were introduced with the sanction of Derby and Disraeli, but no detailed evidence on their attitudes towards their provisions.

67   Whiteside to Naas, 5 November 1852, Mayo papers, 11,020 (39).
68   Whiteside to Disraeli, 4 November 1852, Disraeli papers, B/XXI/W/293.
69   Napier to Eglinton, 9 November 1852, Eglinton papers, GD3/5/51/4432.
70   Napier to Eglinton, 9 November 1852, Eglinton papers, GD3/5/51/4432.
71   The bill did not include any provision for 'retrospective' compensation. For its details, see Gray, *Famine, Land and Politics*, pp. 84–9.
72   See Gray, *Famine, Land and Politics*, pp. 27–8 and p. 39. See also A.D. Kriegel, 'The Irish policy of Lord Grey's government', *English Historical Review*, 86 (1971), pp. 22–45.
73   *Hansard*, CXXIII, 335–7.
74   *Hansard*, CXXIII, 319–20.
75   For agricultural purposes thirty-one-year leases would be granted, for the improvement of waste lands sixty-one-year leases, for mining purposes ninety-nine years leases, and for public buildings, leases of 999 years. See W.N. Hancock, *Two Reports for the Irish Administration on the History of the Landlord and Tenant Question in Ireland, with Suggestions for Legislation, First Report made in 1859: – Second in 1866* (Dublin, 1869), p. 11. Some landlords used leases to specify the types of improvements and the general agricultural practises they wished to see carried out on their land. Napier obviously wished to encourage this practise. Leases were also used to disallow certain practises. For example, the leases on the Duke of Devonshire's property in Cork prohibited subdivision, sub-letting and the removal of crops by the tenants. See James S. Donnelly, *The Land and the People of Nineteenth Century Cork* (London, 1975), pp. 200–2.
76   *Hansard*, CXXIII, 324–28.
77   J.C.Wylie, *Irish Landlord and Tenant Law* (Dublin, 1990), paragraph 1.08.
78   For a discussion of this topic, see E.P.Thompson, *Customs in Common* (London, 1993 edn.), pp. 133–7.
79   J.C. Brady, 'Legal Developments', p. 463.
80   *Hansard*, CXXIII, 330–4.
81   Napier to Disraeli, n.d., Disraeli papers, B/XXI/N/6.
82   T.P. O'Connor, *The Parnell Movement* (London, 1887), p. 126.
83   *Hansard*, CXXIII, 335.
84   *Hansard*, CXXIII, 335–9.
85   See Gray, *Famine, Land and Politics*, p. 88 and p. 92.
86   Whiteside to Disraeli, 4 November 1852, Disraeli papers, B/XXI/W/293.
87   *Hansard*, CXXIII, 339.
88   Sir Charles Gavan Duffy, *The League of North and South: An Episode in Irish history* (London, 1886), p. 231. As early as 1846, both Sharman Crawford and Daniel O'Connell had strongly criticised the Tenants' Compensation Bill introduced by the leading Whig politician, Lord Lincoln, for its 'purely prospective character.' At that time, they had argued that 'only retrospective compensation could satisfy the tenants by providing sufficient protection against immediate landlord oppression.' See Gray, *Famine, Land and Politics*, p. 92.
89   Sir William Shee (1804–68): born Middlesex: educated St Cuthbert's College,

Upshaw and at Edinburgh university: called to the English bar, 1828: became Serjeant-at-law, 1840: MP for Kilkenny County, 1852–57: appointed a Justice of the Court of Queen's Bench, 1863: knighted, 1864.

90   *Hansard*, CXXIII, 343.

91   The 'Irish Brigade' was a nickname used by contemporaries for the Irish Catholic MPs who broke with the Liberal government over the Ecclesiastical Titles Bill.

92   *Dublin Evening Mail*, 26 November 1852.

93   *Hansard*, CXXIII, 1090.

94   *Hansard*, CXXIII, 1126.

95   *Hansard*, CXXIII, 1139.

96   Lennox was MP for Chichester and a close confidant of Disraeli.

97   Naas to Eglinton, 9 December 1852, Eglinton papers, GD3/5/52/4426.

98   This was most likely George Henry Moore, the MP for Mayo. For his friendship with Disraeli see M.G. Moore, *An Irish Gentleman: George Henry Moore, His Travels, His Racing, His Politics* (London, n.d.), p. 195.

99   Henry Reeve (ed.), *The Greville Memoirs: A Journal of the Reign of Queen Victoria*, pt. 3, Vol. I, (London, 1887), pp. 32–3. See also the *Daily Express*, 2 July 1856, which referred to Disraeli's 'personal intimacy' with Moore.

100 In Stewart's account Napier is misidentified as Lord Napier and described as Irish Under Secretary. See Robert Stewart, *The Foundation of the Conservative Party, 1830–1867* (London, 1978), p. 260. See also W.D. Jones, *Lord Derby and Victorian Conservatism* (Oxford, 1956), p. 177. Lord Stanley later claimed that with both Shee's bill and Napier's bills 'being sent before the same committee, it was thought that the latter could not fail to pass, and Shee's to be thrown out, thus guarding our concession from becoming dangerous'. Stanley's diary, 7 December 1852, quoted in John Vincent (ed.), *Disraeli, Derby and the Conservative Party* (Hassocks, 1978), p. 87. See also R.P. Ghosh, 'Disraelian Conservatism: A financial approach', *English Historical Review*, 99 (1984), p. 277, for a judicious discussion of this episode.

101 Gavan Duffy, *League of North and South*, pp. 233–4. The accounts of the negotiations between the Independent Party and the government given by Duffy and Greville do not tally in every respect. For example, Greville dates the beginning of the negotiations to before the committal of the bills to the select committee, while Duffy suggests they began afterwards. Perhaps he was not aware of Moore's initial approach to Disraeli. See fn 98.

102 Naas to Eglinton, 9 December 1852, Eglinton papers, GD3/5/52/4426.

103 *Daily Express*, 11 December 1852.

104 Naas to Eglinton, 9 December 1852, Eglinton papers, GD3/5/52/4426.

105 Eglinton to Derby, 9 December 1852, Derby papers, 148/2. There is a draft of this letter in the Eglinton papers, GD3/5/53/4425.

106 *Dublin Evening Mail*, 10 December 1852.

107 Naas to Eglinton, 9 December 1852, Eglinton papers, GD3/5/52/4426. This letter was the second of two letters written by Naas to Eglinton that day. In his diary for 7 December 1852, Lord Stanley wrote that the committal of Shee's Bill had been agreed because 'of the policy forced upon ministers of securing the Irish vote if possible', quoted in Vincent (ed.), *Disraeli, Derby and the Conservative Party*, p. 87.

108 *Hansard*, CXXIII, 1206.

109 *Hansard*, CXXIII, 1209.

110 *Hansard*, CXXIII, 5.

111 *Hansard*, CXXIII, 1560.

112 *Dublin Evening Mail*, 15 December 1852. See also Edward Lucas, *The Life of Frederick Lucas, MP*, 2 vols (London 1886), Vol. 2, p. 9. See also *The Tablet*, 27 November and 8 December 1852. On 11 December, *The Tablet*, which was edited by Lucas, argued that

'bad as Mr Napier's Bill appeared to be', it had no reason to suppose that 'the Whigs or Peelites would have brought in a Bill one whit better'. *The Tablet*, 11 December 1852.

113   Whyte, *Independent Irish Party*, pp. 95–6.
114   Derby to Disraeli, n.d., Disraeli papers, H B/XX/S/101. I am indebted for this reference to Ms Ellen Hawman of the Disraeli project, Queens University, Kingston, Canada.
115   Blake, *Conservative Party*, p. 87.
116   Gavan Duffy, *The League of North and South*, p. 231. See also Moore, *An Irish Gentleman*, p. 221. Moore describes the Bills as 'designed only to divert attention from other matters'.
117   See Cormac O'Grada, *Ireland Before and After the Famine: Explorations in Economic History, 1800–1925* (Manchester, 1993), p. 65.
118   It was this aspect of the bills that Isaac Butt singled out for praise in his *Land tenure in Ireland: A Plea for the Celtic Race* (Dublin, 1866), pp. 90–3. See also Sir John Pope Hennessey, *Lord Beaconsfield's Irish Policy: Two Essays on Ireland* (London, 1885), p. 30.

THREE

The Irish Conservative Party and the land question

The landlord and Independent Party response to Napier's bills, 1853–60

As DISCUSSED in Chapter 2, the Derby-led government had seriously underestimated the extent of the opposition to Napier's measures, particularly the Tenants' Compensation Bill, among its Irish landed supporters. This opposition was based on a more absolutist view of the rights of property than Napier and those who supported his bills were prepared to accept. It was significant here that Napier came from a non-landed background. As a result, his views on property rights differed significantly from those even of moderate landlords such as Donoughmore and Naas. From the standpoint of his critics, landowners had absolute ownership over their land and should have ultimate control over its disposition. Their principal objection to retrospective compensation sprang from the fact that it would compel Irish landlords to remunerate tenants for improvements, which had been carried out without their consent. The critics of Napier's bills also believed that any prospective improvements should first be sanctioned by the landowner. In their view, it was only those tenants with express contracts with their landlords to carry out specified improvements who should receive compensation.

The Derby-led administration was succeeded by a coalition government made up of Liberals and Peelites led by Lord Aberdeen. Two members of the Independent Irish Party, John Sadleir and William Keogh, accepted minor offices in the new government. Their acceptance of office was regarded by many people in Ireland as a clear violation of the 'Independent' pledge that both men had taken at the Tenant League conference held in September 1852. As a result, it served to seriously undermine the party's position in the House of Commons. It was unlikely, to say the least, that the new government would introduce a measure which would prove acceptable to the Tenant League.

In the course of a re-election speech at Cavan, Sir John Young, the newly appointed Irish Chief Secretary, gave a qualified support to Napier's bills. He suggested that, as amended by the select committee, they might form the basis of a settlement of the land question.[1] Despite Independent Party pressure, this committee had not yet been appointed when the Conservative government fell in December 1852.[2] The composition of the committee was finally agreed in February 1853, despite a last minute effort by Sir Arthur Brooke and other Conservative MPs from the North of Ireland to have it altered in favour of landowners there. Brooke complained that none of the Irish Conservative MPs on the committee had any practical knowledge of the workings of the Tenant Right system in Ulster.[3] In fact, three of the six Conservative MPs who served on the select committee were non-landowners. These three were Napier, Whiteside and Richard Davison. Like Napier and Whiteside, Davison was a member of the legal profession and had practised as a solicitor in Belfast. The other Irish Conservative members of the committee were Lord Naas, Lord Claud Hamilton, whose brother, the Duke of Abercorn, owned extensive estates in Fermanagh and Tyrone, and Edward Grogan, who owned close to 6,000 acres in three Irish counties. The *Daily Express* claimed that four of these men, Napier, Whiteside, Davison and Naas, were committed to the Tenants' Compensation Bill which, it maintained, contained 'a principle that a majority of Irish landlords would not admit'.[4] The committee as a whole consisted of twenty-nine members. The English members of the committee ranged across the political spectrum from Lord Palmerston, who was deeply hostile to the Tenant League, to John Bright, the English Radical MP, who was sympathetic to many of its demands. Shortly after its appointment, *The Nation* newspaper divided the committee's membership into thirteen members whom it labelled 'friends of the Tenant' and 16 members whom it described as 'friends of the Landlord'.[5] However, this proved to be an over-estimation of the pro-tenant forces on the committee.

The committee first considered Napier's Leasing Powers Bill and the Landlord and Tenant Bill, both of which were adopted with minor amendments. It then voted down Shee's Tenants' Compensation Bill by nineteen votes to nine. Among those who voted against Shee's bill was William Kirk, the only Ulster MP sympathetic to the Tenant League elected at the general election. Despite this, Kirk voted with the majority against the clause in Shee's bill that had proposed the legalisation of the 'Ulster Custom' across the whole of Ireland.[6] Indeed the clause was supported by only nine members of the committee and this support came almost exclusively from the Independent Party MPs themselves. Given the scale of this defeat, the party had little option but to withdraw its bill.[7] The committee then considered Napier's bill on the same subject and made a number of important amendments to it. First, it substituted monetary compensation for the compensatory periods that had been recommended by Napier. This appears to have been in response to earlier Independent Party criticism of this proposal. The difference between this and Napier's original scheme was that tenants remained entitled to compensation so long as their improvements continued to increase the value of their holdings rather than for a fixed number of years. As in the earlier bill, a tenant evicted for non-payment or for arrears of rent would not be entitled to compensation.

The committee also drew a distinction between improvements made in and those made on the soil. This was a subtle and technical distinction designed to limit the types of improvements for which compensation would be paid. To receive compensation, a tenant would have to prove that an improvement was 'permanent, visible and not incorporated with the soil'.[8] Improvements which fell under this heading included farm buildings, roads, fences and the reclamation of waste lands. Drainage, 'the improvement most commonly made in Ireland' according to Gavan Duffy,[9] did not fall under the scope of the bill. By limiting the scope of Napier's original measure, the committee had succeeded in drawing much of its sting. It further restricted the bill's operation by specifying that all prospective improvements would have to be made with the landlord's prior consent and under express contract.

Of Napier's four bills the Land Improvement Bill was the only one not to be submitted to the committee. It was read for the third time in the House of Commons on 14 March and sent on to the Lords. There it was strongly opposed by Lord St Leonards, who had been the chief critic of Napier's original bills within the Derby cabinet. St Leonards argued that the bill would discourage landowners from making improvements by allowing limited owners to raise funds to do so themselves.[10] Lord Clanricarde, a Liberal peer and one of the most formidable opponents of Napier's bills, maintained that 'property would not be safe, if the Legislature went on teaching to the tenantry of Ireland that they had rights other than those [which] they legally possessed by their contracts with their landlords'.[11] This bill had been the least contentious of Napier's measures, but the opposition that it encountered in the House of Lords led to its deferral to the next session of parliament.

Nevertheless, in a parliamentary debate on 24 June, Sir John Young declared the government's intention to pass the remaining bills as speedily as possible. The cabinet was, he claimed, 'perfectly united on this point'.[12] However, its position on the bills was less clear-cut than this statement had made it appear. In the select committee, Lord Palmerston had made clear his opposition to Napier's Tenants' Compensation Bill. Indeed, he had argued that there was no necessity for any legislation whatsoever on the Irish land question.[13] As a result, there was to be a persistent ambiguity in the government's handling of the bills, particularly on the question of whether they were to be treated as its own bills or as private bills introduced by Napier.

During June and July, the three remaining bills went through their committee stage in the House of Commons. The amended Tenants' Compensation Bill went through this stage without any major modifications, although its most controversial aspect, the Retrospective Clause, was strongly criticised by both Liberals and Conservatives. Lord Monck, a leading Liberal, considered it 'opposed to all principles of legislation' and warned that it would lead to widespread litigation between Irish landlords and tenants.[14] From a very different political perspective, *The Times* newspaper, at that time seen as representing middle-class 'Free Trade' opinion,[15] also criticised the Retrospective Clause. Its main objection to the bill was its interference with existing contracts. *The Times* argued that the bill's retrospective nature meant that it contained 'a principle... utterly at variance with all our notions of the inviolability of a contract'.[16] The bills had, thus, come under attack from two very different political perspectives; on the one hand, from Irish landowners concerned at their effects on their control over their property and on the other, from middle-class Radicals, opposed to their 'interference', as they saw it, with existing contracts.

After passing through the House of Commons, the bills were introduced in the House of Lords by the Duke of Newcastle. Newcastle had previously accepted Napier's request that he take charge of the land bills once they reached the House of Lords. He was a prominent Peelite, who had served briefly as Irish Chief Secretary under Peel in 1846. After he had agreed to take charge of the bills, Napier advised him of the dangers he believed were posed 'by the narrow and short-sighted views of some who are blind to their own interests and the welfare of Ireland'. This was a clear reference to those Liberal and Conservative peers led by Clanricarde, Roden and Clancarty who opposed the bills. From this group, Napier argued, 'obstruction may be naturally expected. And yet if they were punished by a successful opposition, they would be found only to give zest to a perilous agitation, with a grievance touching the everyday feelings of the people and entangled in the great principles of property'. He assured Newcastle that there were no concessions in his bills which were 'not reasonable, politic and safe'.[17] From Napier's perspective, it was in the landowners' long-term interests to support a moderate measure of land reform, both in order to defuse the tenant agitation in Ireland and to pre-empt a more radical attempt to settle the Irish land question in the future. His fear was that, by so strenuously resisting a measure of land reform stemming from friendly hands, Irish landlords would ensure that a future measure would come from a less friendly source.

Newcastle later claimed that Napier had promised him that, despite the opposition of some Conservative peers, both Derby and Eglinton would give their 'utmost support and assistance' in getting the bills passed in the Lords.[18] Writing to Derby around the same time, Napier again stressed the dangers of postponing legislation on the land question. In his opinion what had 'been proposed and left undecided' would be 'made the basis of very increased demands' while 'at present a reduced plan' would be 'accepted favourably and the question set at rest, so far as the reasonable class are in any way connected with the assertion of claims'. If 'any part of the question' remained unsettled, Napier saw 'no prospect of social peace or quiet progress'[19] in Ireland. His belief in his bills as a comprehensive settlement of the Irish land question was clearly expressed here.

Napier's prediction of Clanricarde's opposition to the bills was borne out in the course of the Lords debate. Clanricarde condemned the Tenants' Compensation Bill for its 'total violation and disregard of all contracts'.[20] This criticism was echoed by Roden, who described the Bill as 'disgraceful and unjust to the holders of property in Ireland'.[21] Given the level of opposition to the bills, Aberdeen accepted Clanricarde's suggestion that they should be read a second time and not proceeded with any further during that session. He also promised that the government would submit them to a Lords select committee in the ensuing session.[22]

During the recess, an important correspondence, both public and private, took place between Napier and Donoughmore. Donoughmore wrote to Napier in late November, expressing his support for the Landlord and Tenant Bill and for the Leasing Powers Bill. However, he made it clear that he could not support the Retrospective Clause in the Tenants' Compensation Bill. He asked Napier if he considered that bill 'really essential' to the settlement of the land question.[23] After the select committee's decision to limit the types of improvements for which compensation could be paid, Napier believed that the Fixtures Clause of his original Compensation Bill was the only part of it that could now be proceeded with. This clause gave tenants under notice to quit the right to remove improvements, such as buildings and gates, if the landlord refused to purchase them. It had been transferred to the Landlord and Tenant Bill and Napier insisted that he had 'nothing further' to propose on the subject.

In Napier's view, the responsibility for the new Tenants' Compensation Bill lay with the government and he would support it only in his capacity as a 'private member'. Significantly, however, Napier argued that the new bill was widely considered to be 'very objectionable, as not sufficiently protective of property'. It had not 'received that sanction from the intelligent part of the community which is indispensable to a measure of this peculiar character'. Napier's intention here, it seems clear, was to distance himself from the Retrospective Clause of the Tenants' Compensation Bill and to give other Conservatives the freedom to oppose it. Yet, in his personal view, Napier had never seen sufficient reason to 'anticipate the peril to property which others apprehend[ed] from this bill'. Its subject matter was 'very limited' and the bill only provided for compensation in exceptional circumstances. Despite this, he suggested that if it generated a 'feeling of insecurity in the country, however unfounded' he believed this to be, it would be better to pass the other two bills on their own. While he would have preferred a separate Compensation Bill, he was willing to work with Donoughmore to pass the two other measures.[24] During the preceding months Napier's bills had been widely criticised in the Conservative press,[25] and it seems from his willingness to compromise on key features of them that this criticism had had some effect.

Napier's sensitivity to this criticism was shown clearly in a letter written to Donoughmore later in November. In relation to the Tenants' Compensation Bill, he claimed that he had never received any intimation from other Irish Conservative MPs that 'any clause [in it] would be opposed as wrong in principle'. Indeed, he had been 'not merely willing but anxious' to accept suggestions from other Conservative politicians for amending his bills. Napier correctly identified 'the real controversy' over the bills as concerning the Tenants' Compensation Bill. He was also critical of the Aberdeen-led government for having fastened the authorship of the amended bill on him.[26] In a letter to Naas, Napier argued that although he disliked it as amended, he thought that it was 'better to pass it – even in this form'. If passed, it would, he believed, 'stop the [land] agitation, at least in so far as agitation can do mischief'. He stressed the limited nature of the bill, and argued that, if the Tenants' Compensation Bill were rejected, it would be more difficult to pass the Landlord and Tenant Bill. That bill was 'eminently favourable to proprietors' and would benefit them far more than the other bill would benefit tenants.[27]

The landlord case against retrospective compensation was stated clearly in a letter from Donoughmore to Napier in late November. He reiterated his distinct opposition to any form of retrospective legislation 'except to give legal effect to previous contracts, which were void from want of power on the part of the landlord'. Donoughmore also argued that the Conservative Party should leave it to the government to introduce its own Tenants' Compensation Bill in the next session of parliament. This would give them more freedom of action than they had had during the previous session, given Napier's authorship of the original bill. From 'the feeling' against it expressed in the House of Lords on its second reading in August 1853, Donoughmore believed that it would be virtually impossible to get a Compensation Bill even 'of the most limited character through that House'. It would be better to 'let the government be defeated on their [own] measure than to bring in ours, be beaten by our own men, and create a split in our own party'. While he would assist Napier in an effort to have the other two measures passed, he could not support the Retrospective Clause.[28]

Replying, Napier agreed with Donoughmore that the Lords would in all likelihood defeat the Tenants' Compensation Bill. Although he could not say that it was 'perilous to property', nevertheless it was 'so dreaded by proprietors' that he would not be 'justified in now asking either House to sanction it as an integral part of the general settlement'. Despite this, Napier believed that 'a contract in good faith' had been made by the Conservative Party with the Ulster tenantry to give them some legal security for their improvements. It was important, therefore, that the Conservatives should show that the other two bills on their own 'were not merely landlord measures – but that in truth [they are] a code at once sufficient' for both landlords and tenants. The Conservative press in Ireland might 'usefully work this side of the case'.[29] It was now clear that, given the level of opposition to the Tenants' Compensation Bill within the Irish Conservative Party and from the Irish Conservative press, Napier was willing to drop it and to proceed with a more limited code than he had originally intended.

Napier confirmed this decision in a letter to Sir Hugh Cairns. It was necessary, he believed, to 'let the Bill for compulsory compensation [the Tenants' Compensation Bill] go by the board'. He had written to Newcastle, telling him that, given 'the manner in which the friends of the Gov[ernmen]t' had fastened on him 'the entire odium of the Comp[ensatio]n Bill', he would 'have nothing further to do with it, by any interference direct or indirect'. It was now 'quite hopeless' to attempt to pass a bill, as this would only 'peril what … [was] prudent [and] safe by insisting on what … [was] suspected disliked & never would be allowed by the peers'. Given the fact that Irish Conservative landowners would support the Fixtures Clause, it would then be up to the government to 'adopt or repudiate the orphan [Tenant Compensation] Bill'. It would 'satisfy the Northern tenantry, and cover the larger cases' while the Leasing Powers Bill would 'provide for the smaller, better than a strict plan of compulsory compensation'.[30] This argument was unconvincing, but it was obviously intended by Napier to justify his abandonment of the Tenants' Compensation Bill. Napier's tone in this letter was strikingly different from that in his letter to Naas in November 1852 quoted above.[31] Then, Napier had maintained that the Tenants' Compensation Bill was an essential element in his landlord and tenant code; to Cairns, he argued for its dispensability. This clearly reflected the change in the political circumstances since November 1852, and the unwillingness of Irish Conservatives, who might otherwise have supported the bill in order to keep a Conservative government in office, to do so any longer.

In a letter to Lord Dunsany in early January, Donoughmore clarified his differences with Napier over the original bills. Dunsany had written to Donoughmore, stressing his acceptance of 'the moral claims of the tenant [to compensation] for bona fide improvements'. However, he was disturbed at the prospect of this moral right being converted into a legal right. If this happened, Dunsany was worried where Irish landlords could 'logically draw the line between such an admission and the rights claimed for the tenant by the Tenant League'. Dunsany's answer to this was to insist that all 'compensation for unauthorised works' should be 'matters of bargain' and not for legislation. He would support a measure that facilitated such contracts, but could not support retrospective legislation.[32] For Dunsany, as for other Irish landowners, it was essential that they should retain control over the types of improvements that were made on their estates. If improvements were made a matter of contract between landlords and tenants, this objective would have been secured.

In response, Donoughmore assured Dunsany that he too had always been opposed to the Retrospective Clause. He described it as 'vicious in principle' and calculated to give rise to 'an infinite amount of litigation'. He also differed with Napier on the propriety of giving compensation for unauthorised improvements. He assured Dunsany that while Napier still maintained 'the safety' of his original bill, he was aware of the extent to which it had 'alarmed many Irish proprietors' and was, therefore, 'willing to abandon it'.[33]

The revised bills were introduced by Donoughmore in the House of Lords on 28 February 1854. In this speech, Donoughmore strongly condemned the Retrospective Clause. He argued that it was impossible to frame such a clause 'which would at the same time guard the rights of property'. The amended bills, by contrast, were based on the principle that improvements should only be made with the consent of the landlord. This principle, could not, he claimed, be made compatible with the payment of compensation for past improvements.[34] Even the revised bills came under attack from some quarters. Lord Desart complained that as 'the land was the property of the landlord', the government should not intervene in its ownership and management 'so long as either were not rendered injurious to the public interest'. Desart baldly stated the essence of the landlord's case: the landlord and tenant stood in the position of 'contractors in a commercial transaction' and their relations should be determined by contract alone and not by the government.[35] At the close of the debate, the revised bills, along with the bills previously introduced by the government, were committed to a House of Lords select committee.

The committee sat between March and May 1854, and collected evidence from a wide range of witnesses, including Napier. His evidence there, although not made public, seems to have been largely along the lines of his previous letters to Donoughmore. He repeated the argument that along with the Leasing Powers Bill, the Fixtures Clause of the Landlord and Tenant Bill would give as large a measure of compensation as was practicable.[36] Not surprisingly, the committee's report issued on 11 May recommended that the Tenants' Compensation Bill be dropped. The other two bills were returned to the Commons with minor amendments. The Fixtures Clause was modified so that it applied only to the cases of tenants with express agreements with their landlords to carry out improvements. The claims of tenants who had been given rent abatements in consideration of improvements, or who had remained in possession for twenty-one years, were also disallowed. Despite these alterations, the revised bills received strong criticism when considered in the Lords on 18 May. Opposing the Leasing Powers Bill, Clanricarde claimed that 'more mischief' had been caused in Ireland by the granting of long leases 'than good prevented' by the lack of them. His argument was that tenants on long leases lacked any incentive to improve their land.[37] This argument was supported by Derby, who argued that a twenty-one-year lease 'afforded ample motive to improvement to an enterprising and intelligent tenant'.[38] Speaking in this debate, Donoughmore regretted that the compensation given to tenants by the committee had been so limited. This ensured, in his opinion, that there would be 'cases of justice and of right' that the measures would no longer meet.

Despite the attacks on the two revised bills, both were passed on the committee stage and were committed for their third reading the following week. On its third reading, Lord Clancarty, a leading Irish Conservative landowner, attempted to have the Fixtures Clause removed from the Landlord and Tenant Bill.[39] The motion to drop the clause was, however, defeated by forty-one votes to ten. After the bills passed through their third reading, a protest against them was signed by a large number of Irish peers. Among the signatories to the protest were prominent Irish Conservative peers like Clancarty and Mayo. Their protest objected to special legislation for Ireland, urging that it was essential that the law in England and Ireland 'should rest on the same fundamental principles'. Any deviation should occur only where 'a difference of circumstances between the two countries' was clearly established. With regard to the Fixtures Clause, this, they argued, had not been done.

The bills were not debated again in the House of Commons until July. On this occasion, Shee asked that the government defer further consideration of them until the next session of parliament. He was surprised that Napier could support the passing of the two approved bills, without a separate Tenants' Compensation Bill. The earlier Compensation Bill had been passed by the House of Commons, and he complained that 'it was not endurable' that 'a few Irish landlords in another House' should set 'aside the deliberate opinion of that House and of the leading statesmen of the country'.[40] Sir John Young admitted that, without the Tenants' Compensation Bill, the other two bills 'by themselves would be unsatisfactory to the people of Ireland'.[41] Given the opposition of Irish Liberal and Independent Party MPs to the amended bills, however, the

Aberdeen government was placed in an extremely difficult position with regard to them.

It had been clear from the outset that the government had little enthusiasm for the proposed bills. A number of senior ministers, most notably Lord Palmerston, had made little secret of their distaste for them.[42] Indeed, in a famous phrase, Palmerston had once described Tenant Right as 'landlord wrong'.[43] The cabinet's ambivalent attitudes to the bills had also been conditioned by the fact it was a Conservative government that had originally introduced them. At the same time, the growing tensions within the Independent Irish Party itself had meant that its ability to influence the government was less than it might otherwise have been. These tensions had originally emerged as a result of Sadleir and Keogh's acceptance of office, but they had been deepened by the ongoing internal conflicts between its leaders. The withdrawal of the Tenants' Compensation Bill also made the bills far less attractive from a Tenant League perspective. By contrast, from Napier's perspective, the dropping of the bill had the effect of lessening his isolation within the Conservative Party. Indeed, there is some evidence that Napier might have been willing to see the Landlord and Tenant Bill pass even without the Fixtures Clause. He justified this flexibility with regard to the bills as being the only way of ensuring that they were passed by the House of Lords.[44]

Between 1855 and 1858, the Irish land question was, in parliamentary terms at least, largely in abeyance. The Tenant League itself fell into a steady decline, largely as a result of the increase in agricultural prosperity in Ireland from 1853 onwards. In the twenty-five years between 1851 and 1876, for example, Irish wheat prices rose by 20 per cent, while barley prices rose by 43 per cent and beef and butter prices by 87 per cent.[45] These price rises principally benefited the more prosperous farmers in the province of Leinster, particularly those in counties like Kilkenny, Kildare and Meath. As it had been farmers from these areas who had provided the backbone of the Tenant League's campaign in the South of Ireland, this rise in agricultural prices served to undermine 'the whole basis of the agitation'.[46] The number of evictions also fell dramatically in these years, as did the number of agrarian outrages.[47] This improvement in the condition of farmers in Ireland was facilitated by the shift from tillage to pastoral farming that occurred in this period, a transition that was largely driven by the rise in the prices which Irish farmers received for their beef and dairy exports.[48] The transition was eased, especially in the province of Leinster, by the decline in the number of smallholdings there during the Famine. Another result of this increase in agricultural prosperity was a growing self-confidence among Irish landowners. As they were now operating from a position of strength, their determination to resist measures, which they saw as damaging to their interests, was reinforced.[49]

Given this decline in the level of tenant agitation in Ireland, there was less pressure on both of the main British political parties to introduce legislation on the land question. There were also growing divisions within the Independent Party itself. After the high point of its electoral success in 1852, the party's structural weaknesses became increasingly evident. These included the divisions between the southern and the northern wings of the movement. These divisions were exacerbated by the fact that the northern wing of the party did not feel the same sense of grievance over the Liberal government's handling of the controversy surrounding the Ecclesiastical Titles Bill, as did its southern wing. As a result, it continued to believe that support for the Liberal Party provided the best opportunity to secure a measure of land reform. Over time, it gradually distanced itself from the southern wing of the Independent Party and sought to achieve its objectives through working from within the Liberal Party.

For different reasons, Paul Cullen,[50] the Archbishop of Dublin and the leading figure in the Irish Roman Catholic Church, who had been a prominent supporter of the Independent Party in its early stages, also began to distance himself from it. Cullen's principal concern was with the extension of the Roman Catholic Church's influence within Ireland. In consequence, he was anxious to see Catholics taking up as many official positions as possible in an attempt to undermine 'Protestant ascendancy' there. To achieve this end, Cullen viewed an alliance with the Liberal Party as essential. Because of his belief in the usefulness of the 'Liberal alliance', Cullen soon lost his enthusiasm for the Independent principle.[51] In 1854, he attempted to prevent other Catholic clerics from campaigning for the Independent Party, a move which seriously weakened it. His attempts to achieve this end also led to a bitter dispute between him and Frederick Lucas. This controversy eventually resulted in Lucas undertaking a 'mission' to Rome to protest against the new policy adopted by Cullen.[52] The mission ultimately ended in failure and its effect was to further damage the credibility of the Independent Party, especially among Irish Catholics. Lucas died unexpectedly in late 1855, not long after the failure of his mission to Rome. Early in the following year, disillusioned by the decline in popular support for the Independent Party and in pecuniary difficulties of his own, Charles Gavan Duffy retired from parliament and emigrated to Australia. This departure of two of its most prominent members from Irish political life further exacerbated the party's difficulties.

Along with these damaging divisions within the party, there was an ongoing debate among its leaders about the tactics that it should use to achieve its demands. There were differing views within the party as to whether it should adhere strictly to the pledges on the land and the Church questions which it had made in 1852 or whether it should accept compromise measures which at least partially fulfilled its demands. This question had, of course, previously been raised at the time of the introduction of Napier's bills in November 1852. However, it had been given added momentum by the wholesale rejection of Shee's bill by the select committee in 1853. These divisions on tactics were brought into the open in early 1854, when, on his own initiative, Shee introduced a compromise Compensation Bill. The measure had not been sanctioned by the Council of the Tenant League, which publicly censured him for not following its instructions. As a result, Shee broke with the party and, from that time on, acted independently from it.[53] Shee's departure, however, did not lead to a resolution of the conflicts within the party. Ultimately, these differences over what tactics the party should pursue led to growing divisions within its ranks, divisions which greatly impeded its effectiveness.

In early 1856, in response to a question from Vincent Scully, the Independent Party MP for Tipperary, Palmerston disclaimed any intention on the part of the government to introduce a Tenants' Compensation Bill, or to support one brought in independently.[54] The land question was low among the government's priorities, with other concerns, not least the Crimean war, taking up most of its time. In addition to this, the government's experience of earlier bills would hardly have inspired much confidence in its ability to pass such a measure. There also was a general lack of political will among both Liberals and Conservatives to broach the question. While abortive Tenant Right Bills were introduced by George Henry Moore[55] in 1856 and 1857, the debates on them took up little parliamentary time, and they did not receive any support from government. This lack of interest in the Irish land question at the official level was reflected in the wish expressed by the Irish Conservative newspaper, the *Daily Express*, in July 1855, that the Tenant Right Bill, having been laid aside, should 'be laid at rest for ever'.[56]

In April 1857, the Palmerston government was unexpectedly defeated in the House of Commons. Palmerston's response to this was to call a general election, at which the government was returned with an increased majority. The election served to revive interest in the Irish land question among some Conservative candidates. Several declared their support for a compensation bill without, in John George's words, 'retrospective and impossible conditions'.[57] In his election address, Pierce Creagh, a Roman Catholic and the pro-Conservative candidate for Clare, attacked Palmerston as 'the enemy of the tenants and of Tenant Right'.[58] Though defeated in Clare, he was representative of a wider strain of Catholic opinion, which preferred the prospect of a Conservative government to that of an administration involving Palmerston and Russell. This view was based, in part, on Irish Catholic dislike of Lord John Russell for his conduct over the Ecclesiastical Titles Bill. It was also based on Irish Catholic opposition to the Liberal Party's policies towards Italy. However, it was also influenced by the perception that Derby was less hostile to a measure of tenants' compensation than was Palmerston. This view had, of course, been given greater strength by the Conservative government's introduction of Napier's original land bills in 1852.

At Napier's election for Dublin University, however, his introduction of the original land bills was used against him by his Liberal opponent. It was argued that Napier's involvement with them had given 'great dissatisfaction' to his constituents. Napier insisted, however, that he had 'abandoned the land bill' which he had found 'not to merit, at least a particular portion of it, the judgement of many of those... [he] respect[ed].' When a heckler called out 'What about Tenant Right?' Napier answered that it was 'dead and gone'. He had 'washed his hands of it'.[59] He qualified this by specifying that he would oppose any land measure 'having provision for retrospective compensation'. This left it open for him to support a measure without such a provision. His private conviction was that it would be 'quite delusive' to reintroduce his original bills and he was not prepared to do so. As they had not satisfied either the landlords or the tenants it was clear that they were not 'practicable' and he would not 'attempt anything more about it'.[60]

In the North of Ireland, the Tenant Right question did not achieve the same prominence as it had done in the 1852 general election. Several candidates, including Lord Edwin Hill in Down County, did not even raise the subject in their addresses.[61] Other candidates, like James Clark in Londonderry County, declared their support for a measure which would secure to the tenant 'the fruit of his toil and outlay'. A similar pledge was made by William Brownlow Forde, one of the candidates for Down County, although he qualified this by referring to 'unexhausted improvements'.[62] Sir William Verner, the combative candidate for Armagh, called on supporters of Tenant Right to define what they meant by it. He had never known 'two persons who advocated Tenant Right that could agree in their views of what it really meant'. If it meant putting the tenant 'in the place of the landlord' he would not vote for it, but he would support a measure giving 'that justice to the tenant[s] to which they were fully entitled'.[63] This was an ambivalent statement by any standards, especially given that Verner had been one of the most vehement critics of Napier's original bills.[64]

As in 1852, candidates sympathetic to the Tenant League did poorly in northern constituencies. In Armagh County, for example, James Caulfield received only six votes in a constituency with some 5,596 voters. As we have seen earlier, landlord influence at elections in Ulster was stronger than elsewhere in the country. After the elections, the *Northern Whig* accused a number of Ulster landlords of having coerced their tenants into voting for Conservative candidates.[65] However, there was another aspect to the 1857 election which was to be a significant pointer to later developments. This was the co-operation which took place between Conservatives and some Independent Party candidates in contests where the other had an opportunity to defeat the Whig–Liberal candidate. In Tipperary, for example, many Conservatives supported The O'Donoghue, the Independent Party candidate, while in Mayo George Henry Moore assisted in the return of Roger Palmer, the Conservative candidate.

While this co-operation was sanctioned by party chiefs in Dublin, like Whiteside and Taylor, it was not necessarily popular with local Conservatives. Writing to Moore, in March 1857, Donoughmore promised him his support in his contest against Laurence Waldron, the Liberal candidate. He admitted, however, that he had been unable to secure 'the united and vigorous action' of the Conservative Party in Tipperary in favour of The O' Donoghue. Many of the gentry there believed that if they voted for him, they would 'be looked upon as approving his [The O'Donoghue's] opinions upon Tenant Right and the revenues of the Established Church'.[66] Against this, Lord Glengall justified his vote for The O'Donoghue by claiming that Moore had promised him, in return, to 'turn out Palmerston for us if he can'.[67] This 'ad hoc understanding'[68] succeeded in most of its immediate aims in the 1857 election, and also laid the groundwork for the co-operation between the Conservatives and a section of the Independent Party in the late 1850s and early 1860s. The results of the election were, however disappointing for the Conservatives and the Palmerston administration remained in office.

The Palmerston government eventually fell in February 1858, after unexpectedly losing a vote in the House of Commons. They were succeeded by the second Derby-led administration, in which Napier was appointed as Irish Lord Chancellor and Whiteside as Attorney General for Ireland. Lord Eglinton and Lord Naas were reappointed as Lord Lieutenant and Chief Secretary respectively. As in 1852, the government was a minority one. Indeed, in parliamentary terms it was weaker than the earlier government had been. Derby's attempts to induce former Peelites, such as Gladstone, to join the government had failed and he was left to form an administration on a purely Conservative basis. The government was therefore placed in the position of trying to gain support from Liberals, disillusioned by Palmerston's performance in government. Along with those Radical MPs dissatisfied by Palmerston's procrastination on the Reform question, the government also attempted to win support from Independent Irish Party MPs aware of his opposition to legislation on the land question. This meant that a number of Independent Party MPs led by John Francis Maguire were prepared to give the Conservative government a 'fair trial' and to support them in the House of Commons on occasion. The absence at this point of any major differences on Irish policy between the Whigs and the Tories made this rapprochement between the

Conservatives and this section of the Independent Party easier to achieve. In this state of 'near equilibrium' it was clear that even minor concessions by the Conservatives might tip the balance in their favour.[69]

The new conciliatory policy was, however, to operate within strictly defined limits. In the debates on a Tenants' Compensation Bill introduced by Maguire in April 1858, both Naas and Whiteside outlined the parameters within which a government measure on the land question would be framed. On 14 April, for example, Naas laid down 'three great objects' which should be kept in mind when considering legislation on the topic. The first was that any proposed bill should be 'entirely prospective' in its operation. This, in effect, ruled out any prospect of the government reintroducing the Retrospective Clause. Second, he proposed that such a measure should be based on the 'compensatory periods' recommended in Napier's original bills. Third, all improvements should 'generally speaking' be made with the landlord's consent. Landlords should also be given the opportunity of making the proposed improvement themselves if they so wished. Naas insisted that the relations between landlord and tenant should be made 'as much as possible a matter of contract'.[70] This speech showed that any measure introduced by the Conservative government would mark a considerable dilution of Napier's original scheme, and would, in most respects, be identical to the bill as amended by the Lords committee in 1853.

In a speech on the second reading of Maguire's bill on 9 June, Whiteside reiterated his support for the introduction of a Leasing Powers Bill. He also favoured the introduction of a consolidation bill to reduce 'the great complexity' of Irish landlord and tenant law. As with Naas, his principal criticisms were reserved for the Retrospective Clause, although he was willing to consider 'a bill carefully framed', shorn of this principle.[71] Following this debate a deputation of Independent Irish Party MPs led by Maguire met with Disraeli. At this meeting Maguire claimed that the support which his group had given to the government 'entitled them to its consideration'. After the large majorities in the House against his bill, Maguire admitted that he did not expect the inclusion of a Retrospective Clause in a government-sponsored measure. However, he did ask for 'a large and liberal measure of Tenant Right'. He pointed out that the deputation was prepared to settle for a bill which gave compensation for prospective improvements only. According to Sir William Shee, Disraeli's reply to the deputation 'abounded in courteous generalities' and he promised, in timeworn fashion, to submit the question to his colleagues. Disraeli could not 'hold out any expectation of an extreme measure', but had 'no doubt' that the government would introduce a land bill.[72]

The meeting did, however, lead to controversy within the Independent Party. According to Maguire, it had enraged the 'thick and thin enemies' of the Conservatives.[73] Shortly after it was held, Patrick O'Brien, the MP for King's County, asked Disraeli in the House of Commons whether the government intended to introduce a measure based on Napier's original bills.[74] In Maguire's opinion, O'Brien's question was designed to embarrass both the government and his section of the Independent Party. To counter this tactic, he advised Disraeli to announce the government's intention to bring in a bill early in the next session or, failing this, to give O'Brien the same answer he had given the deputation. In the event, Disraeli told O'Brien that the government intended to give the question its 'earnest consideration' during the recess. Whiteside had already 'directed his attention to it' and Disraeli hoped that the government would be able to introduce a measure after parliament had reassembled.[75] After Disraeli's reply, Maguire defended his policy of giving the government 'fair play'. In his view, the Conservative government had 'done more for progress than any of their Whig predecessors who had been in office for the last ten years'. It was not his section of the party 'who [had] sold the Irish party to the government of the day, and sacrificed the cause of the tenant to their own selfish purposes'. This was an obvious attack on O'Brien, who was essentially a Liberal and who had only adopted the 'Independent pledge' in 1852 in order to be elected. The acrimonious nature of these exchanges illustrated the depths of the divisions between the Independent Irish Party MPs and their Liberal counterparts.

As in 1852, however, Irish landlords were quick to seize on any possibility of a land measure being introduced. On 5 July in the House of Lords, Clanricarde asked Derby if the government planned to introduce a measure rendering Tenant Right, as it already existed in the North, compulsory by law. Derby naturally denied this, and stated that a government measure would be designed solely to remedy 'acknowledged anomalies and inconveniences' which existed in Irish landlord and tenant law.[76] This reply was clearly intended to dampen down any expectations that the government intended to reintroduce the 1852 bills, or, more specifically, the Retrospective Clause. Derby had earlier told an Independent Party deputation that he had 'burned his fingers'[77] on the question in 1852, and it was quite plain that he had no intention of allowing it to again become a divisive issue within the Conservative Party.

Throughout this session, Whiteside was preoccupied with steering his Sale and Transfer of Land Bill through the Commons. The bill created a new Landed Estates Court in Dublin, which was to take on the powers of the Encumbered Estates Court. The new Court was also given the power to grant legal titles to the owners of unencumbered estates. Despite Whiteside's involvement with the bill, Maguire told a Tenant League conference in Dublin in August that he had promised to take the subject of landlord and tenant law 'in hand' on his return to Dublin for the recess.

For his part, Maguire would support 'any measure introduced by the present government, which...no matter how partially...recognise[d] and establish[ed] the rights of the tenant class' in Ireland. Unless the government failed to keep faith with Whiteside's promise, he would continue to accord them 'the same conditional support' he had given them up to that point.[78]

This policy did not, of course, command unconditional support within the Independent Party. At the Tenant League conference, George Henry Moore had proposed a resolution stating that Disraeli's reply to the deputation had been 'unsatisfactory' and that, in consequence, the Independent Party should hold itself 'independent of, and in opposition to' the Conservative government. He believed that it was 'utterly impossible' that the government would introduce a measure that would be acceptable to Irish tenants.[79] However, Moore's motion had been defeated and Maguire told Naas that, while he had had a 'hard card to play' at the conference, he had 'played it boldly & never quailed for a moment'. John Blake, the MP for Waterford, had, he reported, 'stuck to...[him] like a brick'. He assured Naas that a Tenants' Compensation Bill, even without the Retrospective Clause would 'satisfy the country at large &...be a tower of strength to your government'.[80]

Maguire's letters to Naas took on a more strident and, indeed, almost desperate tone as time advanced and the new session of parliament came closer. On 25 August he assured Naas of his belief that the government would 'not disappoint the anxious hopes of the country and that...[it would] give a good bill'.[81] By September, he was becoming 'nervous', warning of the 'odium and disgrace' which would be heaped on him if those who he had assisted by his 'vote or by...[his] advocacy' did not introduce a Tenants' Compensation Bill. He advised Naas to introduce a bill giving compensation to evicted tenants for all 'useful and permanent' improvements which added to the value of their holdings. By granting such a measure the government would gain the support 'of every man whose mind was not warped by party prejudice'.[82] Maguire's position on this question was close to that previously advocated by Shee. Like him, Shee had been willing to accept a compromise land measure. Ironically, however, Shee was critical of Maguire's willingness to accept a Compensation Bill, without a Retrospective Clause. For Shee, such a bill would 'be worse than no bill'.[83] Indeed, Maguire's stance on the issue had left him and his supporters particularly vulnerable if the government failed to fulfil its promise to introduce a land bill.[84]

The government's hesitancy with regard to the land question was shown clearly in a memorandum on proposed Irish legislation prepared by Napier in October. In it, he warned that the government should 'do nothing which does not provide for the consent of the landlord'. Furthermore,

Napier recommended that any proposed measure should first be submitted to the landed Irish Conservative MPs for their approval before being introduced. Echoing Derby's earlier remarks, he advised that 'the burned child dreads the fire'.[85] Later in October, Spencer Walpole, the Home Secretary, travelled to Dublin where he discussed the government's programme for the coming session with Eglinton, Naas, Cairns and Whiteside. Following this conference, Derby agreed to the introduction of two bills on the Irish land question. These were a consolidation bill on the lines of Napier's original Landlord and Tenant Bill and a Leasing Powers Bill. Derby also approved the Irish administration's decision not to include a Retrospective Clause in the proposed bills. However, he suggested that 'under proper restrictions', tenants should be allowed to request their landlords to drain their holdings. If the landlord refused to do this, an allowance should be given to the tenant to carry out the work himself. Tenants should also be given an 'increased power' to remove fixtures, with the landlord having the right to pre-empt this by paying a money compensation instead. Derby believed that this power should be restricted to cases where there were no express contracts for improvements, as the 'great object' of these provisions was to 'induce the parties to make arrangements for themselves'.[86]

This fear of alienating their Irish supporters was further shown in February 1859, when Naas, Cairns and Whiteside prevailed upon Walpole to omit any reference to the landlord and tenant question from the Queen's speech. Walpole informed Derby that they were 'so strongly impressed with the impolicy of alluding in any way whatsoever' to the question that he had agreed to delete the paragraph referring to it. The government should, he advised, 'avoid raising either undue expectations or fears in Ireland'.[87] On 3 February Naas and Whiteside met with Derby, who agreed to the deletion of this section of the speech. Its inclusion would, Naas told Eglinton, have 'raised false hopes among the Tenant Right people'.[88] In the event, the Queen's speech did not contain any direct reference to Ireland.

On 25 February 1859, in response to a question from William Kirk, Whiteside announced that he intended to introduce a measure on the landlord and tenant issue, although he did not elaborate on the details of what it would contain. As in 1852, however, the broaching of the land question coincided with a period of crisis for the government. The cabinet was seriously divided over the proposed Reform Bill, divisions which finally led to the resignation of three ministers, including Walpole, the Home Secretary, in late February. The bill had also served to unite the opposition parties in the House against the government. Given these circumstances, it was highly unlikely that the government would have been able to pass a Landlord and Tenant Bill. On 7 April, Naas bowed to the inevitable, and told the House of Commons that it would not introduce a bill 'during the present session.' He promised, however, that a measure on the subject would be introduced early in the next session of parliament.[89] A week earlier, the government had been defeated in a vote on its Reform Bill by 330 votes to 291. Instead of resigning, it had decided on the dissolution of parliament, and the elections were due to commence at the end of April.

One of the features of the vote on the Reform Bill had been that Maguire and his supporters again voted with the government.[90] Throughout the month of March, Maguire had been pressing the government to grant a Charter to the Catholic University in St Stephen's Green, Dublin. He also impressed on both Naas and Disraeli the necessity of giving government patronage to Irish Roman Catholics as a way of defusing the 'active hostility' towards it there. It was Catholic apprehensions about the nature of its Irish appointments that had raised the 'strongest clamour' against the government in Ireland.[91] During its term in office, the Conservative government did, however, make a number of minor concessions to secure Catholic support. Salaries were given to Roman Catholic prison chaplains and the remuneration given to military chaplains was increased. Some minor appointments were given to pro-government Catholics in Ireland. Nevertheless, it was the government's failure to make any major concessions to its Catholic supporters that led to the increasingly desperate tone of Maguire's entreaties to both Naas and Disraeli for such measures.

Despite this, the Conservatives were in a better position to gain Irish Catholic support in 1859 than they had ever been previously. Irish Catholic dislike of Palmerston's Italian policy, and his previous government's meagre record with regard to Irish measures, meant that many voters there were prepared to vote for the Conservatives in return for even slim concessions.[92] In addition the Conservatives had the support of Cardinal Wiseman, the Catholic Archbishop of Westminster, who attempted to influence the Irish elections through his protégé Lord Campden.[93]

At the election pro-Conservative Independent Party MPs like John Blake in Waterford, Sir George Bowyer in Dundalk and John Francis Maguire at Dungarvan were either spared contests or given Conservative support to gain re-election. In King's County, John Pope Hennessey, the first Roman Catholic to stand avowedly as a Conservative, was elected. His support for the government was based, in part, on its promise to introduce a measure on the land question.[94] In the northern constituencies, a number of Conservative candidates also gave similar pledges of support for a moderate land bill as they had done at earlier elections.[95] These promises have been well described by K.T. Hoppen as 'nebulous nothings'.[96] Nonetheless, the 1859 elections proved the most successful for the Irish Conservatives since the Reform Act of 1832. They made eight gains there from the 1857 election, and felt assured of the support, at critical divisions. of another seven Independent Irish Party MPs, some of whom owed their election to Conservative support.[97] The party had not fared as well in Britain, however, and it remained in a minority in the House of Commons.

In these circumstances, those Independent Party MPs, who supported the government were in a strong position to exert pressure on it. On 24 May, Maguire wrote to Naas, urging the government 'to give us [Maguire and his supporters] measures or we cannot be with you'. He reiterated his request for the granting of a Charter to the Catholic University, but his main demand was for an 'honest and comprehensive' land bill. A reference to such a bill in the upcoming Queen's Speech would, he argued, 'cut the legs from under your opponents' in Ireland. It would also strengthen the position of those, like Maguire, who 'support[ed] or even occasionally vote[d] for your party, at the risk of their popularity, their influence...[and] the loss of honest friendships'.[98]

Maguire's attempts to influence government policy were rendered largely academic by the Willis's Rooms meeting of 6 June 1859. This meeting signalled a reconciliation between Lord Palmerston and Lord John Russell, the two leading figures in the Liberal Party in Britain. In consequence, it rendered the Conservative government's long-term future extremely doubtful. Up to this point, it had depended on the divisions among its opponents for its survival. In this context, Whiteside's promise on 9 June that he would introduce a land bill on the night after Disraeli introduced the budget was a rather hollow one.[99] In the event, the government was defeated in a vote on an Opposition amendment to the address on 10 June. Neither Whiteside's bill nor Disraeli's budget were ever introduced. In the following session Rickard Deasy, the new Irish Attorney General, introduced two bills relating to landlord and tenant law in Ireland, largely based on Napier's Bills as amended by the House of Lords committee in 1853. The bills contained no provision for retrospective compensation.

The Irish landlord campaign against what they saw as the objectionable aspects of Napier's bills had, thus, proved a successful one. It is, however, clear that this success was, in fact, a pyrrhic one. As we saw earlier, in the long term Napier proved to be more far-sighted than were his opponents. His belief that the landlords' successful resistance to his Tenants' Compensation Bill would mean that a future measure on the subject was likely to stem from a less friendly source turned out to be a correct one. While his bill was limited in its scope, and only part of a wider scheme favourable to the landowners, it might have conciliated the larger tenants who were those most likely to undertake improvements. Like Gladstone's Land Act of 1870, it might also have provided an impetus to further land reform. In the event, it was not until Gladstone's Land Act of 1870 that a provision for retrospective compensation, although restricted to the case of tenants evicted for reasons other than non-payment of rent, was passed by the House of Commons.

Napier's bills did, however, set a precedent for later Conservative measures of Irish land reform, such as the Ashbourne Act of 1885 and the Wyndham Act of 1903.[100] Their introduction also made it possible for Independent Party spokesmen to argue that the leadership of the Conservative Party was less hostile to land reform than were their Liberal counterparts.[101] The bills occupy a peculiar 'half-way' house position in the history of Irish land reform: on the one hand, pointing towards the adoption of a 'contractual' model of landlord–tenant relations which essentially would have benefited Irish landlords[102] and, on the other pointing towards later legislation, like the 1870 Land Act, which displayed a greater concern for the interests of Irish tenants. The bills could be seen as an attempt to synthesise the disparate views on the Irish land question which were discussed in Chapter 2. However, given the landed dominance of parliament at the time the bills were introduced, this synthesis proved to be one that was extremely difficult, and possibly impossible, to achieve.

NOTES

1   *Daily Express*, 11 January 1853.
2   See Walpole to Disraeli, 15 December 1852, Disraeli papers, B/XXI/W/129, enclosing a letter from Shee to Walpole recommending the appointment of Sadleir, Keogh, Lucas, Duffy and Shee himself amongst others to the select committee. Shee to Walpole, 15 December 1852, Disraeli papers B/XXI/W/129a.
3   *Hansard*, CXXIV, 626.
4   *Daily Express*, 26 February 1853.
5   Quoted in Gavan Duffy, *League of North and South*, p. 251.
6   Gavan Duffy, *League of North and South*, p. 258.
7   See *The Tablet*, 14 May 1853.
8   Sir William Shee, *Papers, Letters and Speeches in the House of Commons on the Irish Land Question, with a Summary of its Parliamentary History from 1852 to the Close of the Session of 1863* (London, 1863), p. 20.
9   Sir Charles Gavan Duffy, *My Life in Two Hemispheres*, 2 vols (London, 1898), Vol. 2, p. 87.
10 *Hansard*, CXXV, 588.
11 *Hansard*, CXXVI, 1305. For a discussion of Clanricarde's views on the land question, see J.J. Conwell, *A Galway Landlord During the Great Famine: Ulick John De Burgh, First Marquis of Clanricarde* (Dublin, 2003), pp. 51 4.
12 *Hansard*, CXXVIII, 241.
13 Gavan Duffy, *The League of North and South*, p. 263.
14 *Hansard*, CXXIX, 637.
15 See Vincent, *Formation of the Liberal Party*, p. 63.
16 *The Times*, 17 August 1853.
17 Derby being ill and Eglinton away in Scotland, Napier wrote to Newcastle asking him to take charge of the bills. Napier also enclosed a summary of the bills, which

Newcastle drew on heavily for his speech in the Lords. See Napier to Newcastle, n.d., quoted in Ewald, *Life and Letters of Sir Joseph Napier* (2nd edn, London, 1892), p. 77.

18 *Hansard*, CXXXV, 142.

19 Napier to Derby, n.d., quoted in Ewald, *Life and Letters of Sir Joseph Napier* (2nd edn, London, 1892), p. 77.

20 *Hansard*, CXXIX, 1518. Karl Marx quoted this passage from Clanricarde's speech in an article published in the *New York Daily Herald* on 24 August 1853. Marx described the debate as 'a mere farce, performed for the benefit of the newspaper reporters', as the 'Whig and Tory lords' had already reached 'a secret understanding to throw the bills out'. See Karl Marx and Frederick Engels, *Ireland and the Irish Question* (Moscow, 1971), p. 68.

21 *Hansard*, CXXIX, 1524.

22 *Hansard*, CXXIX, 1533.

23 Donoughmore to Napier, 30 November 1853, quoted in *The Landlord and Tenant Bills: Reply of the Right Hon. Joseph Napier MP to the Letter of the Earl of Donoughmore on the Landlord and Tenant Bills of the Last Session* (Dublin. 1853), p. v. Donoughmore's letter and Napier's reply to it were both included in this pamphlet. There is a draft of this letter in the Donoughmore papers, H/13/1/266. That these letters were not entirely spontaneous is shown by a letter from T.H. Barton to Donoughmore on 6 November 1853. In this letter Barton advised Donoughmore that Napier was 'anxious for an opportunity… to explain his relation [*sic*] with the bills during their transit last session from the committee to the Lords. I should not wonder if he published a letter to you.' See Barton to Donoughmore, 6 November 1853, Donoughmore papers, H/13/1/17. In a subsequent letter, Barton actually enclosed proof sheets of 'Napier's case' in explanation of his relations with 'the government & their Irish land bills', this presumably being a first draft of the letter quoted above. What Napier wanted from Donoughmore was 'an enquiry… for explanation of any portion of his acts seeming to require explanation'. In a significant passage, Barton claimed that Napier's conduct over the bills 'had been the subject of so much unfriendly criticism' from the Irish Conservative press that he feared that his seat was 'imperilled'. The letter to Donoughmore was intended as a defence of his conduct against such criticism. See Barton to Donoughmore, 23 November 1853, Donoughmore papers, H/13/1/19.

24 Napier to Donoughmore, n.d., quoted in *The Landlord and Tenant Bills: Reply of the Right Hon. Joseph Napier*, pp. v–x.

25 The *Dublin Evening Mail* was particularly critical of Napier's bills. A leading article in the paper on 10 December 1852 was headed 'Mr Napier's compromise of Irish property', and the paper was consistently hostile towards Napier's measures, especially the Tenants' Compensation Bill.

26 Napier to Donoughmore, n.d. [but November 1853], Donoughmore papers, H/13/1/266.

27 Napier to Naas, n.d., Mayo papers, 11,017 (14).

28 Donoughmore to Naas, 30 November 1853, Donoughmore papers, H/13/1/266.

29 Napier to Donoughmore, n.d., Donoughmore papers, H/13/1/267.

30 Napier to Cairns, n.d., Cairns papers, Public Records Office, London, PRO 30/51/11.

31 See above, p. 40.

32 Dunsany to Donoughmore, 11 January 1854, Donoughmore papers, H/14/1/97.

33   Donoughmore to Dunsany [probably 2] January 1854, Donoughmore papers, H/14/2/1.

34   *Hansard*, CXXXI, 6.

35   *Hansard*, CXXXI, 35.

36   Shee, *Papers, Letters and Speeches*, p. 74.

37   *Hansard*, CXXXIII, 518.

38   *Hansard*, CXXXIII, 1001.

39   Clancarty implied that only Donoughmore, Lord Wicklow and Lord Dufferin, the latter two being Whig peers, had supported the clause in the Lords committee wholeheartedly. Other Whig peers, such as Clanricarde and Lord Beaumont, had either opposed the clause or distanced themselves from it. His estimate was that nine out of the eleven peers on the committee had opposed the clause, yet it had been retained in the amended bill. This, Clancarty claimed, bore out his earlier criticisms of the committee's lack of Irish representation. See *Hansard*, CXXXI, 518.

40   *Hansard*, CXXXV, 34–5.

41   A deputation from the government's Irish supporters had already asked Young to defer the Bills. See *Hansard*, CXXXV, 39–40.

42   On 6 August 1853, Lord Aberdeen had written to the Queen, stating that there had been 'much doubt…[and] difference of opinion' within the cabinet as to their approach towards the Landlord and Tenant bills. The Irish landlords had, he went on, 'resisted so strongly against them, that it would not surprise him if they were thrown out'. However, the cabinet had finally decided to proceed with the bills, on the basis that 'as they were prepared by Mr Napier…[they] ought to receive the support of his friends'. Aberdeen to the Queen, 6 August 1853, Royal Archives, Windsor Castle, RA 94/88.

43   Quoted in Bull, *Land, Politics and Nationalism*, p. 44.

44   Barton to Donoughmore, n.d., Donoughmore papers, H/14/1/4.

45   Hoppen, *Ireland since 1800*, p. 86.

46   See Lee, *Modernization of Irish Society*, p. 40. See also Hoppen, *Ireland since 1800*, pp. 86–7.

47   While the constabulary had reported 1,362 agrarian outrages in Ireland in 1851 alone, by 1859 they reported only 221 such 'outrages'. Similarly, the number of 'actual' evictions of families in Ireland fell from 5,804 in 1849 to only 615 in 1860. See Vaughan, *Landlords and Tenants in Mid-Victorian Ireland*, pp. 230 and 279.

48   See Hoppen, *Ireland since 1800*, p. 86 See Vaughan, *Landlords and Tenants in Mid-Victorian Ireland*, p. 279.

49   See Hoppen, *Ireland Since 1800*, pp. 87–94.

50   Paul Cullen (1803–78): born County Kildare: educated Shacketon's Quaker School, Ballitore, County Kildare, at Carlow College and at the Urban College of Propaganda, Rome: ordained 1829: appointed professor of Greek and Oriental languages, College of Propaganda, 1830: rector of Irish College, Rome, 1832–50: Archbishop of Armagh, 1850–52: Archbishop of Dublin, 1852–78: became a cardinal, 1866: the dominant figure in the Irish Roman Catholic Church from the mid-nineteenth century onwards and a committed supporter of the extension of Papal influence in Ireland.

51   See R.V. Comerford, 'Churchmen, tenants and independent opposition, 1850–56', in W.E. Vaughan (ed.), *A New History of Ireland: Vol. 5: Ireland Under the Union, 1801–70* (Oxford, 1989), p. 408.

52   See Whyte, *Tenant League and Irish Politics*, p. 17.

53   See Whyte, *Independent Irish Party*, p. 135.

54   *Hansard*, CXI, 90.

55   George Henry Moore (1810–70): born County Mayo: member of a Catholic landowning family: educated Oscott College and at Christ Church, Cambridge: MP for Mayo County, 1847–57 and 1868–70: leading figure in the Independent Irish Party; maintained a personal friendship with Benjamin Disraeli for most of his time in parliament: father of the novelist, George Moore.

56   *Daily Express*, 26 July 1855.

57   *Daily Express*, 16 March 1857.

58   *Daily Express*, 18 March 1857.

59   *Daily Express*, 31 March 1857.

60   *Daily Express*, 1 April 1857.

61   See the *Northern Whig*, 4 April 1857.

62   *Northern Whig*, 26 March 1857.

63   *Northern Whig*, 9 April 1857.

64   *Northern Whig*, 18 April 1857.

65   See Hoppen, *Elections, Politics and Society*, p. 129.

66   Donoughmore to Moore, 4 March 1857, Donoughmore papers, H/17/1/514.

67   Glengall to Donoughmore, 9 March 1857, Donoughmore papers, H/17/1/319.

68   Hoppen, 'Tories, Catholics and the general election of 1859,' p. 49.

69   Hoppen, 'Tories, Catholics and the general election of 1859', p. 50.

70   *Hansard*, CXLIX, 1095.

71   *Hansard*, CL, 1824–8.

72   Shee, *Papers, Letters and Speeches*, p. 211. See also the reports of the deputation's meeting with Disraeli in the *Dublin Evening Mail*, 23 June 1858 and in *The Tablet*, 26 June 1858. The members of the deputation included Maguire, O'Donoghue, J.A. Blake, and Sir George Bowyer.

73   Maguire to Disraeli, 22 June 1858, Disraeli papers, B/XXI/M/66.

74   *Hansard*, CLI, 421.

75   *Hansard*, CLI, 442.

76   *Hansard*, CLI, 913–15.

77   Shee, *Papers, Letters and Speeches*, p. 211.

78   See the reports of the Tenant League meeting in *The Tablet*, 31 August 1858 and in the *Daily Express*, 19 August 1858.

79   *The Tablet*, 31 August 1858.

80   Maguire to Naas, 20 August 1858, Mayo papers, 11,024 (10).

81   Maguire to Naas, 25 August 1858, Mayo papers, 11,024 (10).

82   Maguire to Naas, 25 September 1858, Mayo papers, 11,024 (12). Maguire had attempted to protect his position in Ireland by telling the audience at a Tenant Right meeting in Fermoy in County Cork that if the Conservative government did not introduce a land reform measure, he would become its 'determined opponent'. *The Tablet*, 11 February 1859.

83   *The Tablet*, 10 July 1858.

84   See Whyte, *Tenant League and Irish Politics*, pp. 20–1.

85   'Mem[orandum] for proposed measures given me [Cairns?] by the Chancellor [Napier]', 15 October 1858, Mayo papers, 11,021 (40).

86 Walpole to Eglinton, 21 October 1858, Eglinton papers, GD3/5/56/4438.

87 Walpole to Derby, 2 February 1859, Derby papers, 153/2.

88 Naas believed that the clause would have 'frighted our friends out of their skin'. Naas to Eglinton, 3 February 1859, Eglinton papers, GD3/5/55/44.

89 *Hansard*, CLIII, 1509.

90 Six Independent Party MPs supported the Conservative government in the vote on the Reform bill while five voted against. See Whyte, *Independent Irish Party*, pp. 153–4.

91 Maguire to Naas [probably 29], May 1859, Mayo papers, 11,027 (10).

92 Hoppen, 'Tories, Catholics and the general election of 1859', p. 56.

93 Charles George Noel (1818–81): son of the first Earl of Gainsborough: educated Trinity College, Cambridge: MP for Rutland, 1840–41: converted to Roman Catholic Church, 1851: known by the courtesy title of Lord Campden until he succeeded his father as the second Earl of Gainsborough in 1866: after his conversion was active, through his connections in Whig and Conservative political circles, in promoting the interests of the Roman Catholic Church in both Britain and Ireland.

94 *Daily Express*, 13 May 1859.

95 *Banner of Ulster*, 12 May 1859.

96 Hoppen, 'Tories, Catholics and the general election of 1859', p. 53.

97 See Eglinton to Derby, 17 May 1859, Derby papers, 148/3.

98 Maguire to Naas, 24 May 1859, Mayo Papers, 11,027 (11).

99 *Hansard*, CLIV, 192.

100 For the details of the two measures, see F.S.L. Lyons, *Ireland since the Famine* (London, 1973 edn), p. 181 and pp. 218–19.

101 Even as late as 1864, the Catholic priest, Anthony Cogan, could refer to Napier's Tenants' Compensation Bill as 'the most satisfactory tenant right bill [that] was ever introduced into parliament'. See A.P. Smyth *Faith, Famine and Fatherland in the Irish Midlands: Perceptions of a Priest and Historian, Anthony Cogan, 1826–1872* (Dublin, 1992), p. 170.

102 Peter Gray has argued that Deasy's Act of 1860, which was largely modelled on Napier's Landlord and Tenant Bill, provided for the 'full contractualisation of the landlord-tenant relationship' in Ireland. See Gray, *Famine, Land and Politics*, p. 334. A similar argument is made by Philip Bull in *Land, Politics and Nationalism*, p. 44. By contrast, Napier's biographer, Alexander Charles Ewald, argues that the Tenants' Compensation Bill 'in principle anticipated the chief features of the Land Act of 1870'. See Ewald, *Life and Letters of Sir Joseph Napier* (2nd edn, London, 1892), p. 72.

FOUR

The Irish Conservative Party and the Church question

The Ecclesiastical Titles Bill and its aftermath, 1851–53

A S WE have seen, the defence of the special position of the Established Church was a central tenet of nineteenth-century Irish Conservatism. A number of inter-related arguments were used by Irish Conservatives to support the connection between the Church of Ireland and the British state. For many Irish Conservatives, the Anglican Church, as the 'true' Church, was the only Church that the state could legitimately support. If, as they believed, the Church's role was to serve as the conscience of the state, this purpose could not be served by a Church which the state considered to be in error. From their perspective, the state had a duty to foster and encourage truth in religion, and they believed that this could best be done through the medium of the Established Church. In the context of this argument, the fact that the members of the Church of Ireland were a minority of the Irish population (according to the religious census of 1861, they amounted to just over 11 per cent of the total Irish population) was irrelevant. The 1861 religious census had also revealed that just under one-third of the 1,518 Church of Ireland benefices existing at that time contained 100 or fewer Anglicans. There were 1,406 benefices that contained fewer than 500 members of the Church of Ireland.[1] For Irish Conservatives, however, the Establishment's position was dependent not on numbers, but rather on the fact that the state considered it to be 'the depository and instrument of religious truth'.[2]

Despite the fact that it represented a minority of the Irish population, the Church of Ireland was substantially endowed by the state. Indeed, in the late 1860s its annual income amounted to over £584,000.[3] By contrast, while Roman Catholics amounted to over 77 per cent of the population there (see Table 4.1), the Catholic Church in Ireland was dependent on voluntary subscriptions for its upkeep. However, for Irish Conservatives, the fact that the Roman Catholic Church's primary allegiance was to the Papacy meant that its loyalty to the British Crown was open to question. The Pope's claim to 'ecclesiastical supremacy' was, Joseph Napier maintained, in conflict 'with the common law of the United Kingdom, of which the supremacy of our Monarch' was a central part. Papal authority should, he argued, extend only to religious matters: the British state could not countenance any insinuation that the Pope had any 'temporal power direct or indirect' within its territory.[4] Implicit in this argument was the suggestion that those Catholics who accepted Papal authority in secular matters were politically suspect. The consequences of allowing such divided allegiances were to be feared, its tendency being, Irish Conservatives believed, to subvert the British constitution.

Table 4.1 Religious census 1861

Province	Total no. of inhabitants	Church of Ireland	% of total	Roman Catholic	% of total	Presby- terian	% of total	Other	% of total
Leinster	1,457,635	180,587	12.4	1,252,553	85.9	12,355	0.9	12,140	0.8
Munster	1,513,558	80,860	5.3	1,420,076	93.8	4,013	0.3	8,609	0.6
Ulster	1,914,23	391,315	20.5	966,613	50.5	503,835	26.3	52,473	2.8
Connacht	913,135	40,595	4.5	866,023	94.8	3,088	0.3	3,429	0.4
Ireland Total	5,798,967	693,357	11.3	4,505,265	77.7	523,291	9.0	77,054	1.4

Sources: Figures in this table are based on those in the *Census of Ireland for the Year 1861, Report on Religion and Education*, HC, 1863, lix. See also D.H. Akenson, *The Irish Education Experiment: The National System of Education in the Nineteenth Century* (London, 1970), pp. 218–19.

This contention that Irish Catholics were dominated by foreign influences was a mainstay of Irish Conservative opinion in the mid-nineteenth century. With Irish Roman Catholics having surrendered their political independence to dictation by the papacy, Irish Conservatives could portray themselves as the only truly 'national' party in Ireland. As such, this allowed some Irish Conservatives to maintain the idea that Ireland was a 'Protestant nation', an idea which had been developed by Ascendancy thinkers such as Jonathan Swift and George Berkeley in the later half of the eighteenth century.[5] In July 1852, for example, Joseph Napier complained that Irish Conservatives were faced 'with opposition' from men who had 'no attachment, no nation; their hearts are centred in Rome'. He argued that as Irish Catholic priests had 'no domestic attachment' or 'family ties', all of their 'wasted affection' was directed towards 'the supremacy of a foreign power'. Although this speech referred primarily to the Catholic clergy, it also shed light on Napier's opinion on Irish Roman Catholics generally.[6]

From an Irish Conservative perspective, the 'Glorious Revolution' of 1688 had defeated Papal pretensions in Ireland and established the British constitution firmly on a Protestant basis. Loyal Catholics, therefore, were duty bound to resist any Papal encroachments into secular affairs.[7] Indeed, many Irish Conservatives claimed that it had only been possible to grant Catholic emancipation with safety within the context of the Union. Protestants then had the security of being a majority within the United Kingdom as a whole, and 'civil privileges' could be given to Catholics, which could not 'have been safely granted [previously] to a sectarian majority in the separate country'. Indeed, from 1829 onwards the oath taken by Catholics on entering parliament disavowed explicitly any 'intention to subvert the present Church Establishment as settled by law... or weaken the Protestant religion or Protestant government in the United Kingdom'. In return for emancipation, the argument went, Catholics had accepted the Protestant character of the British constitution. While 'civil and religious privileges' had been extended to them, the 'rights of the Established Church' had also been secured.[8] These arguments were, of course, made mainly after the passing of Catholic Emancipation, as up to that time, Irish Conservatives had, with few exceptions, opposed it.[9]

Nonetheless, by the early 1850s it had become clear that the idea of the 'Protestant constitution' itself had been substantially undermined. Despite the safeguards surrounding it, Catholic Emancipation had altered the foundations on which it rested.[10] The growing strength of the Nonconformist churches in Britain had also made the concept of a 'national' religion there a more problematic one than it had been at the time of the Act of Union. The problem for Irish Conservatives, thus, lay in the fact that the model of Church–state relations that they advocated was coming under increasing challenge, not only in Ireland but also in other parts of Britain itself. Indeed, in the course of the nineteenth century, a number of influential Liberal politicians in Britain had come to consider the position of the Church of Ireland as untenable. They believed that it had done little to justify its existence and that it had proved a continual source of discord within Ireland. Rather than strengthening the Union, it served merely to undermine it.[11] There was also a widespread view among senior British Liberals, a view shared by some leading Conservatives, that it was only through concessions to Irish Roman Catholics that British rule there could be maintained.

The Irish Church Temporalities Act, introduced by the Whig administration in 1834, had already displayed the British government's willingness to directly intervene in the affairs of the Church of Ireland. The act had suppressed ten Church of Ireland bishoprics and reduced the income of the remaining bishops. It had also reallocated incomes within the Church of Ireland, shifting resources away from parishes with particularly small Protestant populations. These measures had been designed to reform the Church of Ireland rather than to interfere with its status as the Established Church. However, for some Irish Conservatives, by demonstrating the British government's willingness to interfere with the property and the administration of the Church of Ireland, the measure had set a dangerous precedent.

The controversy surrounding the introduction of the Ecclesiastical Titles Act in 1851 gave leading Irish Conservatives an opportunity to air publicly many of the ideas discussed above. In late 1850 a Papal brief was issued, appointing Nicholas Wiseman as Archbishop of Westminster and dividing England into twelve bishoprics. Up to that point, Catholic archbishops and bishops in England had gone under the title of 'vicar apostolic'. As a result of the Pope's action, they now took on territorial titles, putting them in competition, or so it appeared, with their Anglican counterparts. Adding to the controversy, the Papal brief had been issued without prior notification to the British government. The ensuing controversy was exacerbated by the tone of Wiseman's pastoral letter of 7 October, which announced that 'Catholic England' had been restored to its 'orbit in the ecclesiastical firmament, from which its light had long vanished'.[12]

The furore over the Papal brief also inspired Lord John Russell to write his celebrated open letter to the Bishop of Durham.[13] Russell's reasons for writing the 'Durham letter' have been much disputed, but, in terms of Irish politics alone, it was to have disastrous consequences for the Liberal Party. The tone of the letter was offensive to Catholic opinion, while the Liberal government's subsequent introduction of the Ecclesiastical Titles Bill undermined its position in Ireland. Shortly after the publication of the letter, Lord Naas met with Cory Connellan, the private secretary to Lord Clarendon, the Whig Lord Lieutenant of Ireland. Connellan told him that, in writing the 'Durham letter', Russell must 'have for a moment forgotten the existence of Ireland'. In his view, it was 'a stultification of the Whig policy towards the country [Ireland] for the last 100 years'. Connellan believed that the Durham letter would 'lead to such a complication as has never even in Ireland been witnessed'. Naas informed Disraeli that 'the whole Papist population' were 'bursting... with fury' over the letter. If they acted up to 'one quarter' of what they said, they would 'never let an Irish member vote for any thing a Whig propose[d]' in future'.[14]

For the Conservatives, this situation presented considerable advantages. As Disraeli pointed out to Stanley on 16 November, Russell was placed in a position from which it would be difficult to extricate himself without estranging at least a section of his supporters. Disraeli believed that if 'in deference' to their Roman Catholic supporters the government were to do nothing in response to the Papal action, then 'the Protestant cry, now legitimately raised... [would] gather to us [the Conservative Party]'. Indeed, there was some evidence that the 'Durham letter' was designed by Russell to prevent the Conservatives out-manoeuvring him on a 'No-

Popery' line.[15] On the other hand, a punitive measure in response to the 'Papal aggression' might lead Irish Roman Catholic MPs to vote against the government. In either case, the Conservatives stood to gain from any such divisions within the Liberal Party.

Disraeli also suggested that the Liberal government's previous policy towards the Roman Catholic Church in Ireland could provide a possible line of attack for the Conservatives. Despite its doubtful legality, the Irish Catholic hierarchy had assumed territorial titles without any interference from government both before and after 1829. The substance of Disraeli's case was that while the government had criticised the establishment of a Catholic hierarchy in England, it had allowed a similar hierarchy to function unhindered for many years in Ireland. Disraeli also claimed that the government had actively colluded with the Irish Catholic hierarchy in the hopes of securing their support for its measures,[16] a line of argument that fitted in closely with Irish Conservative criticisms of Liberal Party policy towards Ireland in the years after 1829.

The initial response of Irish Conservatives to the 'Papal aggression' was to claim that their dire predictions of the dangers of 'coquetting' with the Vatican had been borne out. In January 1851, the *Dublin Evening Mail* declared, in rather overheated terms, that Britain had arrived at 'a crisis in ... [its] history, the importance of which ... [could] not be exaggerated'. The 'days of the revolution of 1688' had returned. It was incumbent on Irish Conservatives to defend their civil and religious liberties or they would be forced to submit to 'the most despicable – the most relentless of tyrants'. The Pope's actions, in giving territorial titles to the English hierarchy, was tantamount to an 'invasion', the paper claimed.[17] At a meeting in Belfast called to denounce the conduct of the papacy, Lord Roden maintained that as Irish Protestants were in 'the van of the combat' against Rome, it was vital that they should defend their 'brethren in England [who were] thus assailed'. Irish Protestants had 'seen in the [British] government ... a desire to communicate and act with the Pope of Rome' which, if persisted in, 'must lead to the ruin and destruction of the Protestant Church in Ireland.' It was no longer possible, Roden maintained, for English public opinion to ignore Irish Conservative warnings about the overweening pretensions of the papacy.[18]

A similar argument was put forward by Lord Donoughmore, who claimed that the 'remonstrances of Irish Protestants ... [who were] suffering in the grip of the tyrant' against concessions to the papacy had been looked upon in England 'as the ravings of a faction enraged by the loss of its ancient ascendancy'. A 'complete unmasking of Rome' had been necessary 'to open England's eyes' and awaken it to the realisation of the 'baneful influence' of the Roman Catholic Church. Irish Protestants had, however, never been 'deceived – the beast [the Roman Catholic Church] had stood before us, face to face, in all its hideous deformity'. As a result of the 'aggression' however, Donoughmore concluded, 'Popery must henceforth ... stand forth in her natural colours ... [as] the enslaver of the human race'. Although the language used by Donoughmore here was undoubtedly exaggerated for effect,[19] it was plain, nonetheless, that some Irish Conservatives saw the 'aggression' as providing a welcome occasion for anti-Catholic, and, in particular, anti-Papal rhetoric.

The Ultramontane views of Paul Cullen, the new Archbishop of Dublin, provided another focus for Conservative attack. At the Synod of Thurles in 1850 Cullen had succeeded in having a resolution adopted denouncing the 'godless' Queen's Colleges established by the Peel government in 1848. There had been considerable opposition from other Irish bishops to this step[20] and Irish Conservatives pointed to the synod as an example of dictation from Rome over-riding the wishes of the domestic Irish Church. The 'Papal aggression' was, thus, seen as merely a symptom of a wider disease.[21]

The Protestant meetings of late 1850 and early 1851 were not, of course, confined to Ireland. Similar meetings were held throughout England, Scotland and Wales. This agitation further intensified the pressure on the Liberal government to introduce anti-Papal legislation, a course of action which could only damage its relations with its Roman Catholic supporters in Ireland. Many Irish Conservatives believed, however, that the government would attempt to exclude Ireland from the operation of any bill it introduced. This course was recommended by a number of senior Irish Liberals, including Lord Monteagle, and by some of the party's MPs, anxious to limit the political damage the government would suffer as a result of any measure seen as hostile to the Catholic Church.[22] Prior to its introduction, however, Derby had come out strongly against the exclusion of Ireland from its provisions. Any violation of the authority of the Crown in England was, Derby asserted, 'an equal violation' of that authority in Ireland. Moreover, the union of the Churches of England and Ireland was such that an attack on one was also an attack upon the other. Understandably, Irish Conservatives were equally insistent that no distinction should be made between England and Ireland in any proposed measure. This was an easy position for them to maintain. It fitted in with both the political and religious prejudices of many party members, while the unpopularity accruing from any such step would fall on the Liberal Party rather than on themselves.

At a meeting in early February, Conservative leaders agreed to support a government measure, so long as it lived up to 'the pledges ... [already] given'. If not, they would 'pin them down' to their earlier promises. It was not the Conservatives' duty to outline any measure of their own: having raised the issue, it was Russell's responsibility to deal with it. Nevertheless,

Derby admitted that, given the reality of Papal influence it might be necessary to sanction it 'to a certain extent by law – to legalise [it], with a view to limiting it'. The creation of an English hierarchy had, he suggested, altered the existing position. If it were to take on a synodical action, this might, as the case of the Queen's Colleges had shown, bring the Catholic bishops into conflict with the government.

Shortly before the re-assembling of parliament, Napier wrote to William Beresford, the Irish-born Chief Whip of the Conservative Party, expressing his gratification that Derby had decided to 'rally us [the Conservative Party] on the great issue between Protestantism and the papacy'. He was concerned, however, that the government intended merely introducing 'some petty bill for England, thereby admitting that the authority of the Queen... [and] the independence of the Constitution... [were] not maintainable in Ireland'. There was, he warned, 'a sorry prospect for an Empire placed in so humiliating a position hating... [and] hitting Popery a slap in England – [while] fearing... [and] giving Popery power... pre-eminence... [and] patronage in Ireland.' The 'arrogant usurpations of the papacy' made it essential that the government should include Ireland in the operation of its bill.[23] Not all Irish Conservatives were as anxious for a comprehensive measure; in early January, Naas confided to Disraeli that he did not 'fancy losing... [his] seat for the mere fun of letting of[f] a random shot at Emancipation and the new system'. While some members of the party believed that 'territorial titles' were of 'little value here [in Ireland] and not worth creating a new Emancipation agitation [over]', others would 'go to the world's end to spit on a Papist if they could do no worse'.

Nonetheless, Naas was aware that the political exigencies of the time meant that some measure was inevitable and he was concerned at the political dangers involved in allowing the Roman 'Catholic Priests [to] get up a religious liberty cry'.[24] Although Naas was notably moderate in his opinions on religious questions, his concerns about these dangers were, of course, also conditioned by the fact that he represented Kildare, a largely Roman Catholic constituency. Sir Lucius O'Brien, another Conservative MP in a similar predicament, reflected around the same time on the difficulties of being a 'zealous Protestant' sitting for a constituency 'almost exclusively Roman Catholic'. As 'their representative' he felt he had no right to 'utter sentiments at variance with their wishes especially in the Senate' unless he was 'likely to be able to carry them with...[him] hereafter'.[25] O'Brien's caution was also based on more pragmatic consider-ations as both he and Lord Naas were dependent on Catholic support to retain their seats.

The government's bill, introduced in February 1851, has been aptly described by Robert Blake as 'absurd and unenforceable'.[26] It reiterated the provision of the Catholic Relief Act of 1829, rendering the assumption of territorial titles by the Catholic hierarchy illegal. It also introduced fines against the use of such titles in any 'public act'. Although it was more moderate than might have been expected from the tone of the 'Durham letter', it nonetheless raised a storm of protest in Ireland. It also gave added impetus to the arguments of those who proposed that Irish Roman Catholic MPs should pursue a policy independent of the two principal British parties. For the remainder of the session, a group of Irish Liberal MPs, whose leaders included George Henry Moore and William Keogh, voted against the government on every possible occasion in protest at its introduction of the Ecclesiastical Titles Act. This obviously involved voting with the Conservatives, a situation which opened up new possibilities for the party.

At a meeting in Dublin on 19 August 1851 some of the leaders of this group joined with prominent Catholic clerics and other Irish Catholic laymen to establish the Catholic Defence Association. Later that month, the leaders of the Catholic Defence Association met with the leaders of the Tenant League to decide on a common platform for the next general election. Their agreement to join forces resulted in the formation of a new party, the Independent Irish Party as it later became known. In the long term, however, this combination of two essentially separate agitations, the one religious and the other agrarian, meant that it proved very difficult to maintain internal unity within the Independent Party.

Even though the Conservatives supported the Titles Bill in parliament, Irish Catholic opinion laid the principal blame for its introduction on Lord John Russell.[27] In October 1861 James Whiteside informed Sir Edward Bulwer Lytton, a prominent Conservative MP, that he would be 'amazed at the rooted dislike' which Irish Roman Catholics felt towards Russell. According to Whiteside, they had 'never forgiven & never will his Durham letter'. He recounted a conversation he had had with Laurence Waldron, the Liberal MP for Tipperary between 1858 and 1863. On that occasion, Waldron had told him that if 'Russell became premier' he would 'instantly cross to our [the Conservative] side of the house'.[28]

In parliament, leading Conservatives continued to argue that the Titles Bill was an inadequate response to the crisis provoked by the 'Papal aggression'. According to Disraeli, it was a 'piece of petty persecution' rather than a considered response to a 'solemn political exigency'. The existence of a 'Roman Catholic hierarchy in a Protestant country, not recognised by law' was, in his view, 'a great political evil'. In order to prevent the occurrence of 'another Papal aggression', it was necessary that the relationship between it and the Vatican should be regulated by the state. Unless this was done, he believed the Whigs would seek to 'govern England again by a continual Popish plot, which . . . [was] never to be brought to a head'.[29] Disraeli did not, in fact, suggest any alternative to the government's scheme, a course that was clearly in line with the Conservatives' desire to gain as much political capital as possible from the embarrassing position in which it found itself. By suggesting a fixed line of policy, the Conservatives might have alienated those Irish MPs willing to vote against the government.

Unsurprisingly, Irish Conservatives took a stronger position on the bill. Speaking in a debate in early February, Napier claimed that a concerted attempt was being made 'to introduce a foreign authority into this land, and to raise it above the constitution and the law'. The Papacy was seeking, he believed, to establish a 'tyranny' over the consciences of Roman Catholic citizens of the United Kingdom. He cited the Synod of Thurles as an example of the way in which Papal authority was used to override even the wishes of the Irish Roman Catholic hierarchy. If the Catholic bishops could thus only 'register... the decrees of the Bishop of Rome', which the laity 'were [then] bound to obey, how could they talk of their [Irish Roman Catholics] being a free people; was it not a solemn mockery?' Irish Roman Catholics should be 'protected by the constitution from all assumptions of authority above the laws, be it ecclesiastical, popular, or Papal'.[30] Indeed, in Napier's view, Roman Catholic pretensions in Ireland posed a greater threat than they did in England. As a result, it was probable, Napier had previously told the National Club, that the 'decisive battles of Protestant truth and Protestant principles would be fought out in the case of Ireland'.[31]

Despite their misgivings about the government bill, however, Irish Conservatives generally supported it as being a necessary, if inadequate, response to the 'Papal aggression'. On its first reading, it was passed by 332 votes, with a large number of Irish Conservative MPs voting in the majority. These included staunchly Protestant MPs such as William Verner and Mervyn Archdall, the MPs for Armagh County, and Edward Grogan, an MP for Dublin City. Naas was notable by his absence from this division. A few days later, in protest against the introduction of the bill, a number of Irish Catholic Liberal MPs voted against the government. Their defection resulted in its being defeated in the House of Commons on a motion introduced by the radical MP, Locke King, for an equalisation of the county and borough franchise. The Conservatives abstained on this occasion, leaving exposed the increasing divisions within the Liberal Party.

The government immediately resigned and Derby was summoned by the Queen. However, given the fact that the Conservative Party was in a minority in parliament, he was unwilling to form a government. As a result, he advised her that a coalition government between the Liberal Party and the Peelites stood a better chance of survival in the House of Commons. Derby also expressed his conviction that the appointment of a parliamentary committee 'to enquire into the position of the Roman Catholic Church'[32] in Britain would have the effect of 'allowing the popular ferment [on the subject] to cool'.[33] In Derby's view, this committee should investigate a range of topics. These would include the manner in which Roman Catholic archbishops and bishops were appointed and the question of whether 'people were detained against their will' in convents. It would also investigate whether undue influence was being exercised by Roman Catholic clerics over the disposal of property by Catholic laymen and by the members of religious orders. The committee would also investigate the operation of Papal bulls and the extent to which they impinged on the supremacy of the Crown and Parliament.[34] While Derby favoured communication between the Vatican and the English Catholic hierarchy being permitted 'for purely religious purposes', he argued that 'mischievous and dangerous ... intervention[s] on the part of the Pope' should not be sanctioned. Like Disraeli, Derby complained that the government had reacted in an ad hoc way to a particular crisis rather than dealing with the question of the relationship between the Catholic Church and the state in a considered fashion.[35] After an abortive attempt to form a government with Peelite support, Derby eventually gave up the task as hopeless. He blamed this failure on the absence of talent in his front bench, while the outcome of the political crisis was that Russell returned to office, with his government seriously weakened.[36]

Although they had supported the first reading of the Ecclesiastical Titles Bill, leading Conservatives were aware that the longer the issue was debated, the longer the difficulties faced by the government would continue. Disraeli himself believed that a prolongation of the controversy would serve to detach both the 'Irish and Peelite MPs from the government'.[37] His suggestion that the Conservatives should also lead 'a combined attack, with the aid of the Irish party' against the bill 'as nugatory and objectionable' received less support from leading Conservatives.[38]

In a letter on 13 March, George Alexander Hamilton outlined to Lord Derby his considered view of the controversy over the bill. Hamilton contended that Irish Catholics generally held 'a strong opinion against the Papal aggression'. They were aware that the 'real question' was not whether restrictions would be placed on the 'legitimate exercise of their religion', but was 'whether the Pope and the Hierarchy ... [were] to be permitted to exercise a jurisdiction in matters ecclesiastical and civil, which would soon be converted into an odious tyranny'. For Hamilton, the strength of the agitation against the bill in Ireland had been principally due to the 'petulant and offensive tone' of the 'Durham letter'. This had, Hamilton suggested, given 'the Ultramontane party' and the 'professional agitators' the opportunity to create a controversy on the issue. He condemned the government's 'miserable vacillation' on the question and recommended that, under the circumstances, the bill should be opposed. Given the Conservatives' position in the House of Commons, he doubted if they could successfully amend it, while the attempt to do so might involve 'the party in some of the odium in this country [Ireland], which at present attaches ... to Lord John Russell'.

The establishment of a committee such as Derby had earlier proposed, would, Hamilton believed, provide an opportunity to introduce a more considered measure.[39] Hamilton's line here was, rather surprisingly, close to that suggested by Disraeli. In the long term, both men believed that state regulation of the Roman Catholic Church would make for better relations between Protestants and Catholics both in Ireland and in other parts of Britain. In the short term, however, they were keenly aware of the political advantage to the Conservative Party of keeping open the divisions within the Liberal Party.

However, they were also anxious to avoid unnecessarily alienating those Irish Roman Catholic MPs who had broken with the government. This was, of course, a delicate balancing act to perform, to satisfy both those Catholic MPs virulently opposed to the bill and those Conservatives in favour of a more stringent measure. The animus felt by Irish Catholic MPs towards Lord John Russell and the Liberal government, however, made this balance easier to achieve than it at first had appeared. According to Lord Stanley, Derby's eldest son, it made 'no difference' to this group of Irish MPs that the Conservatives voted 'for the bill to which they object'. They expected 'no other course' from the Conservatives, while their 'indignation' against Russell was so great that they would seize any pretext on which to turn out the government.[40]

A central argument used by Conservatives against the Titles Bill was that it would prove impossible to enforce. The legislation combined, in Hamilton's words, being 'vexatious and affronting in its spirit' with being 'ineffective in its operation'.[41] It would be 'a mockery', Disraeli maintained, to prosecute Catholic ecclesiastics for assuming titles similar to those, which, in the Irish case, had been used towards them by members of the government.[42] A common thread in Conservative criticisms of the cabinet's handling of the crisis was their contention that it had been its previous policy in Ireland which had provoked the 'Papal aggression'. This contention was expressed clearly in a motion, introduced by David Urquhart, the Radical MP, which explicitly accused the cabinet of having 'encouraged the recent act of the Pope' by their 'conduct and declaration[s]'.[43] Both Derby and Disraeli had, in fact, played a role in drafting Urquhart's motion. The motion also claimed that, by conniving at 'the gradual encroachments of the Roman Catholic Church',[44] the Liberals had, in fact, rendered such a crisis inevitable. The fact that the government had sent Lord Minto, Russell's father-in-law, on a mission to the Vatican was also deemed to be evidence of their collusion with the papacy.[45]

Despite these criticisms, the second reading of the bill was carried by an overwhelming majority, 438 votes to ninety-five votes, with a substantial number of Irish Conservatives supporting it. Naas was again absent from the division. It was on the third reading of the bill that the ultra-Protestant

Conservatives made their most concerted attempt to alter its substance. An amendment moved by Sir Frederick Thesiger, a leading Conservative, extending its provisions to all Papal instruments was carried against the government in early June.[46] On this occasion, those Irish Catholic MPs opposed to the government abstained. Later in June, an amendment excluding Ireland from the operation of the bill was defeated in the House of Commons by 255 votes to 60. According to Napier, it was essential to have 'uniformity of practice' between England and Ireland when dealing with 'great constitutional principle[s]'.[47] In an argument which looked forward to later Irish Conservative criticisms of the disestablishment of the Church of Ireland, Napier claimed that the essence of the Union was that an Irish Protestant had 'an equal right to have his branch of the Church protected in its foundations, as his brother of the same united Church enjoy[ed] . . . in England'. While Irish Roman Catholics had the right to religious liberty, this right was circumscribed by the limits of the British constitution.[48]

In Napier's view, the difficulty in the relations between Britain and the Vatican lay in the dual nature of the papacy, its position as both a temporal and a spiritual authority. Its attempts to assert temporal influence outside its own borders could not but conflict with the British constitution, which rejected 'all foreign jurisdiction, pre-eminence or authority'.[49] Echoing Hamilton's earlier remarks, Napier claimed that there were many Irish Roman Catholics 'in their hearts anxious to be sheltered' by parliament from the threat of Papal dictation.[50]

The bill eventually passed its third reading by a large majority. Its long-term significance, however, did not lie in its practical implications. Indeed, it proved, as its critics had claimed it would, essentially a 'dead letter'. Its real significance lay in its effects on the positions of the various British political parties. In Ireland, it strengthened the position of those advocating the creation of an Independent Irish Party, while it severely damaged Liberal prospects there. The introduction of the bill also encouraged the Irish Catholic bishops to become politically active in order to secure its repeal. For the Conservatives, the new political situation offered the prospect of at least a temporary tactical parliamentary alliance with disillusioned Irish Roman Catholic MPs. Given the parliamentary situation at the time, this alliance, potentially, had the numbers to overthrow the government. The possibility of such an alliance appealed particularly to Disraeli, whose friendship with George Henry Moore was consolidated at this time.[51] Many years later, in a letter to Disraeli, Moore was to claim the credit for having 'broke[n] up the Whig alliance with the Irish popular party'.[52] Whatever the truth of this, the parliamentary situation did provide the Conservatives with openings which had not appeared possible prior to the 'Durham letter'.

In the event, it was internal dissensions on other issues that were responsible for the fall of the Liberal government in February 1852. The Conservative government which replaced it was a minority one, dependent for its survival on support from the other parties in the House. On being appointed Chief Secretary, Lord Naas was obliged to stand for re-election for the largely Catholic seat of Kildare. This election provided an early test of the new government's popularity in Ireland. As we saw earlier, Naas had been keenly aware of the potential difficulties which the Conservative Party's support for the Ecclesiastical Titles Bill might cause him in his constituency. These fears were borne out when the Dublin-based Parliamentary Committee of the Catholic Defence Association issued a circular calling on Catholic electors in Kildare to vote against him at the election. Naas's membership of 'Lord Derby's Protestant Ascendancy government' was cited as a reason for opposing him. He was also condemned as a 'supporter of the infamous Ecclesiastical Titles Bill'.[53] In fact, Naas had been absent from most of the divisions on the measure but it was an indisputable fact that the majority of Irish Conservative MPs had supported it. Naas' position was made more vulnerable by the fact that his return was also opposed by the Earl of Leinster, a leading landowner in the county and a Whig in politics. Leinster had supported Naas on previous occasions, but had turned against him as a result of Naas's moving of a vote of censure against Lord Clarendon, the Whig Lord Lieutenant, earlier in the year.[54]

This 'coalition of parties of the most opposite politics' meant that Naas had no prospect of being returned for Kildare.[55] He eventually retired from the contest there, and was returned for the safe Conservative seat of Coleraine. Disraeli later maintained that he had insisted on Naas's appointment as Chief Secretary, 'against the strong remonstrances of many of the cabinet, who were altogether averse to conciliatory measures [towards Ireland] which they held to be useless'. Their preferred candidate for the position was 'an Orangeman of high standing, who had been twenty years in Parliament and would have given the greatest satisfaction to all the Tories'. Although it has been suggested that this was a reference to Sir William Verner, it seems more likely that it was an allusion to George Alexander Hamilton.[56] Disraeli had pressed for Naas to be appointed to the post, in the belief that this would be more acceptable to Irish Catholic opinion than if Hamilton were given it. As we have seen, Naas was well known for the moderation of his views on religious questions. As a result, Disraeli believed that his appointment would prove 'very agreeable to the R[oman] C[atholic] leaders' of the Independent Party, especially George Henry Moore and William Keogh. The opposition of the Roman Catholic clergy to Naas' re-election, however, had struck Disraeli's hopes of pursuing a policy favourable to Irish Catholics 'a blow' from which it proved 'difficult to recover'. His arguments for 'a mild ... [and] friendly system' had been answered in such a way as 'seemed to prove their utter fallaciousness'.[57] Disraeli did not specify here what exactly a 'mild and friendly system' entailed and clearly underestimated the difficulties which pursuing such a policy would cause within the Conservative Party.[58]

Rather surprisingly, the advent of the new government was welcomed by Paul Cullen, the newly appointed Archbishop of Dublin. Cullen wrote to a friend that while 'the present ministry profess[ed]... itself hostile to the Catholics', it would do 'nothing against them'. He described Eglinton as 'a good man' who would devote himself to 'hunting and horse-racing' and not 'implicate himself in religious matters'. However, 'to please his party' Eglinton would have 'to profess [himself] to be our enemy'. Cullen preferred this simulated enmity to the policy 'of Clarendon and Palmerston' who professed themselves 'favourable to us [the Roman Catholic clergy] and then... [did] everything in secret to promote infidelity and indifferentism'. He considered Clarendon particularly suspect as a promoter of proselytism by Protestant missionary societies in the province of Connaught.[59] Cullen's favourable attitude to the Conservatives was not to last long and surely owed much to the Liberal government's introduction of the Ecclesiastical Titles Act.

The Conservative government's relationship with the Roman Catholic Church was placed under serious strain by its issuing on 15 June of a royal proclamation, which reiterated the illegality of Roman Catholic processions within the United Kingdom. These processions had, in fact, been illegal since 1829, but the law had not been applied in practice. Following a procession through the town of Ballinasloe in County Galway the previous month, John Wynne, the Irish Under-Secretary, sent a public letter to Bishop Derry of Galway, expressing the hope that the violation of the law had occurred 'inadvertently' and warning that any future processions would lead to prosecutions.[60] This letter had been prompted by Walpole and sanctioned by Eglinton.[61] Given that processions had been held for so long without any interference from government, Eglinton feared that to prosecute priests for holding them would be seen as 'an act of extreme persecution even by moderate Catholics'. Nonetheless, he was prepared to run this risk.[62]

For Derby, the issuing of the letter was justified by the fact that the violations of the law on processions had reached 'such a point' that intervention had become necessary.[63] It is not clear how far this letter influenced the subsequent issuing of the royal proclamation. The government defended both, however, by arguing that they were designed to prevent disturbances at the forthcoming elections in Ireland and England. In the atmosphere of heightened sectarian tension caused by the introduction of the Ecclesiastical Titles Act, the holding of Catholic processions would, the argument ran, be viewed as provocative by Protestant opinion.[64] While this was the 'ostensible object' of the proclamation, the real motivation seems to have been to appeal to 'No-Popery' opinion in Britain and Ireland. Stanley, who believed the proclamation to be a 'serious blunder', blamed Napier and Walpole for its introduction. Although Disraeli supported the issuing of the proclamation, he insisted to Stanley that he had only done so in order 'to please the Irish Protestants'.[65] While the proclamation may have gained the Conservatives some support from anti-Catholic opinion in Britain, its main effect in Ireland was to offset a great deal of the advantage which they had obtained from the introduction of the Ecclesiastical Titles Act.

Soon after the issuing of the proclamation, a religious riot took place in Stockport in Cheshire after a Catholic procession had taken place in the town. Over the course of two days, several chapels were destroyed and many Catholics were driven from their homes.[66] In Ireland, many Catholics blamed the disturbances on the government's mishandling of the processions issue. Such criticisms of the government's policy and allegations that it had been directly responsible for the outbreak of the riots became a mainstay of the Independent Party campaign against the Conservatives in the last days of the 1852 election campaign.[67] Several Conservative candidates complained to Naas of the damage that these events had done to their hopes of being elected.[68] The fact that both major British political parties had succeeded in alienating Irish Roman Catholic opinion in the space of less than two years, served to boost the prospects of those MPs willing to take the 'Independent' line. It seems clear that the Irish administration had underestimated the extent of the Irish Catholic reaction to the proclamation. Shortly after it was issued, Naas argued that it would not do the government 'any harm' in Ireland, while it would strengthen it 'greatly' in England.[69]

Unfortunately for Irish Conservatives, however, the proclamation and the Stockport riots ensured that the general election of July 1852 was fought out in an atmosphere of religious controversy, hardly conducive to their prospects. Roman Catholic priests played a prominent part in the campaign and considerable vitriol was directed at the government. A typical example of this invective was an election placard which appeared in County Tipperary, accusing the Derby government of having drawn 'the sword against the altars of Christianity'.[70] While this language was, no doubt, exaggerated, the virulence of Conservative criticisms of the priests' conduct at the election suggests they felt threatened by this exercise of clerical influence. Eglinton's letters to Derby during the election campaign contain a series of indictments against what he considered the 'blackguardism' of the priests. Warning of the 'lawless state of this country [Ireland]', Eglinton accused the Catholic clergy of 'preaching sedition' and raising 'murder bands' to ensure Catholic voters acted at their dictation.[71] Writing to Naas, Lord Charleville described the election in King's County as having become 'a kind of war between Protestantism and Roman Catholicity'.[72]

There were many letters in a similar vein sent from across the country to both Eglinton and Naas. The Conservatives most vulnerable to this type of pressure were, of course, those MPs sitting for constituencies with a substantial Roman Catholic presence. The issue of clerical influence on Catholic voters had continued to preoccupy the Irish administration in the months following the general election. A number of suggestions to reduce the priests' influence had been canvassed, including a proposal that the electoral franchise be raised. Defending such a step, Lord Claud Hamilton complained that 'the franchise bestowed upon the Roman Catholic voters' did not belong to them, but to their 'spiritual pastors'. To counteract this, Hamilton believed that the franchise should be restricted 'to such [voters] as would be above the threats of the priests'.[73] Another proposal, considered by Eglinton, was that it should be made illegal for any clergyman to appear 'within the precincts of a polling booth' at election times.[74] Such suggestions reflected the Irish Conservative fear that the exercise of clerical influence at elections posed a major threat to landlord control over the way in which their tenants voted. However, the members of the Irish administration were agreed that it would be necessary to hold a parliamentary inquiry into the priests' conduct during the election before any such measure could be introduced.[75] However, the practical difficulties attached to the implementation of these measures meant that they had not been introduced by the time the government fell. Nevertheless, the fact that they were seriously mooted reflects the unease felt by Conservatives at the extent of the priests' influence.[76]

Along with the religious issue, the government also faced the threat of the Independent Party's popularity with Roman Catholic voters. The Independent Party's success at the election was due to a shrewd combination of religious and agrarian issues. Shortly after the election, a new body calling itself the Friends of Religious Freedom and Equality was formed at a meeting in Dublin. The meeting was attended by twenty-six Independent Party MPs, who pledged themselves to oppose any government which did not include the repeal of the Ecclesiastical Titles Act and the disestablishment of the Church of Ireland in its programme.[77] In theory at least, the party now seemed to be on the brink of becoming a genuine force in Irish politics. The very raising of religious issues in this way, however, threatened, in the long term, to disrupt the unity which existed between the northern and southern wings of the movement.

Ironically, considering the criticisms which they had made of Minto's mission to Rome, the Conservative government itself sent a similar informal envoy there in the autumn of 1852. The envoy chosen was Sir Henry Bulwer, a brother of Sir Edward Bulwer Lytton, the novelist and Conservative politician. The government had appointed Bulwer as British Minister in Florence, and it was from that post that he undertook his mission to the Vatican. The decision to send Bulwer to Rome was taken by Lord Malmesbury, the Foreign Secretary. Reflecting the concerns of the Irish administration, Derby was anxious that Bulwer should obtain a Papal denunciation of the Catholic clergy's involvement in electioneering in Ireland.[78]

In late September, Bulwer met with Cardinal Antonelli, the leading diplomat at the Vatican, in Rome. Antonelli assured Bulwer of his opposition to the conduct of the Irish Roman Catholic priests at the general election and offered to write to the Irish Catholic bishops, expressing 'his strong disapproval' of such behaviour. He also criticised the land bill introduced by William Sharman Crawford as being 'destructive of the rights of property... [and thus] leading directly to robbery which was breaking a commandment'. Bulwer concluded from the meeting that the Vatican authorities might not be altogether hostile to some form of state provision for the Roman Catholic clergy, 'possibly [with] some conditions annexed'.[79] This idea of acquiring some political control over the Catholic Church in Ireland through state endowment had been raised at the time of the Act of Union, though it had not then been acted upon. In the political climate of the 1850s, with the controversy over the Ecclesiastical Titles Act still fresh in people's minds, Bulwer was keenly aware of the political difficulties involved in making such a proposal. Accordingly, he advised Malmesbury that any such an 'arrangement would require great preparation' and could not, in his opinion, be attempted at that time.

Shortly after this meeting, Bulwer wrote to Lord Stanley, asking for the name of a moderate Roman Catholic bishop in Ireland to whom Antonelli could write his proposed letter. Stanley forwarded this request to Naas, asking him to recommend someone who had conducted himself 'properly' by not 'abetting violence... [or] meddling in politics'.[80] However, Eglinton was unconvinced of the value of such a letter. If written in general terms, for example calling on the Catholic Church 'on all occasions' to be 'moderate in their language, obedient to the laws, [and] respectful to the constituted authorities', it would differ little from the pastoral issued by Archbishop Cullen prior to the election. Despite this pastoral, however, the 'priestly agitation' during the election campaign had, Eglinton believed, been 'commenced under his [Cullen's] instruction'. While the letter proposed by Antonelli would reassure moderate Catholic opinion, 'disgust[ed]' at the outrageous conduct of the priests', it would have little practical effect. It would not prevent priests from exercising electoral influence or denouncing voters who acted contrary to their instructions. He maintained that 'no good' had ever come from 'coaxing the Roman Catholic priesthood or [from] any negotiations that...[had] ever been entered into with them'. Nevertheless, Eglinton did suggest three names, William Delaney, the Bishop of Cork, John Ryan, the Bishop of Limerick, and Cornelius Denvir, the Bishop of Down and Connor. He characterised them as the 'least violent' of the Irish Roman Catholic bishops. He advised that any negotiations with the Catholic bishops should be carried on 'your side of the water [in England]' and the first approaches made by an Irish Roman Catholic such as John Howley, a prominent barrister, friendly to the government.[81]

Eglinton's pessimism about the results of Bulwer's mission was shared by other senior members of the cabinet, and, most significantly, by Derby. This pessimism was borne out when Antonelli withdrew his offer to write to the Irish bishops at a second meeting with Bulwer. He justified this on the grounds that to do so would be 'an interference with the affairs of another country', a declaration, Derby observed, 'which it must have been difficult even for an Italian cardinal to make with a grave face'.[82] This convinced the government that Bulwer was unlikely to achieve anything concrete in Rome and he was, consequently, advised to return to his mission at Florence. The outcome of these negotiations convinced Malmesbury that the British government should 'establish a recognized diplomatic agent' in Rome, as a means of exercising some influence over Papal policy towards Ireland.[83] The thrust of Bulwer's mission, although it had proved abortive, had been in this direction. The political exigencies of the times, however, made this an extremely difficult policy to pursue.

Although Derby himself viewed the question of state endowment of the Roman Catholic Church as one of 'policy' rather than 'principle', any attempt to move in this direction would have incurred serious opposition from within the Conservative Party. Derby also questioned whether such a move would achieve its 'real object, that of diminishing the community of feeling between the R[oman] C[atholic] Priest and his flock, and bribing him to allegiance and to exertion in favour of the constituted authorities'.[84] While pragmatic considerations drove Conservative leaders towards some form of rapprochement with the Vatican, it was always necessary for them to consider the state of feeling on the subject within the Conservative Party. It was only seven years earlier that the Maynooth grant had created serious divisions within the party and Derby was naturally unwilling to risk a similar schism in the party.

As we saw previously, the Conservative government fell on 17 December in a vote on Disraeli's budget. Derby was succeeded as Prime Minister by Lord Aberdeen, who presided over a coalition of Liberals and Peelites. Two Independent Irish MPs, William Keogh and John Sadleir, accepted office under Aberdeen, in defiance of the 'Independent' pledge which both had taken. Their promotion led Irish Conservatives to complain that they had been rewarded for their attacks on the Established Church. The *Daily Express*, a Dublin-based Conservative newspaper, asked if Sadleir and Keogh had insisted on the government's pledging to 'destroy the Irish Church' as a condition of accepting office. If not, the paper continued, they had 'disregard[ed] . . . all truth and honesty' in disavowing their former principles, merely in order to gain advancement. The accession of Gladstone and Sidney Herbert, two of the most outspoken critics of the Ecclesiastical Titles Act, to the cabinet was also perceived by Irish Conservatives as proof that the new government was overly sympathetic to Roman Catholicism.[85] These claims, exaggerated as they were, hit the mark in one respect. Sadleir and Keogh had accepted office without being offered any substantial concessions, a proceeding which obviously cast doubts on their sincerity in adopting the 'Independent' pledge.[86] There was also a good deal of irony involved in two leading members of the Independent Party accepting office in a government in which Lord John Russell served as Foreign Secretary.

This chapter has concentrated on Irish Conservative responses to the controversy over the introduction of the Ecclesiastical Titles Act. In particular, it has looked at the way in which this response was conditioned by their wider beliefs as to the correct relationship which should exist between Roman Catholic citizens and the British state. For Irish Conservatives, the 'Papal Aggression' had come as a welcome confirmation of their long held conviction in the hostile designs of the Vatican. In political terms, the crisis also gave the Conservative Party leadership an ideal opportunity to embarrass the Liberal government. Russell's miscalculation in writing the 'Durham letter' helped lay the foundation for the Independent Irish Party successes at the 1852 general election and opened up the possibility of Independent Party–Conservative Party co-operation, which reached its height at the 1859 general election. However, the Ecclesiastical Titles Act itself had little tangible effect and the ultimate effects of the agitation around the subject were, in Irish Conservative eyes, disappointingly small. In Chapter 7 we will go on to consider the implication of this. In Chapters 5 and 6, however, we will examine the Education question in Ireland in more detail, a question that was intimately connected with the ongoing struggle for religious supremacy between the Church of Ireland and the Irish Roman Catholic Church.

NOTES

1   See P.M.H. Bell, *Disestablishment in Ireland and Wales* p. 33. See also McDowell, *Church of Ireland*, p. 17.

2   From a speech by George Alexander Hamilton, 10 July 1849, *Hansard*, CXII, 149.

3   According to the Royal Commission of 1869, this income was divided as follows; land rental amounting to £204,932, tithe rent charges of £364,224 and £15,530 raised from other sources. See Akenson, *The Church of Ireland: Ecclesiastical Reform and Revolution 1800–1885* (New Haven, CT, and London, 1971), p. 224. See also Bell, *Disestablishment in Ireland and Wales*, p. 29.

There was some controversy over whether this figure accurately represented the annual income of the Church of Ireland: Bell estimates that the actual figure may have been closer to £680,000 per annum. See Bell, *Disestablishment in Ireland and Wales*, p. 30. In 1868, the *Freeman's Journal* estimated the annual expenditure of the Roman Catholic Church at over £762,000. In 1861 there were 1,036 Roman Catholic parish priests in Ireland, supported by 1,491 curates. There were four Catholic archbishops and thirty-three bishops. See Hoppen, *Elections, Politics and Society*, p. 171. Hoppen estimates that there were 1,873 Roman Catholics for each parochial clergyman. See also E.R. Norman, *The Catholic Church and Ireland in the Age of Rebellion, 1859–1873* (London, 1965), pp. 14–15. By comparison, the hierarchy of the Church of Ireland consisted of two archbishops and ten bishops. See R.B. McDowell, *The Church of Ireland, 1869–1969* (London, 1975), p. 7.

4   From a speech by Napier on 29 August 1849, *Hansard*, CI, 616.
5   For a discussion of this subject see Spence, 'The philosophy of Irish Toryism', in particular p. 10.
6   This speech is quoted in the *Dublin Evening Mail*, 14 July 1852.
7   For a discussion of these ideas, see Hill, *From Patriots to Unionists*, pp. 10–11. See also G.F.A. Best, 'The Protestant constitution and its supporters, 1800–1829', *Transactions of the Royal Historical Society*, 5th Series, 8 (1958), pp. 105–27 and Sean Connolly, *Religion, Law and Power: The Making of Protestant Ireland, 1660–1760* (Oxford, 1992), pp. 156–9.
8   Joseph Napier, *England or Rome? Which Shall Govern Ireland?: Reply to the Letter of Lord Monteagle* (2nd edn, Dublin, 1851), pp. 37–8.
9   See O'Ferrall, *Catholic Emancipation*, pp. 207–15.
10   See O'Ferrall, *Catholic Emancipation*, pp. 319–20.
11   In Lord Macaulay's view, the Church of Ireland had produced 'twice as many riots as conversions'. See Richard Shannon, *Gladstone: Peel's Inheritor, 1809–1865* (London, 1999 edn), p. 83. Jonathan Parry has also noted that many Liberals saw the Church of Ireland as 'the greatest obstacle to popular acceptance [in Ireland] of the benefits flowing from the British connection'. See J.P. Parry, *The Rise and Fall of Liberal Government in Victorian Britain* (New Haven, CT, and London, 1993), p. 266.
12   Quoted in D.A. Kerr, *'A Nation of Beggars'? Priests, People, and Politics in Famine Ireland 1846–52* (Oxford, 1994), p. 244.
13   In this letter, Russell denounced the Pope's 'aggression' against England, describing it as 'insolent and insidious . . . inconsistent with the Queen's supremacy . . . [and] the spiritual independence of the nation'. Russell also warned that the 'present state of the law' would be examined with a view to preventing such 'assumption[s] of power' in the future. See G.I.T. Machin, *Politics and the Churches in Great Britain, 1832 to 1868* (Oxford, 1978), p. 217.
14   Naas to Disraeli, 12 November 1850, Disraeli papers, B/XX/BO/1. See also Monypenny and Buckle, *Life of Benjamin Disraeli*, Vol. 3, pp. 267–68 and M.G. Wiebe, J.B. Conacher, and J. Matthews (eds), *Benjamin Disraeli: Letters*, Vol. 5 (Toronto, 1993), pp. 376–8.
15   See Machin, *Politics and the Churches in Great Britain, 1832 to 1868*, p. 231.
16   Disraeli to Stanley, 16 November 1850, quoted in Monypenny and Buckle, *Life of Benjamin Disraeli*, Vol. 3, pp. 267–9.
17   *Dublin Evening Mail*, 1 January 1851.
18   *Dublin Evening Mail*, 3 January 1851.
19   Donoughmore wrote as a prospective candidate for Portarlington and the

letter was probably written to secure the club's support for his candidacy. In other words, it seems likely that Donoughmore was writing what he thought the club wanted to hear. Suirdale [Donoughmore] to Wolsely, 27 August 1851, Donoughmore papers, H/11/1/121. Wolsely was the Secretary of the Portarlington Club, which, as he informed Donoughmore, had been formed 'to secure among other matters a fit and proper Representative for Parliament', one who would 'promote the best interests of the Borough [Portarlington], and especially endeavour by his vote and influence to uphold the paramount authority of the word of God in the government of this great Empire'. J. Wolsely to Donoughmore, 23 August 1851, Donoughmore papers, H/19/1/121.

20   The resolution was passed by only one vote. See J.H. Whyte, 'Political problems, 1850–60', in Patrick Corish (ed.), *A History of Irish Catholicism*, Vol. 5, fascicule 3 (Dublin, 1967), pp. 7–9.

21   See Napier, *England or Rome?*, pp. 5–6.

22   See Napier, *England or Rome?*, pp. 3–4. See also Hewett (ed.), '...*and Mr Fortescue*', p. 10.

23   Napier to Beresford, n.d. [but January 1851], Trinity College, Dublin, Ms. 6235/3.

24   Naas to Disraeli, 11 January 1851, Disraeli papers, B/XX/BO/2.

25   Sir Lucius O'Brien's notes on 'Papal Aggression', 2 February 1851, Inchiquin papers, National Library of Ireland, 21,203 (IV).

26   Robert Blake, *Disraeli* (London, 1966), p. 301.

27   See Whyte, *Tenant League and Irish Politics*, p. 11. Whiteside to Lytton, 9 October 1861, Lytton papers, County Records Office, Hertford, D/EX/C7/6.

28   Whiteside to Lytton, 9 October 1861, Lytton papers, D/EX/C7/6.

29   *Hansard*, CXIV, 261.

30   *Hansard*, CXIV, 460–1.

31   Ewald, *Life and Letters of Sir Joseph Napier* (London, 1887 edn), p. 41.

32   Memorandum by Prince Albert, 27 February 1851, quoted in Benson and Esher (eds), *The Letters of Queen Victoria*, Vol. 2, p. 365.

33   Stanley diary, 16 May 1851, quoted in Vincent (ed.), *Disraeli, Derby and the Conservative Party*, p. 65.

34   See the 'Resolutions on Papal Aggression' of which Derby was probably the author in the Disraeli papers, B/XX/S/24. See also memorandum by Prince Albert, 28 February 1851, quoted in Benson and Esher (eds), *Letters of Queen Victoria*, Vol. 2, p. 367.

35   *Hansard*, CXIV, 1027.

36   Blake, *Disraeli*, pp. 305–6.

37   Stanley diary, 15 April 1851, quoted in Vincent (ed.), *Disraeli, Derby and the Conservative Party*, pp. 61–2.

38   Stanley diary, 9 March 1851, quoted in Vincent (ed.), *Disraeli, Derby and the Conservative Party*, p. 54.

39   Hamilton to Derby, 13 March 1851, Derby papers, 150/9.

40   This group comprised only a minority of the Irish Roman Catholic MPs, with their parliamentary strength being variously estimated at between 18 and 24 MPs. Stanley diary, 8 February 1851, quoted in Vincent (ed.), *Disraeli, Derby and the Conservative Party*, p. 39.

41   *Hansard*, CXIV, 660.

42   *Hansard*, CXIV, 601.

43   *Hansard*, CXIV, 830.

44   *Hansard*, CXIV, 1027.
45   See Disraeli's speech of 7 February 1851, *Hansard*, CXIV, 259. See also Napier's speech of 12 February 1851, *Hansard*, CXIV, pp. 463–4. The Pope had, in fact, given Minto a hint of his intention to restore the English hierarchy, a hint that Minto had not pursued. See Blake, *Disraeli*, p. 299 and Kerr, '*A Nation of Beggars?*' p. 251.
46   See Machin, *Politics and the Churches in Great Britain, 1832 to 1868*, p. 224.
47   *Hansard*, CXVII, 337.
48   Napier, *England or Rome?*, p. 36.
49   Napier, *England or Rome?*, p. 45.
50   Napier to Derby, n.d., [but probably June 1851], quoted in Gardiner (ed.), *Lectures, Essays and Letters*, p. 80.
51   See Moore to Disraeli, n.d., Disraeli papers, B/XXI/M/503. For Moore's friendship with Disraeli see Moore, *An Irish Gentleman*, p. 195.
52   Moore to Disraeli, 20 July 1868, Disraeli papers, B/XIII/M/201.
53   *Dublin Evening Mail*, 13 March 1852.
54   See Leinster to Naas, 27 February 1852, Mayo Papers, 11,019 (29).
55   Letter from Naas to his 'leading supporters in Kildare', March 1852, quoted in the *Dublin Evening Mail*, 13 March 1852.
56   Arabella Kenealy, *Memoirs of Edward Vaughan Kenealy, LLD* (London 1903), p. 157. See also Disraeli to Sir Henry Bulwer, n.d. [but October 1852], draft in Disraeli papers, Bodleian Library, Oxford, H B/11/026b. I am indebted for this reference to Ms Ellen Hawman of the Disraeli Project, Queen's University, Kingston, Canada. The *Dublin Evening Mail*, of 3 February 1852, actually lists Hamilton as Irish Chief Secretary. In early February Napier wrote to Sir James Emerson Tennent, expressing his disappointment 'at the arrangement which is announced as to Hamilton. No man on the score of services, sacrifices, & personal merit has so strong a claim [to the office] as he has – & the passing him over & appointing Lord Naas over his head will be felt by his numerous and influential friends as an unmerited and ungenerous superseding of as good & as honest a man as ever came from Ireland'. Napier to Tennent, n.d., Tennent papers, Public Records Office of Northern Ireland, Belfast, D2922/B/27/7.
57   Disraeli to Bulwer, n.d. [but October 1852], draft in Disraeli papers, H B/11/026b. I am indebted for this reference to Ms Ellen Hawman of the Disraeli Project, Queen's University, Kingston.
58   For obvious reasons, the evolution of Disraeli's attitudes towards Ireland has not received anything like the same attention, as has the development of Gladstone's ideas on the same subject. While some recent writers (a recent example is T.A. Jenkins, 'Benjamin Disraeli and the spirit of England', *History Today*, 54 (2004), pp. 9–15) have attempted to stress the elements of consistency in Disraeli's political career, it is difficult to trace a coherent pattern in the attitudes he adopted towards Ireland in the course of his political career. As Robert Blake has pointed out, in some of his early writings, Disraeli had displayed 'a virulent racial and religious political prejudice against Ireland'. However, from his 'Young England' days onward, with the exception of his vote against the increase in the grant to Maynooth in 1845, he generally adopted a much more conciliatory tone towards Irish Catholics. Throughout the period covered by this book, he was to make repeated attempts to win over Irish Catholic MPs to support of the Conservative Party. This approach was conditioned in part by his wish to conciliate English Catholic political opinion, which, he believed, was

generally sympathetic to the Conservatives. It was also conditioned to a large extent by tactical political considerations. See Blake, *Disraeli*, pp. 131–2 and p. 342. See also Jane Ridley, *The Young Disraeli, 1804–1846* (London, 1996), pp. 306–7 for a discussion of the reasons for Disraeli's opposition to the increase in the Maynooth grant in 1845.

59   Cullen to Dr Bernard Smith, 8 March 1852, quoted in Peadar MacSuibhne, *Paul Cullen and his Contemporaries with their Letters from 1820–1902*, 5 vols (Naas, 1961–77), Vol. 3, p. 113. For a very different characterisation of Eglinton see Stanley's diary for June 1852, quoted in Vincent (ed.), *Disraeli, Derby and the Conservative Party*, p. 62.

60   Wynne to Derry, 7 May 1852, quoted in the *Dublin Evening Mail*, 21 June 1852.

61   See Walpole to Eglinton, 5 May 1852, Eglinton papers, GD3/5/52/4428.

62   Eglinton to Derby, 28 June 1852, Derby papers, 148/2. There is a copy of this letter in the Eglinton papers, GD3/5/53/4425.

63   Derby to Eglinton, 28 June 1852, Eglinton papers, GD3/5/53.

64   See Stanley's diary for June 1852, quoted in Vincent (ed.), *Disraeli, Derby and the Conservative Party*, p. 73. Disraeli later claimed that the proclamation had been introduced 'for the protection of Roman Catholics.' See Courtenay to Naas, 9 July 1852, Mayo papers, 11,018 (30).

65   See Stanley's diary for June 1852, quoted in Vincent (ed.), *Disraeli, Derby and the Conservative Party*, p. 73.

66   See Donald MacRaild, *Irish migrants in Modern Britain, 1750–1922* (London, 1999), pp. 173–4.

67   See Whyte, *Tenant League and Irish Politics*, p. 13. See also Machin, *Politics and the Churches in Great Britain, 1832 to 1868*, p. 239.

68   See, for example, Clayton Browne to Naas, n.d., Mayo papers, 11,018 (11), Daly to Naas, 31 July 1852, Mayo papers, 11,018 (42), and Herbert to Naas, 18 July 1852, Mayo papers, 11,019 (17).

69   Naas to Eglinton, 16 June 1852, Eglinton papers, GD3/5/53/4426.

70   *Dublin Evening Mail*, 14 July 1852.

71   Eglinton to Derby, 16 July 1852, Derby papers, 148/2. There is a copy of this letter in the Eglinton papers, GD3/5/53/4425.

72   Charleville to Naas, 16 July 1852, Mayo papers, 11,018 (29).

73   *Dublin Evening Mail*, 2 August 1852.

74   See Eglinton to Walpole, 23 October 1852, Holland papers, 894c. There is a copy of this letter in the Eglinton papers, GD3/5/51/4433.

75   See Eglinton to Walpole, 23 October 1852, Holland papers, 894c. There is a copy of this letter in the Eglinton papers, GD3/5/51/4433. See also Derby to Eglinton, 2 October 1852, Eglinton papers, GD3/5/53/4424 and Whiteside to Eglinton, 27 October 1852, Eglinton papers, GD3/5/51/4433.

76   See Derby to Eglinton, 1 August 1852, Eglinton papers, GD3/5/53/4424. At Derby's instructions, the Irish administration compiled a dossier of the more inflammatory speeches made by the Irish priests during the election to be given to Bulwer to use in Rome. This dossier was also made available to Sir Francis Head, the former Lieutenant Governor of Canada, for use in his travel book *A Fortnight in Ireland*. The government eventually decided against allowing Head to make direct reference to these reports, although he did make indirect use of them by quoting newspaper reports of some of the speeches they contained. See Head to Naas, n.d., Head papers, National Library of Ireland, Dublin, 18,513.

77   Whyte, *Tenant League and Irish Politics*, p. 14.

78   See Stanley diary for 2 August 1852, quoted in Vincent (ed.), *Disraeli, Derby and the Conservative Party*, p. 79.

79   Bulwer to Malmesbury, 21 September 1852, Eglinton papers, GD3/5/51/4434.

80   Stanley to Naas, 25 September 1852, Mayo papers, 11,020 (26).

81   Eglinton to Malmesbury, 22 October 1852, Eglinton papers, GD3/5/51/4433.

82   Derby to Malmesbury, 3 October 1852, quoted in Earl of Malmesbury, *Memoirs of an Ex-Minister: An Autobiography*, 2 vols (London, 1884), Vol. 1, p. 353.

83   Malmesbury suggested to Eglinton that 'France & other powers' were opposed to the British government sending a 'diplomatic agent' to Rome as they feared this would '*tranquilize Ireland*' and thus strengthen Britain's position internationally. Malmesbury to Eglinton, 27 October 1852, Eglinton papers, GD3/5/51/4433.

84   Derby to Disraeli, 21 December 1848, Disraeli papers, B/XX/S/2.

85   *Daily Express*, 4 January 1853.

86   Whyte, *Tenant League and Irish Politics*, pp. 15–16.

FIVE

The Irish Conservative Party and the national education question, 1852–53

O F ALL the questions facing the Irish administration in 1852 that of education was to prove one of the most problematic. The National Board system of primary education established in 1831 was deeply unpopular with many Irish Conservatives. Their opposition to the system rested principally on the restrictions placed on religious instruction, in particular on the use of the Bible, in the board's schools. Its schools had, however, proved more successful in attracting Irish Roman Catholic children than had the earlier Kildare Place Society. Despite its beginnings as a non-denominational body, the society had gradually become a Protestant-dominated one. As a result, a widespread suspicion grew up among Irish Roman Catholics that its schools were being used for proselytising purposes. This Catholic sense of grievance about the character of the religious teaching in the society's schools was further increased by the fact that it received a substantial degree of government support. At the same time, a number of other Protestant proselytising societies operating in Ireland, including the London Hibernian Society, were also receiving some financial assistance from the British government. As a result, from the mid-1820s onwards, both Roman Catholic clerics and politicians began to campaign against the government's expenditure of public money to subsidise bodies of this kind.[1]

The emergence of these proselytising societies had been one of the characteristic features of the so-called 'Second Reformation' (sometimes described as the 'New Reformation') of the late eighteenth and early nineteenth centuries. At that time, a group of Irish Evangelicals, with support from their counterparts in Britain, had launched a concerted effort to secure the mass conversion of Irish Roman Catholics to Protestantism. When the campaign was launched, Irish Evangelicals were optimistic that it stood a good chance of success. However, their belief was that it could only succeed if the British state and the Irish landed elite were to provide the financial resources that would be necessary to secure conversions on such a wide scale. Indeed, from the Evangelicals' perspective, it was the moral duty of the British state to bring the benefits of the Protestant religion to the Irish Catholic population. Furthermore, those who supported the 'Second Reformation' contended that mass conversions to Protestantism in Ireland would help win over the population there to support of the Union with Britain. In consequence, they maintained that there would be clear advantages to the British government, in both political and religious terms, if it were to support their campaign in Ireland.[2]

The effects of the conversion campaign in Ireland, however, were, in many ways, the reverse of what the Evangelicals had hoped to achieve. Despite their best efforts, neither the British government nor the majority of Irish landowners proved willing to provide them with the level of financial support that they felt was necessary to ensure the success of their campaign. The militancy of some of the advocates of the 'New Reformation' also helped to convince many members of the Catholic hierarchy and clergy in Ireland that they should throw their weight behind Daniel O'Connell's campaign for Catholic Emancipation. A consequence of this was that in the course of the campaign for Emancipation, the Catholic Church in Ireland had emerged as a powerful political force in its own right, with the ability to challenge and, indeed, to defeat landlord electoral influence there.

Indeed, the success of the campaign was largely due to the emergence of a new more militant Catholic middle-class political leadership in Ireland, the most notable of whom was Daniel O'Connell. The securing of Emancipation had also instilled a new sense of self-confidence among Irish Roman Catholics, a self-confidence that was cemented by the failure of the 'Second Reformation' to achieve the level of conversions that it had initially sought.[3] The increased political strength of the Catholic community in Ireland helped convince many leading British Whig politicians that it was necessary to address its concerns across a range of areas, including in relation to education. The Whig government, which came to power in Britain in 1830, also hoped that concessions to Roman Catholic opinion in Ireland would undercut support for O'Connell's campaign for the Repeal of the Union, launched in the same year.

In consequence, the national system of education, as introduced by the Whig government in 1831, was designed to meet Roman Catholic concerns about the existing provision of elementary education in Ireland. The new system was designed to be a mixed one, providing combined non–denominational classes in most subjects with separate religious education for Catholic and Protestant children. As part of the government's scheme, a National Board of Education was established to administer the system at the national level. The new board was to include representatives from all of the main religions in Ireland. At the time of the foundation of the system, three of these commissioners appointed to the board were members of the Church of Ireland, two were Presbyterians and two were Roman Catholics. The

Board had varying degrees of responsibility for the different types of schools within the system. The first type of schools, the model schools, came directly under its control. These schools were fully funded by the board, which had sole control over the appointment of teachers, the books used, and the curriculum followed. After his visit to the model school in Marlborough Street in Dublin shortly after his arrival in Ireland, Eglinton described it 'as one of the most magnificent institutions' he had ever seen. It appeared to him to be 'a perfect specimen of the united system'.[4] Critics of the system were, however, quick to warn against the dangers of judging the system as a whole on the basis of the model schools.[5]

The second level of schools, the vested schools, had more independence from the system. In the vested schools the role of the state was limited to providing a maximum of two-thirds of the expense of the initial foundation of the school. The rest of the money necessary for the maintenance and upkeep of the schools was provided by local patrons. In the case of Roman Catholic schools, such patrons were often the local Roman Catholic bishops. In general, these patrons left the day-to-day running of the schools to the local managers, usually the Roman Catholic priest in the parish in which the school was located. In the case of those Church of Ireland schools which joined the system, the patrons were usually either the local landowner or the Church of Ireland bishop. In return for its financial investment in the vested schools, the board demanded that these patrons adhered to its rules regarding religious education. It also retained the right to send inspectors to gauge the quality of the education given in such schools. The patrons were, however, responsible for the appointment of the teachers who taught in the schools and the determination of the curriculum to be followed in them. In both of these types of schools, separate religious instruction could only be given on one day per week or outside regular school hours. On that day, clergymen from the different denominations had the right to attend the schools to give religious instruction to the children of their respective faiths.

The third, and the most controversial, type of schools were the non-vested schools. These schools had not formed part of the original scheme and had, in fact, been won from government as a result of intense pressure from the Presbyterian synod in the course of the 1830s.[6] The state's responsibility for these schools was restricted to the payment of the teachers' salaries and the provision of schoolbooks. The Board also had a power of veto over the books used in the schools and in relation to the appointment of teachers. While the teachers in the non-vested schools were debarred from using any compulsion in relation to religious instruction, the board's regulation restricting religious instruction did not apply to these schools. There was no obligation on the patrons of these schools to allow clergymen of other faiths to attend their schools, although children from those denominations could attend religious instruction elsewhere, if their parents so wished.[7] Critics of the non-vested schools claimed with some justice that these schools were run, more or less openly, as denominational schools, pointing particularly to the fact that some were convent schools.[8]

Within the Irish Roman Catholic hierarchy itself, there were three main viewpoints on the education question. The first of these points of view, best represented by John McHale, the Archbishop of Tuam, opposed the national system and favoured the institution of an explicitly denomin-ational system funded by the state. The second point of view, supported by David Moriarty, the Bishop of Kerry, favoured the restoration of the system as it had originally been established in 1831 without the changes that had been subsequently introduced to it, as a result of pressure from the Protestant churches, particularly the Presbyterian Church, in Ireland. The third and the majority view among the Irish Roman Catholic bishops, and that maintained by Cullen himself, was that, while the national system was 'indefensible from a Catholic point of view', they should work within it until they could persuade the state to grant a 'separate system'. They justified this course on the grounds that the Roman Catholic Church was simply not capable of maintaining a separate system from its own.

From the outset, the national system as a whole was opposed by the vast bulk of the Church of Ireland bishops and clergy, who refused to connect their schools with it.[9] The crux of their opposition to the system lay in their belief that, as the 'National' Church in Ireland, the Church of Ireland had an inherent right to control over any system of education established by the state. Indeed, from their perspective, the foundation of the system marked another break with the idea, supported by most Irish Conservatives, that the state should endow one form of religion, and that form alone. The supporters of the society were also concerned at the implications that the appointment of Roman Catholic commissioners to the National Board had for the future relations between the Church of Ireland and the state.[10]

This concern was closely related to the even more fraught question of whether the Church of Ireland was to be a 'missionary church' intent on gaining converts from the Roman Catholic Church or, alternately, whether its concern should be to consolidate its own position in Ireland and achieve some sort of rapprochement with that church.[11] While, as we have seen, Anglican Evangelicals had been disheartened by the failure of their attempts to secure the mass conversion of Roman Catholics in Ireland to the Church of Ireland through the 'New Reformation', they were not yet prepared to admit defeat in their ongoing struggle for religious supremacy in Ireland with the Roman Catholic Church.[12] They also continued to believe that it was the duty of the British state to provide them with the funds that they required to carry on their educational work.

The extent of the opposition to the national system within the Church of Ireland led to the foundation of the Church Education Society in 1839. The rules of the society admitted the use of the Bible and instruction in the Church of Ireland catechism on a regular basis in its schools.[13] Its schools were designed to provide an alternative to the national schools and were reliant on voluntary subscriptions rather than on state support.

The levels of these subscriptions ran at a surprisingly high level in the late 1840s and early 1850s, when the society spent some £50,000 to £60,000 annually on its primary schools. In 1849, for example, it ran 1,868 schools, which catered for 112,000 pupils. It was organised across the country, with 'the real power base of the system' lying in the local societies organised on a diocesan basis.[14] A number of prominent Conservative landowners including Lord Clancarty in Galway, Lord Donoughmore in Tipperary, and Lord Roden in Down were closely associated with such local bodies. They were also supported by the bulk of the Church of Ireland hierarchy and clergy.[15] Despite this, it was clear that this level of expenditure would be difficult to maintain, unless there was some prospect of winning government support for the society's schools. In consequence, the attempt to win government support for these schools was motivated by financial considerations well as by considerations of principle. However, many Irish Conservatives continued to believe, on grounds of principle, that the British government should grant financial support to the schools run by the Church Education Society. The main difference of opinion among them was over whether this should be done by a modification of the rules of the National Board, which would appease Church of Ireland opinion, or by a complete abandonment of the system.

The demand for state assistance for the society's schools was given a further impetus in 1845, with the Conservative government's decision to increase the grant to Maynooth College. The college was a Catholic seminary in County Kildare, which had been established in 1795. Its foundation was a result of the closure of the great continental seminaries, where most Irish Catholic priests had previously been trained, in the wake of the French revolution. The disturbed state of the European continent between 1795 and 1815 had made it impossible, in any case, for Irish clerical students to make the journey to the continental centres, like St Omer and Louvain, which they had previously undertaken. In 1795, the Pitt government had allocated an annual grant of £8,000 to the college. The grant was designed to ensure the Catholic Church's loyalty to the British connection, at a time of heightened tensions both across Europe, and, indeed, within the United Kingdom itself. In 1845 Sir Robert Peel, the Conservative Prime Minister, proposed that the grant should be increased fivefold to £40,000 a year and that it should be made permanent. Peel's belief was that the increase in the grant would conciliate moderate

Roman Catholic opinion in Ireland and, in consequence, would undermine radical agitation there.[16] However, the proposal created major divisions within the Conservative Party itself and it proved especially unpopular with the Irish members of the party.[17]

In the debates on the Maynooth question, Irish Conservatives referred constantly to the contrast between the government's increase in the grant to Maynooth and its failure to give any assistance to the Church Education Society. William Verner, the staunchly Protestant MP for Armagh, protested at the government's unwillingness to aid 'Scriptural' schools, while at the same time heaping 'a fivefold bounty... [on] a system, not merely suspected but accused, on evidence which has never been contradicted, of circulating principles and fostering a spirit which it ought to be the object of every good government... to discountenance and extinguish'.[18] This stress on the supposedly 'disloyal' nature of the teaching carried on at Maynooth was commonplace among the opponents of the grant. For example, George Alexander Hamilton maintained that the majority of the Irish Catholic clergy had 'already declared themselves the enemy of [the] British connexion'. But this was not his essential objection to the Maynooth grant, which rested on his conviction that 'it was the duty of every state' to acknowledge 'some intelligible system or principle of religious truth'. In Britain, this system was the Protestant religion, and it was

> most inconsistent, and a great dereliction of the homage that was due to [the] truth in religion, for the state to countenance and support any two systems of religion diametrically opposed to one another; and still more so, to pay for the promulgation of doctrines held by the state to be erroneous.

As the Protestant religion was 'conformable to God's revealed will, and the Roman Catholic religion opposed to it', Hamilton believed that he would be 'guilty of a great sin' if he were to vote for any measure, which would encourage the spread of doctrines he believed to be untrue.[19]

As we saw in Chapter 4, this view of Church–state relations was widely held among Irish Conservatives and, indeed, within the Conservative Party itself more generally. Followed to its logical conclusion, this view would, of course, have led to the state funding of the Church Education Society's schools and, in all probability, to the withdrawal of the Maynooth grant.

Although Peel succeeded in passing the Maynooth bill, this was only done at the cost of creating deep-seated divisions within the party. On the second reading of the bill, for example, 159 Conservatives voted for the increased grant, while 147 voted against.[20] An important result of these divisions was the foundation of the National Club in June 1846. Its membership was largely made up of Protestant clergymen and those ultra-Protestant Conservatives who had been disillusioned by Peel's handling of the Maynooth question.[21] In its principles and membership, the club reflected that combination of Evangelical beliefs and defence of the Established Church in both England and Ireland with which both Napier and Hamilton were associated. Among the club's objectives, as stated in its first annual report, were 'the maintenance of the Protestant principle of the Constitution in the administration of public affairs', the 'upholding of a system of national education, based on Scripture', and the preservation of 'the United Church of England and Ireland in its true Protestant faith as the established religion of the country'.[22] In its first general statement issued in November 1845, the club made clear its opposition to the Maynooth grant, arguing that 'no connection [should exist] between the state of England and the Church of Rome'. Such a connection was, it claimed, 'opposed to our civil polity, and to our religious principles'.[23]

From its inception, the club had a large and influential Irish membership. Among those who joined it were Evangelical landowners such as Lord Roden and Lord Lorton, Irish Conservative MPs such as George Alexander Hamilton and James Hans Hamilton, the MP for Dublin City, and prominent Irish Evangelical clergymen such as Mortimer O'Sullivan and R.J. McGhee. John George Beresford, the Primate of the Church of Ireland, was also an early member of the club. By 1848, it had 451 members and these included twenty-nine MPs, thirteen peers and 253 clergymen. The MPs involved also included such leaders of English ultra-Protestant opinion as Richard Spooner and Charles Newdegate.[24] After his election for Dublin University in February 1848, Napier was also to play a prominent role in its affairs.[25]

At the general election of August 1847, Napier had stood unsuccessfully for election as MP for Dublin University. His campaign was particularly directed against Frederick Shaw, Hamilton's colleague as sitting MP, who had alienated Irish Conservative opinion by voting for the Municipal Reform Act of 1840, and by voting against Lord George Bentinck's proposals for loans for the extension of Irish railways in 1846.[26] In his election speech, Napier had outlined a view of Church–state relations that bore a good deal of similarity to that outlined by Gladstone in his *The State in its Relations with the Church*, published in 1838.[27] As with a household, Napier argued, 'a nation...must have a religion' which ought to be 'encouraged and acted on'. While the state should display 'tenderness for the consciences of those who differ[ed] from it', 'no encouragement by active support' should be given 'to anything at variance with it'. Following logically from this, Napier would 'firmly testify' against the principle behind the Maynooth grant and the restrictions on religious education in the National Board schools. In parliament, he would 'act on the requirement of truth – truth as stereotyped in the word of God, and engraven on the British constitution'. Holding these beliefs, he would 'testify against any public assistance to any system essentially opposed' to what he considered to be the 'household faith of the Empire'.

After a fiercely contested and often bitter campaign, Napier was defeated but by the slimmest of margins. As a sitting member, Shaw had had a considerable advantage over Napier, and the closeness of the result meant that his was something of a Pyrrhic victory. In any event, Shaw's retirement of the seat in February 1848 led to a by-election in which Napier was elected without a contest. The closeness of Napier's ties to the Evangelical wing of the Irish Church at this point in his political career was illustrated by the fact that two of its leading clerical representatives, Joseph Singer and Mortimer O'Sullivan acted as his proposer and seconder at the nomination of candidates. In nominating him, Singer singled out Napier's 'uncompromising [advocacy] . . . of the great principle of scriptural education' for praise.

At the Church Education Society's annual meeting in April 1848, Napier reaffirmed his support for its principles. He even went so far as to argue that 'where spiritual education existed [in Ireland] there was prosperity, and where ignorance [of the Scriptures] was prevalent, famine and destitution abounded'. The 'word of God' was, he claimed, at the root of the relative prosperity of the North of Ireland. He also proposed that education for both Roman Catholic and Protestant children should be based on the Bible,[28] a suggestion which went beyond the society's own stated aim of providing 'scriptural' schools for 'the children of the Church'.[29]

Shortly after his election for Dublin University, Napier was elected to the committee of the National Club. From that time on, he regularly attended committee meetings, and in July he was commissioned by the club to write an address on the subject of Irish national education. This address was eventually published as a pamphlet by the club in November 1848. Napier began by claiming that there '[was] no fact unhappily more capable of proof with regard to Ireland than that, generally speaking, the Irish Protestants are loyal subjects, and that the Roman Catholicks [*sic*] are comparatively disloyal'. Consequently, Napier claimed that the government's policy, in treating 'its loyal and attached subjects with contempt, setting at naught their conscientious scruples, whilst respecting that of every other religious body in the United Kingdom' was 'as unnatural and ungrateful' as it was 'unintelligible and unwise'.

As unrestricted access to the Bible was 'the essence of Protestantism', Napier maintained that the restrictions on its use meant that the national system was founded on a 'Romanist' basis. The system had been founded in a misguided attempt to purchase the loyalty of Irish Catholics, while Irish Protestants, whose 'fidelity was undoubted', had their objections to the whole basis of the system overruled. In conclusion, Napier called on the government 'to cease to encourage the Popish creed, which ... [was] as politically dangerous as it was religiously false'. The government should 'honestly support and foster the Protestant faith; not, however, because it happens to be the faith of the majority in these islands – But, because, based on the Bible, the whole Bible, and nothing but the Bible, its foundation rested on uncontaminated truth'.[30] Napier's pamphlet reflected the view, held by many Irish Conservatives, that their loyalty to the connection with Britain was not being rewarded in the way that it should have been.

Napier's identification with the cause of the Church Education Society was further strengthened in August 1848, when he supported George Alexander Hamilton's motion calling for government assistance to be given to its schools. Echoing Napier's earlier argument, Hamilton made the claim that the national system was based on an essentially 'anti-Protestant principle'. The restrictions on the use of the Bible 'negatived the great principle of all Protestant churches ... the free use of the Holy Scriptures'.[31] As Protestants could not, in conscience, attend schools where the Bible was not freely used, Hamilton argued that the national system 'was essentially a separate one, and could never be otherwise'.[32] In a sparsely attended House, however, Hamilton's motion was easily defeated by 118 votes to fifteen votes. The scale of the defeat was probably due to the timing of the motion, the vote being taken on the eve of the recess. Many Irish Conservatives had already returned to Ireland by this time, which accounted for the small number of them who voted in the division.

This defeat did not prevent Hamilton from raising the question again in June of the following year. Although the motion was again defeated, the vote on this occasion gave a truer reflection of Irish Conservative opposition to the National Board system. The motion was supported by 102 MPs, an increase of eighty-seven from the previous session. This increase was largely made up of Irish Conservative MPs, who were present in greater force than they had been on the previous occasion. The motion was also supported by leaders of English Protestant opinion such as Spooner and Newdegate, and, more surprisingly, by Disraeli. The National Club had issued a whip on the motion to those MPs who were members,[33] a practice which it adopted regularly in divisions on Church questions.

A year later, in June 1851, Hamilton reintroduced the same motion. On this occasion, it was seconded by Spencer Walpole, a prominent English Conservative, who claimed that state assistance was due to the Church Education Society, as an 'act of justice ... to a loyal, faithful and devoted set of men'.[34] Walpole's Evangelical views had already brought him into contact with Irish Conservative MPs such as Napier and Whiteside, with whom he developed close personal friendships. These contacts were to prove significant during Walpole's terms as Home Secretary in 1852 and in 1858–59. Significantly, however, the national system was defended by

Edward Stanley, Lord Derby's son, who had been MP for King's Lynn since 1849. Stanley challenged the opponents of the national system to suggest a realistic alternative to it, given the religious divisions in Ireland. He warned prophetically that the effect of creating separate schools would be to leave Protestants in isolated and mainly Roman Catholic areas with either inferior schools or none at all. In such areas, the parents would simply be unable to raise the funds for a viable 'scriptural' school.[35] Stanley's comments were important, as they indicated that there were influential members of the Conservative Party opposed to any tampering with the national system.

By the time of their appointments to the Derby government in February 1852, both Napier and Hamilton had clearly identified themselves with the aims and objectives of the Church Education Society. This was less true of the other leading members of the Irish administration. Although Naas' father was a prominent Evangelical, and he was related to Lord Roden, the leading Evangelical peer in Ireland, he had the reputation of being a moderate Conservative and was a supporter of the Maynooth grant. As he sat for the largely Catholic constituency of Kildare County, these views were no doubt tempered by susceptibilities of the voters there.[36] He had, however, supported Hamilton's motion on national education in June 1850. As we saw earlier, Naas's appointment as Chief Secretary had been designed to diminish Catholic suspicions of the new government.

As the incoming government was a minority one, its scope for manoeuvre on the Irish education question was correspondingly limited. There was, however, a widespread feeling among Irish Conservatives that the new government would be more sympathetic to the claims of the Church Education Society than its predecessor had been. Despite this, however, Lord Derby's position on the education question was an ambivalent one. He had entered political life as a Whig and he had played a major role as Irish Chief Secretary in the foundation of the Irish national education system. Consequently, he was unlikely to support any measure that might threaten its continued existence.

Shortly after his appointment as Attorney General, Napier had met with Derby, who reassured him that his acceptance of office did not interfere with his freedom of action on the Irish education question. Hamilton also received a similar assurance,[37] while Derby expressed his willingness to support an 'honest' inquiry into the system. The inquiry would be designed to see what deviations had taken place from the original rules of the board, and to gauge the extent to which its schools were united across religious lines.[38] A common criticism of the National Board schools was that most of them were essentially run on sectarian lines, the exception being the model schools run at various centres across the country. Derby's proposal for an inquiry served a double purpose. It would operate as a useful safety valve against Irish Conservative criticism of government inaction on the education question, while the result of such an inquiry might win over opposition MPs to some minor adjustments in the rules of the Board. It would also help to conceal the divisions within the Conservative Party on the question, as even those MPs who supported the system could vote for an inquiry.

At an election meeting at Dublin University on 12 March, Napier stressed the fact that his opinions on the education question had not changed with his acceptance of office. To strengthen this claim, Napier told his audience that he had won an assurance from Derby that the Conservative government would not continue the policy, informally adopted by the Whigs, of barring supporters of the Church Education Society from ecclesiastical preferment. At his meeting with Derby, Napier had warned him that the system was neither 'comprehensive... [nor] united' and that it was essential that that 'sphere of education... [be] enlarged'. He suggested that this should be done by bringing 'the piety and intelligence of the clergy of the Established Church throughout the country' into 'harmonious action' with the National Board.[39] Implicitly, this was a call for state funding for the Church Education Society's schools. Indeed, Napier's speech was so worded that it could have been interpreted as implying that the whole object of the proposed inquiry was to facilitate this end.

This interpretation was, in fact, taken by Lord Clanricarde, a leading Irish Whig, in a question he put to Lord Derby in the House of Lords. Clanricarde paid tribute to Derby for his part in founding the system, a tactic obviously designed to embarrass the government and Derby himself in particular. He also criticised Napier for having given the impression that he wished to 'induce the government to change the [national] system'. As the system was designed to be a united one, it was 'clearly impossible that a separate system', such as the Church Education Society provided, could co-exist with it. On account of this, Clanricarde 'took exception to the whole tone of... [Napier's] speech for going forth to the people of Ireland upon such authority, and addressed as it was to the highest educational institution in Ireland it could not fail to give the impression' that the government was prepared to 'extend its support to other systems of education' besides that conducted by the National Board.[40]

As a political manoeuvre, Clanricarde's question was well judged. It was obviously designed to force Derby into a repudiation of Napier's speech, and, by implication, into a defence of the national system. Derby's reply, however, skilfully avoided the traps Clanricarde had laid for him. He expressed his gratification at the 'progressive increase' that had taken place in the numbers attending National Board schools since its formation. The system had become so well established that 'no step' could be taken which

would 'have any effect in weakening the influence and hold' which it had
established in Ireland. He qualified these remarks by arguing that, since its
foundation, various alterations had been made in the 'minor arrangements
of the Board, and even in some matters which may be considered of
primary importance'. This situation had arisen, in Derby's view, from the
fact that the management of the schools had increasingly been left to the
discretion of the school managers at the local level.

Following on from this, Derby argued that it was essential that the
question whether 'the system, as it at present exists, is practically a system
of combined education' should be investigated. The inquiry would also
consider whether 'any possible modification of the existing rules' could
remove the objections raised against the national system. Once the inquiry
had reported, it might be possible for the government to grant 'some,
perhaps, a minor degree of assistance to schools, be they Protestant or
Roman Catholic' which did not 'come under the strict rules of the Board'.
If exclusively Protestant schools were to receive assistance, Derby did not
dissent from the logical corollary of this, which was that exclusively Roman
Catholic schools should also receive state assistance. However, he explicitly
declined to pledge the government to anything beyond the appointment
of a committee, 'fairly chosen', to inquire into these questions.[41]

Shortly before this debate, Derby instructed Eglinton to obtain an
official return of the religious denominations of the children attending the
national schools. One of the principal motives behind this was to discover
whether it would be possible to establish alternative schools for Protestants
in areas where the attendance at the Board schools was almost exclusively
Roman Catholic.[42] On 19 March, Eglinton complained to Derby of the
difficulties he was having in procuring such a return. He warned that
granting state aid to exclusively Protestant schools would have a damaging
effect on the national system. On the other hand, even the possibility of
funding being given to exclusively Catholic schools would lead to 'a far
worse outcry from the Church Education [Society] people than . . . [would
their] adherence with perhaps some modifications to the present system'.[43]
Eglinton appears here as a defender of the national system, a stance he
maintained throughout his time as Lord Lieutenant. His support for the
system was largely based on pragmatic grounds. In October 1852 Eglinton
conceded to Derby that he was 'far from saying that the system . . . [was]
perfect because I can apply that term to no system of Education, in which
religion is not the first object, and the reading of the Bible is not enforced'.
Nevertheless, he considered the system to be 'the best which under the
peculiar circumstances of the country could have been adopted, and having
been adopted . . . its overthrow would be a grievous national calamity'.[44]

These views had been shaped soon after his arrival in Ireland. As early
as 26 March 1852, Eglinton had advised Naas that the 'best chance [the

government had] of obtaining a fair trial' for the national system lay in removing the exclusion of Church Education Society supporters from Church patronage.[45] Although Eglinton was sympathetic towards its objectives, he was realistic enough to determine that if the modifications to the system demanded by the Church Education Society were made, it would have the effect of driving 'away from it the Archbishop of Dublin [Whately], and those [Protestants supporters of the system] who follow him'. The Roman Catholics would, he believed, seize on this pretext 'for breaking it [the national system] up altogether'. He was also critical of the Protestant clergy's initial decision not to join the system, as it had led to the 'patronage of the schools' falling so heavily into 'the hands of the R[oman] Catholics'.[46]

Eglinton was a Scottish landowner, owning some 29,000 acres in Ayrshire and Lanarkshire. He had first come to prominence as a leading Protectionist. In his early years in parliament, he had also been closely associated with the 'Protestant' party there. In 1848, for example, he had moved a successful amendment to the Whig government's Diplomatic Relations with Rome Bill, barring Roman Catholic clerics from being appointed as Papal ambassador to London. This was necessary, Eglinton claimed at the time, in order to prevent the proposed embassy becoming 'a nucleus for the Jesuits'.[47] At the time of his appointment, Lord Stanley had worried that Eglinton had too 'strong… [a] leaning towards the Orange faction, which… [was] too much identified with Conservatism in Ireland' for affairs there to be safe in his hands. Stanley later revised this judgement of Eglinton's position, praising him as 'a fair, liberal and popular administrator'.[48] Although Stanley's judgement was obviously a partisan one, in general, Eglinton took a pragmatic line on Irish issues. As a result, with a few minor exceptions, he managed to avoid religious controversy during his time in office.[49] His sensitivity to Irish concerns may have owed something to his experiences in Scotland. In 1853 he became President of the National Association for the Vindication of Scottish Rights, an organisation that campaigned for greater rights for Scotland *within* the framework of the Union.[50] Its demands included an increase in the number of the Scottish MPs sitting at Westminster. Although the association only lasted for a brief period, its complaints of English politicians' neglect of Scottish interests bore a good deal of resemblance to the similar claims made in the Irish context by Irish Conservatives.

Although the government had by this point pledged itself to an inquiry into the national system of education, it had not yet clarified its position on the Maynooth grant. The question was, of course, a controversial one, and was a divisive issue even within the cabinet. Given its minority position, it was necessary for the government to tailor its policy on Maynooth to the views held by the other parties in the House of Commons. In early February

Derby reported to Disraeli that he had heard that the ultra-Protestant party in parliament intended to raise the question of Maynooth in the upcoming session. This made it necessary that the leadership 'be prepared with our line' and that a decision be made whether or not Derby should move for a House of Lords committee 'on the whole R[oman] Catholic question', which he thought might prove a 'useful safety valve'.[51] The idea of a committee to investigate the legal position of Roman Catholics 'with reference to the pretensions of Rome, their civil rights, the affairs of their Church and the condition of their schools, charities & religious establishments'[52] had already been mooted by Derby at the height of the controversy over the Ecclesiastical Titles Act in the previous year. At that time, Derby had seen the appointment of such a committee as a useful means by which to defuse 'the popular ferment'[53] in Britain over the supposed 'Papal aggression' of that year. By 1852, however, the proposed committee was principally designed to pre-empt criticism of the government's policies from the ultra-Protestant section of the Conservative Party. Its appointment was further discussed at a meeting of senior Conservatives, attended by Napier, Hamilton and Whiteside, in February 1852.[54] The government's short term in office and its minority position in the House of Commons ensured, however, that such a committee had not been appointed by the time that it fell in December 1852.

As the proposal for the appointment of this committee showed, both Derby and Disraeli believed that state regulation of the Roman Catholic Church would have considerable long-term advantages for the British government. They hoped that its ultimate effect would be to reduce the tensions between it and the Roman Catholic Church in Ireland. By doing so, it might also reduce Irish Roman Catholic antagonism to the Established Church there. State regulation would also have the advantage of giving the British government some form of control over the actions of the Catholic Church in Ireland. It might also make it possible for the British government to 'drive a wedge' between the Catholic hierarchy and future radical movements in Ireland.[55] Some form of rapprochement with the Catholic Church would also, it was hoped, make it easier to win over middle-class Irish Catholic opinion to support for the Union with Britain. Conservative leaders also hoped that the regularisation of the relationship between the state and the Vatican would conciliate English Catholic opinion. Disraeli placed particular emphasis on this objective, describing the English Catholics as a 'most powerful body' who were 'naturally Tories'.[56] Furthermore, state regulation of the Catholic Church would also bring Britain into line with the practise adopted in most other European countries. It also might prevent issues like the Maynooth grant, for example, from again becoming a source of contention in British politics.

The Maynooth question had a special significance for Irish

Conservatives both for those opposed and those in favour of it. In late January 1852, for example, a public meeting calling for the repeal of the grant had been held in Dublin. The meeting was chaired by Edward Grogan, the Conservative MP for Dublin City.[57] It was held under the auspices of the Dublin Protestant Association, a militantly anti-Catholic organisation dominated by the Reverend Tresham Dames Gregg, an erratic but formidable leader of extreme Protestant opinion in Dublin. Gregg had been active in the foundation of the Protestant Operatives Society in the 1840s and had a populist appeal unmatched by any other leader of Irish Conservative opinion in this period.[58]

Shortly before the meeting, Hamilton had written to Derby, asking for his advice as to whether he should attend. While Hamilton believed that 'the arrogant conduct of the [Irish] Roman Catholic hierarchy' had helped to provoke the campaign against Maynooth he was not convinced of 'the prudence of an agitation on this subject among the Protestants of Ireland'. He was worried that a general agitation against Maynooth by them would only serve to inflame sectarian tensions in Ireland.[59] Indeed, he told Derby that, if he had found out about the meeting sooner, he would have dissuaded the organisers from holding it. Hamilton's reference to the 'arrogance' of the Roman Catholic hierarchy was probably an allusion to the Synod of Thurles, which had condemned the 'godless' universities established by Peel. It may also have been influenced by the rumoured appointment of Paul Cullen as Archbishop of Dublin, an appointment felt by many Irish Protestants to presage greater control by Rome over the Irish Roman Catholic Church. In the event Hamilton did not attend the meeting, nor was it attended by either Napier or Whiteside. All three, however, sent letters explaining their absence.[60]

As we saw earlier, Napier had pledged himself to agitate for the repeal of the Maynooth grant during his first election contest for Dublin University in 1847.[61] Hamilton had also made clear his opposition to the increase of the grant in 1845. At that time he had described the endowment of Maynooth as 'virtually an abnegation of the Protestantism of the Empire'.[62] As members of the National Club, both men were closely associated with leaders of the anti-Maynooth movement in England such as Spooner and Newdegate. Aside from this, the issue was one of great political sensitivity as any decision to withdraw the grant was likely to raise a storm of protest among Irish Roman Catholics. The sensitivity of the Maynooth issue meant that the leaders of the Conservative Party were reluctant even to go as far as the granting of a committee. This approach was put under strain, when a motion calling for an inquiry into the system of education carried on in Maynooth was introduced in the House of Commons on 11 May. The motion was sponsored by Richard Spooner, the staunchly Protestant MP for North Warwickshire. Spooner described the grant to Maynooth as a 'a national sin' and stated his belief that the system of education there was 'antagonistic to the Word of God'.[63] His motion was seconded by Lord Blandford, the future Duke of Marlborough and a Conservative MP for Woodstock, who bluntly stated his belief that the grant should be 'absolute[ly] and unconditional[ly]' withdrawn.[64] There can be little doubt that this was the ultimate objective of most of the ultra-Protestant party in the House, but they were usually more diplomatic in their language than Blandford had been.

Walpole denied that the motion had the support of the government. However, the tone of his speech left little doubt of his personal support for it. In his opinion, the Maynooth grant had failed to fulfil the purpose for which it had been originally granted. While the original intention of the grant had been to produce 'a well-educated, loyal and domestic priesthood, ' Walpole felt that it had failed to achieve that objective. Instead, the Irish Roman Catholic hierarchy had 'assumed an aggressive character, 'constituting 'a confederacy' against 'the British Crown and the British connexion'. In his belief the 'conditions' on which the grant had been made had 'not been adequately or completely fulfilled'. As a consequence, it was open to parliament to insist that public funds should not be applied 'to any other purpose' than those for which they had originally been intended.[65] As a prominent member of the National Club and the leading English Evangelical in the cabinet, Walpole's position on Maynooth was hardly surprising. It did, however, point to the difficulties which the cabinet was having in presenting a united front on the question. The implication of his speech was that the grant should be repealed, a stance which, given his position as Home Secretary, was bound to raise controversy.

The government's policy of leaving the Maynooth grant intact was restated by Disraeli, in reply to a question from Lord John Russell on 19 May. However, Disraeli stressed his willingness to support an inquiry into the system of education there, provided it was restricted to 'ascertaining whether the [original] objects of that institution [Maynooth] had been fulfilled'. This, he claimed, was also Walpole's opinion,[66] although the clear implication of the latter's speech had been that the inquiry should be a preliminary to the repeal of the grant. Despite this, Walpole complained on 20 May that his original speech had been 'misrepresented' and that Disraeli's interpretation of it was the correct one.[67] Two days later, in the House of Lords, Derby reiterated this line taken by Disraeli. He emphasised the fact that he regarded the question of the Maynooth grant as 'one purely of policy' and disagreed with those who saw the grant as being a 'national sin'. The government's policy on the question would be determined not by 'any specific principle of right or wrong' but merely 'with regard to the public welfare, the maintenance of the public peace and the general well being of the country'. He insisted that the cabinet 'must be left to act with perfect liberty' on the subject and that it had no immediate intentions of repealing the grant.[68] This was Derby's clearest statement of government policy on Maynooth and was in all likelihood designed to counteract the equivocal character of Walpole's speech.

Despite this speech, the Maynooth question was to rumble on in parliament right up to its dissolution in the middle of June. These debates were repeatedly adjourned, although Disraeli claimed that this was due to the pressure of other business rather than from a desire on the part of the government to 'evade discussion' upon the subject.[69] Napier was the most senior member of the Irish administration to speak on the question during that session of parliament. In common with other Conservatives, he was critical of the behaviour of the Irish Roman Catholic clergy since 1845. Its behaviour had, Napier suggested, 'placed the Maynooth grant in a totally different light'. Using similar language to Walpole's, Napier argued that the initial policy of creating a 'well educated loyal and peaceable priesthood' had apparently failed. In his view, 'the policy [they] now pursued' only succeeded in 'putting funds derived from the public treasury into the hands of foreign agents for their own purposes'. Despite this indictment, Napier denied that he was advocating the immediate repeal of the grant. What he proposed was an inquiry along the lines originally suggested by Disraeli. While on principle, Napier might believe that the grant was one that 'ought ultimately to be repealed', he nonetheless conceded that this could only be done 'after a dispassionate and careful consideration of all the circumstances connected with the case'.[70] This speech signalled a retreat from Napier's position in 1847, when he had pledged himself to agitate in parliament for the immediate repeal of the grant. The speech was ambivalent enough, however, to sustain his position as a leader of Irish Protestant opinion.

These 'unsatisfactory discussions about Maynooth'[71] finally terminated for the session on 15 June, when Spooner interpreted a division in favour of an adjournment of the debate as having 'evinced clearly' the feeling of the House on the subject.[72] The government's vacillating policy on Maynooth had been determined by two factors. The first was their unwillingness to pledge themselves to any definite policy on the issue. In a letter to Eglinton on 26 May, Naas expressed his hope, 'between ourselves', that the discussion of Maynooth was over for that session. He believed that there was a 'very great danger in meddling with it at all' and had 'very much dreaded speaking on it'. As we saw earlier, Naas had supported the grant, a stance not universally popular among Irish Conservatives. He was also concerned that the controversy over Maynooth might draw attention towards the financial position of the Church of Ireland, an Established Church whose members were very much a minority of the Irish population.[73] The second factor determining the government's policy was the impending general election.

As even supporters of Spooner's motion conceded, it was unlikely that a committee appointed so close to the dissolution of parliament would be able to achieve anything very substantial. The debates did, however, give Conservative MPs from constituencies where there was a strong anti-Catholic vote an opportunity to reaffirm their 'Protestant' credentials. As Derby wrote to Disraeli, many of those who supported the motion for an inquiry did so with the 'impending elections' in mind. As a result, the government should 'not be hard upon men, even in office' who voted for Spooner's motion.[74]

From an electoral point of view, these debates were not wholly unwelcome to the government. The problem for the Irish administration was that any benefits which the Conservative Party might gain in the rest of Britain by the expression of anti-Maynooth sentiments were likely to be offset by the negative impact this would have in Ireland. This perceived ambivalence in the government's approach to the Maynooth question was criticised in an editorial in *The Globe*, an English Liberal newspaper, on 14 June. According to *The Globe*, Derby was willing to let voters in England believe that the government intended 'to aim a death blow at Maynooth', the proposed inquiry being merely a means to that end. In Ireland, on the other hand, the paper claimed, the inquiry was presented merely as 'a sop to appease Protestant antipathy [towards Maynooth] – a side door by which members may slip into the next parliament'[75] without having declared themselves against the principle of the grant. Although this article over-simplified the true position, nonetheless, it contained a grain of truth. It was the case that many English Conservatives advocated the repeal of the grant in the course of their election campaigns.[76] Several of those who did so supported an inquiry as the first step in this process. While other candidates were less forthcoming, they nevertheless expressed their support for an investigation into the system of teaching carried on at Maynooth.[77]

One of the exceptions to the predominant tone of English Conservative statements on Maynooth at the 1852 general election came from Seymour Fitzgerald, the candidate for Horsham in Sussex. Fitzgerald's family owned land in Tipperary and he admitted that his Irish connections had influenced his views on Maynooth. While he was prepared to vote for Spooner's motion if elected, he would not support the immediate withdrawal of the grant. He believed that such a move would cause 'serious hostility' towards the government in Ireland and would not be popular with British opinion.[78] At the opposite extreme to Fitzgerald's conciliatory comments were the abrasive statements made by William Beresford, the Secretary at War. Like Fitzgerald, Beresford had Irish connections, his father being a cousin of the Marquis of Waterford. The Beresfords were also prominent in the Church of Ireland, two members of the family serving successively as Archbishops of Armagh in the latter half of the nineteenth century.

Beresford himself had a reputation for irritability and a general lack of tact. Disraeli described him as

> a tall, coarse man, who could blend with his natural want of refinement, if necessary, extreme servility; very persevering, capable of labour, prejudiced, & bigoted. Protection and Protestantism were his specifics for all the evils of the state, & the only foundation for strong & lasting governments.[75]

Beresford's comments at Essex North bore out Disraeli's description of him, as he called on the voters there not to turn against a 'man who has bearded Popery to the face, and who will do it again, whether it be in Ireland, or the House of Commons or anywhere else'.[80] The character of Beresford's speech inspired a letter from Henry Herbert, the Conservative MP for Kerry, to Lord Naas, in which he complained that 'your friends in England seem determined to make it impossible for a Protestant to be elected in the South of Ireland'. Beresford's comments had, he complained, put him, as the representative of a Roman Catholic constituency who was 'anxious to support the government... in a very awkward position'. In Herbert's opinion, the language used by Beresford was

> disgraceful... even if the government intended to bring forward stringent measures against Roman Catholics (which I do not believe)... It is very well for you and I to laugh who know that his chief qualification for the place which he [Beresford] occupies is a temper which renders him unfit to occupy a subordinate one, but that will not go down either in this country or even in England.[81]

Herbert's letter shows clearly the difficulties which Conservative expressions of anti-Catholic sentiments caused for Irish Conservatives, who required Roman Catholic support in order to be elected.

The election campaign also revealed a disparity in attitudes between those Conservatives who had sizeable numbers of Roman Catholic voters in their constituencies and those chiefly dependent on Protestant support. In Dublin City, for example, one of the few constituencies outside the North of Ireland to have a considerable working-class Protestant element, Conservative politics had a populist and sectarian flavour, unlike that found elsewhere in the South of Ireland. Both of the Conservative candidates there, Edward Grogan and John Vance, made no secret of their opposition to the Maynooth grant and the national education system.[82] An indication of the tone of these election meetings was the fact that Tresham Gregg, the noted anti-Catholic polemicist, was one of the principal speakers at one of them.[83] At an earlier meeting, Grogan had suggested that, as Irish Roman Catholics had sufficient funds with which to maintain the Catholic University in Dublin, they should now be able to maintain Maynooth from their own resources. Speaking on the same platform, Vance expressed his support for separate grants for the Church Education Society schools.[84] The most likely outcome of such a policy would have been to create a system of denominational grants, a policy which had the support of some of the Roman Catholic critics of the system. It would also have put an end to any real possibility of the national system operating as a genuinely united one. Following a lively and often polemical campaign, both candidates for Dublin City were returned, the Conservatives regaining the seat which had been lost to John Reynolds, the Independent Party candidate, in 1847.

An interesting example of the divergent ways in which Conservative candidates in different parts of the country campaigned in the 1852 general election is provided by a comparison between the pre-election speeches of Mervyn Archdall, the MP for Fermanagh since 1834, and those of Francis Bernard, the unsuccessful candidate for King's County. Ironically, both of these candidates quoted passages from Derby's speeches in parliament that session to support widely divergent positions on the Maynooth grant. In his election address, Archdall, a prominent member of the Orange Order, described himself as 'a firm supporter of Protestant Ascendancy'.[85] At the nomination of the candidates, he quoted Derby's speech earlier that year, in which he had suggested that the conduct of the Roman Catholic clergy since 1845 had rendered it more difficult for the government to support the grant. Archdall hoped that the speech had increased the likelihood that the proposed inquiry would recommend the repeal of the Maynooth grant.

In Archdall's view, Maynooth was a 'pernicious nest of idolatry and sedition' a description hardly likely to appeal to the Catholics in his constituency. The system of education carried on there was, in his opinion 'highly prejudicial to the religious, social and moral interests of the country'. Archdall was also opposed to the national system of education, urging the necessity of a modification of 'its present unscriptural state'. He claimed that the main advantage of the system was that threatening letters and 'Ribbon notices...were better written, spelt and expressed than formerly'.[86] As an MP of long standing, whose family had controlled the Fermanagh seat for many years before his election, Archdall probably had more freedom to articulate his real opinions than did candidates elsewhere in the country. Nevertheless, his comments provide a clear contrast to those made by Francis Bernard, in the course of his election speeches. Unlike Archdall, Bernard countered his opponents' claims that he supported the withdrawal of the Maynooth grant by pointing to Derby's pledge that the government had no intention of interfering with it.[87] This use of Derby's statements to justify two completely opposed positions on Maynooth was revealing in itself, the government's reluctance to declare itself unambiguously on the subject being one of the constants of the parliamentary session. One of the chief factors determining this reticence had been its unwillingness to alienate potential supporters on both sides of the sectarian divide in the run-up to the election.

Despite the attempts by some Conservative candidates to conciliate Irish Catholic opinion, the election results in Ireland were particularly notable for the strong showing of Independent Party candidates in constituencies outside the North of Ireland. Of the 105 MPs returned from Ireland, some forty-eight, with varying degrees of sincerity, had pledged themselves to the policy of remaining independent from all British parties. A number of commentators, not least Lord Stanley, attributed the Independent Party's successes at the elections to the government's mistaken policy in issuing the proclamation against Roman Catholic processions.[88] Stanley had also found the 'No-Popery' tone of some of the Conservative candidates in England distasteful. On 19 July Stanley had written to Disraeli, describing such speeches as 'a case of playing to the pit'. However, echoing his father's earlier comments, he claimed that 'reasonable people... [were] tolerant of such measures at election time, and all the unreasonable people are mostly with us'.[89] In a letter to Stanley in mid-July, Disraeli blamed the Conservative losses at the elections on their taking up of the 'Protestant cry'. This claim exasperated Stanley, who complained that Disraeli had been largely responsible for that 'cry... [being] raised'.[90] The issuing of the proclamation was a clear case of the government failing to maintain its complex balancing act between Irish Protestants and Irish Catholics. It was also the case that senior members of the Irish administration, including Naas, had seriously underestimated the effect which the proclamation would have on Irish Catholic opinion.[91]

There were forty-one Irish Conservative MPs returned in the 1852 general election, a disappointing return for party leaders who had hoped for more substantial gains. After the elections were concluded, two separate conferences were held in Dublin, one organised by the Tenant League and the other by the newly formed Friends of Religious Freedom and Equality. At the latter meeting, which was attended by some twenty-six Independent Party MPs, resolutions were passed, calling for the repeal of the Ecclesiastical Titles Act and the disestablishment of the Church of Ireland. The MPs at the conference also pledged themselves to remain independent of any government that did not concede these demands. These conferences brought the Independent Party 'to full strength' and, given the Conservative government's minority position in the House of Commons, seemed to have given them a position of some influence there.[92] The question that remained to be answered, however, was what influence, if any, the emergence of this new bloc would have on the government's Irish policy.

Earlier in the session, Walpole had advised Eglinton that, even though the government had 'postponed' dealing with the education question until after the elections, he should reflect on it 'with great care'.[93] In the event the government's attention was forcibly drawn to the subject as the terminal illness of Thomas Stewart Townshend, the Church of Ireland Bishop of Meath, and the death of Daniel Murray, the Roman Catholic Archbishop of Dublin, left it with the politically delicate task of filling two vacancies in the National Board. The appointment of a replacement for Murray presented the government with particular difficulties. An obvious candidate for the position was Paul Cullen, the Archbishop of Armagh, who was widely tipped to be Murray's successor. Cullen's ultramontanism was, however, anathema to many of the government's supporters. The condemnation of the 'godless Colleges' at the Synod of Thurles in 1851 had also revealed Cullen's opposition to the principle of mixed education. At a meeting with Eglinton in April 1852, Richard Whately, the Archbishop of Dublin and the most prominent Church of Ireland supporter of the system, informed him that Cullen's appointment would 'probably force him to retire' from the Board.[94]

In these circumstances, the government decided on appointing a Catholic cleric other than Cullen to the post. This proved more difficult to achieve than the government had expected, with the position being refused by a number of senior Catholic clerics, including Edward Walsh, the Bishop of Ossory, and Cornelius Denvir, the Bishop of Down and Connor, and by a number of prominent Catholic laymen like Richard Corballis.[95] In October Whately informed Eglinton that it had proved difficult to find a Roman Catholic bishop who would accept the office, 'except such as would be dangerous Commissioners'.[96] A few weeks later, Eglinton complained to Derby that the Roman Catholic members of the Board 'were attempting to force Cullen on us, which is quite out of the question'.[97] The protracted nature of the government's search for a replacement for Archbishop Murray meant that an appointment had still not been made by the time it fell in December 1852. It was plain that leading Irish Catholics were more concerned to avoid Cullen's displeasure than to accept the poisoned chalice of membership of the National Board. The second vacancy, caused by Townsend's illness, had been filled much earlier by Francis Blackburne, the Irish Lord Chancellor and a staunch Protestant. This appointment had been made at the insistence of Archbishop Whately.[98]

Townsend's illness and subsequent death left the government with the difficult task of filling his position on the ecclesiastical bench. There were two principal candidates for the situation, Edward Pakenham, the Dean of St Patrick's, and Joseph Singer, the Archdeacon of Raphoe. Even though both men supported the Conservative Party, the choice between them did have implications for government policy. While Pakenham favoured the

National system, as one of the leaders of Evangelical opinion in Ireland, Singer was a prominent advocate of 'scriptural' education. He had also been one of Napier's intellectual mentors at Trinity College and a major contributor to both his and Hamilton's electoral success there. Not surprisingly, both Napier and Hamilton pressed Singer's claim for the bishopric strongly.[99]

His candidacy was also supported by Naas, who believed that Singer's appointment would 'be taken by the Church as the first decided step in showing that the present gov[ernmen]t abhor the rule that debarred opponents of the national system from preferment'. As such, it would 'smooth the way for a settlement of the National Education question', as Singer's appointment would 'disarm [any] suspicions' which the supporters of the Church Education Society had of government policy on the question. Naas conceded that it was 'true... [that] we [the government] appoint a no-Popery man in Singer and why should we not? After the open declaration of war upon our [Church] Establishment by the Political and Clerical Magnates of the Romish Party are we bound to conciliate [?]'The 'ultra' party to which Singer belonged, Naas claimed, numbered 'among it every man of honesty and ability who heartily supports us'. The appointment would, he concluded, 'be taken as proof of Protestantism and it is by Protestantism we exist'.[100] Although, the tone of these remarks belied Naas' reputation as a moderate Conservative, it should be noted here that his upbringing had been strongly coloured by Evangelical Protestantism and that he grew more moderate as a politician as his career progressed. He was also keenly aware of the political advantage that would accrue to the Irish Conservative Party from Singer being chosen for Meath.

In early June, Eglinton sought Derby's advice on the appointment. He questioned him as to 'which party in the Church [of Ireland]' should be placated when selecting the new bishop. The Church Education Society's supporters had, he believed, already 'been very much gratified... [and] their views [towards the national system] modified' by the government's promise to grant them an equal share of ecclesiastical patronage. Up to that point, however, this had not gone beyond 'a verbal understanding'. Eglinton counselled that it would greatly strengthen the government's position if it were to give the Church Education Society a tangible proof of its good will. The only danger he saw arising from this policy was that it might lead to speculation that the government was intent on 'abandon[ing] the National Board system altogether'. This could be avoided, he suggested, by selecting 'as eminent and moderate a man as we can find'.[101] This description was presumably intended to refer to Singer, although, given Naas's description of him, his moderation might have been in some doubt.

Eglinton returned to the same theme on the death of the Bishop of

Meath in late September 1852. He again stressed the necessity of conciliating the supporters of the Church Education Society who, he asserted, 'formed by far the most numerous and the most distinguished portion of the clergy'.[102] On 2 October, Derby advised Eglinton to consult with Whately and John George Beresford, the Archbishop of Armagh and Primate of the Church of Ireland, on the subject. The Irish administration should ensure that whatever choice it made would be such 'as might least embarrass' Whately.[103] Not surprisingly, Whately proposed that Pakenham should be the preferred candidate, although he did not 'entirely approve' even of him.[104] Another alternative candidate, proposed by George Alexander Hamilton, was James Thomas O'Brien, the combative Bishop of Ossory.[105] Like Singer, O'Brien was a partisan of the Church Education Society, but he was a younger man than Singer and his talents as a polemicist would have made him a more controversial choice. The suggestion here was that Singer would be transferred to Ossory, with O'Brien going to Meath.

In the event, however, the Irish administration decided to appoint Singer.[106] The decision to nominate him for the Meath bishopric was, obviously, based as much on political as it was on religious considerations. In Eglinton's view, at least, the decision would make it easier for the government to maintain the national education system by conciliating its critics within the Church Education Society.[107] In any case, Singer's term as Bishop of Meath was distinguished less by Evangelical zeal than by 'a tendency towards nepotism'. Already an old man at the time of his appointment, Singer lived the life of a 'scholarly... recluse' and fulfilled neither the fears of his critics nor the hopes of his supporters.[108]

Both Eglinton and Hamilton had related the question of Singer's appointment to the need for the government to decide its policy on the whole question of national education. In early September Hamilton had impressed upon Naas the necessity for government action on the subject. The settlement of the question would, he argued, 'be considered as the test by the Protestants in Ireland of the principles of Lord Derby's government'. Referring back to the elections, Hamilton contended that as 'open war' had been declared and would 'be carried to the knife by the R[oman] C[atholic] clergy it would seem an act of fatuity not to have the cordial support of the Protestants'. Their support could, he believed, be won by even minor concessions. On principle, he was opposed to the granting of a committee of inquiry, as he thought that it would be both difficult to manage and would delay a resolution of the question. Given the Conservatives' minority position in the House, it would also be difficult to ensure that the proposed committee would reach conclusions acceptable to Irish Conservative opinion. Hamilton's preferred option was that the National Board would adopt a new set of supplementary rules,[109] allowing the Church Education Society's schools to adhere to the national system as non-vested schools.

Unlike in the other non-vested schools, however, there would be no restrictions placed on the use of the Bible in these schools. The new rules would, however, prohibit the use of Church of Ireland catechisms or formularies during regular school hours. The new rules would also leave it open to those schools, which wished to retain the original rules of the Board, to do so.[110] In essence, this was a proposal for the creation of an implicitly denominational system. It was doubtful, to say the least, that the Roman Catholic clergy would have agreed to such a radical alteration in the rules of the National Board. If such a scheme were adopted it would most likely have led, as Eglinton had earlier suggested, to demands by Roman Catholic patrons for increased control over the religious education in their schools.

Writing to Derby in late September, Eglinton emphasised the importance of the government determining its educational policies before the next session began. He suggested there were three options open to the government; the first being to leave the national system intact as it then stood, the second to appoint a committee of inquiry into the whole subject of national education in Ireland, and the third to themselves 'make such changes [in the system], as might remove the opposition of our [the Church of Ireland] clergy, without breaking up the system'.[111] Eglinton's primary concern was to prevent such an eventuality. While he 'earnestly wish[ed] that such modifications could be devised [to the national system], as would satisfy the scruples of the Evangelical clergy', he was unwilling to introduce them if their effect would be to drive away the Roman Catholics and lead to 'the destruction of the best system of secular education any country ever possessed'. If an inquiry were held, Eglinton recommended that the government should go before it unpledged to any definite scheme for amending the system, as it would 'then [not] be answerable for the failure, which would probably ensue'.[112]

Nonetheless, Eglinton believed that a committee should be appointed, as the Evangelical wing of the party would be 'grievously offended' if the government refused all inquiry into the system. As the Evangelical 'party' represented an important element of Conservative support in Ireland, that was an outcome which the government could not afford. Eglinton also pointed to the fact that many Conservative MPs, both in Britain and Ireland, had already pledged themselves to the holding of such an inquiry. He was sceptical, however, about the prospect of its leading to any practical result. Another advantage of the government's pursuing this line was that 'some suggestion' might be made in the course of the inquiry that it might 'think it right to adopt'. Up to that point, he had not heard any scheme for the reform of the national system that he could advise the government to accept.[113]

In the course of October, Eglinton was in regular contact with John

George Beresford and Whately, both of whom sought to influence government policy on education. Between them, these two men represented the
poles of Irish Protestant opinion on the issue. Beresford defended the
Church Education Society's schools as being based on the same principle
maintained by the National Society in England,[114] this being that
'instruction in the Holy Scriptures...[was] an indispensable part of the
education of a Christian child'. He saw it as the duty of the Church of
Ireland clergy to give such instruction in their schools. They could not, in
conscience, agree to the restrictions on Bible-reading enforced by the
National Board. Their objection to the system was, therefore, one of
principle, not 'a political, nor an intolerant one'. Beresford suggested that
the increasing opposition to the system expressed by the Roman Catholic
hierarchy, particularly by Cullen, meant that there was 'less prospect than
ever of united education becoming general'. In these circumstances, he felt
that Eglinton should give his 'powerful assistance...[to] bringing about a
satisfactory settlement of this vexed question'.[115] Beresford's preferred
solution was that the rules of the national system should be so modified as
to allow the society to join it.

Such a solution to the controversy was, however, anathema to Whately.
In his view, the low level of Bible-reading in the national schools was a
direct result of the refusal by the Protestant gentry and clergy of 'all
connection' with it. As a result, the majority of the schools were under
Roman Catholic patrons, while the board's opponents blamed the
government 'for the consequences of their own procedure'. If the Church
of Ireland clergy were to connect themselves with the system, then, as
patrons, they would have had the right to have the Bible read in their
schools, 'only excluding from the school those whose parents object[ed]
to it'. As Whately had pointed out, it was the case that individual patrons
generally had more freedom in the conduct of religious instruction in
their schools than a strict reading of the Board's rules would have
suggested.

Whately was also concerned at the practical consequence of any
change in the rules of the National Board. Those supporters of the
Church Education Society who recommended that patrons of vested and
non-vested schools should be left free 'to introduce whatever religious
instruction' they thought fit had not, he believed, considered the effect
this would have on schools under Roman Catholic patrons. These
patrons would now be left free to 'introduce & to render compulsory the
R.C. Catechisms, & prayers in a majority of the [National Board]
schools'. He also warned that if government assistance were given to
exclusively Protestant schools, in which the children were compelled to
receive religious instruction decided on by a Protestant patron, the
government would be accused 'not without some shred of reason' of

employing 'public money in compulsory proselytism'. Such a perception would, Whately warned, be disastrous for the government's standing in Ireland.[116]

At a meeting with Eglinton in early October, Whately again made plain his absolute opposition to any state aid being given to the Church Education Society's schools. If such aid were given, even with 'the National schools . . . [being] left untouched', he would immediately retire from the Board.[117] This outright opposition to any concession to the society from the leading Church of Ireland defender of the national system indicated the difficulties which Eglinton faced in shaping education policy. Essentially, the government had to attempt to square the circle by framing a policy which would maintain the system and, at the same time, satisfy the advocates of 'scriptural education'.

The system's success in attracting Roman Catholic children also meant that the government could not lightly tamper with it. According to figures supplied to Eglinton in July 1852, there were some 424,717 Roman Catholic children out of a total of 493,018 children on the rolls of the national schools. This contrasted with some 40,618 Presbyterian children and 24,684 Church of Ireland children.[118] These figures did not, of course, indicate actual attendance at the schools, which was considerably lower.[119] The existence of alternative 'scriptural' schools had the effect of lowering the number of Church of Ireland children attending national schools and accentuating the predominance of Roman Catholic children in the system. In terms of patronage, Roman Catholic patrons controlled some 3,376 schools, compared to 708 schools under Presbyterian control and 751 under Church of Ireland patrons.[120] By way of comparison, in 1849 the Church Education Society claimed to have 1,868 schools, educating 111,877 children. Of these children, 37,857 were Roman Catholics and 15,562 non-Anglican Protestants.[121] These figures can be contrasted with the figures for the religious composition of the country as a whole, given in Table 4.1.

As D.H. Akenson has pointed out, the society's success in siphoning off Protestant children played a large part in determining the denominational nature of the national system.[122] For the government, however, its principal dilemma lay in determining whether the gains it would make by conciliating the Church Education Society would offset the losses incurred by interfering with a system, which had grown steadily since its inception in 1831. It also had to bear in mind that any attempt to effect the latter option would have been likely to unite the opposition parties against it in the House of Commons.

Despite this ongoing debate, the government had in fact already approved a substantial increase in the grant to the national schools. This increase was in line with those given in previous years and would, in all probability, have been given by a Liberal administration. This increased subsidy for the national schools passed the House of Commons without opposition. Even opponents of the system conceded that the holding of an inquiry into it was an essential first step before the grant could be withdrawn. The central weakness of the case made by the critics of the national system was their inability to propose a viable alternative to it. Although many Conservatives were unhappy with aspects of the system as it stood, they were unwilling to sacrifice the concrete benefits it provided for the prospect of a renewed sectarian wrangle over the future of Irish primary education. While Derby could complain to Eglinton that the system, as it operated in practice, was 'a sham [one] – [theoretically] united but really a separate Education, and except in particular localities destitute of all religious teaching', the government was eventually to come to the conclusion that it should be left intact, without any modifications in favour of the Church Education Society. As late as October, Derby still hoped that the government could devise a scheme to achieve that end which would be accepted by the proposed inquiry. He even suggested to Eglinton that the institution of an avowedly denominational system similar to that which existed in England would be preferable to 'the present working of the [national] scheme'.[123] The Lord Lieutenant's reports of his dealings with Whately and with Beresford and his consistent support of the national system seem, however, to have dissuaded Derby from this course. In November, Naas gave the first indication of the government's new line, in response to a question from Bernal Osborne. Naas denied that the government intended to make any alteration in the system, particularly if this would 'interfere with its efficiency'. He coupled this defence of the national system, with a promise to carefully consider any scheme suggested to remove the Church of Ireland objections to it.[124]

The government's failure to act on the education question meant, however, that it ran the risk of alienating the Evangelical wing of the Conservative Party in Ireland. Napier commented on this danger in a letter to Eglinton on 4 December. After discussing the frayed conditions of his nerves and his hopes for a judicial appointment, Napier disclosed that he was 'somewhat the more anxious to retire [from political life], in consequence of the resolution...[reached] by Lord Derby as to the Education question'. A large majority of his constituents believed the issue to be one 'of vital importance'. When they saw 'the estimates come on, [with] the National system & Maynooth provided for & nothing given to the faithful friends of scriptural Education,' Napier feared that his position as a member of the government would become untenable. He would, he warned, 'be expected to take a course, which as a man of honour', he would 'find difficult to avoid'. This was an obvious signal by Napier of his willingness to make the question a resigning issue. He sugared this, however, by stressing his unwillingness to embarrass 'those who differing from me on this, have so consistently acted towards me in a spirit which must ever be remembered with sincerest gratitude'.[125] In the event, Napier did not have an opportunity to carry this threat into force, as the government fell within two weeks of his writing this letter.

The Conservative government's handling of both the education and Maynooth questions had obviously been circumscribed by its minority position. On neither issue was it free to initiate policies, without first weighing the possibility of their attracting support from the other parties in parliament. This difficulty was compounded by the divisions within the Conservative Party's ranks on both questions. In these circumstances, occasional playing to the gallery was, perhaps, inevitable. Both the issuing of the Royal proclamation in July 1852 and the stridently anti-Maynooth tone adopted by many Conservative candidates at the 1852 general election were designed as much to draw attention away from the government's inaction in other areas as for any other reason. Even the Evangelical members of the party, like Napier, were prepared to accept that the government's freedom of action was limited. Earlier in its life, he had warned that if Irish Conservatives insisted on its pursuing a 'sectional policy', it was unlikely that it would survive very long.[126] He advised that they practice 'forbearance and acquiescence' and give Derby an opportunity to strengthen the government's position. By the time that the government fell, however, even Napier was critical of its equivocation over both questions.[127]

Nevertheless, given its position in the House of Commons, it is difficult to see how the government could have successfully pursued a more definite policy on either issue. The government also had to consider the effects that a withdrawal of the Maynooth grant or an alteration of the national system might have had on Irish public opinion and, more specifically, on Conservative support in largely Catholic constituencies. The education question was, however, one which the Conservatives could use to embarrass the incoming Aberdeen government. In opposition, the party could also hope to avoid having to deal with the thorny question of proposing a viable alternative to the existing system.

NOTES

1   See D.H. Akenson, *The Irish Education Experiment: The National System of Education in the Nineteenth Century* (London, 1970), pp. 80–93.
2   See S.J. Brown, *The National Churches of England, Ireland and Scotland, 1801–1846* (Oxford, 2001), pp. 120–36.
3   See Brown, *National Churches*, p. 141.
4   Eglinton to Walpole, 24 April 1852, Eglinton papers, GD3/5/51/4429a.
5   Speaking in the House of Commons in April 1853, George Alexander Hamilton described the model schools as being deliberately designed to

'mislead Parliament' as to the true nature of the National system, *Hansard*, CXXVl, 571.

6   See Akenson, *Irish Education Experiment*, pp. 161–86.

7   For a fuller discussion of the nature of the different types of schools see Akenson, *Irish Education Experiment*, pp. 147–8, pp. 158–60 and pp. 186–7. A useful contemporary account, published in pamphlet form, is '*The Irish Education Question*': *Reprinted with Additions from the Westminster Review* (London, 1860).

8   Akenson points out that, in 1850, some 2,310 out of a total of 3,076 non-vested schools were under clerical management. Of these 1,746 were under Roman Catholic management. Akenson derived these figures from the *Appendix to the Seventeenth Report of the Commissioners of National Education in Ireland, for the Year 1850*, p. 479. Akenson, *Irish Education Experiment*, p. 221. Akenson discusses the problems involved in gauging the accuracy of these figures on p. 220 of the same book.

9   For a detailed account of the founding of the system see D. H. Akenson, *Irish Education Experiment*. The same author's *Church of Ireland*, pp. 202–6, provides a concise account of the controversy over the national system and the issues involved. For the views of an influential Church of Ireland critic of the system, see Earl of Clancarty, *Ireland: Her Present Condition and What it Might Be* (Dublin, 1864), pp. 1–32.

10   The *Quarterly Review* complained in June 1852 that the national system had caused 'a disastrous separation between [the] Government and the Established Church'. See 'The new Reformation in Ireland', *Quarterly Review*, 91 (1852), p. 60.

11   See Bowen, *Protestant Crusade in Ireland*, pp. xii–xiiii. See also Brown, *National Churches*, pp. 404–6.

12   See Brown, *National Churches*, pp. 404–6.

13   See the 'Fundamental laws' in the *Sixteenth Report of the Church Education Society for Ireland, Being for the Year 1855* (Dublin, 1856), p. 19.

14   See Akenson, *Church of Ireland*, p. 204.

15   In a speech at the Church Education Society's annual meeting in April 1852, James Thomas O'Brien, the Bishop of Ossory, claimed that, at most, one quarter of the Church of Ireland clergy supported the National system. See Akenson, *Irish Education Experiment*, p. 191.

16   Gash, *Peel*, p. 237.

17   The political controversy over Maynooth is dealt with in detail in Donal Kerr's, *Peel, Priests and Politics: Sir Robert Peel's Administration and the Catholic Church in Ireland* (Oxford, 1982).

18   *Hansard*, LXXIX, 702.

19   *Hansard*, LXXIX, 764–5.

20   See Norman Gash, *Reaction and Reconstruction in English Politics, 1832–1852* (Oxford, 1965), p. 151.

21   For the motivation behind the formation of the Club, see J. Wolffe, *The Protestant Crusade in Great Britain, 1829–1860* (Oxford, 1991), pp. 210–16.

22   See the 'First Annual Report of the National Club', in the National Club papers, Bodleian Library, Oxford, Dep. d. 754/2.

23   See the 'First General Statement' of the National Club, National Club papers, Dep. d. 755.

24   These figures for the membership of the National Club are taken from Wolffe, *Protestant Crusade in Great Britain*, p. 211.

25   Napier was elected to the General Committee of the National Club on 23

March 1848. See 'National Club General Committee Minute Book No.2' for that date in the National Club papers, Dep. b. 235. In 1850 steps were taken to establish an auxiliary branch of the club in Dublin. Although this went as far as the appointment of a Dublin-based committee, the Irish branch of the club does not seem to have lasted very long. The committee's membership included familiar names like Roden, George Alexander Hamilton, Napier, Singer and Mortimer O'Sullivan. As it turned out, all of these continued to take an active part in the English branch of the club, and the Irish version seems to have died a natural death. See 'National Club General Committee Minute Book No. 2' in the National Club papers, Dep. b. 235.

26 See *The Warder*, 3 July 1847.
27 For a discussion of the ideas contained in Gladstone's book, see Perry Butler, *Gladstone, Church, State and Tractarianism: A Study of His Religious Ideas and Attitudes, 1809–1858* (Oxford, 1982), pp. 80–5.
28 *The Warder*, 20 April 1848.
29 See Rule No. 2 of the 'Fundamental Laws' in the *Sixteenth Report of the Church Education Society for Ireland*, p. 19.
30 Pamphlet dated 14 November 1848, *On the Injustice done to the Irish Branch of the United Church of England and Ireland by the Refusal of all Aid from the State for the Protestant Schools*, in *A Selection from the Second Series of the Addresses of the National Club* (London, 1849), National Club papers, Dep. d. 755. Napier had been commissioned to write such an address on 11 July 1848. See 'National Club General Committee Minute Book No. 2', National Club papers, Dep. b. 235.
31 *Hansard*, CLI, 320–1.
32 *Hansard*, CLI, 332.
33 See 'National Club General Committee Book No. 2' for 28 May 1850, National Club papers, Dep. b. 235.
34 *Hansard*, CXII, 163.
35 *Hansard*, CXII, 179.
36 For Naas' family background and early political career see W.W. Hunter, *A Life of the Earl of Mayo: Fourth Viceroy of India* (London, 1875). See also George Pottinger, *Mayo: Disraeli's Viceroy* (Salisbury, 1990), pp. 1–15. This work is principally concerned with Mayo's time in India and adds little to Hunter's account of his Irish background. A short account of Mayo's career is given in Mark Bence-Jones, *The Viceroys of India* (London, 1982), pp. 59–75.
37 See Hamilton's speech at the annual meeting of the Church Education Society in April 1857 quoted in the *Daily Express*, 17 April 1857.
38 See report of Napier's speech at the Dublin University election in *The Warder*, 10 March 1852. See also Napier to Clanricarde, n.d. [but April 1852], quoted in the *Dublin Evening Mail*, 24 April 1852.
39 *The Warder*, 13 March 1852.
40 *Hansard*, CXIX, 1131–3.
41 *Hansard*, CXIX, 1135–9.
42 See Eglinton to Derby, 11 March 1852, Derby papers, 148/2. There is a copy of this letter in the Eglinton papers, GD3/5/53/4425.
43 Eglinton to Derby, 19 March 1852, Derby papers, 148/2. There is a copy of this letter in the Eglinton papers, GD3/5/53/4425.
44 Eglinton to Derby, 21 October 1852, Derby papers, 148/2. There is a copy of this letter in the Eglinton papers, GD3/5/53/4425.
45 Eglinton to Naas, 26 March 1852, copy in the Eglinton papers,

GD3/5/52/4427.

46 Eglinton to Walpole, 8 October 1852, Holland papers, 894c. There is a copy of this letter in the Eglinton papers, GD3/5/51/4429a.

47 *Hansard*, XCVI, 284. See also Machin, *Politics and the Churches in Great Britain, 1832 to 1868* (Oxford, 1977), p. 215.

48 Vincent (ed.), *Disraeli, Derby and the Conservative Party*, p. 71.

49 See Hoppen, *Elections, Politics and Society*, pp. 294–5.

50 See T.M. Devine, *The Scottish Nation, 1700–2000* (London, 1999), p. 287.

51 Derby to Disraeli, 5 February 1852, Disraeli papers, B/XX/S/44. See also Machin, *Politics and the Churches in Great Britain, 1832 to 1868*, p. 230.

52 Derby to Disraeli, 26 September 1851, Disraeli papers, B/XX/S/39.

53 See Stanley's journal for 16 May 1851, quoted in Vincent (ed.), *Disraeli, Derby and the Conservative Party*, pp. 65–6.

54 Derby suggested that Walpole, Sir Frederick Thesiger, the English Attorney General, Lord Lyndhurst, a former Conservative Lord Chancellor, Lord Redesdale, Deputy Speaker of the House of Lords, J.C. Herries, the President of the Board of Trade, and Lord Granby attend the meeting. See Derby to Disraeli, 5 February 1852, Disraeli papers, B/XX/S/44.

55 There is an interesting discussion of an earlier attempt to achieve these ends in Gash, *Peel*, pp. 236–8.

56 Disraeli to Corry, 16 October 1866, Disraeli papers, B/XX/D/22.

57 See the *Dublin Evening Mail*, 28 January 1852.

58 For Gregg's career see Spence, 'The philosophy of Irish Toryism' pp. 134–6. See also Hill, 'The Protestant response to Repeal: the case of the Dublin working class', pp. 35–68 and the same author's, 'Artisans, sectarianism and politics in Dublin, 1829–48'.

59 Hamilton to Derby, 15 January 1852, Derby papers, 150/9.

60 *Dublin Evening Mail*, 28 January 1852.

61 See above, p. 118.

62 *Hansard*, LXXIX, 765.

63 *Hansard*, CXXI, 502.

64 *Hansard*, CXXI, 524.

65 *Hansard*, CXXI, 537–8.

66 *Hansard*, CXXI, 797–8.

67 *Hansard*, CXXI, 848.

68 *Hansard*, CXXI, 876.

69 *Hansard*, CXXI, 798.

70 *Hansard*, CXXI, 1146–9.

71 Disraeli to Sir Henry Bulwer, n.d. [but early October 1852], Disraeli papers, H B/11/026b.

72 *Hansard*, CXII, 763.

73 Naas to Eglinton, 26 May 1852, Eglinton papers, GD3/5/52/4426.

74 Derby to Disraeli, 11 May 1852, Disraeli papers, H B/XX/S/56. I am indebted for this reference to Ms Ellen Hawman of the Disraeli Project, Queen's University, Kingston, Canada. The letter is quoted in Monypenny and Buckle, *Life of Benjamin Disraeli*, Vol. 3, p. 374.

75 Quoted in the *Dublin Evening Mail*, 5 June 1852.

76 See, for example, the reports of the addresses or speeches of the following Conservative candidates; Sir Fitzroy Kelly for East Suffolk in *The Times*, 3 May 1852, Campbell Swinton for Haddington Borough in *The Times*, 26 May 1852, Henry Drummond for Surrey West in *The Times*, 10 June 1852, J. Talbot Clifton for Peterborough in *The Times*, 12 June 1852, R.A.

Christopher, the Chancellor of the Duchy of Lancaster, for Lincolnshire North in *The Times*, 26 June 1852, Lord Burghley also for Lincolnshire North in *The Times*, 26 May 1852, Lord Blandford for Woodstock in *The Times*, 9 July 1852 and William Beresford for Essex North in *The Times*, 14 July 1852.

77   See, for example, the reports of the speeches or addresses of the following Conservative candidates; Seymour Fitzgerald for Horsham in *The Times*, 7 July 1852, John Wilson Patten for Lancashire North in *The Times*, 14 July 1852, R.H. Clive and Viscount Newport, the two Conservative candidates for Shropshire (South), all of whom supported the proposed inquiry into Maynooth. See *The Times*, 13 July 1852.

78   *The Times*, 7 July 1852. In the event Fitzgerald was elected, and for a brief period was seen as a rising light within the Conservative Party. His subsequent career did not live up to his early promise, although he was to hold office as Under-Secretary for Foreign Affairs in the short-lived Conservative government of 1858–59.

79   H.M. Swartz and Marvin Swartz (eds), *Disraeli's Reminiscences* (London, 1975), p. 49.

80   *The Times*, 14 July 1852.

81   Herbert to Naas, 18 July 1852, Mayo papers 11,019 (17).

82   See the addresses of both Grogan and Vance in the *Dublin Evening Mail*, 23 June 1852.

83   *Dublin Evening Mail*, 6 July 1852.

84   *Dublin Evening Mail*, 9 July 1852.

85   *Dublin Evening Mail*, 12 July 1852.

86   *Dublin Evening Mail*, 23 July 1852.

87   *Dublin Evening Mail*, 23 July 1852.

88   See Stanley's diary entries for 19 and 21 July 1852, quoted in Vincent (ed.), *Disraeli, Derby and the Conservative Party*, p. 76.

89   Stanley to Disraeli, 19 July 1852, quoted in Machin, *Politics and the Churches in Great Britain, 1832 to 1868*, p. 243.

90   Vincent (ed.), *Disraeli, Derby and the Conservative Party*, p. 76.

91   On 16 June 1852 Naas had written to Eglinton, expressing his belief that the proclamation would not 'do... [the government] any harm in Ireland and I have no doubt will greatly strengthen us here [in England]'. Naas to Eglinton, 16 June 1852, Eglinton papers, GD3/5/52/4426.

92   Whyte, *Tenant League and Irish Politics*, p. 14.

93   Walpole to Eglinton, 29 March 1852, Eglinton papers, GD3/5/52/4428.

94   See Eglinton to Derby, 11 April 1852, Derby papers, 148/2. There is a draft of this letter in the Eglinton papers, GD3/5/53/4425.

95   See Whately to Eglinton, 22 October 1852, Eglinton papers, GD3/5/50/4434. Also Eglinton to Derby, 4 December 1852, Derby papers, 148/2. There is a draft of this letter in the Eglinton papers, GD3/5/53/4425.

96   Whately to Eglinton, 22 October 1852, Eglinton papers, GD3/5/50/4434.

97   Eglinton to Derby, 4 December 1852, Derby papers, 148/2. There is a draft of this letter in the Eglinton papers, GD3/5/53/4425.

98   See Whately to Eglinton, 3 June 1852, Eglinton papers, GD3/5/50/4434. Blackburne's principal recommendation for the position seems to have been his legal expertise. He had been Irish Attorney General during Derby's term as Chief Secretary there. See Eglinton to Derby, 22 June 1852, Derby papers, 148/2. There is a draft of this letter in the Eglinton papers, GD3/5/53/4425.

99   See Napier to Eglinton, 29 September 1852, Eglinton papers, GD3/5/51/4432.

Also Hamilton to Naas, 12 October 1852, Mayo Papers, 11,019 (20).

100 Naas to Eglinton, n.d. [but March 1852], draft in Mayo papers, 11,020 (1).

101 Eglinton to Derby, 7 June 1852, Derby papers, 148/2.

102 Eglinton to Derby, 28 September 1852, Derby papers, 148/2. There is a draft of this letter in the Eglinton papers, GD3/5/53/4425.

103 Derby to Eglinton, 2 October 1852, Eglinton papers, GD3/5/53/4424.

104 See Eglinton to Derby, 6 October 1852, Derby papers, 148/2. There is a draft of this letter in the Eglinton papers, GD3/5/53/4425.

105 See Hamilton to Naas, 1 October 1852, Mayo papers, 11,019 (20).

106 Quoted in the *Daily Express*, 16 October 1852.

107 See Eglinton to Walpole, 8 October 1852, Holland papers, 894c. There is a draft of this letter in the Eglinton papers, GD3/5/51/4429.

108 Bowen, *The Protestant Crusade in Ireland*, p. 68.

109 Hamilton to Naas, 1 September 1852, Mayo papers, 11,019 (19).

110 Hamilton expanded on the specifics of this scheme in a speech in the House of Commons in June 1856. See *Hansard*, CXLII, 1624.

111 Eglinton to Derby, 28 September 1852, Derby papers, 148/2. There is a draft of this letter in the Eglinton papers, GD3/5/53/4425.

112 Eglinton to Derby, 6 October 1852, Derby papers 148/2. There is a draft of this letter in the Eglinton papers, GD3/5/53/4425.

113 Eglinton to Walpole, 8 October 1852, Holland papers 894C. There is a draft of this letter in the Eglinton papers, GD3/5/51/4429a.

114 In England, unlike Ireland, the state gave a degree of support to schools run on explicitly denominational lines. The main bodies that ran such schools were the National Society, an Anglican body established in 1811, the British and Foreign Schools Society, a non-denominational body whose schools were principally attended by Nonconformist children, the Wesleyan Methodist Education Committee and the Roman Catholic Poor School Committee. For a discussion of the English system see Owen Chadwick, *The Victorian Church*: Pt 1 (3rd edn, London, 1971), pp. 336–46.

115 Beresford to Eglinton, 12 October 1852, Eglinton papers, GD3/5/50/4434.

116 Whately to Eglinton, 18 October 1852, Eglinton papers, GD3/5/50/4434.

117 See Eglinton to Derby, 6 October 1852, Derby papers, 148/2. There is a draft of this letter in the Eglinton papers, GD3/5/53/4425.

118 See Eglinton to Derby, 9 July 1852, Derby papers, 148/2. There is a draft of this letter in the Eglinton papers, GD3/5/53/4425. These figures can be compared with the official returns for 1851, which record that there were some 490,027 children on the rolls of the national schools. This number included 390,840 Roman Catholics, 23,629 Church of Ireland children, 39,751 Presbyterians and 2,083 other Protestant dissenters. Another 33,724 children did not have their religious denomination recorded. See the *Report from the Select Committee of the House of Lords into the System of National Education in Ireland*, pp. 22–3.

119 D.H. Akenson gives a figure of 282,575 for the average daily attendance at the national schools in 1852. See Akenson, *The Irish Education Experiment*, p. 276.

120 These figures are taken from Eglinton's letter to Derby of 21 October 1852, Derby papers, 148/3. There is a draft of this letter in the Eglinton papers, GD3/5/53/4425.

121 Akenson, *The Irish Education Experiment*, p. 98.

122 Akenson, *The Irish Education Experiment*, p. 199.

123 Derby to Eglinton, 2 October 1852, Eglinton papers, GD3/5/53/4424.

124 *Hansard*, CXXIII, 247.
125 Napier to Eglinton, 4 December 1852, Eglinton papers, GD3/5/51/4432.
126 Napier to Walpole, n.d., Holland papers, 928g.
127 See Napier to Eglinton, 9 December 1852, Eglinton papers, GD3/5/51/4432.

SIX

The Irish Conservative Party and the national education question, 1853–60

IN Chapter 5, we looked at the way in which the Irish Conservative Party dealt with the national education question in the period up to the fall of the Conservative government in December 1852. Here we will look at the way in which the question developed between 1853 and 1860, concentrating, in particular, on the Conservatives' period in office from 1858–59. However, it may be useful at this point to look at the way in which the parameters of the question had changed in the years after the formation of the Church Education Society in 1839. At that time the central plank of the society's opposition to the national system had been that it was not under the control of the Church of Ireland. The leaders of the society believed that, as the Established Church in Ireland, it was entitled to exercise full control over any system of education funded by the state. Furthermore, from their perspective, unrestricted instruction in the scriptures was an essential part of a child's education.

Although a few Evangelical spokesmen, like Lord Roden, continued to maintain this position, by the early 1850s the bulk of Irish Conservative opinion no longer saw this as a realistic possibility. The growth of the national system over the previous two decades had ensured that there was little likelihood that any government would disturb it by insisting on these terms. In these circumstances, it became necessary for the supporters of the Church Education Society to devise an alternative scheme whereby its schools could receive state funding. One solution, proposed by George Alexander Hamilton among others, was that an alteration should be made in the National Board's regulations to allow the society's schools to come under its umbrella.

The alternative to this scheme, favoured by the Evangelical clergy, and most closely associated with James Thomas O'Brien, the Bishop of Ossory, was that the state should concern itself only with secular education, leaving religious education solely to the discretion of the patrons. This scheme's attractiveness to Evangelical opinion lay in the fact that it would remove all restrictions on religious instruction. It was this second option that Lord Derby denounced in a debate on the national education system early in 1853. Given the Roman Catholic majority in Ireland, Derby believed that the institution of an openly denominational education system would principally benefit that Church. He feared that the effect of such a scheme would be to throw 'the education of the large bulk of the Roman Catholic population...into the hands of the most violent and bigoted of the Roman Catholic clergy'. Ultimately, this would result in 'a most complete spiritual despotism'. In Derby's view, 'in endeavouring to avoid a partial evil', there would be 'inflicted on Ireland a great calamity, by the sacrifice of...[the national] system which...was working for the good of the people'.[1] Derby also argued that the original decision by the Church of Ireland clergy to remain aloof from the national system had been a 'lamentable error'. By doing so, they had ensured that the system had fallen under Roman Catholic control.

By the mid-1850s it was also becoming clear that the Church Education Society was steadily drifting towards financial crisis. After a period of sustained growth, there was a decline in both the number of its schools and in the number of pupils attending them between 1851 and 1855. The root of its problems lay in the fact that, as a voluntary society, it could not compete with the kind of resources which the state was able to provide for the national system. It was also the case that the supporters of the society were not prepared to continue to subscribe to it indefinitely, unless there was some prospect that it would receive some state support. The society's increased willingness from the early 1850s onwards to make compromises in order to receive state aid was, thus, based on a realistic appraisal of its prospects. While the Church Education Society was in decline, the national school system continued to expand. By 1859 there were some 5,496 national schools, with 803,610 children on their rolls. With the growth of the system, the parliamentary grant was also regularly increased, rising from £164,577 in 1852 to £223,530 in 1857.[2]

The perceived success of the national education system had, however, rendered it difficult for a British government to interfere with it. There was little temptation for a British cabinet to risk the break-up of a rapidly expanding system in order to placate a voluntary society, which was having increasing difficulty in maintaining its schools. There was, however, a considerable body of opinion within the Church Education Society which remained hostile to any compromise with the national system. They continued to insist that they would not accept any settlement to the controversy which would fall short of its central tenet of the free use of scripture during regular instruction.

Despite this, there was a feeling among some of the senior members of the Conservative Party, including Eglinton and Walpole, that it should attempt to reach a settlement of the education question. At the same time, Irish Conservatives were naturally sensitive to the claim that having avoided the issue while in government, the party was now employing the issue simply in order to use it as a weapon with which to attack the new government. Napier and Hamilton were, of course, particularly vulnerable to this kind of attack, both having significantly advanced their careers through their closeness to the Evangelical clergy. These accusations were given added point through the admission by Derby and Eglinton that, while in government, they had not been 'able to see their way to any satisfactory alteration' to the national system.[3]

However, throughout the 1850s, many leading Irish Conservatives remained, at least outwardly, supportive of the aims of the Church Education Society. At the general election of April 1857, for example, Joseph Napier, James Whiteside and George Alexander Hamilton, its most prominent Irish Conservative supporters, reiterated their support for the society. In his election address, Napier declared that he would continue to 'uphold the great principle of a free and unrestricted use of the Bible'.[4] On this occasion, however, Napier's seat was contested. His Liberal opponent, James Fleetwood Wilson, used Napier's conduct on the Education question as a weapon with which to attack him. According to Charles Blackwood, Wilson's seconder at the nomination of candidates, Napier's behaviour on that question and on the issue of Maynooth had caused 'great dissatisfaction' to many of the Trinity College electors. Despite his earlier pledges, Wilson argued, Napier had not used his influence, when in government, to forward a settlement of the controversy. More worrying for Napier was the fact that his opponent was supported by the Reverend Daniel Foley, a prominent Evangelical clergyman and a zealous supporter of the Church Education Society. According to Foley, however, it was Derby, not Napier, 'who [had] sold the revered cause of truth and education'. Foley also praised the English ecclesiastical appointments made by Lord Palmerston, the Liberal Prime Minister. Under the influence of his son-in-law, Lord Shaftesbury, these appointments had generally been of an Evangelical character. Foley also drew attention to the widespread unease among Irish Conservatives at the policies towards Italy then being advocated by the leaders of the Conservative Party. According to Foley, the Irish Protestant clergy had, 'struggled hard to get Lord Derby into power, and when he did get in he turned round and betrayed them'.

Napier responded to these criticisms by arguing that the Conservative Party remained pledged to giving some financial assistance to the Church Education Society, providing that this could be done without breaking up the national system. He contended that his critics, outside the House of Commons, did not know the difficulties which he and Hamilton had encountered in advancing the society's case. The pledges he had made in 1848, especially in relation to Maynooth, had been made at a time when he was 'earnest and enthusiastic, but without experience of parliamentary life'.[5] Napier's admission of the difficulties which Irish Conservatives faced, in having their priorities reflected in the policies adopted by the party leadership at Westminster, injected a dose of realism not overly common in these campaigns. As it transpired, however, Napier and Hamilton were returned comfortably, although the campaign itself was a frequently acrimonious one.

The return of Derby to office in February 1858 was, as in 1852, a result of divisions within the Whig–Liberal leadership rather than of Conservative strength. As we have seen, in parliamentary terms, the new government was in a weaker position than the previous Conservative government had been. If the opposition were to unite against it, it was certain to be defeated. The only major change in the Irish appointments from 1852 was that Napier was promoted to Lord Chancellor, with Whiteside being appointed as Attorney General. Hamilton resumed the position of Financial Secretary to the Treasury, although he left that office and accepted a non-political appointment at the Treasury in January 1859. Walpole, who was by this time closely identified with the interests of the Church Education Society, returned to the Home Office. On the other hand, there were some members of the cabinet, particularly Lord Stanley, the Colonial Secretary and Sir John Pakington, the First Lord of the Admiralty, who were hostile to any interference with the national system. The presence of acknowledged partisans of the Church Education Society in senior positions within the Irish administration was, nevertheless, a substantial boost for the organisation.[6]

A number of statements made by Disraeli and Derby in parliament in mid-March 1858 further increased Irish Conservative optimism about the government's intentions. Disraeli's comments were, not uncharacteristically, more equivocal than those made by Derby. Speaking in response to a question from Ralph Bernal Osborne, Disraeli remarked that the government intended to maintain the national system 'inviolate'. However, if a means could be found whereby the Church Education Society's schools could receive state aid, 'without in the least impugning the principles' of the system, the government would 'not preclude' itself from introducing it.[7] Derby went further than this, arguing that the cabinet might consider furnishing 'encouragement' to such schools, 'even though to a certain extent' this might be 'in violation' of the principles under which the national system was run. 'Encouragement' was a key word here, as it implied that those schools would not receive the same amount of state aid as did bona-fide national schools. Although the government had not yet come to any determination on the subject, it would not do anything to 'imperil' the existing system. Any modifications in the distribution of the state grant for education would first have to be discussed and approved by parliament.[8]

Soon after his re-appointment as Lord Lieutenant, Eglinton began the delicate task of gauging opinion within the different camps of the Church of Ireland on the possibility of a compromise with the national system. By this time he had firmly committed himself against the idea of separate grants for education. These would, he told Naas on 20 March, 'upset' the national system and bring the government into 'difficulties with the R[oman] Catholics'. He was, however, intent on making a final effort 'to reconcile the Church Education people to the system'.[9] This was to prove a more difficult task than Eglinton had anticipated.

A meeting with James Thomas O'Brien, the Bishop of Ossory, on 24 March proved a reminder of the obstacles involved in reaching a settlement. Eglinton told O'Brien that the government considered itself 'bound in good faith' to attempt to introduce a settlement of the Education question. It was essential, however, that such an arrangement should have some prospect of success in parliament. The circumstances of the government's accession to office meant that this was an impossibility 'during the present session'. Given these circumstances, he urged the Church Education Society to exercise 'forbearance towards us [the government] in the mean time'. Eglinton stressed the problems which he felt the administration would have in 'inducing Parliament' to agree to Derby's proposals. He asked O'Brien, in the light of this, whether it was possible that 'such modifications might be made which would make it possible for him to join the national system'. His reply was a categorical negative. He could not foresee 'any circumstances' in which it would be possible for him and his supporters to do so.[10] This meeting seems to have left Eglinton with a lingering dislike for the Bishop of Ossory, whom he described as an 'overbearing bigot'.[11]

By 1858 there was a widespread consensus, even among supporters of the Church Education Society, that a large number of its schools were inferior in terms of secular education to the schools in the national system. Indeed William Dwyer Ferguson, a supporter of the society and a close associate of Napier's, described their schools in the North of Ireland as being 'in general in a state of collapse'.[12] A similar view was taken by Eglinton who complained that, as a result of their failure to join the national system, the Church Education Society's schools were 'starved of funds'.[13] This in turn added a sense of urgency to the attempts being made by the more moderate members of the society to achieve an accommodation with the government.

On 5 July, it was decided at a meeting between Eglinton, Napier, Blackburne and Greene that the 'only course' for the government to pursue was that earlier determined upon by the Lord Lieutenant. They had considered a number of courses which the government could adopt; the main ones being either to leave the system intact as it then stood and the other, which had previously been suggested by Derby, being to grant a limited form of state aid to the Church Education Society's schools, while the remainder of the system continued under the existing rules. If the first option were taken, Eglinton believed, it would 'leave the great body of the Protestants of Ireland without funds for decent education'. Meanwhile, convent schools which were even 'more exclusive and denominational' than the 'scriptural' schools would remain within the national system. In Eglinton's view, the second course offered an opportunity both to 'satisfy the Protestant clergy' and to improve the standard of education for Protestant children in Ireland. Eglinton accepted that by taking this option, the government might find it necessary to grant aid to 'exclusively Catholic schools'. However, he maintained that the restricted nature of this assistance would mean that few Catholic schools would 'abandon the national system for the privilege of receiving ... humbler assistance under the new system'.[14] The government's scheme was, therefore, primarily designed to benefit the Church Education Society's schools. Nevertheless, it would be open to Catholic patrons to avail themselves of this scheme, if they were prepared to suffer a drop in income in return for freedom from National Board regulation.

The negotiations for a resolution of the education dispute took on an added impetus in the latter half of 1858. In September, Eglinton proposed that the government should introduce a resolution, early in the next session of parliament, to the effect that training for teachers and school requisites should be given to those schools then outside the system which were willing to submit to inspection by the National Board. They should also announce their intentions of including proficiency allowances for those schools as an item in the financial estimates to be introduced later in the year. A defeat on the estimates, would, Eglinton suggested, expose the government to 'less risk' than if it were 'a regular government measure' which was defeated.[15]

A visit to Ireland in early October gave Spencer Walpole, the Home Secretary, an opportunity to discuss the education and other Irish questions with leading members of the Irish administration. While in Ireland, Walpole also met with several prominent Church of Ireland clergymen, spending a number of days in Armagh with John George Beresford.[16] He was readily converted to the scheme proposed by Eglinton and given a strong recommendation in a memorandum prepared for him by Napier, who was out of Ireland for the duration of his visit.[17]

Walpole's attempts to negotiate an acceptance of these terms by the National Board were compromised by a misunderstanding which arose between him and Alexander Macdonnell, its Resident Commissioner and a member of the Church of Ireland. During a conversation with Macdonnell, Walpole believed that he had won his approval for all the elements of the government's plan, including the granting of proficiency allowances. In this view he was mistaken. In fact, Macdonnell had expressed his willingness to accept such allowances only for schools within the national system. While Macdonnell was ready to accept the other planks of the government's plan, his willingness to do so was based on the assumption that the Church Education Society would accept this as a final settlement.[18] This misinterpretation of Macdonnell's position led Walpole to give an overly optimistic report on the position of the question to Derby on his return to England. Derby's natural caution, however, led him to take a more sceptical view of the situation. Writing to Eglinton on 31 October, Derby warned that he 'rather doubted' the prospect of parliament agreeing to the society's teachers receiving training in the model schools run by the National Board. Proficiency allowances would perhaps, be more acceptable as they could be set at such a level to prevent the schools which received them from becoming 'rival[s]' to the national schools. He was 'surprised' to hear from Walpole that Macdonnell had agreed to the government's proposals. Even so, he was at pains to stress the necessity of proceeding cautiously with them. Nevertheless, he believed that it would be a major coup for the Irish administration if they were able to win a declaration from the members of the National Board that their proposals 'would not injuriously interfere with the present system'.[19]

This letter was, of course, written before it became clear, at a meeting between Eglinton and William Higgins, the Bishop of Derry, that Walpole had misread Macdonnell's opinions on the question of proficiency allowances. At this meeting, Higgins had 'started' at the mention of the subject and he insisted to Eglinton that 'neither he nor any of the other Commissioners had any idea of consenting to this point'. Following this meeting, Eglinton saw Macdonnell, who confirmed that he and the members of the National Board were 'strongly opposed' to the granting of such allowances. After these meetings Eglinton concluded that there no longer was any possibility of the government securing the assistance of the Board in carrying through all of their proposals. He had no doubt that an 'extraordinary mistake'[20] had occurred, but disclaimed all responsibility for it. The 'mess'[21] that had been made was Walpole's responsibility alone. In an attempt to extricate the government from this quandary, Eglinton suggested to Macdonnell that the Board should approve the granting of school requisites to Church Education Society schools. He also wanted it to allow its inspectors to visit the society's schools. However, the awarding of proficiency allowances would be left to a new body independent of the National Board. Not surprisingly, Macdonnell rejected this proposition, restating his position that he would only concede the other points if they were accepted by the Church Education Society as a final settlement of the question. There would have to be an express understanding that once these were granted, the 'contention' between the board and the society would be at an end.[22]

In any case, the amount which the Church Education Society would have obtained from the government's plan, particularly without proficiency allowances, was quite small. The total sum involved was estimated by Naas at no more than £6,000, 'or a little more than £3 a school'. Given these circumstances, he was convinced that it would be impossible for the society to accept the government's recommendations as anything other than 'an instalment'.[23] One way around this problem, advocated by Eglinton, was to proceed with the Irish administration's original scheme, while accepting that the most likely outcome was that the bestowing of 'proficiency' allowances would be defeated in the House of Commons.[24] Aside from these problems, Walpole cautioned Eglinton that there was a group within the cabinet who would be unwilling to accept any settlement of the question, which did not have the sanction of the National Board.[25] This group included Lord Stanley and Sir John Pakington, both of whom were advocates of what was termed a 'secular system' of education in Britain. This would have involved the creation of an essentially non-denominational system of education there, intended particularly for working-class children.[26] Holding these views, they were extremely reluctant to see the national system undermined in Ireland. Disraeli was also wary of any meddling with the question, particularly given the government's precarious position in the House of Commons. Nonetheless, Walpole was so convinced that the proposals were 'clearly right' that he concluded that they should be brought before the cabinet, leaving it with the responsibility for either accepting or rejecting them.[27]

At this point, Derby introduced a cautionary note into the Irish administration's proceedings. He disputed Eglinton's view that the government was under 'any obligation' to deal with this question. This would only have been the case, if they were in a position to 'deal with it satisfactorily'. As matters stood, Derby did not believe that they would even be able to obtain the cabinet's consent to Eglinton's proposals. If the government went forward with the scheme under the existing circumstances, Derby warned that its effect would be to disappoint the expectations of the Church Education Society.[28] At the same time, the government would also run the risk of incurring the 'active hostility' of the National Board. Despite this admonition, Eglinton continued his negotiations with senior members of the society during November and December 1858. These negotiations involved Beresford, O'Brien, Singer and Robert Daly, the influential Evangelical Bishop of Cashel. Hamilton Verschoyle, an honorary secretary of the Church Education Society, acted as the channel between Eglinton and the bishops. Eglinton's intention in commencing these discussions was to establish what concessions the society was willing to make in return for the limited amount of state aid on offer.

In the event, these discussions were to prove more productive than Eglinton had originally anticipated. At meetings with Verschoyle and Beresford, Eglinton made it clear that he could not expect cabinet support for the granting of 'proficiency allowances'. He recommended that they should settle for those concessions that it would be possible to obtain.[29] Although both he and Derby were favourable to the provision of proficiency allowances, they were concerned that to propose these would 'endanger the success of the more limited measure[s]'.[30] As he reported to Derby on 10 January 1859, this warning had the desired effect, and he had won the support of all the leading members of the society for the government's other recommendations. This acceptance was conditional upon a number of concessions by the government, which Eglinton believed, they 'ought to close with', and which, he hoped, would 'not deter the other party [the National Board] from coming to an arrangement'. The first of these was that, as the proposed grants were not sufficient to maintain its schools, the society should remain in existence, if only 'for the collection of funds'. Other conditions were that the inspectors' reports on its schools should be sent to the central council of the society rather than to the Board, that the books and school requisites should be distributed by the society itself, and that its student teachers should be permitted to receive religious instruction from Church of Ireland clergymen at the model schools.[31] Their final demand was that while they accepted government assistance, they did 'not in the least depart from . . . [their] fundamental principle' with regard to the use of the scriptures. The society would continue to publicly oppose the restrictions on religious education in the national schools.[32]

The society also reserved the right to complain 'of the inadequacy of the assistance' which it received from the state. This was the only demand which Eglinton felt was 'of any importance'. The difficulty was that this clashed with the National Board's insistence that the society should accept the government's proposals as a final settlement. Eglinton was reassured, however, by Verschoyle's pledge that the society would consider the government as having fulfilled its pledges to it by proceeding with the 'the three [agreed] points'. Verschoyle also acknowledged that it would not immediately press for 'any further grants'.[33] This was, no doubt, a highly welcome prospect for the leaders of the Conservative Party, freeing them from a political pressure applied on it for the previous twenty-five years. The difficulty that remained was to secure the assent of the National Board to the proposed arrangement.

Derby outlined some of the problems he foresaw in achieving this end in a letter to Eglinton on 12 January. He pointed out that several members of the National Board remained adverse to 'any assistance being given to the Church Education schools' and he was concerned that they would 'catch at any plea to escape concurrence' with the proposed scheme. Turning to the demands made by the society, Derby considered that it would be difficult for the Board to allow religious instruction to be given in the model schools. This would have to be provided by the society itself, without the Board's involvement.[34]

The religious composition of the National Board was such that it was difficult for the government to secure majority support for its scheme. At that time, the Board had fifteen members, six of whom were Roman Catholics, six were members of the Church of Ireland, two were Presbyterians and one a Unitarian. Of these fifteen members, Eglinton estimated that there were only six who could be counted on as 'favourable' to the government's scheme. This group was made up of four Church of Ireland representatives, Alexander Macdonnell, Lord Kildare, Mountifort Longfield and William Higgins, the Bishop of Derry. The two other supporters of the government scheme were Dr Andrews, a Presbyterian, and Dr Henry, the Unitarian member of the board. Of the remaining Church of Ireland members of the board, Eglinton considered one, Francis Hatchell, to be 'doubtful', while the other, Maziere Brady, who had been Irish Lord Chancellor under Palmerston, was 'at present unfavo[u]rable'. James Gibson, the second Presbyterian representative on the board, was also 'decidedly opposed' to the government's plan.

The Protestant members of the board thus divided into six who were favourable to the government's position, two who were opposed and one who was 'doubtful'. The six Roman Catholic members were, Eglinton admitted, all opposed to the suggested changes. There was little real enthusiasm for these even among the 'favourable' members of the board. Macdonnell told Eglinton that several members of the board would 'as soon see matters left where they are'. Despite the fact that there was an adverse majority against his proposals, Eglinton nevertheless felt that this constituted 'a far more hopeful result than could have been anticipated'. There were two reasons for Eglinton's hopefulness; the first being that he had secured the support of more members of the board than he had originally anticipated. His second ground for optimism was the assurance he had been given by Macdonnell that, even if the Catholic members of the board were to resign, the vast majority of Roman Catholic patrons would choose to keep their schools within the system.[35]

Feeling convinced that these proposals offered hopes for a viable settlement of the education question, Eglinton continued to press both Derby and Walpole to submit them to the cabinet throughout January and February 1859. He was anxious that the grants to the Church Education Society should be included in the estimates to be introduced in the autumn, although he conceded that it was possible that the government might not then 'be in a position' to bring them forward.[36] However, as

Derby informed Eglinton on 28 January, there were other issues which preoccupied the attention of the cabinet at this time. Chief among these was the government's proposed Reform Bill, itself the source of divisions within the party. The government also faced the threat of a war breaking out between France and Austria, over the latter's Italian possessions. Confronted with these concerns, Derby claimed he had little time to devote to Irish education. He also pointed to the opposition felt by senior members of the cabinet to any tampering with the question. To bring the question before the cabinet under such circumstances would, in Derby's view, only add to the difficulties it was experiencing.

It was at this point that Eglinton's hopes of securing cabinet approval for his plan received another, perhaps fatal, blow. Walpole, who had been a consistent critic of the government's proposed Reform Bill, resigned from it when it was introduced on 28 February. This altered the balance of forces within the cabinet and rendered it increasingly unlikely that Eglinton's scheme would receive its sanction.

As the foremost champion of the Church Education Society among English Conservatives, Walpole had been an invaluable ally particularly given his position at the very centre of the government. His retirement as Home Secretary could only, as Derby informed Eglinton, 'operate unfavourably' on the prospects of the education proposals 'of which he was the warm advocate'.[37] Walpole was replaced by Thomas Sotheron Estcourt, a politician without any of his commitment to the Irish education question. The second vacancy in the cabinet, left by Joseph Warner Henley, the President of the Board of Trade, who had resigned at the same time as Walpole, was filled by Lord Donoughmore. Although Donoughmore was as strong a supporter of the Church Education Society as Walpole had been, he did not have anything like the latter's influence within the Conservative Party. To convince the cabinet to accept the Irish administration's scheme would have been an uphill task in any case; without Walpole's backing, the difficulty was increased immensely.

Despite this setback, Eglinton continued to press Derby to at least bring the subject before the cabinet for discussion. He underlined his personal commitment to the proposed settlement by threatening to resign if the scheme was not adopted as government policy.[38] Derby succeeded in dissuading him from this course by a piece of well-timed flattery. He could not accept his resignation 'from a post for which ... [Eglinton] was so peculiarly qualified'.[39] It had become clear, by this point, that Eglinton was far more committed to the proposals than was Derby. Through his dealings with the Church Education Society, Eglinton felt personally pledged to the plan agreed between them. Derby, on the other hand, believed that the government was only pledged to introduce a measure if it had a reasonable chance of success. He was also unwilling to risk the government's already uncertain position by bringing the proposed measure forward. His prevarication in submitting the topic to the cabinet was thus based both on pressures of business and on wider political considerations. The difficulties under which Derby laboured were compounded on 31 March when the government's Reform Bill was defeated in the House of Commons. His response to this defeat was to dissolve parliament, the decision being announced in both houses on 4 April.

The dissolution of parliament gave Eglinton an opportunity to bring his scheme before the cabinet. He travelled to London in early April, although Derby warned him that he was unlikely to find government ministers 'in a very fit state of mind' to discuss the subject.[40] While Eglinton was in London, the Church Education Society's annual meeting was held in Dublin. At this meeting, Hamilton Verschoyle made a general reference to the agreement reached between the Irish administration and the society. He emphasised the fact that the plan would not give the society 'the full measure of relief' to which it believed it was entitled. Nevertheless, it would give it 'substantial relief' and the proposed measure had 'obtained universal acquiescence' from its leading members. Although the plan had not yet been accepted by the cabinet, Verschoyle hoped that, given Eglinton's 'powerful influence', it soon would be. Even as matters stood, Verschoyle felt that the society was 'under...peculiar obligations to the present Irish administration', as it was the first 'for twenty-five years which...[had] stretched out a helping hand in the smallest degree without at the same time expecting us to surrender our principle'. This statement was, of course, a double-edged one; while it served as a useful boost for the Conservatives as they faced into a general election, it was also intended to keep the Irish administration up to the mark on the issue. Thus, for example, the Dublin ultra-Protestant paper, *The Warder*, interpreted Verschoyle's statement to mean that the government had pledged itself 'to a decided course of action on the most momentous of Irish questions'. It had made a 'distinct promise' to the Church Education Society, which ought to be fulfilled. The article went on however to criticise the members of the Irish administration and other Irish Conservative MPs for failing to attend the meeting and 'make the statement that fell from Mr Verschoyle'.[41]

A number of Irish Conservative candidates in the 1859 election, including Whiteside and Anthony Lefroy, expressed their hope that the education question might be settled in the near future, without going into specifics on what a settlement would entail.[42] As we saw earlier, the election was also notable for the return of John Pope Hennessey, a Roman Catholic, as Conservative MP for King's County. Hennessey was an outspoken critic of 'mixed' education which, he argued was essentially a Whig policy. By contrast, he favoured the creation of an explicitly denominational system of primary education in Ireland. As a result, he made common cause in parliament with the opponents of the national system. Hennessey played an important role in the years that followed, being close to leading members of the Independent Party and to the Irish Roman Catholic hierarchy.[43] His return as a Conservative MP bore out Derby's prediction to Eglinton that the party had 'every reason to expect a large measure' of Roman Catholic support at the election. Derby felt that this fact further complicated the government's position *vis-à-vis* Irish education. It was important, he believed, that the Conservatives should do nothing to alienate that support, prior to the election.[44]

For reasons outlined in Chapter 7,[45] the 1859 general election proved to be the most successful for the Irish Conservatives since the Reform Act of 1832. They made eight gains there from the 1857 election, going from forty-seven seats to fifty-five. They also felt assured of the support, at critical divisions, of another seven Independent Irish Party MPs, some of whom owed their election to Conservative support. The party was less successful in Britain, however, and remained in a minority position in the House of Commons. The constraints which had restricted the government's approach to the question remained very much in place.

Although Eglinton had been present for the cabinet's discussion of the subject in early April, the exigencies of the election campaign meant that it was late May before Sotheron Estcourt, the new Home Secretary, took any initiative in the matter. He then circulated a memorandum on the question to the other members of the cabinet. This circular prompted a lengthy response from Donoughmore, giving his views on Eglinton's plan. In it, he warned Estcourt against thinking that the Church Education Society were 'satisfied' with the proposed arrangements. Although willing to accept them in order to free themselves from the dilemma of being 'a state church ... [in] a position of hostility to the government of the country', it was not possible for them to 'rest satisfied with such a settlement'. Donoughmore restated his personal preference for an explicitly denominational system, which he believed, was 'desired' by all the churches in Ireland. He believed that the increased hostility to the national system expressed by the Roman Catholic hierarchy meant that in the long term its supercession was inevitable. An openly denominational system would, in any case, only permit 'the Roman Catholics & Presbyterians ... to do ... avowedly and openly what they now do in fact'. Donoughmore was particularly disappointed at the government's failure to grant salaries to teachers in the society's schools, especially as it was willing to give them to 'chapel clerks in the rural parishes of Munster and Connaught who teach their children little else besides the Roman Catholic catechism and the library of the Virgin'. The strength of Donoughmore's language showed that there were some members of the Church Education Society who had not been completely won over by Eglinton's proposals. While he was willing to support the government's plan, he viewed it as the first step towards a system based on separate schools for the children of the various creeds in Ireland.[46]

It was at this point that outside events again conspired to render the government's efforts on the Irish education question ineffectual. A meeting at the Willis's Rooms in London on 6 June signalled a reconciliation between Lord Palmerston and Lord John Russell, the two leading figures in the Whig–Liberal Party. It was the divisions between the two men that had been one of the chief reasons for the Conservatives' accession to office. From that point on, there was a strong possibility that the government would not survive for long once parliament reconvened. In the event it was narrowly defeated on a motion of no confidence on 10 June. It was succeeded by a Liberal government under Lord Palmerston.

Despite the fact that the Irish administration's education scheme had ultimately proved abortive, it nonetheless represented the best opportunity that arose, during its existence, for a settlement favourable to the Church Education society being reached. Circumstances would never again arise as favourable to the interests of the society. The two most senior members of the Irish administration, Lord Eglinton, the Lord Lieutenant, and Joseph Napier, the Lord Chancellor, were strongly committed to the scheme, as was James Whiteside, the Irish Attorney General. Throughout most of the lifetime of the government, the Church Education Society also had the powerful backing within the cabinet of Spencer Walpole, the Home Secretary. Despite this advantageous combination of circumstances, there remained severe obstacles to the achievement of a resolution of the question along the lines that Eglinton had envisaged. The Conservative government's minority position ensured that it was difficult for it to guarantee that any measure it introduced on the subject would pass through the House of Commons. It was also intensely wary of doing anything which might lead to the break-up of the national system. These contradictory pressures, combined with the unwillingness of some of its members to tamper with the question, meant that Lord Derby indulged in a good deal of prevarication before eventually submitting it to the cabinet. Whether Eglinton's plan would have been adopted by the cabinet remained doubtful, even before its fall; by the time it came before ministers, the government was already in crisis and its priorities lay in areas other than Irish education. Despite this, the defeat of the government also represented a defeat for the Church Education Society, as it was extremely unlikely that a Liberal government would be as amenable to seeking an accommodation with it as the Conservative government had been.

During the years 1858–59, the Maynooth question never attained the same level of prominence as it had done during the tenure of Derby's first government. This was partly attributable to the decline in the virulence of anti-Catholic sentiment in England in the years after 1851. The government's minority position in the House of Commons also meant that it was difficult for it to take the initiative on the question. Maynooth remained, of course, a divisive subject, both within the Conservative Party and in Ireland. In the years between the fall of Derby's first government and 1858, Richard Spooner had regularly re-introduced his motion for a committee of inquiry into the system of education there. Indeed, he brought forward this motion in February 1853, only two months after the fall of the Conservative government. This debate saw an important speech from Lord Stanley, who referred to the 'general desire' in the House of Commons that the discussion of the subject should be wrapped up speedily, and 'being concluded, [that] it should not again be resumed'. Stanley believed that the issue had been debated so often that all which was 'original and valuable, whether in the way of opinion, or argument, or of fact ... [had] long since been elicited, leaving behind little except matter for theological disputes and mutual recrimination'. He feared that the continued agitation of the subject served only to 'embitter the animosity' with which the question was 'unhappily regarded' in Ireland, and to 'keep open that sore which it was the object of the settlement of 1845 to heal and to close up for ever'. While he was not opposed to an inquiry into the system of teaching at Maynooth, his conviction was that there would be 'no security for the Established Protestant Church of Ireland', unless it dealt 'in a fair and liberal spirit with the claims of the Irish Roman Catholic population'.[47] Writing in his diary soon afterwards, Stanley admitted that he had long since 'abandoned' the idea that the Irish Roman Catholic Church should be endowed by the state. While he had once favoured this notion, he had become convinced that it would prove unacceptable to British public opinion. Holding this view, he had been persuaded that it would be ultimately necessary to withdraw the Maynooth grant. Prophetically, however, Stanley felt that the determination 'on the part of England not to sanction or recognise the religion held by the Irish must react on the general principle of [religious] establishments'. This would, he concluded, lead 'directly to a voluntary system in Ireland'.[48] It was hardly surprising, therefore, that Stanley should have opposed Spooner's attempts to undermine the Maynooth grant.

Like Stanley, Donoughmore was unconvinced of the wisdom of polemical attacks on Maynooth. Writing on 14 April 1853, he told Derby that he felt 'constrained to withhold' his vote on an anti-Maynooth motion introduced by Lord Winchilsea[49] in the House of Lords. He warned that 'the consequences of the agitation of the Maynooth question' had not been 'sufficiently considered'. The conduct of the priests at the 1852 election had, in Donoughmore's opinion, 'alienated from them a very large portion of the respectable Roman Catholics'. In Donoughmore's view, it was in the long-term interests of the Conservative Party to win over the support of this section of Irish opinion. This could be achieved, he maintained, with 'a little management'. If, however, the Conservatives continued to attack the Maynooth grant, they would drive sympathetic Catholics 'back again into the arms of the priests'. While he remained 'utterly opposed to Popery', he believed that 'the Catholic clergy were 'still too strong for anything but mischief to result from the present agitation of the Maynooth question'. Donoughmore assured Derby that the massive and sustained emigration of the Famine and post-Famine years was 'drawing away the priests' life blood'. Within a 'few years,' they would 'no longer be formidable'. As a consequence, it would then be possible to withdraw the Maynooth grant with impunity.[50] This claim that emigration would strengthen the position of the Church of Ireland, the bulk of the emigrants being Roman Catholics, was regularly used by Irish Conservatives. Occasionally the wilder claim that this would eventually result in a Protestant majority in Ireland was made.[51] In fact, the Church of Ireland population did increase slightly between 1834 and 1861, from 10.7 per cent to 11.9 per cent of the Irish population.[52] This increase, however, should be placed in the context of the decline in the overall population there. It has been estimated that between 1845 and 1870 no fewer than three million persons left Ireland.[53] Even given these figures, Protestants remained a minority of the Irish population, particularly outside the north of the country.

Throughout the decade of the 1850s neither Liberal nor Conservative governments were willing to run the political risks which a unilateral withdrawal of the Maynooth grant would have involved. This was admitted by Derby in a letter to Henry Lambert, an Irish friend of his, in January 1856, when he observed that any attempt to pursue that course would have the effect of 'displeasing all parties and overthrowing the government which should attempt it'.[54] The Conservative Party was itself divided on the question. Prominent English Conservatives, such as Stanley and Sir John Pakington, were opposed to any precipitate withdrawal of the grant. In a debate on Spooner's motion in June 1856, Pakington accused him of attempting to 'reverse the policy towards Ireland' pursued by British governments for the previous fifty years. He asked if the supporters of Spooner's motion wished to see the Roman Catholic population of Ireland 'left without a priesthood'. It was preferable, in his view, that the Catholic priesthood should be educated 'under our own eyes' rather than on the continent. Pakington argued that not 'even the most zealous Protestant' could wish for a situation to arise where there would be a shortage of properly trained priests in Ireland.[55]

Differences of opinion on the question were not, of course, solely confined to English Conservatives. Such were these divisions on the issue within the Irish Conservative Party that, as early as 1854, Napier had argued that it was one on which Irish MPs should be left 'freedom of opinion and action'. Electoral pressures meant that some candidates for Irish seats would find it necessary to approach the question 'on different grounds from those which others must take'.[56] It was, however, open even to supporters of the grant to criticise the type of education given at the college. The extent of Conservative divisions on the issue persuaded Thomas Barton that Maynooth should be left a 'completely open question' during the 1857 election campaign.[57] A similar view was taken by James Whiteside. Rather disingenuously, he asserted that the Maynooth grant had 'never be[en] made a party question' by Irish Conservatives. As for himself, he claimed he had 'never [been] pledged about it' and saw no difficulty in a candidate stating he would 'not vote against it. '[58] This course was, in fact, taken by a number of Irish Conservatives at the election. Among those who acted in this fashion were John Wynne, the defeated candidate for Sligo County, John Alexander, successfully returned as Conservative MP for Carlow, and Sterne Ball Miller, elected as Conservative MP for Armagh City.[59] These were all candidates who had a sizeable number of Roman Catholic voters in their constituencies. There were of course other successful candidates, such as Edward Grogan and John Vance for Dublin City, and George Alexander Hamilton for Dublin University, who expressed themselves in favour of the repeal of the Maynooth grant. While Napier played down the Maynooth issue in his own campaign, he did make the admission that, as he was in favour of 'the endowment of truth', he could not support 'the endowment of error'.[60]

Given the divisive nature of the Maynooth question, it was hardly surprising that Derby adopted a tentative approach toward it in the years 1858–59. One avenue he did explore was the payment of a lump sum to the authorities in Maynooth in return for a discontinuance of the grant. Derby first suggested this as a possibility to a deputation on the subject which visited him in April 1858. This deputation included long-term anti-Maynooth campaigners such as Spooner and Newdegate, and a number of clergymen from the Anglican, Methodist and Presbyterian churches. Derby's reply to their request that the grant be terminated was that this would encourage those who objected to 'all state endowments'. This remark pointed to a central weakness of the campaign against the grant, in that it included Anglicans, who were opposed specifically to the payment of a subsidy to the Roman Catholic Church and Nonconformists, who were opposed in principle to any state support for religion. According to Derby, it would not be possible to 'capriciously remove' a grant that had been maintained for such a length of time. He could only agree to an 'equitable and fair compromise' that was acceptable to all parties as a resolution of the question. Derby's language was carefully judged and was designed not to alienate either ultra-Protestant or Irish Roman Catholic opinion.[61]

Shortly after receiving the deputation, Derby met with Sir Culling Eardley, one of the prime movers in the original anti-Maynooth agitation in 1845, to discuss the subject. Derby told Eardley that he was willing to see the question settled by a money payment, provided all of the parties involved accepted this. The compensation paid should, Derby maintained, take into account Roman Catholic expectations that the grant would be continued. While Spooner's suggestion was that compensation should only be paid to students then enrolled at Maynooth, Eardley was prepared to accept that the authorities there should be recompensed by a sum based on eight years' purchase of the annual grant. The first plan involved a payment of £100,000 while the second involved a sum of close to £240,000.[62] In early May, Walpole suggested to Derby that a sum based on ten years' purchase of the grant, or approximately £300,000, might be more acceptable to the governing body of Maynooth. Any decision to proceed on these lines should, Walpole argued, first be agreed by the cabinet. He also advised that the sum should be paid in instalments, rather than as a lump sum, so as to forestall ultra-Protestant opposition to the move.[63]

At this point, Derby felt a degree of optimism about the proposal's chance of success. He informed Eglinton that he considered the point at issue reduced to one 'of money'.[64] In a reversal of their roles on the education question, Eglinton proved more sceptical about the scheme than was Derby. He was concerned that the anti-Maynooth wing of the Conservative Party would react unfavourably to such a large payment being given to the college. This might, he warned, excite more controversy than the continued payment of the annual grant. Despite this, he agreed to Derby's request to sound out Irish opinion on the proposal.[65] By November, Eglinton reported that he doubted if the buying out of the grant would have much impact in Ireland. In his opinion, it was more a 'question of parliamentary tactics than of national policy'.[66] The scheme eventually floundered as a result of the government's failure to reconcile the conflicting aspirations of the two sides in the dispute. On the Roman Catholic side, the ruling body of Maynooth was unwilling to accept a payment of less than £500,000. Derby could not, however, get Eardley and his supporters to raise their initial offer of £300,000. Unwilling to impose a settlement which would alienate either side, Derby eventually decided that it was preferable to leave the grant unchanged.[67] The government's decision to leave things as they stood was also influenced by the fact that a group of Irish Roman Catholic MPs, led by John Francis Maguire, the Independent Party MP for Dungarvan, had given them a general support in the House of Commons since their accession to office. Without the assurance of support from a majority in parliament, the government was unwilling to risk its continued existence on so volatile an issue as the Maynooth grant. Indeed, the difficulties inherent in taking the initiative on an issue of such political and religious sensitivity meant that, ultimately, the Conservatives had little choice but to maintain the grant intact, as it then stood.

A major turning point in the history of the Church Education Society took place in February 1860, when John George Beresford issued a circular to the patrons of its schools in the diocese of Clogher. This circular advised those patrons in areas where there were insufficient funds to maintain a viable Church Education Society school to place their schools under the National Board. While Beresford still supported the principle on which the society was based, he believed that it was better that Protestant children should receive an adequate education at a national school rather than an inadequate one at a Church Education Society one. It would also be preferable, he believed, that Protestant parents should not be forced to send their children to national schools under Roman Catholic patrons for want of any satisfactory alternative. Beresford's shift in opinion was prompted by the refusal by Edward Cardwell, the newly appointed Chief Secretary, to sanction the granting of state aid to the society's schools. Cardwell gave this negative response during a meeting with Hamilton Verschoyle in January 1860. Cardwell had earlier refused a similar appeal from the Roman Catholic hierarchy, who had asked that they be given control over the funds allocated for the education of Catholic children. The Liberal government's obvious unwillingness to abandon the national system in favour of a system of 'separate' grants convinced Beresford that it was no longer viable for the Church Education Society to maintain as extensive a system of schools as it had done up to that point. The failure of Eglinton's earlier initiative on the question may also have influenced Beresford in this direction. The Primate's position was supported by Napier in a pamphlet published in April 1860.[68] This apparent volte-face by Napier was severely criticised by those Irish Conservatives who remained unyielding in their opposition to the national system.[69] Other supporters of Beresford's change in opinion also suffered similar attacks. Beresford himself was likened to Judas Iscariot by the *Dublin Evening Post*.[70]

The virulence of this campaign, however, could not alter the significance of Beresford's circular. Once a public split had occurred within the society, particularly one inspired by a figure of Beresford's prominence, there was no longer a realistic possibility that its schools would receive state assistance. It was, of course, arguable that, by 1860, there was little likelihood that this would happen in any case, and that Beresford's initiative simply represented a belated acceptance of reality. Whether this was the case or not, the years after 1860 did see the society fall into a steady decline, both in the numbers attending its schools and in its funding. For example, the number of students attending its schools fell by some 17,000 between 1863 and 1870 to 52,166.[71] While some senior Irish Conservatives, particularly James Whiteside, continued to press the society's claims in parliament, they no longer had the ear of government in the same way as they had done in the earlier period. The society's political influence, which had been by no means insubstantial during the periods of Conservative government in 1852 and, from 1858 to 1859, dwindled significantly in the years that followed.

The controversies over the national education system and the grant to Maynooth College are illustrative of some of the wider problems facing the Irish Conservative Party in the decade of the 1850s. A central difficulty facing the party was the fact that its priorities did not necessarily reflect those of the party leadership at Westminster. The importance attached to both issues by Irish Conservatives did not mean that all shades of English Conservative opinion felt as strongly on them. Moreover, the advances that the national system had made in Irish primary education rendered it exceedingly difficult for any British government to tamper with it. As a result, there was a series of contradictory pressures on the leaders of the Conservative Party in Britain during this period. Among these pressures was the need to conciliate Irish Catholic opinion, particularly in the years after 1857, when this seemed to be yielding concrete results. As a result, even the Conservatives' most concerted attempt to reach a settlement of the national education question favourable to the Church Education Society in 1858–59 was preceded by a serious attempt to win the backing of the National Board for their proposals. Furthermore, even if the government's scheme had been introduced, the Church Education Society schools would still have received considerably less state aid than schools under Roman Catholic patrons would have done. It was unlikely, in any case, that Eglinton's scheme would have won unanimous backing from the Conservative cabinet.

The developments within the Irish national education system in this period also show a gradual move by the Church of Ireland away from the conception of itself as the 'National Church' of Ireland. The initial demand made by the Church Education Society had been that the Established Church should have complete control over the national system of education. This claim was founded on the argument that, as the state church, the Anglican Church had responsibility for all the people of Ireland. Its retreat from this position in the decades between the 1830s and 1850s reflected both the British government's unwillingness to accede to such demands and a more realistic appraisal by the Church of Ireland of its position *vis-à-vis* the Roman Catholic Church than had originally been taken.[72] By accepting the Catholic Church's right to control over the education of Roman Catholic children, the Church of Ireland could be perceived as abdicating a responsibility which it had previously claimed.

This also had obvious implications for its position as the Established Church in Ireland.[73] In Chapter 7 we will consider in more detail the Irish Conservative conception of the nature of the British state and at the way in which this affected their view of the relationship which that state should have with the Irish Roman Catholic Church.

NOTES

1   *Hansard*, CXXIV, 1215–17.
2   These figures are taken from Akenson, *The Irish Education Experiment*, p. 276.
3   See Derby to Wilson 3 February 1853, quoted in the *Daily Express*, 1 April 1857.
4   *Daily Express*, 24 March 1857.
5   *Daily Express*, 31 March 1857.
6   *The Warder*, 10 April 1858.
7   *Hansard*, CXLIX, 200.
8   *Hansard*, CXLIX, 403–4.
9   Eglinton to Naas, 20 March 1859, Mayo papers, 11,031 (18).
10 Eglinton to Derby, 24 March 1858, Derby papers, 148/3. There is a draft of this letter in the Eglinton papers, GD3/5/56.
11 Eglinton to Derby, 14 April 1858, Derby papers, 148/3.
12 Ferguson to Donoughmore, 10 February 1858, Donoughmore papers, H/18/1/572. See also Clancarty, *Ireland: Her Present Condition*, p. 19.
13 Eglinton to Derby, 19 June 1858, Derby papers, 148/3. There is a draft of this letter in the Eglinton papers, GD3/5/56.
14 Eglinton to Derby, 6 July 1858, Derby papers, 148/3. There is a draft of this letter in the Eglinton papers, GD3/5/56.
15 Eglinton to Derby, 27 September 1858, Derby papers, 148/3.
16 See G.A. Hamilton to Naas, 9 October 1858, Mayo papers, 11,028 (6).
17 'Memorandum for proposed measures given me [Cairns?] by the Chancellor [Napier]', 15 October 1858, Mayo Papers, 11,021 (14).
18 See Eglinton to Walpole, 14 November 1858, Holland papers, 894c. Also Eglinton to Derby, 14 November 1858, Derby papers, 148/3. There is a draft of this letter in the Eglinton papers, GD3/5/56/4437.
19 Derby to Eglinton, 31 October 1858, Eglinton papers, GD3/5/56.
20 See Eglinton to Derby, 14 November 1858, Derby papers, 148/3. There is a draft of this letter in the Eglinton papers, GD3/5/56/4437.
21 Eglinton to Naas, 16 November 1858, Mayo papers, 11,031 (14).
22 See Eglinton to Derby, 17 November 1858, Derby papers, 148/3. Also Eglinton to Walpole, 17 November 1858, Holland papers, 894c.
23 Naas to Walpole, 22 November 1858, Holland papers, 128g. See also Eglinton to Derby, 17 November 1858, Derby papers, 148/3.
24 Eglinton to Derby, 22 November 1858, Derby papers, 148/3.
25 Walpole to Eglinton, 20 November 1858, Eglinton papers, GD3/5/56/4438.
26 See Vincent (ed.), *Disraeli, Derby and the Conservative Party*, p. 144.
27 Walpole to Eglinton, 20 November 1858, Eglinton papers, GD3/5/56/4438.
28 Derby to Eglinton, 3 December 1858, Eglinton papers, GD3/5/56.
29 Eglinton to Derby, 22 January 1859, Derby papers, 148/3.

30   See Beresford to Eglinton, 20 January 1859 [enclosure with Eglinton to Naas, 8 February 1859], Mayo papers, 11,031 (15). There is a copy of this letter in the Donoughmore papers, H/19/3/7.

31   Eglinton to Derby, 10 January 1859, Derby papers, 148/3. There is a copy of this letter in the Holland papers, 894c, enclosed with Eglinton to Walpole, 10 January 1859.

32   See Beresford to Eglinton, 20 January 1859 [enclosure with Eglinton to Naas, 8 February 1859], Mayo papers, 11,031 (15). There is a copy of this letter in the Donoughmore papers, H/19/3/7.

33   Eglinton to Derby, 10 January 1859, Derby papers, 148/3. There is a copy of this letter in the Holland papers, 894c, enclosed with Eglinton to Walpole, 10 January 1859.

34   Derby to Eglinton, 12 January 1859, Eglinton papers, GD3/5/56.

35   Eglinton to Derby, 23 January 1859, Derby papers, 148/3. There is a copy of this letter in the 'Confidential Memorandum' on Education in the Donoughmore papers, H/19/3/7.

36   Eglinton to Walpole, 24 January 1859, Holland papers, 894c.

37   Derby to Eglinton, 16 February 1859, Eglinton papers, GD3/5/56/4436.

38   See Eglinton to Naas, 17 February 1859, Mayo papers, 11,031 (16).

39   Derby to Eglinton, 21 February 1859, Eglinton papers, GD3/5/56/4436.

40   Derby to Eglinton, 6 April 1859, Eglinton papers, GD3/5/56/4436.

41   *The Warder*, 9 April 1859.

42   *Daily Express*, 2 May 1859.

43   For Hennessey's political career and a brief discussion of his views on 'mixed' education see James Pope Hennessey, *Veranda: Some Episodes in the Crown Colonies, 1867–1889* (London, 1964), pp. 27–37 and John Biggs-Davison and George Choudhary-Best, *The Cross of St Patrick: The Catholic Unionist Tradition in Ireland* (Abbotsbrook, 1984) pp. 183–4. See also Hennessey to his father, 2 April 1859, Pope Hennessey papers, Rhodes House Library, Oxford, Box 2/1 fs. 93.

44   Derby to Eglinton 6 April 1859, Eglinton papers, GD3/5/56/4436.

45   See below, pp. 178–80.

46   Estcourt's memorandum incorporated Eglinton's letter to Derby of 23 January, which gave a detailed outline of the Irish administration's proposals, and Beresford's letter to Eglinton of 20 January, which gave the Church Education Society's response. See Donoughmore to Estcourt, 27 May 1859, Donoughmore papers, H/19/1/436.

47   *Hansard*, CXXIV, 508–13.

48   See Stanley's diary for 22–3 February 1853, quoted in Vincent (ed.), *Disraeli, Derby and the Conservative Party*, pp. 99–100.

49   Winchilsea had been one of the founding members of the National Club. See Jones, *Lord Derby and Victorian Conservatism*, p. 31.

50   Donoughmore to Derby, 14 April 1853, Derby papers, 158/6.

51   See for example the article on 'Conversion and persecution in Ireland', *Dublin University Magazine*, 40 (August 1852), pp. 244–8.

52   Akenson, *Irish Education Experiment*, p. 285.

53   Foster, *Modern Ireland*, p. 345.

54   Derby to Lambert, 5 January 1856, Derby papers 183/2. See also Stewart, *Foundation of the Conservative Party*, p. 341.

55   *Hansard*, CXLII, 1952–4.

56   Napier to George Alexander Hamilton, 28 November 1854, Disraeli papers, H B/XX/H/31.

57 Barton also described Maynooth as 'the great rock ahead, which threatens disunion'. Barton to Donoughmore, 16 January 1857, Donoughmore papers, H/17/1/40.

58 Whiteside to Donoughmore, 22 March 1857, Donoughmore papers, H/17/1/706.

59 See Whiteside to Donoughmore, 22 March 1857, Donoughmore papers, H/17/1/706. See also the *Daily Express*, 4 April 1857.

60 See the *Daily Express*, 26 March and 31 March 1857.

61 See the *Dublin Evening Mail*, 30 April 1858. See also Machin, *Politics and the Churches in Great Britain, 1832 to 1868*, p. 290.

62 See the letters from Eardley to Derby, 29 October 1858, Derby to Eardley, 31 October 1858 and Eardley to Derby, 3 November 1858, reprinted in the *Daily Express*, 16 November 1858.

63 Walpole to Derby, 12 May 1858, Derby papers, 153/2.

64 Derby to Eglinton, 25 May 1858, Eglinton papers, GD3/5/56.

65 Eglinton to Derby, 11 June 1858, Derby papers, 148/3.

66 Eglinton to Derby, 2 November 1858, Derby papers, 148/3.

67 See Derby to Eglinton 6 June 1858, Eglinton papers, GD3/5/56 and Derby to Eglinton, 31 October 1858, Eglinton papers, GD3/5/56.

68 The background to Beresford's issuing of the circular is discussed in Akenson, *Irish Education Experiment*, pp. 289–91. See also Napier's pamphlet, *The Education Question: Thoughts on the Present Crisis* (2nd edn, Dublin, 1860), pp. 7–10.

69 On 12 January 1861 *The Warder* reported that a resolution had been moved at a meeting of the Dublin Protestant Association removing Napier from the position of Vice-President in consequence of 'his recent conduct in the matter of education'. See *The Warder*, 12 June 1861. See also *To the Right Hon. Joseph Napier Late Lord Chancellor of Ireland, The Address of the Committee of the Dublin Protestant Association*, dated 20 September 1860 and published as an appendix to *The Report of the Dublin Protestant Association* (Dublin, 1861), copy in the Cullen papers, Dublin Diocesan Archives. The address condemned Napier for having 'betrayed … [his] trust' and abandoned his 'friends'. Napier had 'quit the camp of the Lord and the standard of our God'. *The Warder* published a series of leading articles attacking Napier's change of opinion on the Education question and perhaps the most virulent of these was published on 4 May 1861. Equally critical articles appeared in the *Dublin Evening Mail*, see in particular the leading article of that paper for 9 February 1865, which sharply attacks Napier's entire political career. See also the pamphlet, *Some Remarks on a Pamphlet Entitled 'The Education Question: Thoughts on the Present Crisis'* (Dublin, 2nd edn, 1860), published in reply to Napier's one, by James Thomas O'Brien, the Bishop of Ossory.

71 *Dublin Evening Post*, 10 April 1860, quoted in Akenson, *Irish Education Experiment*, p. 291.

72 Akenson, *Irish Education Experiment*, p. 289.

73 See Brown, *National Churches*, p. 405.

74 For a discussion of this subject see Akenson, *Irish Education Experiment*, pp. 285–94.

SEVEN

The Irish Conservative Party and the Church question

The position of the Church of Ireland, 1853–68

A S PART of their defence of the position of the Church of Ireland, some leading Irish Conservatives were at pains to stress its historical antiquity, tracing its origins back to the time of St Patrick. In their belief, it was it, rather than the Roman Catholic Church, that carried on the traditions of the 'primitive Church' in Ireland, while its bishops could trace back an unbroken line of succession to the early Church.[1] Irish Conservative thinkers also emphasised the independence of the early Christian Church in Ireland from Papal authority. Whatever the merits of the historical arguments used to back up these assertions, their main purpose was to bestow legitimacy on the claims of the Church of Ireland to be the 'national' Church in Ireland. On a more pragmatic level, Irish Conservatives argued that the Act of Union had secured the future of the Established Church. In particular, they pointed to the fifth article of that treaty which deemed 'the continuance and preservation of... the United Church, as the Established Church of England and Ireland... an essential and fundamental part of the Union'. According to Joseph Napier, the Union was an 'international treaty in its very nature permanent, because on each side there was the giving up of the separate and independent existence of a state, a legislature and a national Church'. Irish Conservatives had, he claimed, only accepted the Union on this basis. As a result, any attempt to undermine the position of the Church of Ireland would call the Union itself into question.[2] Indeed, James Whiteside claimed, in March 1865, that 'on the day upon which the Church of the Protestants of Ireland... [was] struck down [by a British Parliament]... the Union is at an end'.[3] Whiteside argued that the effect of this would be that Irish Conservatives would then be at liberty to 'reconsider the terms of [their] connexion with England'.[4] The strengthened connection between the Irish and English branches of the Established Church, created by the Act of Union, also led some Irish Conservatives to claim that any weakening of their Church would also undermine the position of the Church of England. In Napier's words, the 'strength of the beam... [lay] in the weakest part'.[5]

Another central plank of the Irish Conservative defence of the Established Church was the argument that any interference with its property would weaken the 'rights' of property in Ireland generally. They doubted the wisdom of questioning the legitimacy of titles to property in Ireland. If some Church property owed its origins to the land confiscation of the seventeenth century, then so too did the estates of many large landowners in Ireland. This point was made explicitly by Napier in a debate in February 1849, when he stressed that the Church's title to its property was 'as good as the title by which any landlord held his land'.[6] Its connection with the settlement of land in Ireland was reinforced by the fact that it was members of the Church of Ireland who owned the bulk of the larger estates there. Furthermore, in most parishes in Ireland, the local Anglican clergy were dependent on the local landlords for their own livelihoods and for the upkeep of their parishes.

Despite these arguments, Irish Conservatives still felt it necessary to defend the seemingly anomalous position of an Established Church, which served only a minority of the Irish population. Even Napier admitted that the Reformation had been 'partial and limited' in its operation in Ireland. This he attributed to the 'historical antecedents' of Ireland and the way in which 'national feeling' there had come to be associated with Roman Catholicism.[7] He also blamed the British state for its failure to actively support the Church of Ireland as a missionary Church. No 'adequate provision' had been made by government 'for giving the [Irish] people the benefits and blessings of the Reformation'. Rather than supporting a policy of wide-scale conversion to Anglicanism, earlier governments had, he claimed, instead relied on the policy of 'penal laws and legislative prohibition[s]' against the practice of the Roman Catholic religion.[8] The Church of Ireland had been used as a political instrument, a buttress for the power of the ruling elite in the country, rather than as a vehicle for disseminating religious truth. Nevertheless, Napier argued that this latter was the true role for the Church and one which deserved state support.

The social utility of having Church of Ireland clergymen spread across the country was also stressed. As 'resident gentlemen' they were, according to James Whiteside, 'ministers of peace... and of loyalty' to the British connection. In his view, the Church of Ireland clergyman was incapable of being a 'disloyal man'. He preached and taught 'loyalty' in his district and the English government would fail in 'their first duty' if they failed 'in recognising the value of... [his] services'.[9] Implicit in this argument was the suggestion that the 'loyalty' of the Roman Catholic priests was suspect. The clergymen of the Established Church played a critical role, therefore, as a counterweight to their influence.

Underlying many of these arguments was the 'providential' sense of history shared by many of the leading figures within the Irish Conservative Party. Like many contemporaries, they believed that history exhibited plainly 'the course of God's moral government'.[10] Thus, for example, in the history of Britain, Napier believed that it had been providential that the Reformation had preceded the revolution of 1688. The Reformation had 'settled the faith of the Church upon the abiding truth of the sure Word of God' while the 'Glorious Revolution' had 'settled the freedom of the state upon the basis of the Protestant Religion'.[11] Napier's belief was that for as long as England continued to support and encourage the Established Church, it did not need to fear 'from any knowledge derived from the causes of decline [of earlier states] under paganism, and [under] the temporary Jewish dispensation'.[12] In consequence, they saw the Established Church as a vital institution, both as a guarantor of national religion and as an essential element in Britain's success as a nation.

As we saw in Chapter 4, from an Irish Conservative perspective, the Ecclesiastical Titles Act itself had had little tangible effect. Indeed, from their viewpoint, the ultimate results of the agitation around the subject had been disappointingly small. In the early 1850s, however, they remained intent on dealing with what they saw as the unfinished business left between the British state and the Catholic Church in the wake of the Titles Act. This intention was clearly displayed in a series of debates on religious questions that took place from early 1853 onwards to the outbreak of the Crimean War in March 1854. While these debates covered a wide range of topics, from attempts to amend the form of oath taken by Catholic MPs to a bill designed to protect the rights of nuns to freely dispose of their own property, there was a common thread that ran through them. Their common concern was with what Irish Conservatives saw as the problem of reconciling Papal authority over the Roman Catholic Church in Ireland with the maintenance of the supremacy of British laws and the British constitution there.

Irish Conservatives were given another opportunity to raise these issues when Thomas Chambers, the Liberal MP for Hertford, introduced a motion in late February 1854 calling for the appointment of a committee to inquire into the number and rate of increase of convents and monasteries throughout the British Isles. This motion was seconded by Napier, who argued that 'even Roman Catholic states had very jealous codes of law' with respect to such institutions. According to Napier, the vows of obedience taken by the inmates of convents and monasteries had bound them to obey 'an authority [the papacy]' over which the laws of England had no control. He insisted that it was not legal under the British constitution for a 'foreign authority' without responsibility to 'the law of the land' to direct the behaviour of British citizens. As monasteries and convents were conducted under rules devised by a 'foreign power' it was important to ensure that their regulations did not conflict with British law.[13]

The Property Disposal Bill, dealing directly with this point, was introduced by Whiteside soon afterwards. He maintained that it was designed 'to secure perfect freedom in the alienation of their property' for people in religious orders. The vows of poverty and obedience taken by monks and nuns, he argued, prevented them from exercising 'free will' in this area. To counteract this, under the terms of Whiteside's bill, it was incumbent on the superior of a monastery or convent to prove that they had not exercised 'undue' influence over the wills made by inmates under their supervision. This provision applied only to cases where substantial legacies had been left to the institution of which the monk or nun was a member.[14] Not surprisingly, the bill encountered severe opposition from Irish Roman Catholic MPs. Its introduction was also condemned by Sir George Bowyer, the MP for Dundalk, who had regularly voted with the Conservatives.[15] Like their Irish counterparts, some senior members of the English Roman Catholic aristocracy and gentry, including Lord Edward Howard, also opposed any state interference with convents.[16]

The introduction of the bill led to the holding of a series of protest meetings in Ireland. At these meetings, Napier and Whiteside were regularly accused of religious bigotry, with Whiteside being described as a 'great Inniskilling [*sic*] Dragoon' by a speaker at a meeting in Dublin.[17] Some senior Conservatives also doubted the wisdom of alienating Roman Catholic opinion in this manner. Whiteside's polemical attacks on the Roman Catholic Church had previously led Lord Stanley to complain that his speeches in parliament were never complete without 'some attack on the Pope or the R[oman]. C[atholic]. priesthood'.[18] However, these tactics did succeed in embarrassing the government, when Chambers' motion for an inquiry into convents was passed by fifty-seven votes in a thinly attended House of Commons on 24 March. This victory was, however, to be a short-lived one. Under government pressure to avoid raising controversial issues given the outbreak of the Crimean War, Chambers eventually agreed to postpone the appointment of the proposed committee to the ensuing session.[19]

Whiteside had also agreed previously to the sending of the Property Disposal Bill to this committee. However, when it became clear that it was not going to be appointed that session, he attempted to have the bill read a second time. In supporting it, John George, the Conservative MP for Wexford, distanced both himself and Whiteside from Chambers' motion. Whiteside's measure would not, he stressed, involve Protestant inspectors visiting Catholic convents. His own opinion was that the law of habeas corpus should be extended to cases where it was suspected that an individual was being held in a convent without her consent. Unlike

Chambers' motion, which involved 'interference in a private residence', George argued that Whiteside's bill was designed only to protect property.[20] Ultimately, however, facing government hostility to the measure and the prospect of obstructive tactics from the Independent Irish Party, Whiteside withdrew it for the session.

While the controversy over convents continued, an attempt was made by the Liberal government to introduce a single oath for all members of parliament. The principal object of this motion was to make it easier for Jewish MPs to enter the House of Commons, but the measure also involved the abolition of the special oath taken by Roman Catholic MPs. Irish Conservatives were adamantly opposed to any change in the terms of the oath. As Catholic Emancipation had been granted on certain conditions, Napier insisted that any alteration of the terms on which it had been granted would 're-open the [whole] question of 1829'.[21] The primary purpose of the oath was, in Whiteside's view, 'to repel Papal usurpation, and [to] preserve to the Sovereign of England complete and undisputed sway in her dominions'. So long as the papacy aspired to 'interfere... [in] the internal concerns' of Britain and Ireland, so long would it be necessary to maintain the Roman Catholic oath as it stood.[22] As a 'state assuming dominion over independent kingdoms throughout the world', the papacy was a continual threat to the supremacy of the Crown and Parliament.

Napier questioned the motivation of those who wished to have the oath repealed or amended. Any concession on this issue would, he claimed, only inspire a full-scale attack on the Church establishment in Ireland and England. He described the Roman Catholic Church as a 'confederacy [designed to] enslave opinion, to coerce conscience, and thus, by the exercise of an assumed spiritual jurisdiction, to acquire dominion in temporal things'.[23] In the event, the motion to amend the oath was narrowly defeated in the House of Commons. A large number of Irish Conservative MPs voted in the division. While ultra-Protestants such as Mervyn Archdall, Edward Grogan and John Vance were present, more moderate Conservative MPs such as Lord Naas, Thomas Edward Taylor and John George also voted against the motion. The high level of attendance by Irish Conservative MPs reflected their sensitivity to any perceived threat to the position of the Church of Ireland.

The close of the session of 1854 was particularly notable for a surprise intervention by Disraeli on the subject of the 'Protestant Constitution'. In a debate on Maynooth, Disraeli argued that, rather than dealing with religious issues in a piecemeal fashion as had happened that session, the government should propose a comprehensive measure dealing with the broad question of the relationship between the Roman Catholic Church and the British state. The government should, Disraeli argued, bring forward legislation defining the 'attributes... the influence... [and] the bearing of the Protestant Constitution'. While the rights of the individual should be clearly defined in any proposed legislation, the limitations on these freedoms should also be clearly demarcated. Rather than leaving these questions in 'perpetual controversy', Disraeli maintained that the government had the duty to resolve them in as broad a fashion as possible. If not, the eventual result of constant sectarian quarrelling would be, Disraeli warned, 'internal dissensions, perhaps violence, and disorder'.[24] While a similar proposal had been made by Walpole earlier in the session,[25] the delivery of this speech had the unlikely effect of making Disraeli a 'Protestant hero', at least for a brief period. Stanley was concerned by this turn of events, cautioning Disraeli against repeating the mistake made at the time of the issuing of the Royal Proclamation against processions in June 1852. Indeed, Disraeli had previously told Stanley that the Conservatives had 'ruined' their chances at the 1852 election by taking up 'high Protestant politics'. Stanley queried whether the Conservatives would 'gain in 1854' by repeating the blunders of 1852.[26]

On the face of it, Disraeli's adoption of a 'Protestant' line also contradicted his earlier attempts to reach an accommodation with the Independent Party. His decision to take this course was, however, influenced by the 'relative success' that the ultra-Protestant party had achieved in the 1854 session.[27] The speech could be seen as an attempt by Disraeli to placate Protestant opinion in the House of Commons. It also provided him with an opportunity to embarrass the government, by playing on the divisions within its ranks. These divisions had previously been exposed by Lord John Russell's forthright criticisms of the Roman Catholic Church and the papacy.[28]

The close of the 1854 session saw a period of intense activity by the ultra-Protestant members of the Conservative Party. Disraeli's speech seems to have initiated this process, by giving them renewed hopes of support from the party leadership. While Disraeli was principally concerned with short-term political advantage, the ultra-Protestant MPs were anxious to use the political momentum stemming from his speech to forward their own ideas. They were also concerned to prevent the leadership on 'Protestant' issues falling into the hands of Liberals such as Chambers. The Crimean War, however, acted as a powerful barrier against raising religious controversies in Parliament. Walpole cautioned Disraeli against doing so, arguing that it would leave the Conservatives open to charges of 'making differences or disunion among the people, when there ought to be nothing but concord and harmony'.[29]

Nevertheless, in late 1854 Disraeli was obviously playing with the idea of preparing a comprehensive measure along the lines he had earlier suggested. In October, Whiteside advised him that if the Conservative Party did not 'take up the general Protestant question', it would be 'seized on by some man like Chambers' and they would be 'dragged at his heels'. Chambers had, in fact, already given notice of a motion couched in language very close to that used in Disraeli's speech.[30] Whiteside believed that it was essential for the Conservatives to have their own measures prepared before Chambers' motion came on for discussion. Disraeli's speech had, he suggested, 'prepared the public mind for something of this kind'. All that remained was to 'have the work prepared by practical men in good time before Parliament so that you may have the boat ready to launch when you wish'.[31] Disraeli's reply to this letter has not survived, but as Whiteside's response was to consult with Napier on the proposed measure, it seems likely that he encouraged him to do so.[32]

Whiteside outlined the nature of the proposed bill in a letter to Disraeli soon afterwards. The first object of the measure would be to regulate the introduction of Papal bulls into England. These bulls would be submitted, in the first instance, to the Home Secretary, who could, if he wished, submit them to the legal officers of the Crown for an opinion on their legality. Second, the proposed bill would have placed restrictions on the appointment of Roman Catholic bishops. In order to check 'ultramontane' influences, Napier proposed that 'the native clergy' in each diocese should be given control over the election of local bishops. In a clear reference to the manner of Cullen's appointment, he condemned the nomination of a bishop by the papacy, against the wishes of the local clergy. Indeed, similar suggestions about the 'domestic nomination' of the Catholic hierarchy had been made at the height of the debate on Catholic Emancipation in the late 1820s. At that time, Irish Conservatives had argued that this would reduce Papal influence on the Roman Catholic Church in Ireland and would reduce the likelihood of clashes between the Catholic hierarchy there and the British government. The proposed bill also covered similar ground to the Property Disposal Bill, rendering 'all gifts made or to be made' to monasteries and convents 'null...[and] void to all intents and purposes'. Finally, Napier and Whiteside proposed that all 'Jesuit establishments ...[and] monastic institutions' within the British Isles be required to make a return of their inmates by a given date. Those institutions which provided returns would be granted an indemnity for their breaches of the Catholic Relief Act, which had required such institutions to be licensed by the state. Napier explained the necessity for these regulations on the grounds that 'the agency of these orders had always been a most important element in the policy of Rome'. Given the controversy which had surrounded the convents issue, it is difficult to see, however, how such a measure could have been introduced without causing a similar furore.

Nevertheless, Napier was concerned that the Conservatives should attempt 'to bring the [Catholic] laity with...[them] as far as possible...

[and to] divide the Papal from the domestic section of the Church'. The 'crude... [and] ill-considered assaults on the convents' by some MPs had made this task more difficult. Napier believed that 'domestic associations of religious females, not under orders from Rome' should be left untouched by the provisions of his measure. If, however, their regulations derived from 'Papal orders', they should be classified with monastic institutions and come under the same regulations. Napier's language here reflected the Irish Conservative eagerness to draw a distinction between their opposition to 'Popery' as a political position and their tolerance for the practise of Roman Catholicism itself as a religion. For Napier, the essential thrust of the proposed bill was to 'shut out external... [and] foreign influence [from Britain], with a firm... [and] independent hand'.[33]

At this stage, Disraeli appears to have concluded that these measures went a good deal further than he had originally intended them to do. He told Whiteside that he feared taking the initiative on the question at a time of war. The need for caution was also stressed by Hamilton. He warned that to bring forward a measure at a time when the news from the Crimean War was at the forefront of people's minds would be unwise. Any movement in this direction 'originating from you [Disraeli], or any of the opposition leaders... without any cogent cause' would be 'ill-timed'. Hamilton suggested that it might be best to wait and see how Chambers' motion was received in parliament before taking any further steps. Nonetheless he praised the 'great constitutional knowledge and large views' of both Napier and Whiteside, and expressed his belief that 'Napier's prudence... [would] restrain Whiteside's impetuosity' when preparing their bill.[34]

At this point, however, Disraeli's initiative was overtaken by a wider political crisis. On 29 January 1855, the Aberdeen-led government was defeated on a motion censuring its conduct of the war introduced by John Arthur Roebuck, the Radical MP for Sheffield. The cabinet immediately resigned, and, as the leader of the largest party in the House of Commons, Derby was sent for by the Queen. Palmerston's broad support across the country meant that Derby was anxious to secure his adhesion to a Conservative cabinet. As an Irish landowner himself and as a politician whose conservatism in matters of domestic policy was well known, Palmerston was popular with Irish Conservatives. As early as August 1853, Napier had looked to an arrangement between Palmerston and Derby as being essential for the formation of 'a really good... [and] efficient [Conservative] party'.[35] Palmerston did, in fact, provisionally agree to join a Conservative cabinet, on the condition that Lord Clarendon remained as Foreign Secretary. However, Clarendon's refusal to serve under Derby led Palmerston to withdraw his acceptance of office.[36] While Derby's approach to Palmerston was uncontroversial among Conservatives, there was more opposition to his attempts to induce Gladstone and Sidney Herbert, both of whom had been leading Peelites, to join his cabinet. Thomas Edward Taylor, the Conservative Chief Whip and an MP for Dublin County, admonished Derby that 'the admission of Gladstone to... [the] cabinet' would cause the 'Protestant party... to leave us to a man'. He warned that if Napier and Whiteside took office with Gladstone, they 'would lose their seats'. The coalition with the former Peelites would be 'a source of... weakness' not of strength to the Conservative Party.[37] Gladstone's unpopularity with Irish Conservative opinion stemmed from their suspicions of his Anglo-Catholic leanings. These suspicions had been further increased by his opposition to the Ecclesiastical Titles Act. As events transpired, however, Gladstone and Herbert refused to accept office in a Derby cabinet and their refusal prompted Derby to abandon his attempts to form a government. Palmerston eventually returned as Prime Minister, with the Conservatives remaining in opposition.

Writing to Derby soon afterwards, Napier referred to the 'strong remonstrance and stronger repugnances [*sic*]' he had found at the National Club against 'the rumoured proposal about Mr Gladstone and Mr Herbert'. This had been succeeded by 'thankfulness that... [Derby had] escaped the junction'. Opinion there had also been gratified by the fact that the terms of Gladstone's refusal of office made it unlikely that he would accept, or be offered, office by the Conservatives in the future. Napier recommended that Derby reassure Protestant opinion by 'making clear... the absence [on his part] of all sympathy with the school in which Gladstone has been trained'. While some of the ultra-Protestant MPs were not 'very reasonable' they were 'still manageable and open to the admonition of friends'. Their very unreasonableness made it imperative that the Conservatives should have clearly worked out policies on religious issues. If not, those 'great questions' could fall into the hands of 'overheated men'. The party ought to have 'intelligent, well considered' policies on such issues, and ensure that party members were united in support of them.[38]

It is clear that Napier's principal concern here was the need for greater party discipline on religious issues. As Disraeli had done earlier, Napier was attempting to grapple with the difficulties caused by the long drawn out and generally inconclusive nature of parliamentary debates on religious questions in the early 1850s. Napier was also suspicious of the radical tendencies within the Nonconformist community in Britain. Writing to a friend around this time, he conceded that 'the formation of a party purely and properly Protestant, however desirable' was not practicable. He could not see 'where... the men [were] to guide and lead' such a party. As a strong supporter of the Established Church, Napier feared the voluntaryist strain within British Nonconformism. He was also worried that 'the Protestantism of England which would prevail in Parliament... [was]

largely Nonconformist, and might rapidly become Cromwellian'.[39] Indeed, it was these divisions between Anglican Evangelicals and their Nonconformist counterparts that had been one of the key reasons for the decline of 'Protestant' activity in parliament in the late 1850s.[40]

Palmerston's appointment as Prime Minister had also presented the Conservatives with considerable problems. As we saw earlier, his conservatism in terms of domestic policy was well known, while on religious issues, he was strongly influenced by Lord Shaftesbury, his son-in-law. As Shaftesbury was a leading Evangelical, most of the bishops appointed by Palmerston came from that wing of the Church. Palmerston was also a strong supporter of the Church of Ireland and he was as suspicious of the intentions of the Roman Catholic Church as any Irish Conservative. In September 1864, for example, he told Chichester Fortescue, a leading Irish Liberal, that while Irish Catholics professed 'a desire for religious equality', in reality they 'aimed at nothing less than political domination'.[41] Palmerston's popularity as a war minister also made it difficult for the Conservatives to find a convincing line of attack against him. These circumstances meant that the years 1855–57 were to prove exceptionally difficult for the Conservative opposition.[42]

By the mid-1850s, the 'no-Popery' ferment which had been inspired by the 'Papal aggression' had greatly subsided. As we have seen, this was partly a result of the mutual suspicion that existed between Nonconformist Evangelicals and their Anglican counterparts. In consequence, as the issue of the relationship between the British state and the Roman Catholic Church became less politically pressing, other issues rose to prominence. Among them was the question of the future position of the Church of Ireland, an Established Church, which served only a minority of Ireland's population.

Despite the fact that the campaign for the disestablishment of the Established Church was only 'in incubation' in the 1850s, Irish Conservatives had begun to feel threatened by the possibility of a unified campaign by Roman Catholics in Ireland and Nonconformists in other parts of Britain against the position of the Church of Ireland.[43] British Nonconformists would, they argued, only use this agitation as the thin end of the wedge with which they hoped to overturn the Church of England.[44] Nonconformist hostility to the established churches in England, Ireland and Wales was, of course, a long-standing one. Indeed, many Nonconformists had a principled opposition to the concept of state endowment of *any* religion and, as a result, they favoured a 'voluntary' system for the support of all the churches in both Britain and Ireland.[45] In 1844, this had led to the formation of the largely Nonconformist body, the Anti-State Church Association, in Britain. The association had the declared objective of seeking the disestablishment and disendowment of the existing state churches in the

British Isles. In 1853, the organisation changed its name to the Society for the Liberation of Religion from State Patronage and Control, but this title was generally shortened, in practice, to the Liberation Society.

An early attempt to raise the question of the future status of the Church of Ireland was made in May 1853, when George Henry Moore introduced a motion calling for an inquiry into its revenues to see if these were disproportionate to its actual requirements. On this occasion, Whiteside made a strong defence of the Irish Church as being 'pure in doctrine ... [and] tainted by no pestilent heresies'. In a clear reference to the Oxford movement, Whiteside argued that the Irish Church had 'adopted no spurious form of Romanism ... [and] had adhered unswervingly to the doctrine and principles of the Reformation'. This argument that 'Irish Protestantism ... was a healthier, stronger plant than the English variant'[46] had been used regularly by Irish Conservatives from the 1820s onwards. Whiteside further asserted that by raising the issue of the Church establishment, Catholic MPs were breaking the terms of their oath. He contended that Moore's pledge to oppose any government that did not support the disestablishment of the Church of Ireland implied that his ultimate object was not merely to 'spoliate' but to 'annihilate' it.[47]

This debate prompted Lord Stanley to confide in his diary that he believed 'the permanent maintenance of the Irish [Church] Establishment ... [could not] be defended'. An adjustment of the question should, however, wait, until 'the cessation of emigration [from Ireland] had settled the 'relative numerical strength of the two creeds and races [*sic*]'.[48] Although he consigned a settlement of the question to a future date, Stanley's expression of this opinion was important as it revealed that the Conservative Party was not completely united in defending the Irish Church.

The potential for an alliance between the opponents of the Established Church in Ireland and in other parts of Britain was shown in May 1856, when Edward Miall, the Radical MP for Rochdale and a leading member of the Liberation Society, brought forward a motion for the redistribution for secular purposes of the surplus revenues of the Established Church in Ireland. Miall was a leading member of the Liberation Society. There was, of course, a certain irony in even an *ad hoc* parliamentary alliance between radical Nonconformists and Irish Roman Catholics. The Roman Catholic Church across Europe had no opposition *per se* to the concept of state endowment of religion. It was the peculiarity of the Irish situation, the fact of being a majority Church without state support, which forced it into the position of looking for a severance of the ties between the Established Church and the state.[49] By contrast, as we have seen, the majority of the Nonconformist opponents of the Church of Ireland, were opposed in principle to any state endowment of religion. As a result, there was a wide difference in outlook between the two groups.

Speaking in the debate on Miall's motion, Napier contended that the property of the Church of Ireland 'was the most sacred of all properties . . . [and] the most ancient of any in the country'. As part of the 'settlement of property' referred to in the oath taken by Roman Catholic MPs, it should 'not be interfered with'. The Church of Ireland's legal title to its property had, he argued, been copperfastened by the fifth article of the Union, which had secured it 'for all time – for after ages, as well as the present'. Any attempt to interfere with this property would, Napier warned, 'light the flame of religious discord from one end of [Ireland] to the other'. Irish Protestants would, he maintained, resist strenuously any attempt to undermine the privileges secured to them by the Union.

In the course of his speech, Napier had appealed to government ministers to use the debate to reaffirm their support for the Church of Ireland.[50] The only government minister to answer this appeal was Palmerston, who expressed his conviction that a Church Establishment was 'a proper part of the organisation of a civilised country'.[51] The significance of Palmerston's speech was increased by the conspicuous absence of Conservative leaders, such as Disraeli and Stanley, from the debate and the subsequent division. While Miall's motion was defeated by seventy votes, only 256 out of the 654 MPs in the House of Commons took part in the division. A high number of Irish Conservatives voted on this occasion, as did MPs such as Augustus Stafford and Evelyn Shirley, who had close connections with Ireland although they sat for English constituencies. Unsurprisingly, leading English ultra-Protestants, such as Richard Spooner and Charles Newdegate, also voted against the motion.

The failure of Disraeli, Stanley and Sir John Pakington to attend this debate was taken by some Irish Conservatives as evidence of the luke-warmness of their support for the Irish Church. Noting Disraeli's regular attendance in the House of Commons, the parliamentary correspondent of the *Dublin Evening Mail* implied that he had made a conscious decision not to be present. At the very least, he continued, 'the subject [of the Church of Ireland] was one which it was discreditable to any one claiming the position of the leader of a party to evade'.[52] An obviously angry Napier wrote to Sir William Jolliffe, the Conservative chief whip, complaining that he had never felt 'more humiliated . . . [and] discouraged than last night'. For the 'greater part' of the debate, he complained, there 'was not one of our leading men beside us [on the front bench] . . . [and] scarcely one of our party behind us'. The 'most indecent . . . [and] insulting proposal[s] of confiscation' had been made without any reply from the leaders of the Conservative Party. This would 'not do,' Napier insisted. If the Conservatives were to retain any credibility, the motion should, in his view, have been met with 'a bold decided and united opposition'. He accused the Conservative leadership of having 'evaded' the Maynooth question and of having 'avoided the support of the Irish Church'. If the party did not take up the Irish national education question in the next session of parliament, he could not see 'any purpose' being served by the Conservative Party 'continuing to be in name what . . . [it] would not be in reality'.[53]

Whiteside wrote to Jolliffe in a similar vein, complaining that 'not one English [Conservative] statesman [had] uttered a word' in support of the Church of Ireland. What was 'worse still', Whiteside believed, was that of the leading members of the party in Britain, only J.W. Henley had voted in the division. He contended that 'no greater blunder could have been committed than that of abandoning the Irish Church on such an occasion'. To Irish Conservatives, it displayed 'an utter absence of feeling, of sincerity . . . [and] of consistency . . . [and although] this was only in appearance yet appearance in politics can not be disregarded'. Any repetition of this disregard for their concerns would 'assuredly [be] resented'.[54] As we saw earlier, this conviction that party leaders at Westminster did not sufficiently consider their interests was frequently expressed by Irish Conservatives.[55]

These criticisms of Conservative leaders obviously had some effect, with the excuses of senior party members, like Disraeli, Lord John Manners and Walpole, for their non-attendance being given in the Dublin *Daily Express* on 6 June.[56] Regardless of the truth of these statements, they did not completely appease Irish Conservative opinion. Significantly, in the light of future events, the *Dublin Evening Mail* singled out Palmerston for praise for his part in the debate, contrasting his speech with the silence of Edward Horsman, the Irish Chief Secretary. The paper called for a 'reconstruction' of parties 'on a sound basis' with Palmerston and other conservative-minded Liberals joining with the Conservative Party, leaving the radical element within the Liberal Party to go its own way.[57]

Disraeli again alienated Irish Conservative opinion later that session when he voted in favour of the abolition of the oath of abjuration, a move designed principally to allow Jewish MPs to enter parliament. In the debate on the question, Napier warned that any tampering with the oath would render 'the propriety of the Protestant succession [to the throne] as by law established, and the truth of the Christian faith, open questions'. In his view, it was not consistent with the British constitution 'to admit any one into Parliament who denied the truth of the Christian religion'.[58] Irish Conservative opinion had long been hostile to Jewish Emancipation. In 1854, for example, both Whiteside and Napier had been prominent in the opposition to the Jewish Relief Bill. They defended this position on the basis of their belief in the 'Protestant Constitution'. Whiteside claimed that, as Christianity was the basis on which the 'whole system of . . . [British] laws, monarchy, and constitution' rested, to deny it was to strike at the foundations of the British state.[59] The providential theory of history was invoked by Napier as an additional reason for the exclusion of Jews from parliament. If, he warned, Britain was to 'renounce Christianity as the basis of . . . [its] law' it would leave itself open in consequence 'to Divine . . . displeasure'.[60]

It was on the issue of Jewish 'disabilities' that Disraeli was most out of step with opinion within the Conservative Party. His support for their removal made him unpopular with ultra-Protestants and added to their suspicions of him politically. Indeed, in June 1856, the *Dublin Evening Mail* suggested that his differences with the bulk of the party were such that he should be 'deprived of . . . [the] leadership by a formal vote'.[61] From this time on until the election victory of 1874, Disraeli was to be the subject of regular attacks, both personal and political, from the Irish Conservative press. These attacks reflected Conservative disillusionment at the party's failure to win office in these years. They also reflected a broader feeling of unease at Disraeli's leadership which was widespread within the Conservative Party. He was frequently accused of lack of political principle and the sincerity of his attachment to the 'Protestant' cause was frequently questioned.[62] It was also contended that Palmerston was, in some respects, a steadier Conservative than Disraeli himself. These difficulties in Disraeli's personal position were particularly marked in the late 1850s and early 1860s and had a considerable effect on Conservative politics in this period.[63]

The political outlook, which had appeared bleak for the party, was temporarily brightened with the unexpected defeat of the Palmerston government in the House of Commons in April 1857. Its defeat followed a debate on the bombardment of Canton by the British navy.[64] Palmerston immediately called a general election and the Liberal government was returned with an increased majority. At the Dublin University election the Liberals attempted to capitalise on Palmerston's popularity with Irish Protestants by standing two candidates, Wilfrid Lawson and George Fleetwood Wilson, the first time the election there was contested since 1848. Both of the Liberal candidates criticised Napier for not having lived up to the pledges he had made on religious issues when he was first elected to parliament in 1848. Napier responded by criticising Palmerston's political record, claiming that he had never known him 'to state any religious conviction, or put any proposition on a religious basis'. He also defended his own conduct on Maynooth and on the national education question. Speaking in support of Napier's candidacy, Whiteside criticised Palmerston's support for Jewish Emancipation and his participation in government with Keogh and Sadleir, both of whom had been pledged to the disestablishment of the Church of Ireland.[65] Although Napier and Hamilton retained their seats comfortably, it was apparent that the Liberal Party had deliberately set out to portray Palmerston as being sounder on religious issues than Derby. Irish Conservatives were wary of this strategy, fearing that Palmerston's long-term intention was to divide the party.[66]

The elections were also notable for the first tentative attempts by Conservative and Independent Party candidates to co-operate in contests where the other had an opportunity to defeat the Whig/Liberal candidate. This 'ad hoc understanding'[67] succeeded in most of its immediate aims in the 1857 election, and laid the groundwork for the co-operation between the Conservatives and a section of the Independent Party between 1858 and the early 1860s. Despite these successes, the elections saw the strength of the Liberal government increased, with the Conservatives remaining a minority in the House.

The Palmerston government suffered a second unexpected defeat in the House of Commons in February 1858 when the Conservatives and a group of disaffected Liberals combined against its introduction of the Conspiracy to Murder Bill. Palmerston resigned soon afterwards and Derby was called on to form a government. As in 1855, Derby approached Gladstone to join his government, but the offer was again refused. The new government owed its position primarily to divisions within the Liberal leadership rather than to any increase in Conservative strength. In consequence, it was placed in the position of seeking support from whatever quarter of the House that it could be gained. Derby's Irish appointments were much the same as they had been in 1852, with Naas resuming his previous position as Chief Secretary, Napier being promoted to the Lord Chancellorship and Whiteside being appointed Attorney General.

For several years prior to 1859, Irish Catholic MPs had been seeking a Royal Charter for the Catholic University in Dublin, which would give it the power to grant degrees. The university had been founded by John Henry Newman in 1851. As they had failed in obtaining any firm pledge on this question from Palmerston, they viewed the accession of the Conservative government to office as giving them a fresh opportunity to secure this goal. At this time, a small group of Independent Irish Party MPs led by John Francis Maguire were already giving the Conservative government a general support in the House of Commons. This group argued that the granting of a charter would both ensure their continued support for the government and conciliate Roman Catholic opinion in Ireland. The case for the granting of a charter was also supported by the Irish Roman Catholic hierarchy. In May 1858 Archbishop Cullen had approached William Monsell, a leading Irish Liberal MP, asking him to raise the issue with the government. Monsell sounded out Disraeli on the subject and his reply was sufficiently ambiguous for Monsell to believe that he would bring it before the cabinet.[68] Matters rested on this understanding until October when Ralph Earle, Disraeli's private secretary, pressed George Alexander Hamilton to obtain a final decision on the subject from the Irish administration. From the tone of this approach, it seems evident that Disraeli had not informed Eglinton or Naas of the vague promise he had made to Monsell. While claiming that he was not 'at all bigoted on such matters', Hamilton advised caution. For 'all his experience', he contended, Disraeli was not 'sufficiently alive to the machinations... and real objects of the parties he is dealing with'.[69]

At the beginning of the new year, Maguire put increased pressure on both Disraeli and Naas to grant a charter. To refuse it would, Maguire asserted, put the government 'in the wrong with the Catholics of the Empire' in general and, more particularly, with Irish Roman Catholics. If, on the other hand, it were to act on the question, it would secure the support of those Irish MPs who up to then had voted with the Liberals. Maguire also warned that government inaction 'would cut the legs from under your Catholic friends who had stood by you last year'.[70] At the same time he also recommended that the Irish administration should appoint Roman Catholics to some of the offices in its gift. As the session progressed, Maguire's appeals became increasingly desperate in tone. The government was bound to 'have days of storm before' it and ought to 'make friends against the evil day'. By refusing to grant the charter, the government would, Maguire warned, eventually force the group led by him to vote against it.[71] He stressed the fact that they were not seeking any endowment for the Catholic University, only the power to grant degrees. By issuing it, the government would impose 'a deep obligation on the "Catholic nation" of Ireland which would be profoundly felt'.[72]

Maguire reinforced these appeals by leading a large deputation, which met with Disraeli to press the claim for a charter in March 1859. The deputation included a number of MPs, including John Blake and Sir George Bowyer, who, along with Maguire, had given the government a general support in the previous session. It also included senior Irish Liberals such as Rickard Deasy and William Monsell, and, more surprisingly, James Spaight, the unsuccessful Conservative candidate for Limerick at the 1857 general election. Disraeli's reply to the deputation was couched in studiously ambiguous language. He described the existence of the Catholic University as a 'memorable example of the zeal and liberality of the Roman Catholics of Ireland' and carried on this conciliatory tone by promising to bring the issue before the cabinet. However, he did not give any pledge as to what the cabinet's decision would be on the subject, although he did promise, in an equivocal phrase, that the issue would be considered with 'a full sense of the importance due to it'. The ambiguity of this reply caused some alarm among Irish Conservatives, with the *Dublin Evening Mail* asking what 'Whig clothes... had he [Disraeli] stolen?' The paper's animus against Disraeli was displayed in its contention that it would 'prefer to have open foes' rather than 'traitors in[side] the fortress' to contend with.[73] The alarm expressed in this article was, however, misplaced. The measured tone of Disraeli's language was carefully chosen to avoid alienating Irish Catholic opinion while leaving the government unpledged on the question of the charter. Even before the deputation met Disraeli, Eglinton had advised Naas that it would be 'impossible' for the Irish administration to consent to the granting of a charter as this would 'disgust... [their] friends' and would, most likely, be opposed by the Whigs.[74] With a general election pending, however, the Irish administration saw no need for an immediate declaration of its policy on the subject.

The general election was called in April 1859, after the government was defeated on a resolution on reform brought forward by Lord John Russell. As we have seen, this election marked the high point of the co-operation between the Independent Irish Party and the Conservative Party on electoral matters. A number of factors were responsible for this; these included Palmerston's lack of a positive Irish programme in government, which meant that the Conservatives could hope to win Independent Party support with comparatively minor concessions. The Conservative Party's prospects in Ireland were also enhanced by events in Italy, where moves towards unification threatened Papal control over its dominions. These considerations impelled some Roman Catholics in both Ireland and Britain, notably Cardinal Wiseman, to support the Conservatives at the election. The government's decision to remunerate Catholic chaplains in prisons and to recognise the position of their counterparts in the military had also been designed to win Catholic support. Some Independent Party MPs also took Disraeli's equivocal pledge on the charter question as proof that the government intended to grant it. The government's award of a transatlantic packet station to Galway had also proved popular with Irish MPs across party lines.[75]

Irish Conservative leaders consolidated their alliance with Maguire's group of MPs by preventing local Tories from undertaking contests against him in Dungarvan and against Sir George Bowyer in Dundalk. Pressing his claims for support, Maguire told Naas that his election address had gone 'the whole length for Lord Derby's foreign policy... and against Russell and Palmerston'.[76] He argued that, if he were opposed by a Conservative, 'a blow' would be struck 'at independent action on the part of Irish Catholics for the future'. After having supported the Conservatives 'both by votes and addresses' in the previous session, Maguire believed he deserved their assistance at the election 'as a right'.[77] A local Conservative backed up Maguire's claims, adding that he had 'very materially damaged his position and prospects, with what is termed the Liberal Party, by some of his late votes, as well as by the known fact that he has influenced those of Mr [J.A.] Blake and other members [of parliament] – six or seven I believe'.[78] These appeals led Donoughmore to use his influence to persuade Sir Nugent Humble, the prospective Conservative candidate, to withdraw from the contest.

Conservative support also played a role in the return of other Independent Party MPs including Blake in Waterford and Patrick McMahon in Wexford. However, an appeal by George Henry Moore to Donoughmore for support in his contest for Kilkenny received a less favourable response. While Maguire, Bowyer, Blake and McMahon had supported the Conservatives in the division which had precipitated the general election, Moore had not. He attempted to back up his case for Conservative support by insisting that it would 'surely... [be] better' for the party to have an Independent Party member like himself in parliament, who would support it on occasion, than to have 'two Whigs – who [would]... oppose... [it] on all party questions'.[79] Donoughmore replied by claming that his influence in Kilkenny was 'very small' but that Moore's action in voting against the government meant he would not have supported him in any case. The division had been a critical one and Russell's motive in introducing the resolution had been to gain 'political power'. If the government had to fall, Donoughmore concluded, he would prefer that it would be 'succeeded by [a government under] Lord Palmerston... [and] his friends than by [a government including] Lord John Russell, Mr Bright... [and] Sir James Graham'.[80] Donoughmore believed, no doubt, that a government led by Russell would be more radical in its domestic policy than would a government under Palmerston. He was also making it clear that Conservative support was dependent upon a sense of reciprocal advantage, a condition which Moore's withdrawal of support in a crucial division had clearly breached.

The 1859 election was also unusual in the fact that a number of Conservative candidates received public support from Catholic clerics. A notable example was the manifesto issued by over seventy priests in County Meath, which praised the Conservative government's policy of non-interference with regard to Italy. The manifesto also endorsed the government's concessions to Roman Catholic chaplains in the military. They contrasted the government's position with that of Palmerston and Russell, from whom 'no prospect of good whatsoever to the Irish tenant' could be hoped, and who threatened 'the most certain prospect of evil on the largest scale to the interests of the church at home and abroad'.[81] It was, perhaps, no coincidence that both Meath MPs, Matthew Corbally and Edward MacEvoy, had supported the Conservatives in the previous session of parliament.

In King's County, John Pope Hennessey, the Conservative candidate and himself a Catholic, attracted considerable support from the local Catholic clergy. In his election address, Hennessey described the 'present disorganisation of Irish parties' as traceable 'to the unnatural efforts' which had been made 'to infuse Liberalism into Ireland'. The 'old traditions, the natural habits, the generous impulses, and above all, the religious faith of the Irish people' would, he insisted, 'never allow them to sympathise with English Whigs or continental Republicans'.[82] Hennessey laid considerable stress on his support for the papacy and his dislike of the Whigs. The Liberal Party's two principal objects were, he claimed, 'the degradation of Ireland, and the degradation of the religion to belong to which was his [Hennessey's] proudest boast'.[83] This anti-Whig rhetoric proved effective with Hennessey being returned at the top of the poll. Indeed, it was partly due to the strength of this anti-Whig sentiment across the political spectrum in Ireland that the Independent Party and the Conservatives could co-operate in the manner they did at the 1859 general election. Hennessey was the first Irish Catholic to be returned as a Conservative MP and his role as a link between the Conservative leadership and Independent Irish Party MPs was to be of considerable importance in the years that followed.

Cardinal Wiseman also played an active part in the elections in support of the Conservatives. He did this, indirectly, through his protégé, Lord Campden,[84] and openly, through a letter written to Thomas Strange, the former mayor of Waterford. In this letter, Wiseman defended John Blake for his support of the Conservative government in the division on Russell's motion. He expressed his 'decided approval' of Blake's conduct on that occasion. In Wiseman's view, the real motivation behind that vote had been Blake's desire to maintain the Conservative government, a course which, given the situation on the continent, the Cardinal believed to be a wise one.[85] Wiseman also sought to enlist the support of Bishop Furlong of Wexford for John George, the embattled Conservative candidate there. This intervention may possibly have aided George in winning the seat.[86]

The 1859 election saw the Conservative Party achieve considerable success in Ireland. For the first time since the 1832 Reform Act, the party, with fifty-five seats out of 105, held the majority of the Irish representation. The party gained some eight seats, which with the addition of their Independent Party allies, estimated by Eglinton at seven,[87] added fifteen votes to the Conservative strength in the House of Commons. Despite these gains, however, the Conservatives remained in a minority in the House of Commons, and were still threatened with defeat if the opposition could find an issue on which to combine.

The exigencies of the parliamentary situation had the effect of increasing the leverage which Maguire and his supporters held over the government. Soon after the election, Sir George Bowyer had a meeting with Disraeli, where he informed him that 'while he . . . [and] his friends 15 in number . . . [were] most anxious to support the government', the nature of its appointments in Ireland made it difficult for them to do so.[88] Bowyer was apparently including a number of Liberal MPs in the calculation of his 'friends' here. At the meeting, Bowyer argued that the government's failure to give any patronage to Catholics had made his and his supporters' position in Ireland 'scarcely tenable'. They had, he claimed, 'been accused of supporting an Orange Gov[ernmen]t'. Unless some Catholics were given office immediately, Bowyer warned that they would be forced 'against their will to take a position hostile to ... the government'.

The question of the nature of the government's appointments had been raised by Eglinton himself in a letter to Derby late in the previous year. At that time, he had reminded him that the Irish administration had 'not yet given a single appointment to a Roman Catholic'. However, he made it clear that the Irish administration had already decided to appoint Richard Coppinger to the Chairmanship 'of a first class county' at the first possible opportunity. Coppinger was, Eglinton told Derby, '... [that] rare ... [and] praiseworthy curiosity ... a Conservative Roman Catholic'.[89] This isolated appointment did not satisfy Irish Catholics, however, and in the following month Maguire again impressed upon Naas the importance of appointing Roman Catholic magistrates.[90] At his meeting with Disraeli, Bowyer had insisted that his group wanted nothing 'for themselves or for their immediate friends' but merely wished for Roman Catholics to be given government patronage, regardless of their politics.[91]

After this meeting Disraeli wrote a strong letter to Naas, claiming that the 'Orange system of Napier ... [and] Whiteside ... [had] done the government incalculable injury'. The priority for the government was survival and unless they were supported by the Independent Irish Party MPs, they would 'be beat[en] on the address'. He recommended a number of individuals who he believed were suitable for promotion and cautioned Naas 'not [to] wait for Roman Catholics who ... [were] members of the Carlton Club'. They would 'become so in time', he maintained.[92] Writing to Naas, Donoughmore agreed that the government's difficulties were such that it would be necessary to take immediate steps to satisfy Bowyer and the other Independent Party MPs. He recognised that these would create difficulties for the Irish administration – first, 'from the anger of ... [their] own ultra [Protestant] friends' and second, 'from the unwillingness of Napier and Whiteside to agree to such a policy'.[93] The reality was, however, that the government had no choice but to follow this course if it 'wished to stay' in office.

Naas responded to Disraeli's letter by claiming that the Irish administration had 'made no Orange app[ointmen]ts'. That was 'only the hustings cant of the Whigs infuriated' by Conservative success at the elections. The government's policy had been, he contended, 'to appoint competent men' to the offices in their gift. He claimed that 'ten years of Whig rule had crammed every department [of state] with Catholic incapables – appointed solely on account of their religion'. While he was willing to appoint qualified Catholics to government office, he was determined to 'appoint the best man to all the offices in . . . [his] gift'. Naas also pointed to Irish Conservative success at the elections as proof of the correctness of the policies pursued by him and Eglinton.[94] Eglinton cautioned Disraeli not to accept Bowyer's calculation of Independent Party support, arguing that the number could not be more 'than ten at the outside'. He also warned him of the dangers of alienating Irish Conservatives by giving government patronage to Roman Catholics who had previously been 'decidedly opposed' to the party. The party's long period in opposition meant that its supporters were naturally anxious for office and Eglinton believed that it would not be wise to disappoint them to too great an extent. While willing to give advancement to 'moderate . . . [and] respectable' Roman Catholics, he warned that 'to go farther than that' would risk losing 'many more votes' than that policy would gain.[95]

A similar line was taken by Whiteside, who told Disraeli 'not to imagine (for it would be a delusion) that the party which . . . [could] alone sustain us in Ireland was any other than the Conservative Party'. While he had 'no prejudices', he did have 'convictions'. These would not prevent him from supporting the granting of office to qualified 'Roman Catholic gentlemen . . . who had not actually assailed the government'. He had supported the decision to promote Coppinger and reminded Disraeli that it was on his advice that the Irish administration had decided against appointing Rickard Deasy, a prominent Irish Liberal, as a judge in the Landed Estates Court. In that instance, Whiteside conceded, Disraeli's advice had been correct, 'as there was not 'a more active partizan [*sic*] in the House or out of it against us than the same Deasy'. The 'draw[ing] in of Roman Catholics' had to be done 'with judgement' or it might have disastrous effects on the position of the Conservative Party in Ireland. Like Naas, he referred to the 'incredible exertions' undertaken by Irish Conservatives at the elections and suggested the fact that they had won an overall majority there was a vindication of the conduct of the Irish administration.

However, Whiteside's argument that the elections represented an Irish Conservative victory over 'priestcraft'[96] was criticised, in strong terms, by Disraeli. Rather than looking at the elections in this light, Disraeli had hoped that Irish Roman Catholic priesthood had been 'somewhat on our [the Conservatives] side' at the elections. He also expressed his belief that 'the time had gone by' for Irish Conservatives to speak of them 'in this vein'.[97] In 1865, Lord Stanley recorded in his diary that Disraeli had 'long detested'[98] Whiteside on political grounds, an attitude reflected in this letter to Naas. Disraeli's attitude to Whiteside also reflected the fact that, throughout this period, many of the senior leaders of the party in Britain, notably Disraeli himself and Lord Stanley, were more moderate in their opinions on religious questions than were the majority of Irish Conservatives, and indeed, the bulk of the party as a whole.

The Irish administration responded to Disraeli's entreaties by promoting Coppinger to a more senior appointment and giving Sir Colman O'Loghlen, a member of a prominent Roman Catholic family, the Chairmanship of County Mayo. Eglinton also offered a vacant judgeship in the Bankruptcy Court to John Howley, who refused the offer. Even these minor appointments, however, caused an outcry in the Irish Conservative press. O'Loghlen's promotion was, the *Daily Express* commented, 'one of those deep seated mysteries which plain honest men cannot pretend to explain'. Describing O'Loghlen as a 'Radical', the *Express* accused the government of having abandoned 'principle, consistency, character and conscience' in the search for parliamentary support.[99] This characterisation of O'Loghlen as a 'Radical' was hardly accurate, as even Eglinton described him as 'a fit & respectable man though politically opposed to us',[100] while Napier believed that his appointment was 'by far the most popular promotion we could make in the Dizzy [Disraeli] direction'.[101] The Irish Conservative press also linked these appointments with the possibility of further concessions to Irish Roman Catholic opinion by the government. During the elections, Bowyer had claimed that the government was intent on dealing with the question of the charter and this assertion had been taken up by the Conservative press in Ireland. In particular, these journals were concerned that the government would trade the granting of a charter to the Catholic University for short-term support. On 3 June, the *Dublin Evening Mail* warned of 'how deeply injurious to the stability of a professedly Conservative Ministry' such a course would be.[102] The ultra-Protestant newspaper *The Warder* went further in arguing that if the 'Newman seminary' were given a charter, 'the Protestant public would indignantly hurl the cabinet from their place, even though they had little hope of getting better men in the room of the expelled'.[103]

The government responded to these criticisms through a reply that Derby gave to a parliamentary question from Lord Shaftesbury. In it, he categorically denied that the government had any intention of granting a charter to the Catholic University.[104] Prior to making this statement, Derby had received a letter from Walpole, outlining his involvement with the issue. During his visit to Ireland in October 1858, it had been decided at a meeting between Naas, Eglinton and himself that 'it was out of the question' for the government to 'grant such a charter'. They had agreed that such a step 'would be totally contrary to the policy pursued in Ireland for 20 years – namely the policy of joint [united] education and that our party was ... the last party which ought to consider it'. Walpole believed this to be the end of the matter and had been disturbed 'to hear from so many quarters' that some intimation had been given by government members to the contrary.[105] The implication here was that these intimations had been made by another member of the government, probably Disraeli. By the time Derby made his statement in the Lords, the government's hold on political power was very precarious and he may well have believed that, under these circumstances, there was no advantage to be gained in alienating Irish Conservative opinion.

In any case, the Conservative Party scarcely had the parliamentary strength to carry a measure on the subject in the House of Commons. Three days previously, a meeting held at the Willis's Rooms in London had signalled a reconciliation between Lord Palmerston and Lord John Russell. This meeting further diminished the government's prospects of survival and, on 11 June, it was defeated in a division on its proposed Reform Bill. Despite Derby's statement, a number of Independent Party MPs supported the government on this occasion, but given the Liberal Party's superior numbers, this was not enough to save it. Derby was succeeded as Prime Minister by Palmerston, who went on, unexpectedly, to hold office for the next six years.

The defeat of the government was not regretted by all Conservatives. Shortly after its defeat, Napier wrote to Walpole that he was 'better pleased' that the party should have lost office than that it should be 'reduced to a mendicant dependence on men who had no sympathy with the Conservative cause'. This appears to have been a reference to Independent Party MPs, particularly as Napier went on to argue that the Conservatives 'might by imprudent concessions made to secure support... [have] eaten in upon... [their] moral capital – and damaged the best interests of the great cause... [they had in charge'. While he would 'not name names', Napier conceded 'that there were in the late cabinet men, whom... [he] would not follow in the field as leaders' of the party. The party's strength, Napier maintained, was 'moral' or it was 'nothing' and he could not be a party to any 'barter[ing] away of any of the great principles, which... [were] the elements of Conservative life'. Napier's distrust of what he saw as opportunism on Disraeli's part comes through clearly here. Napier concluded by hoping that the Conservatives would regard 'the responsible duties of 'being in opposition as something higher than the manoeuvres of faction'.[106] Again, the suggestion here was that, unless persuaded by party opinion to change course, Disraeli would continue to seek alliances in quarters distrusted by 'Protestant' opinion. Napier would certainly not have been reassured by a letter that Disraeli wrote to Sir George Bowyer shortly after the fall of the government. In the letter, Disraeli thanked Bowyer for 'the valuable and truly independent support' he had given the Conservative government during its period in office. He also requested Bowyer to 'convey' to Wiseman his sense of 'the generous and courageous manner in which . . . [he] accorded us his assistance'.[107] This letter showed that Disraeli still hoped to win support against the Palmerston government from both Irish and English Roman Catholic MPs in the House of Commons.

The years between 1860 and 1865 proved frustrating ones for the Conservative Party. Palmerston's position as a Liberal Prime Minister who, in terms of domestic policy, was closer to the Conservatives than to many of his own party members was a central reason for these difficulties. On a number of occasions in these years, it was the Conservative Party that kept Palmerston in office, when his position was threatened by the Radical wing of his own party. The situation in Italy in these years did, however, allow Disraeli to cement his tentative alliance with Independent Irish Party and English Roman Catholic MPs. Ultimately, however, this alliance rested on slight foundations. It was Palmerston's peculiar combination of inertia on the domestic front combined with an active foreign policy, which allowed it to develop in the manner that it did. So long as he remained in office, it was clear that the Church of Ireland would remain free from serious attack and that reform of parliament would remain a low priority. Both of these issues had the potential to break up the elements within this 'alliance', but while they remained in abeyance this informal alliance was able to co-operate on issues of common concern in parliament. Disraeli's lack of sympathy with Italian nationalism, and his support for the Pope's retention of at least part of his temporal dominions, had also increased his popularity with sections of Irish and English Roman Catholic opinion. Inevitably, however, these very stances further increased Irish Conservative suspicions of him.

These suspicions were increased in late February 1860 when, largely at John Pope Hennessey's prompting, Lord Campden contested the Cork County by-election against Rickard Deasy, the newly appointed Irish Attorney General. Campden's election address bore clear signs of Hennessey's influence. In it, he described the Whigs as 'the avowed enemies of the Holy See', who 'wished to despoil the Holy Father of his temporal possessions'. Campden, however, wished to see these 'preserved for him [the Pope] in all their integrity'. His address condemned the Liberal government for its support of the National Education system in Ireland, arguing that this ran contrary to the wishes of the Roman Catholic hierarchy. The general tone of the contest was exemplified by Hennessey's criticism of Deasy for having failed 'to go to any meetings held for expressing sympathy' with the Pope.[108] Campden's position as a convert to Roman Catholicism, however, made him a suspect figure to Irish Conservative opinion. *The Irish Times* advised Conservative voters in Cork to remain neutral in the contest, although it expressed the opinion that Campden was even 'less acceptable' than Deasy.[109] The *Dublin Evening Mail* went further, describing Campden as coming forward 'professedly, as the champion of [the] Pope against [the] Queen'. Conservatives should, the *Mail* concluded, support Deasy against Campden, who was 'the devoted servant of Roman agents in Ireland'.[110] This ill-conceived venture ended in Deasy's being returned by a majority of more than 2,000 votes. Campden did not succeed in winning over enough Catholic or Conservative support to carry the contest, and, in the event, probably alienated both groups.

The result of the election revealed the difficulties involved in holding together a coalition of such disparate elements as the Conservative–Independent Party 'alliance' represented. Later in the year, Cardinal Cullen described Hennessey's behaviour at the election as 'strange'. He could not understand how Hennessey could contemplate a reconciliation between Catholics and 'that wicked faction so hostile to all our interests'.[111] Cullen's distrust of Hennessey was shared by Disraeli, who later described him as a 'slippery customer'.[112] He also criticised his conduct of the Cork election, claiming that this resulted in 'the greatest fiasco on record: not only losing a seat that might have been won', but almost ruining Campden 'by the wildest, most reckless . . . [and] most foolish expenditure, in wh[ich]. a candidate was ever involved'.[113] Nevertheless, despite this, Disraeli continued to use Hennessey as a channel of communication with the Roman Catholic hierarchy and the Independent Party up until the latter's loss of his seat in the general election of 1865.

Despite his criticisms of Hennessey's actions, Disraeli remained sufficiently convinced of the political advantages to be gained from the 'ultramontane alliance' to make informal approaches to Wiseman through Ralph Earle, his private secretary. Earle visited Wiseman in Rome in April 1861 and reported back to Disraeli that the Cardinal had promised 'to do all in his power' to aid the Conservatives. Wiseman told Earle that there was 'a very good feeling' towards the party in Ireland as a result of its policy towards Italy. This had convinced some Irish Liberal MPs, who had rejected Wiseman's 'invitation' to support the Conservatives in 1859, to hold out hopes that they might eventually do so. He advised Earle that, both for his importance within the Irish Liberal Party and for ' his great influence with the Irish bishops and clergy', William Monsell was a key figure for the Conservatives to win over. Along with Hennessey and Bowyer, both of whom already voted with the Conservatives, Monsell could play a vital role in winning over MPs hesitant to break with the Liberal Party.

In any case, Wiseman assured Earle that Disraeli was 'quite right in looking to the R[oman] C[atholic]s for . . . [his] majority', as they were in a position to provide it. If, Wiseman insisted, a Conservative government could be formed 'that would carry out a respectable foreign policy', it would be supported by the Roman Catholic MPs in the House of Commons.[114] Although Monsell occasionally showed his dissatisfaction with the government's foreign policy by abstaining from divisions on it, his primary loyalty remained with the Liberal Party, and he never came close to giving the Conservatives the consistent support that Bowyer had done. Nevertheless, on some parliamentary votes during the period between 1859 and 1865 the Conservatives succeeded in drawing a number of Irish Liberal MPs away from the government's ranks. Their most notable success in this direction was in a division on the Schleswig- Holstein question in July 1864, when the bulk of the Irish Catholic MPs voted with the party and Palmerston's government survived by only eighteen votes.[115]

The hostility felt by Irish Conservative opinion to the Papacy meant that they felt considerable enthusiasm for the prospect of Italian unification. This enthusiasm led Irish Conservatives to feel considerable disquiet at the foreign policy being pursued by Derby and Disraeli. One concerned supporter of the party wrote to Donoughmore in February 1861, complaining that its leaders were cutting 'their own throats...by running counter to the all but unanimous feeling of England [*sic*] respecting the noble struggle, now being made for freedom' in Italy.[116] In early 1862 Whiteside warned Disraeli of the danger to the Conservative Party of being associated with an 'illiberal foreign policy' or of being seen as wishing to uphold 'the Papal power'. Most Irish Conservatives were sympathetic at heart to Palmerston's foreign policy and if they became convinced that the party's leaders did not support it, the divisions within the party might become serious. If Palmerston used the opportunity to try and win over elements within the Irish Conservative Party disillusioned by Derby's stance on Italy, Whiteside feared that he might, given time, 'split the party'.[117] A number of senior Conservatives, including Lord Stanley, believed that Palmerston had already decided on this course. The appointment of Sir Robert Peel, the son of the former Prime Minister, as Irish Chief Secretary earlier in the year had helped foster this suspicion. From the time of his appointment onward, Peel had engaged Cullen in a series of public controversies, a course which Stanley attributed to Palmerston's wish 'to break with the Catholic party ostentatiously and openly, in such a manner as to secure a considerable amount of Protestant opinion'. Stanley's opinion was that this 'device' would cost the government 'nothing' as it had already lost Catholic support through its Italian policy. Disraeli's 'coquetting with the Pope's party' had, Stanley concluded, given Palmerston this opportunity to assert the government's 'Protestant' credentials.[118]

In November 1861 Stanley himself alienated Irish Conservative opinion by describing the Church of Ireland as the Church of a 'very inconsiderable minority' of the Irish population. He admitted that he 'look[ed] forward with uneasiness and apprehension to the discussion which some day or other...[would] arise on ecclesiastical affairs' there.[119] This was the first occasion on which Stanley had publicly expressed his doubts about the 'permanent maintenance' of the Irish Church Establishment, and the speech raised considerable controversy in Ireland. Whiteside told Disraeli that Irish Protestants would 'infinitely prefer Palmerston' to continue in office than to see him replaced by 'any Ministry in which Stanley had influence'. He had also heard that 'Spooner...[and] his set...[had] expressed the same resolution at the National Club'.[120] *The Warder* argued that Stanley's speech together with Conservative co-operation with Independent Party MPs in parliament would only serve to increase the 'grave suspicions' of the party leadership felt by Irish Conservatives.[121]

Throughout the parliamentary session of 1862, Irish Conservative newspapers regularly denounced what they described as the 'Ultramontane alliance'. These attacks were coupled with praise for Palmerston's foreign policy, with *The Warder* going so far as to describe the government as 'safe a one as the Protestant public could have at present'.[122] In a similar vein the *Daily Express* contended that the Conservatives would have to 'shake off the Ultamontane alliance, before they...[could] again be intrusted [*sic*] with the reins of government'. It went on to praise Palmerston as a complete 'man of the people – so popular and yet so aristocratic –, so liberal and yet so Conservative, – thoroughly tolerant while earnestly Protestant'. So long as the Conservative leaders embraced 'the temporal sovereignty of the Pope' and opposed 'the freedom of Italy' the *Daily Express* would favour Palmerston's continuance in office.[123]

These criticisms reached a more sustained pitch in April 1863 when Disraeli, Derby and a number of other senior Conservatives, including Lord John Manners and Sir John Wilson-Patten, voted for a government measure, which granted salaries to chaplains attending Roman Catholic prisoners. Replying to a request from Lord Campden to support the bill, Disraeli told him he would do so as it was conceived 'in the spirit of the policy of the late [Conservative] government'. However, he went on, his attempts to pursue a conciliatory policy towards Roman Catholics had been rendered more difficult by 'the systematic hostility always shown by the Catholic members of the House of Commons to the Church of England'. He cited their support for the abolition of Church rates as evidence of this. If, he suggested, Catholic members abstained in divisions on such issues, there would no longer be any 'difficulties' involved in introducing measures like the Prison Ministers Bill. If the Catholic and Protestant members combined together on religious issues, Disraeli believed that the 'following' of no-Popery advocates like Newdegate 'would sink into insignificance'.[124] In the event, only nine Irish Conservatives voted against the measure, a fact seized on by the Conservative press as evidence of the corrupting nature of the 'Ultramontane alliance'. *The Warder* stressed the failure of senior Irish

Conservatives like Naas, Whiteside and Taylor to vote in the division, informing its readers that their failure to do so had displayed 'the utter untrustworthiness, the hollow-heartedness and wretched pliancy, of that clique of...politicians who...[had] entered with...Disraeli into the immoral compact with Rome'.[125]

Soon after this vote, Lewis Llewelyn Dillwyn, the Radical MP for Swansea, who was a Quaker himself, introduced a motion, calling for the appointment of a select committee to inquire if 'the present endowments for religious purposes throughout Ireland...[could] be so amended as most to conduce to the welfare of all classes of Her Majesty's Irish subjects'.[126] Prior to the debate on this motion, Napier wrote to Disraeli, suggesting that if the Conservatives presented a strong front against it, this would undermine the 'suspicion [Napier found] rife everywhere' that Conservative leaders were 'prepared to compromise the interests of...Protestants for [the sake of] an Ultramontane alliance'. From this point of view, it was important, Napier believed, that Disraeli should take 'a leading part' in the debates on the motion. If he were to put up 'a good resistance to this [motion]', as an attack on the United Church, to be met with a flat negative', this 'would be of much service to you [Disraeli] with many influential and intelligent men in Ireland'. It would also have the effect of neutralising the criticisms made of his leadership by the Irish Conservative press. While Napier was not opposed to reform of the Church of Ireland designed to make it more efficient and to 'remedy a few local anomalies', he considered Dillwyn's ultimate objective to be disestablishment and disendowment, and, hence, believed that the motion should be vigorously opposed.[127]

The language of Dillwyn's motion was notably ambiguous and was designed to attract support from a wide range of opinion within the House, from those who supported disestablishment to those who merely wished to see a re-allocation of resources within the Church of Ireland. Dillwyn himself believed that 'the time had come when a great change should be made in...the temporalities of the Irish Church' and he criticised the Liberal government for its failure to address the issue. He maintained that, as a missionary Church, the Irish Church had been a 'signal failure' and quoted Disraeli's celebrated description of it as an 'alien Church' in support of this argument.[128] Despite Napier's entreaties, Disraeli did not take part in the debate.

The main speaker on the Conservative side was Whiteside, who argued that any interference with the parochial system of the Established Church would give the Roman Catholic Church, with 'its organization, its missionaries, its priests, its friars and its Jesuits,'[129] free rein in large parts of Ireland. While categorically opposing Dillwyn's motion, Whiteside also disapproved of an amendment to it tabled by Digby Seymour, another

Liberal MP. Seymour proposed the setting up of a Royal Commission to inquire into the revenues of the Established Church in Ireland and to suggest ways in which clerical incomes there could be more equitably distributed. Seymour's scheme involved the dissolution of parishes where Church membership fell below a certain level and the amalgamation of parishes which, while above this level, were too small to employ the services of a full-time clergyman. Whiteside believed that the ends sought by Seymour could best be achieved in other ways than through 'a Royal Commission invested with prodigious powers – it might be for good, it might be for mischief'. It would be difficult, Whiteside argued, to ensure that the members of the commission would be 'friends' of the Church of Ireland who had not formed 'a preconceived idea of the existence of a surplus'. If they had done so, then it was likely that the commission's findings might undermine the parochial system of the Church and pave the way for further attacks on its endowments. Whiteside considered the presence of Protestant clergymen in parishes throughout Ireland as vital to the maintenance of the Church of Ireland's claims to be a 'national' Church. He was worried that an abandonment of this principle would prove fatal, in the long term, to the existence of the Church Establishment in Ireland. He was also concerned that the defence of the Church of Ireland should be based on 'high principle... principles interwoven with the monarchy, with the Constitution, with the maintenance of religious truth, and with the settlement of property in these Kingdoms' rather than on considerations of expediency.[130]

After this debate was adjourned, Dillwyn withdrew his motion in favour of one in a similar vein, brought forward by Ralph Bernal Osborne, for the appointment of a select committee 'into the ecclesiastical settlement in Ireland'. As Whiteside had predicted, Osborne recommended the substitution of a 'congregational' for the parochial system of organisation of the Church of Ireland.[131] Under this system, the distribution of parishes would be based on the number of Anglicans living in a particular area. This left open the possibility of some districts being left without a resident clergyman other than the local Catholic priest. Under this scheme, the status of the Church would be directly related to the numbers of its members, a suggestion strongly opposed by senior Irish Conservatives. While willing to see a 're-adjustment' of ecclesiastical incomes in the Church of Ireland, Sir Hugh Cairns, like Whiteside, stressed his complete opposition to the use of Church funds for any purpose other than those for which they had originally been intended. Cairns argued that where clerical incomes were disproportionate to the work undertaken, the incomes should be reduced and the remainder distributed among other parishes.[132] For many supporters of Osborne's motion, however, the ultimate goal was the reduction of the endowments given to the Church of Ireland and the use of any surplus funds left over from this for objectives decided upon by the government itself.[133]

Although it did not succeed in its objectives, Dillwyn's motion did provide a pointer towards future events. It encouraged the development of an alliance between Irish Roman Catholics and Nonconformists in Britain against the Established Church in Ireland, an alliance that was to bear fruit in the formation of the National Association later in the year. Having realised that the disestablishment of the Church of England was unlikely to be attained in the foreseeable future, Nonconformist organisations such as the Liberation Society began to see the Established Church in Ireland as being far more vulnerable to attack. Under the centralised leadership of Cullen, the Roman Catholic Church was also in a strong position to launch a concerted assault on the position of its main rival in Ireland.

In these circumstances, some senior members of the Church of Ireland began to believe that it would be wise to pre-empt future attacks on its position by putting forward their own schemes for reform. In late 1863 the Irish bishops devised a scheme, along the lines of that earlier proposed by Cairns, to be submitted to Lord Palmerston, providing for the transfer of income from the more affluent parishes to poorer ones. The proposals also included provisions for the suppression of a number of deaneries and a reduction in the number of cathedrals, which were 'cathedrals in name only', held by the Church of Ireland. Given the divisions within his cabinet and in the Liberal Party generally on the question, Palmerston refused to bring the bishops' measure before parliament.[134] The bishops also sought Derby's approval for their suggestions, but he advised extreme caution in raising the issue of Church endowments. He was particularly concerned at the bishops' recommendation that a number of parishes, particularly in the North of Ireland, should be unified. The principal motivation behind this was to raise the income of clerics in those parishes whose income was below that of their southern counterparts. Like Whiteside, Derby believed that to take such a step would undermine one of 'the essential characteristics' of a 'national' Church, that was the existence of a parochial structure covering the entire country. Derby believed that to retreat from this principle would undermine the foundation of the Established Church in Ireland.[135]

The dilemma posed for the Irish hierarchy, however, was to reconcile the 'high' view of the role of the Church taken by Derby and Whiteside with the reality of their minority position within Ireland. Their very willingness to suggest measures for the reform of the Establishment indicated that they were aware that it had become necessary to defend the scale of their endowments and the manner in which they were distributed. Although it was clear that their position was not under immediate threat for as long as Palmerston remained Prime Minister, it was the question of what would happen after he left office that disturbed the supporters of the Irish establishment.

In an attempt to capitalise on the growing anti-establishment sentiment among Nonconformists in Britain, a new Irish political organisation, the National Association, was founded at a public meeting in Dublin in late 1864. This meeting was attended by Archbishop Cullen and by a number of leading Irish Catholic MPs, including John Francis Maguire and William Monsell. The meeting also received a message of support from John Bright, a Nonconformist himself, who was the leading Radical politician in Britain. The objectives of the association were declared to be the disestablishment of the Church of Ireland, the promotion of denominational education there and the introduction of a comprehensive measure of land reform. Cullen saw the association as providing a forum for moderate Catholic opinion and a means of strengthening the links between the Roman Catholic Church and Liberals in Britain. Although the association proved, at best, only moderately successful, its very existence was perceived as a threat by Irish Conservative opinion.[136] Writing to Derby, Whiteside insisted that 'the movement of the Papal Legate [Cullen] ... [and] his followers against the very existence of the Established Church in this country' rendered it imperative that the Conservatives should 'liberate ourselves unequivocally from all connection with the party who advocate these Papal doctrines'. He contended that Conservative Party supporters in Ireland and the rest of Britain would brook no 'hesitation' upon the subject. If the Established Church were disendowed, he warned that England's hold over Ireland, which was dependent upon Irish Protestants, would 'be lost for ever'.[137] Whiteside was arguing here for a clear line to be drawn between the Conservative Party and those Catholic MPs such as Bowyer and Maguire who continued to support it on occasion. In this respect, John Pope Hennessey was in an even more equivocal position, as a Conservative who had been in regular close contact with many of the MPs involved in the association.

Under these circumstances, the tabling in March 1865 by Dillwyn of a motion, describing the state of the Church of Ireland as 'unsatisfactory' and calling on the government to devote its 'early attention' to the question, took on a more threatening aspect in Irish Conservative eyes.[138] On 10 March, Derby reported to Disraeli on a meeting he had had with Cairns and Whiteside. They had stressed their anxiety that 'the debate on our [the Conservative Party] side should not be confined to the Irish members; but that some of our leading English members should take a part' in it. This request was, no doubt, based on their experience of earlier debates on the topic. Derby's own opinion was that the motion should be 'resisted to the uttermost'. This conclusion was based on his belief that 'the abolition of the Established Church would be fatal' to English rule in Ireland and 'an injury to Ireland itself'. He also believed that the attack on the Irish Church was a prelude to a concerted attack on the Church of England. Any 'slackness' on the Conservatives' part with regard to this question would, Derby contended, lose the party 'a large amount of Protestant support in Ireland without gaining us any from the R[oman] Catholics'. Derby pointedly suggested that the debate on Dillwyn's motion would provide a 'not unfitting occasion' for Disraeli to end his 'profound silence' of the parliamentary session up to that point.[139]

A second approach to Disraeli to take part in the debate was made by Napier. This appeal reflected the anxiety felt by Irish Conservatives that senior English Conservatives should speak in the debate. Napier stressed the importance of not dealing with the issue 'as a mere Irish squabble about the Irish Church but on its own merits as a movement of dissent and democracy against a religious Establishment and a landed gentry'. The campaign against the Church of Ireland had, Napier maintained, 'originated in England'. He saw it as the first step in a campaign by the advanced Liberals to undermine the established institutions of that country. Dillwyn's motion was cleverly devised to separate the Church of Ireland 'from the United Church' and leave it open to a 'local assault' with the ultimate objective of disestablishment. This was, in Napier's opinion, 'a fraud upon the treaty of Union' which had guaranteed equal treatment to the established Churches in both England and Ireland. Napier stressed his conviction that 'English government' could not be maintained in Ireland 'without the Established Church' and 'that any betrayal of it would alienate…Protestant feeling' in both England and Ireland. He conceded that there was a necessity to soften 'the antagonism of the Churches [in Ireland] by encouraging toleration and co-operation'. For his part, he believed that the Church of Ireland had exhibited too much 'polemical bitterness… [and] Puritan exclusiveness' in the past, while he accused the Catholic Church of being overly 'Papal and Ultramontane'. The comparatively moderate tenor of these remarks may have been due to Napier's clash with the more extreme Irish Protestants on the issue of national education, which we discussed earlier. He concluded by stressing his support for any concessions to the Catholic Church, which were 'just and liberal' and would leave the status of the Established Church unaffected.[140]

Prior to the debate on Dillwyn's motion a rumour circulated Westminster that the government was going to support it. The credibility of this rumour was enhanced by the suspicion that leading members of the government, including Gladstone, the Chancellor of the Exchequer, and Sir George Grey, the Home Secretary, were unhappy with the condition of the Church of Ireland. These reports led Stanley to approach Sir Charles Wood, the Secretary for India, to ascertain what the government's intentions were with regard to the motion. Wood denied there was any truth in these suggestions and confessed that the cabinet had not 'even . . . seriously discussed' it. His personal conviction was that the 'Irish Establishment [was] an abomination' but at the same time he believed that the political risks involved meant that it 'would be madness . . . [to] meddle with it'. However, he told Stanley that he could not say 'what Gladstone might or might not do' on the question.[141] Wood was not the only member of the cabinet who was concerned with what Gladstone's stance on the issue might be. Palmerston himself wrote to Gladstone, warning him of the dangers of expressing his individual opinions on such a question while still a member of the government.[142]

Despite the appeals made by Derby and Napier, Disraeli did not take part in the debate. The most notable speech made by a senior English Conservative was that made by Gathorne Hardy, who had been an Under-Secretary for the Home Department in the 1858–59 Conservative government. Since that time Hardy had developed a considerable reputation as a parliamentary speaker and as a strong defender of the Established Church. Hardy's speech gave a robust defence of the position of the Church of Ireland, repeating many of the arguments put forward on previous occasions by Irish Conservatives. Like them, Hardy defended it as upholding the 'tenets' and carrying out the 'views of the primitive Church' in Ireland. In his belief, the essence of the parochial system of the Church of Ireland was that Irish Protestants should be able 'to find in every parish or place a pastor and a church, and the means of grace in connection with the Established Church'. Hardy contended that this right was common to Church members in both England and Ireland, 'for it was upon that basis' of the equality between the Churches that Irish Protestants had assented to the Union. To alter that arrangement after Ireland had lost its 'national Parliament' would be 'unreasonable and unfair'. Through this speech, Hardy identified himself as the leading English Conservative defender of the Irish Church establishment, a position he maintained in the years that followed.

An equally significant pointer to the future came in Gladstone's speech on the motion. Although Gladstone declared that the government did not 'concur' with Dillwyn's motion, he did not contest the accuracy of the latter's assertion that the state of the Church of Ireland was 'unsatisfactory'. He also repeated Dillwyn's criticisms of the Irish Church for its failings as a missionary Church. The anomalous position of being an Established Church, which served only a minority of the Irish population had, in Gladstone's opinion, hindered rather than helped it in this role.[143] Earlier in the year, Gladstone had told Robert Phillimore that he was no longer loyal to the 'Irish Church . . . as an Establishment' and this was the essential thrust of his speech in the debate.[144] However, he was careful to point out that he viewed the question of the future of the Established Church as one which could only be settled after careful consideration. It was, for the time being at least, outside the scope of practical politics.

This assertion was picked up on by Whiteside, who coupled it with recent statements made by Gladstone on the reform question, as evidence that he was laying

> the foundation[s] of another scheme, a policy of another and not very distant day, when he [Gladstone] might be able to say the time had come and a change of feeling had been provoked out of doors that would enable him to do then what he now fears to do.

Whiteside found it significant that he had not defended the Church of Ireland on grounds either of 'principle' or of 'conviction'. Essentially, he maintained, Gladstone's tone had been 'hostile' to the Irish 'branch' of the Established Church, leaving open only the question of when the right time would come to attack it. It had laid down 'the seeds of...[the] future policy' which would be pursued once Palmerston had left the political arena. Whiteside was especially aggrieved that Gladstone, as 'the author of a book in defence of [the connection between] the Church and state', should have spoken in such a fashion.[145]

Reporting on the debate, the *Dublin Evening Mail* commented that Gladstone's speech had shown him to be a 'most dangerous enemy' of the Church of Ireland. The speech had, the paper claimed, been motivated by Gladstone's desire to win Radical support in order to boost his campaign to succeed Palmerston as Prime Minister.[146] A similar claim was made by Whiteside soon after the debate. He argued that by his criticisms of the Irish Church, Gladstone had placed himself at the head of a 'numerous and active party' whose ultimate ambition was to 'level' the establishment in both Ireland and England 'in the dust'. Given Gladstone's 'great abilities, high position and surpassing eloquence', Whiteside considered him an extremely dangerous adversary. To counter this new threat, he called for unity among Irish Protestants in order to 'safeguard...their liberties'.[147] Behind these exchanges lay a growing sense among members of both parties that Palmerston's retirement from political office, when it came, would open up a whole range of possibilities which had been suppressed so long as he remained in office. This allowed Irish Conservatives to revive the 'Church in danger' cry, which had fallen into disuse during the heyday of Palmerston's administration.

The Irish Protestants' sense of being under attack was reinforced in March 1865, when William Monsell brought forward a motion calling for the revision of the oath taken by Roman Catholic MPs. Monsell wanted to remove those parts of the oath unacceptable to Roman Catholic opinion. These objectionable provisions included those, noted above, which pledged Catholic MPs not to take any steps to weaken the position of the

Established Church or overturn the settlement of land in Ireland. Although Monsell did not suggest an alternative form of oath, both Whiteside and Anthony Lefroy, his colleague as MP for Dublin University, accused him of seeking to modify it in order to clear 'the way for an attack on the Established Church'.[148] They linked Monsell's motion and Dillwyn's motion together as being part of a concerted plan to undermine the 'Protestant' character of the British constitution. Whiteside warned that he would give 'the most unqualified resistance' both 'in...and out' of Parliament to any attempts to re-open 'the Catholic question', as it had been settled in 1829.[149]

On 19 May, Monsell succeeded in having his bill read a second time in the House of Commons. The effect of this vote, with the deletion of those clauses Monsell had wished to see discarded, was to transform the oath into a simple pledge of allegiance to the Monarch and to the Protestant succession. The Conservative response to this defeat was to seek to amend Monsell's bill by restoring that section of the oath relating to the Established Church and to the settlement of property. According to Cairns, by taking away the 'impediment' posed by their oath, Roman Catholic MPs had been left 'perfectly free...to subvert the Church Establishment if they please[d]' to do so. It was also necessary to realise, he contended, that those sections of the oath not only guaranteed the preservation of the Church Establishment in Ireland but also referred to the Church of England. To undermine one would, of necessity, be to undermine the other.[150]

However, the Conservative amendment to the bill was defeated by nineteen votes in a thinly attended House of Commons, with a number of Conservatives, including John Pope Hennessey, Samuel Dickson, the MP for Limerick, and Crofton Vandeleur, the MP for Clare, opposing it. Dickson and Vandeleur sat for predominantly Catholic constituencies, and this may have influenced their votes on this occasion. Despite the bill's successful passage through the House of Commons, Derby was able to secure its defeat in the House of Lords. While he was prepared to accept an alteration of the oath which would leave intact 'the security provided for the Established Church in Ireland', Derby was not prepared to accept the proposed changes. The removal of those securities would, he believed, 'open the door to serious attacks' upon the Church. It was already clear to Derby, from the statements made by the National Association and by the MPs associated with it, that a concerted campaign along these lines was being planned. Given these circumstances and with a general election pending, it was not the time 'to leave the walls of the fortress absolutely undefended'.[151] Derby's prestige in the Lords was such that the bill was defeated by twenty-one votes, with a considerable number of Irish Conservative peers voting in the division.[152]

The general election of July 1865 left the parties in much the same position as they had been before it was called. While the Conservatives had lost ground in Ireland from the high point of 1859, they still succeeded in returning forty-seven MPs there. As in 1859, the Dublin University seat was contested by a Liberal, but on this occasion the party's candidate, John Thomas Ball, was a confidante of Marcus Beresford, the Primate of the Church of Ireland. Ball's campaign was particularly directed against Anthony Lefroy, a sitting Conservative MP, who rarely attended the House or spoke in debates. While Whiteside was confident that Lefroy would retain the seat, he told Derby that many Church of Ireland clergymen had come to see support for Palmerston as a route to clerical preferment. He was concerned that this did not bode well for Conservative prospects, particularly as Palmerston also controlled patronage of a more secular kind. Unless the Conservatives could show reasonable prospects of a return to office, it would be difficult for the country gentry, 'unrequited ... [and] unacknowledged', to continue to support them.[153] Although some commentators have seen Palmerston's attempts to win over Irish Protestant support as misguided,[154] the tone of Whiteside's comments on this occasion show clearly that he feared this strategy was working and, that given time, it would pose a serious threat to the party's position in Ireland.

Ball based his campaign for the Dublin University seat on the argument that the future of the Church of Ireland would be safer in Palmerston's hands than it was in Derby's. He contrasted Palmerston's support for the Church of Ireland with the failure of both Disraeli and Stanley to speak in its defence in any of the debates on its position over the previous two years. Referring to his vote against Church rates, Ball asked Whiteside if he could vouch for Stanley's 'friendship for any ecclesiastical establishment'.[155] Whiteside responded to such attacks by praising Palmerston 'for the political dexterity' with which he had 'disappointed the expectations of those who brought him into power and baffled the designs of his colleagues' with regard to parliamentary reform and the Church of Ireland. This 'system of management' could not, however, last much longer and 'a contest of principles must ensue'. In this contest, Whiteside contended, the opposing parties would be 'the great Conservative Party ... the sure defence of the Church, the Constitution and the Throne' and the Radical section of the Liberal Party, led by Gladstone, which threatened to undermine all three institutions. Whiteside feared that, under pressure from this group within the party, the disestablishment of the Irish Church would eventually become Liberal government policy. A vote for Ball would thus, Whiteside argued, only serve to weaken the position of the Irish Church Establishment.[156] After a sharply fought contest, Whiteside and Lefroy were re-elected, this election campaign providing the last example of Palmerston's attempt to draw away Protestant voters from the Irish Conservative Party.

Palmerston's death, three months after the election, dramatically altered the political landscape. He was succeeded as Prime Minister by Lord John Russell, whose attempts to introduce a Reform Bill split the Liberal Party. These divisions resulted in the government's measure being defeated in the House of Commons and the subsequent formation of a Conservative government under Derby in June 1866. As with the previous governments of 1852 and 1858–59, it was a minority one, dependent upon support from other parties in the House of Commons for its survival. The 1866–68 Conservative government made a more concerted attempt to appeal to Irish Catholic opinion than any earlier Conservative administrations had done. An early indication of this was given when, at Disraeli's instigation, Whiteside was passed over for the position of Irish Lord Chancellor. To soften this blow, he was offered the purely legal position of Lord Chief Justice, which, after some initial reluctance, he accepted.[157] Disraeli had hoped to give the Lord Chancellorship to the more moderate Abraham Brewster, a one-time Peelite who had been Irish Attorney General under Lord Aberdeen. The rumour of Brewster's appointment, however, created an outcry among Irish Conservatives and the appointment was given on an interim basis to Francis Blackburne, who had held the office in the 1852 government. Brewster eventually replaced Blackburne in the post in March 1867. Napier, who had not sat in Parliament since 1859, was also given a judicial post, but resigned soon afterwards when his partial deafness caused controversy.[158] Of the senior Irish Conservative politicians of the 1852–66 period, only Naas, always a moderate in Irish Conservative terms, held office in the government. Indeed, in its moderation and in its attempts to conciliate Roman Catholic opinion, the Irish administration of 1866–68 bore the imprint of Naas' political personality to a far greater extent than had the earlier Conservative governments of 1852 and 1858–59.

The change in the nature of the government's Irish appointments was clearly shown in July 1866 when Michael Morris, a Roman Catholic and former Liberal, was appointed as Irish Solicitor General. The government also attempted to win over Irish Catholic opinion by such concessions as granting a charter to the Catholic University, the introduction of a diluted version of Napier's land bills and by a vague, if subsequently withdrawn, hint that they were willing to consider some form of endowment for the Catholic Church.[159] It also sought to forestall Liberal Party attacks on the Church of Ireland by appointing a Royal Commission to inquire into the manner in which its property was distributed. It was imperative, argued John Thomas Ball, the newly appointed Irish Attorney General, that reform of the Church of Ireland should be 'undertaken by its friends . . . [and] not [by] its enemies'.[160] In fact, the commission's report, published in June 1869, resembled, in broad outline, the proposals drawn up by the Church of Ireland bishops in 1864. It recommended that the number of archbishoprics

JUSTICE -FOR IRELAND.

4. '*Justice for Ireland*': cartoon satirising Napier's appointment, given his partial deafness, as Irish Lord Justice of Appeal from *Punch*, 28 July 1866.

in the Established Church be reduced from two to one, that parishes across the country should be amalgamated, and that clerical incomes be reduced in localities with few Protestants. The report, however, proved to be too moderate for those who favoured disestablishment and too radical for the Church of Ireland clergy to accept.[161] In any case, its publication had been rendered largely academic in the wake of Gladstone's introduction in March 1868 of his celebrated resolutions on the position of the Church of Ireland. By raising the spectre of disestablishment, Gladstone effectively drove the Conservatives into a defensive posture in the election which followed and ended Disraeli's attempts to achieve a rapprochement with Irish Roman Catholics. It also rendered redundant the Conservative's belated attempts to achieve reform of the Church of Ireland from within.

The terms of the disestablishment settlement were surprisingly generous to the Church of Ireland. While 'technically expropriated',[162] the Irish Church was, in fact, substantially re-endowed. However, the real significance of disestablishment was symbolic, as a belief in the 'national' character of the Church of Ireland had been one of the central tenets of Irish Conservatism. Disestablishment had, however, decisively altered this status, as the Church of Ireland was, now, merely one among the competing Churches in Ireland. Its main rival for dominance in Ireland, the Roman Catholic Church, had steadily grown in discipline and coherence throughout the course of the nineteenth century. Under Cullen's centralised leadership, it was now a force to be dealt with and one that British governments were increasingly willing to conciliate. After 1868 Irish Conservative leaders became notably more moderate in their religious views than their predecessors, such as Napier and Whiteside, had been.

Gladstone followed disestablishment with the 1870 Land Act. This measure, though largely ineffective, paved the way for the more radical land bills of 1885 and 1903. The ultimate effect of these measures was to effect a revolution in Irish landownership, which ultimately led to the breakdown of landlord influence in the South of Ireland. This influence had been the backbone of the Irish Conservative Party's electoral strength there. Land-lord influence was to prove more resilient in Ulster where the Conservative Party retained a strong presence up to the 1880s. After 1885, the party there was subsumed into the Ulster Unionist party, which brought together a wide spectrum of pro-Union forces in the North of Ireland. Ulster Unionism, as it developed, was to have a visceral and populist character, quite unlike that of Irish Conservatism. This may have been related to the fact that it had the support of a strong urban working-class constituency in the North of Ireland. In the long run, Unionism there was able to garner support across class lines in a way that never had been achieved by Irish Conservatism. Like their Irish Conservative predecessors, however, Ulster

Unionist MPs often proved to be troublesome allies for their Conservative counterparts elsewhere in Britain.

NOTES

1 See Napier's lecture on 'The Irish difficulty' delivered in Dublin on 7 February 1865, quoted in Ewald, *The Life of Sir Joseph Napier* (2nd edn, London, 1892), p. 226. The classic work in this vein was J.H. Todd's *Saint Patrick, Apostle of Ireland: With an Introductory Dissertation on Some Early Usages of the Church in Ireland, and its Historical Position from the Establishment of the English Colony to the Present Day* (Dublin, 1864).

2 *Dublin Evening Mail*, 15 June 1864.

3 *Hansard*, CLXXVIII, 448.

4 Whiteside, *Essays and Lectures*, p. 475.

5 *National Club; A Report of Speeches Delivered at the Annual Meeting of the Members and Friends of the National Club held in the Club House, Whitehall, May 9, 1855* (London, 1855), p. 11.

6 *Hansard*, CII, 1429.

7 Napier's lecture on 'The Irish Difficulty' delivered in Dublin on 7 February 1865, quoted in Ewald, *Life and Letters of Sir Joseph Napier* (2nd edn, London, 1892), p. 231.

8 *Daily Express*, 1 September 1853.

9 *Daily Express*, 12 February 1859.

10 From a speech by Napier on 4 May 1848, *Hansard*, XCVIII, 640.

11 Gardiner (ed.), *Lectures, Essays and Letters*, p. 345.

12 *Daily Express*, 24 January 1854.

13 *Hansard*, CXXXI, 78–9.

14 *Hansard*, CXXXXI, 796–807. See also the *Daily Express*, 17 March 1854.

15 *Hansard*, CXXXXI, 809.

16 See *Hansard*, CXXIII, 842.

17 See the *Dublin Evening Mail*, 28 March 1854. See also the *Daily Express*, 16 May 1854.

18 Stanley diary, 5 May 1851, quoted in Vincent (ed.), *Disraeli, Derby and the Conservative Party*, p. 64.

19 See Wolffe, *The Protestant Crusade in Great Britain, 1829–1860*, pp. 269–71.

20 *Hansard*, CXXXIII, 852–4.

21 *Hansard*, CXXXIII, 915.

22 *Hansard*, CXXXIII, 940.

23 *Hansard*, CXXXIII, 903–7.

24 Quoted in Monypenny and Buckle, *Life of Benjamin Disraeli*, Vol. 3, p. 544.

25 *Hansard*, CXXXI, 117.

26 Quoted in Monypenny and Buckle, *Life of Benjamin Disraeli*, Vol. 3, p. 544.

27 Wolffe, The *Protestant Crusade in Great Britain, 1829–1860*, p. 273.

28 See J.B. Conacher, *The Aberdeen Coalition, 1852–1855: A Study in Mid-Nineteenth Century Party Politics* (Cambridge, 1968), pp. 107–10.

29 Walpole to Disraeli, n.d., quoted in Monypenny and Buckle, *Life of Benjamin Disraeli:*, Vol. 3, pp. 544–5.

30 The motion called the attention of parliament 'to the relations at present subsisting between Her Majesty's Roman Catholic subjects and the laws and constitution of this realm, with a view to ascertain in what manner the full political and religious freedom

now enjoyed by them may best be brought into harmony with the principles and provisions of our common and statute law, and be made compatible with the safety and integrity of our institutions'. See the *Daily Express*, 29 November 1854.

31   Whiteside to Disraeli, 20 October 1854, Disraeli papers, B/XXI/W/320.

32   Whiteside assured Disraeli that George Alexander Hamilton would be their 'only confidante' until 'the thing... [took] shape'. Whiteside to Disraeli, 25 October 1854, Disraeli papers, B/XXI/W/295.

33   The details of the bill are outlined in Whiteside to Disraeli, 30 October 1854, Disraeli papers, B/XXI/W/296 and in Napier to Hamilton, 28 November 1854, Disraeli papers, B/XX/H/31. Hamilton was staying with Disraeli when he received this letter and it was intended as much for Disraeli's eyes as his own.

34   Hamilton to Disraeli, 4 November 1854, Disraeli papers, B/XX/H/27.

35   Napier to Naas, n.d. [but probably August 1853], Mayo papers, 11,017 (14).

36   See Jasper Ridley, *Lord Palmerston* (London, 1972 edn), p. 584.

37   Stanley diary, 30 January 1855, quoted in Vincent (ed.), *Disraeli, Derby and the Conservative Party*, p. 132.

38   Napier to Derby, n.d. [but probably January/February 1855], quoted in Ewald, *Life and Letters of Sir Joseph Napier* (London, 1887 edn), pp. 126–7.

39   Napier to 'a friend... [a] pillar of the National Club', n.d., quoted in Ewald, *Life and Letters of Sir Joseph Napier* (London, 1887 edn), pp. 122–3.

40   See Wolffe, *The Protestant Crusade in Great Britain, 1829–1860*, p. 48.

41   Palmerston to Fortescue, 11 September 1864, quoted in E.D. Steele, *Palmerston and Liberalism, 1855–1865* (Cambridge, 1991), p. 329. See also Ridley, *Lord Palmerston*, pp. 270–2 and G.L. Bernstein, 'British Liberal politics', pp. 59–60.

42   The divisions between Derby and Disraeli on what the party's policy should be in opposition further exacerbated its problems. See Blake, *Disraeli*, p. 364.

43   Machin, *Politics and the Churches in Great Britain, 1832 to 1868*, p. 255.

44   See Napier to Naas, n.d. [but probably August 1852], Mayo papers, 11,020 (15).

55   See Bell, *Disestablishment in Ireland and Wales*, pp. 17–21. See also D.M. Thompson, "The Liberation Society, 1844–1868' in P. Hollis (ed.), *Pressure from Without in Early Victorian England* (London, 1974), pp. 210–38.

46   Spence, 'The philosophy of Irish Toryism', p. 46.

47   *Hansard*, CXXXIII, 921–5.

48   Stanley diary, 31 May 1853, quoted in Vincent (ed.), *Disraeli, Derby and the Conservative Party*, p. 107.

49   See O'Ferrall, *Catholic Emancipation*, p. 284. See also E.R. Norman, *The Catholic Church and Irish Politics in the Eighteen Sixties* (Dundalk, 1965), p. 5 and pp. 16–17.

50   *Hansard*, CXLII, 762–4.

51   *Hansard*, CXLII, 768.

52   *Dublin Evening Mail*, 2 June 1856.

53   Napier to Jolliffe, n.d. [but probably 28 May 1856], Jolliffe papers, Somerset Records Office, Taunton, DD/HY/18/5.

54   Whiteside to Jolliffe, 28 May 1856, Jolliffe papers, DD/HY/18/5.

55   See below, pp. 5–6.

56   Disraeli claimed a prior engagement at the Turkish ambassador's, while Walpole had been 'really ill' and was advised to 'pair' by George Alexander Hamilton. See the *Daily Express*, 6 June 1856.

57   *Dublin Evening Mail*, 7 June 1856.

58   *Hansard*, CXLI, 736.

59   *Hansard*, CXLV, 1844.

60   *Hansard*, XCVIII, 641.

61   *Dublin Evening Mail*, 11 June 1856.

62   See, for example, *The Warder*, 2 May 1862, which depicted Disraeli as not being 'in earnest... He makes points but seems to have no principle of action'. Whiteside made a similar assessment of Disraeli many years later, doubting if he 'ever had any deep & settled convictions on political questions'. See Whiteside to Lytton, 23 June 1870, Lytton papers, D/EK/C18/123.

63   See Blake, *Disraeli*, pp. 368–69. See also John Ramsden, *An Appetite for Power: A History of the Conservative Party since 1830* (London, 1999 edn), p. 89.

64   After this debate, Napier wrote to Gladstone, praising him for his 'great effort on the China question'. He claimed he had never given a vote on any issue 'with a clearer conviction of its foundation in justice, humanity... [and] Christian obligation'. He concluded the letter by regretting 'the course of events which had changed the apparent relation in which we stood'. From the time of his entry into Parliament, Napier had felt that his views 'of sound policy both foreign ... [and] home, substantially agree[d]' with those held by Gladstone. He assured Gladstone that he knew of 'no man, for whose personal character and parliamentary ability... [he] had more unaffected regard'. Napier to Gladstone, 13 March 1857, Gladstone papers, British library, Add. Ms. 44,387, fs.155. It is interesting to contrast the tone of this letter with that of Napier's letter to Derby quoted above, p. 147. It was, of course, no coincidence that this letter was written at a time when Gladstone was co-operating closely with the Conservatives against Palmerston's government. See Shannon, *Gladstone: Peel's Inheritor*, p. 327. There was a good deal of similarity, in character, temperament and family background between Napier and Gladstone. The two men also shared a common interest in the ideas of Bishop Joseph Butler. For Gladstone's interest in Butler's thought, see Richard Shannon, *Gladstone: Heroic Minister, 1865–1898* (London, 2000), pp. 573–4. See also Napier's lectures on Butler's *Analogy of Religion* in Gardiner (ed.), *Lectures, Essays and Letters*, pp. 383–421.

65   See the *Daily Express*, 31 March 1857.

66   See Napier to Derby, 25 March 1857 and 4 April 1857, quoted in Ewald, *Life and Letters of Sir Joseph Napier* (London, 1887 edn), pp. 156–7.

67   Hoppen, 'Tories, Catholics and the general election of 1859', p. 49.

68   Cullen to Newman, 20 July 1858, quoted in Mac Suibhne, *Paul Cullen and his Contemporaries*, Vol. 2, p. 259.

69   See Earle to Hamilton, 4 October 1858, and Hamilton to Naas, 4 October 1858, Mayo papers, 11,023 (6).

70   Maguire to Disraeli, 14 January 1859, Disraeli papers, B/XXI/M/66.

71   Maguire to Naas, 5 March 1859, Mayo papers, 11,027 (6).

72   Maguire to Disraeli, 8 March 1859, Disraeli papers, B/XXI/M/68. See also Maguire to Disraeli, n.d. [March 1859], B/XXI/M/72.

73   *Dublin Evening Mail*, 23 March 1859.

74   Eglinton to Naas, 8 March 1859, Mayo papers, 11,031 (18).

75   See Hoppen, 'Tories, Catholics and the General Election of 1859', pp. 48–57.

76   Maguire to Naas, 16 April 1859, Mayo papers, 11,036 (4).

77   Maguire to Donoughmore, 16 April 1859, Donoughmore papers, H/19/1/6.
78   O'Dell to Donoughmore, 19 April 1859, Donoughmore papers, H/19/1/1208.
79   Moore to Donoughmore, 4 May 1859, Donoughmore papers, H/19/1/1801.
80   Donoughmore to Moore, 9 May 1859, Donoughmore papers, H/19/1/1802.
81   Referring to the Durham letter and the Ecclesiastical Titles Bill, the manifesto condemned the Whig leadership for having heaped 'injuries and insults' on the Roman Catholic Church throughout Europe. From the Conservative side, however, it concluded, there had never been any danger 'to the independence of the Irish party'. See the copy of this manifesto in the George Henry Moore papers, National Library of Ireland, Dublin, Ms. 894.
82   *The Irish Times*, 10 May 1859.
83   *Daily Express*, 13 May 1859.
84   Lord Campden informed Naas that Cardinal Wiseman was 'quite on your side' and supported the government in the belief that they would 'do justice to Roman Catholics'. Campden to Naas, 10 May 1859, Mayo papers, 11,036 (3).
85   *Dublin Evening Mail*, 29 April 1859.
86   Hoppen, 'Tories, Catholics and the general election of 1859', p. 56.
87   These seven MPs would, Eglinton told Derby, 'not vote against us if they... [could] possibly help it'. Eglinton to Derby, 17 May 1859, Derby papers, 148/3.
88   See Donoughmore to Naas, 12 May 1859, Mayo papers, 11,036 (5).
89   Eglinton to Derby, 22 December 1858, Derby papers, 148/3.
90   Maguire to Naas, 14 January 1859, Mayo papers, 11,027 (2).
91   Donoughmore to Naas, 12 May 1859, Mayo papers, 11,036 (5).
92   Disraeli to Naas, 12 May 1859, Mayo papers, 11,036 (4).
93   Donoughmore to Naas, 12 May 1859, Mayo papers, 11,036 (5).
94   Naas to Disraeli, 17 May 1859, Disraeli papers, B/XX/BO/10.
95   Eglinton to Disraeli, 11 May 1859, Disraeli papers, B/XXI/E/110.
96   Whiteside to Disraeli, 16 May 1859, Disraeli papers, B/XXI/W/30.
97   Disraeli to Naas, 20 May 1859, Mayo papers, 11,025 (35).
98   Stanley diary, 17 February 1865, quoted in Vincent (ed.), *Disraeli, Derby and the Conservative Party*, p. 228.
99   The *Express* pointed out that O'Loghlen had voted for Francis Calcutt, the Liberal candidate for Clare, at the general election in preference to Crofton Vandeleur, the Conservative candidate. See the *Daily Express*, 30 May 1859.
100   Eglinton to Derby, 30 May 1859, Disraeli papers, B/XX/S/227.
101   Napier to Eglinton, 28 May 1859, Eglinton papers, GD3/5/57/44442.
102   *Dublin Evening Mail*, 3 June 1859.
103   *The Warder*, 11 June 1859.
104   *Hansard*, CLIV, 1861.
105   Walpole to Derby, 8 June 1859, Derby papers, 153/2.
106   Napier to Walpole, n.d. [but June 1859], Holland papers, 894c.
107   Disraeli to Bowyer, 25 June 1859, quoted in William Ward, *The Life and Times of Cardinal Wiseman*, 2 vols (London 1897), Vol. 2, p. 447.
108   *Dublin Evening Mail*, 29 February 1860.
109   *The Irish Times*, 29 February 1860.
110   *Dublin Evening Mail*, 5 March 1860.
111   Cullen to William Monsell, 24 December 1860, quoted in MacSuibhne, *Paul Cullen and his Contemporaries*, Vol. 3, p. 313.

112   Disraeli to Corry, 16 October 1866, Disraeli papers, B/XX/D/22.

113   Disraeli to Corry, 19 October 1866, Disraeli papers, B/XX/D/24.

114   Earle to Disraeli, 26 April 1861, Disraeli papers, B/XX/E/219. See also Monypenny and Buckle, *Life of Benjamin Disraeli*, Vol. 4, p. 325.

115   See Steele, *Palmerston and Liberalism*, p. 327.

116   Saurin to Donoughmore, 9 February 1861, Donoughmore papers, H/21/1/768.

117   Whiteside to Disraeli, 13 January 1862, Disraeli papers, B/XXI/W/303.

118   Stanley diary, 17 November 1861, quoted in Vincent (ed.) *Disraeli, Derby and the Conservative Party*, pp. 177–8.

119   *Daily Express*, 25 November 1861.

120   Whiteside to Disraeli, 13 January 1862, Disraeli papers, B/XXI/W/303.

121   *The Warder*, 12 November 1861.

122   *The Warder*, 24 May 1862.

123   *Daily Express*, 4 June 1862.

124   Disraeli to Campden, 10 April 1863, quoted in Monypenny and Buckle, *Life of Benjamin Disraeli*, Vol. 4, p. 367.

125   *The Warder*, 25 April 1863.

126   *Hansard*, CLXX, 1988.

127   Napier to Disraeli, 15 May 1863, quoted in Ewald, *Life and letters of Sir Joseph Napier*. (2nd edn, London, 1892), pp. 202–5.

128   *Hansard*, CLXX, 1989.

129   *Hansard*, CLXX, 2015.

130   See Whiteside to Stopford, 20 May 1863, quoted in *The Warder*, 4 June 1863.

131   See *Hansard*, CLXXI, 1560.

132   See *Hansard*, CLXXI, 1699–703. See also Cairns' speech at the Diocesan Church Conference in Belfast, quoted in the *Daily Express*, 25 October 1863.

133   See, for example, Monsell's speech in the same debate, *Hansard*, CLXXI, 1716.

134   For details of this scheme and the government's reaction to it see Beresford to Mayo, 2 June 1867, Mayo papers, 11,216 (1). See also Beresford to Donoughmore, 5 December 1863, Donoughmore papers, H/23/1/58. Whiteside informed Derby that in rejecting the proposals of the Irish bishops, Sir George Grey, the Home Secretary, told Marcus Beresford, the recently appointed Primate, that to 'a very large party in the House of Commons...it would be no recommendation of any Bill that it...[tended] either to purify or strengthen the Irish Church'. See Whiteside to Derby, 8 January 1865, Derby papers, 154/6A.

135   Derby to Donoughmore, 18 November 1863.

136   See E.R. Norman, *The Catholic Church and Ireland in the Age of Rebellion, 1859–1873* (London, 1965), pp. 139–43. See also Patrick Corish, 'Cardinal Cullen and the National Association of Ireland' in Alan O'Day (ed.), *Reactions to Irish Nationalism, 1865–1914* (London, 1987), pp. 117–65 and Emmet Larkin, *The Consolidation of the Roman Catholic Church in Ireland, 1860–70* (Dublin, 1987), pp. 291–311.

137   Whiteside to Derby, 8 January 1865, Derby papers, 154/6A.

138   *Hansard*, CLXXVIII, 385.

139   Derby to Disraeli, 10 March 1865, Disraeli papers, B/XX/S/332. See also W.D. Jones, *Lord Derby and Victorian Conservatism*, p. 337.

140   Napier to Disraeli, 25 March 1865, quoted in Ewald, *Life and Letters of Sir Joseph Napier* (2nd edn, London, 1892), pp. 206–7.

141   Stanley diary, 16 March 1865, quoted in Vincent (ed.), *Disraeli, Derby and the*

Conservative Party, p. 229.

142   See Shannon, *Gladstone: Peel's Inheritor*, p. 535.

143   See Shannon, *Gladstone: Peel's Inheritor*, p. 536.

144   Gladstone to Phillimore, 13 February 1865, quoted in J. Morley, *The Life of William Ewart Gladstone*, 3 vols (London, 1903), Vol. 2, pp. 141–2.

145   *Hansard*, CLXXVIIII, 443–4. Gladstone quoted part of this exchange in his *A Chapter of Autobiography* (London, 1868), p. 41.

146   *Dublin Evening Mail*, 25 March 1865.

147   Whiteside's lectures on 'The Church in Ireland' given at the Dublin Young Men's Christian Association on 28 April 1865 and 4 May 1865, quoted in Whiteside, *Essays and Lectures*, p. 378. See also the *Daily Express*, 28 April and 4 May 1865.

148   *Hansard*, CLXXIX, 1435.

149   *Hansard*, CLXXIX, 466.

150   *Hansard*, CLXXX, 48.

151   *Hansard*, CLXXX, 787–91.

152   Among those who voted against the bill were the fifth Lord Mayo, Lord Bandon, Lord Bantry, Lord Da Vesci, and, naturally enough, the Archbishop of Dublin.

153   Whiteside to Derby, 8 January 1865, Derby papers, 154/6A.

154   See, for example, Vincent, *Formation of the British Liberal Party*, pp. 50–1.

155   *Daily Express*, 14 July 1865. A satirical account of this campaign was published under the name John Figwood by the novelist, Joseph Sheridan Le Fanu. See *The Prelude, Being a Contribution Towards a History of the Election for the University, by John Figwood esq., Barrister at Law* (Dublin, 1865).

156   See Whiteside's election address in the *Daily Express*, 8 July 1865.

157   See Maurice Cowling, *1867: Disraeli, Gladstone and Revolution: The Passing of the Second Reform Bill* (Cambridge, 1967), p. 304.

158   The motivations behind these appointments are discussed in Daire Hogan, '"Vacancies for their Friends": judicial appointments in Ireland 1866–67', in Daire Hogan and W.N. Osborough (eds), *Brehons, Serjeants and Attorneys* (Dublin, 1990), pp. 211–29.

159   For the government's negotiations with the Roman Catholic hierarchy on the question of a charter for the Catholic University see *Copy of [the] Correspondence Relative to the Proposed Charter to a Roman Catholic University in Ireland*, H.C. 1867–68 (779, 791), liil. See also Naas to Derby, 26 December 1867, Derby papers, 155/4 and Derby to Naas, 1 January 1868, Mayo papers, 11,164. For their plans for a land bill, see Napier to Naas, n.d., Mayo papers, 11,211 (1) and Naas to Roberts, 2 March 1867, Mayo papers, 11,211 (22). The hint that the government might consider some form of concurrent endowment was contained in a speech given by Naas in the House of Commons on 10 March 1868. See *Hansard*, CXC, 1390–1.

160   Ball to Mayo. n.d. [but probably 12 October 1867], Mayo papers, 11,216 (1). The government had considerable difficulty in inducing Liberal politicians to sit on the Commission, Naas informing Derby on 10 October 1867 that the 'Whig peers steadily turn[ed] their face from the Church Commission'. He believed that they were waiting to see 'whether some party capital . . . [might] not be made out of the Irish Church'. See Naas to Derby, 10 October 1867, Derby papers 155/3.

161   See Akenson, *Church of Ireland*, p. 232.

162   Foster, *Modern Ireland*, p. 396.

Conclusion

IN RETROSPECT, the years between 1852 and 1865 can be seen as the Indian summer of Irish Conservatism. As we saw in the Introduction, it was during this period that the party achieved its greatest electoral success.[1] This success was, however, achieved on the basis of a restricted franchise, with an electorate vulnerable, especially in the county constituencies, to landlord influence. The exceptional nature of Irish politics in the 1850s and early 1860s also contributed to the success of the Irish Conservative Party in those years. Lord John Russell's introduction of the Ecclesiastical Titles Act, whatever its effects might have been in other parts of Britain, seriously undermined Liberal prospects in Ireland in the early 1850s. The rise of the Independent Party, although it never achieved the cohesion which the Home Rule party was to have under Parnell, occurred principally at the expense of the Liberals rather than the Conservatives.

As the principal party of the Irish landowners, the Irish Conservatives had an internal unity unmatched by either the Liberals or the Independent Party. Its internal coherence meant that the party never suffered from the type of divisions which plagued the Irish Liberal Party.[2] Such divisions as did exist within the party generally arose from patronage disputes within its own ranks or from concerns that it was not upholding the interests of Irish Protestants or of the Irish landed class to a sufficient extent. Throughout the period covered by this book Irish landlords retained their predominant position within Irish society. They dominated the Irish parliamentary representation and played a significant role in Irish local government. As a body, they strongly supported the Conservatives.[3]

Landlord influence in Ireland had, in some respects, been strengthened during the Famine years. Indeed, K. T. Hoppen has argued that by weeding out the more inefficient and indebted landowners, the Famine actually strengthened the position of Irish landlords in general.[4] The Conservatives' position in Ireland had also been strengthened by the decline and demise of O'Connell's nationally organised and widely supported Repeal Association in the course of the Famine years. The resurgence of landlord influence in Ireland also contributed to a revival of Conservative self-confidence there, following the series of political reverses that the party had suffered in the years between 1829 and 1845. These reverses had included the introduction of Catholic Emancipation in 1829, the creation of the

National Education system in 1831 and the passing of the Irish Church Temporalities Act in 1834. Along with the increase in the Maynooth grant in 1845, all of these measures were seen by Irish Conservative opinion as being detrimental to their interests. These measures and the increasing political militancy of Irish Catholics from the early 1820s onwards convinced many Irish Conservatives that they needed to organise to resist this threat to their position in Ireland. It was this conviction that led party leaders to develop the extremely effective electoral machinery, which was discussed earlier in the book.

The revival of landlord electoral influence in Ireland in the mid-nineteenth century was facilitated by the fact that none of O'Connell's political successors had anything like his ability to mobilise mass support. The consequent resurgence of the Irish Conservative Party in this period was aided, however, by the unpopularity accruing to the Liberal Party from the introduction of the Ecclesiastical Titles Act and from Lord Palmerston's failure to develop a constructive policy towards Ireland during his periods in office. As we have seen, Palmerston was, in fact, more opposed to Irish land reform than was Derby. The general Liberal sympathy with Italian unification in the years after 1859 also persuaded some influential Catholics that support for the Conservatives was the lesser of two evils. It was within this context that Conservative leaders could hope to win Catholic support through concessions, which, in other circumstances, would have appeared trivial.

Palmerston's death in 1865 altered the context in which Irish Conservatives operated. The advent of Lord John Russell and subsequently of William Ewart Gladstone to the leadership of the Liberal Party enabled trends that had been suppressed while Palmerston was alive to come to the surface of British politics. It also rendered easier the establishment of clear demarcation lines between the two main British political parties. In particular, Gladstone's adoption of the disestablishment of the Church of Ireland as Liberal policy in 1868 put an end to Conservative attempts to woo Irish Roman Catholic support. In essence, the party could not hope to outbid Gladstone on the issue.

Disestablishment also struck at one of the central props of Irish Conservative identity. The position of the Church of Ireland as the 'national' Church had been of crucial symbolic importance to Irish Conservatives. It had enabled them to portray themselves as the truly 'national' party in Ireland, while criticising Irish Catholics for being dominated by a priesthood, whose primary loyalty was to Rome. On occasion, Conservative rhetoric had even reverted to the idea of the 'Protestant nation' developed in the eighteenth century by Anglo-Irish thinkers such as Jonathan Swift and George Berkeley. As late as 1866, for example, James Whiteside could object to the definition of Ireland as a

Catholic nation on the grounds that it 'excluded five-sixths of the landed gentry, the greater portion of the aristocracy, forty nine out of every fifty of the manufacturers... and all the skilled artizans'. He denied that Ireland 'as a nation, was a Roman Catholic country'.[5] While this position was a comforting one for some Irish Conservatives, the leaders of the party in Britain could not so blithely dismiss the Roman Catholic population living there.

Before the Act of Union, the Anglo-Irish Ascendancy's dominance of Irish political life had been based on the exclusion of Roman Catholics there from political life. After Catholic Emancipation, however, it became necessary for Conservative leaders, both in Britain and in Ireland, to devise alternative strategies towards the Roman Catholic population in the country. As we have seen, all three Conservative governments of this period made at least token attempts to win over a section of the Irish Catholic middle class. The more far-sighted leaders of the party recognised that this was imperative if the Conservatives were to maintain their strength in Ireland. Their problem lay in conceiving policies which would win Catholic support without alienating their Protestant base. Even at the height of the Conservative success at achieving this, the balance proved to be a difficult one to maintain. For example, even a limited measure of land reform, such as Napier attempted in 1852, provoked fierce opposition among Irish Conservative backbenchers. Indeed, some of its most vocal critics in the House of Lords were Conservative peers, who, in opposition, effectively neutered a bill brought in by the party when in government. The difficulty involved in conciliating Irish Catholic opinion was further increased by the defensiveness which, as we have seen, was a marked characteristic of Irish Conservatism. Their minority status in Ireland convinced many Irish Conservatives that every concession made to Roman Catholics there represented a further erosion of their privileged position in the country. Indeed, many of them would have agreed with James Whiteside's assertion, made in March 1865, that every concession given to Irish Catholics only laid 'the foundation... [for] further demands'.[6] The Irish Conservative tendency to view every concession as the thin end of the wedge, however, meant that they tended to resist reforms even when, as in the case of Catholic Emancipation, popular pressure had made them all but inevitable.

Another problem facing the party was that, in the long term, the Protestant upper and middle class was not large enough to provide it with a viable base, particularly if there were to be a large-scale extension of the electoral franchise. For this reason, Irish Conservatives, notably James Whiteside, regularly opposed electoral reform. In April 1866, Whiteside complained that revision of the Irish franchise would cause 'the meaner sort' to prevail. As they were 'generally ignorant', this would result in their being led 'by faction or affection rather than by right understanding' in casting their votes.[7] The franchise should, he believed, be restricted to those who had 'sufficient property' to exercise 'a free and independent will'.[8] Behind this rhetoric lay the Irish Conservative fear that the extension of the right to vote and the introduction of the secret ballot would undermine the landlord influence, upon which their strength lay.

From 1852 onwards, the Conservative Party as a whole was in a minority position within the House of Commons. This, in itself, limited its ability to act independently of the other parties there. Furthermore, throughout the party's existence, leading Irish Conservatives operated under constraints not shared by their British counterparts. Irish MPs were a minority within the party as a whole and they needed the co-operation of the party leadership in Britain in order to pursue their policy objectives. As we have seen, on certain issues, for example on national education and on the Maynooth grant, party leaders were generally out of sympathy with Irish Conservative aspirations. Even when they shared such concerns, pragmatic political considerations could lead them to act in ways which Irish Conservatives found objectionable. Thus, Disraeli's attempts to secure Independent Irish Party support stemmed as much from party political considerations as from his own personal predilections.

A constant factor in the beliefs of Irish Conservatives was their ambivalent attitude towards the Union, which they saw as both securing their position and, at the same time, limiting their freedom of action. They were frequently critical of English misgovernment of Ireland, the failures of Liberal policy during the Famine being a favourite point of attack. They were also unsure of the extent to which even the leaders of the Conservative Party were committed to upholding their interests, a scepticism which owed much to what they saw as Sir Robert Peel's double-dealing over both Catholic emancipation and the Maynooth grant. However, the exigencies of the British political system left Irish Conservatives little option but to remain loyal to the leadership of the party at Westminster.

Irish Conservatives also suffered from a dilemma which has recurred frequently in the history of Irish Unionism. While calling for closer integration with Britain, they were also concerned that 'the marked peculiarities' of Ireland should be taken into account when framing Irish legislation.[9] On the one hand, for example, Joseph Napier argued in 1850 that the 'great object' of the British government ought to be 'to identify Ireland as much as possible with England'. This could best be done, he argued, by establishing a 'uniform [legal] system' for both countries.[10] In contrast, when faced with cabinet opposition to his land bills, Napier complained bitterly of the 'bigotry of the Saxon clique'.[11] Indeed, Napier's Tenants' Compensation Bill was a clear example of an Irish measure that differed markedly from anything that might have been proposed for the rest of Britain. Napier justified this by citing Irish exceptionalism as a reason for the introduction of the bill, specifically the under-capitalised nature of agriculture there.

The ambivalence, which lay behind such attitudes, was coloured by the myths Irish Conservatives had built around the Union. Irish Conservatives regularly argued that it had been an international agreement, agreed on terms of equality, between two separate kingdoms. In 1853, the *Daily Express* complained that it had been forgotten that 'Ireland was an ancient kingdom,' which had maintained 'a separate existence with her own army, her own treasury, her own fiscal arrangements, and peculiar system of taxation' up to the time of the Union.[12] Ireland was, thus, an equal partner in the Union, with the right to have its economic position and national interests safeguarded. Irish Conservatives also regularly argued that Ireland was entitled to 'Imperial equality', to an equal right to share with England in the benefits of the British Empire.[13]

Unfortunately, for Irish Conservatives, they simply did not have the weight within the British political system to sustain this position in practise. As A.P.W. Malcolmson has pointed out in relation to an earlier period, the relationship between the British government and the Anglo-Irish Ascendancy was, ultimately, a profoundly 'unequal' one. While the Ascendancy was dependent upon the British government for the maintenance of its position in Ireland, the British government had nothing like the same attachment to it.[14] As events proved, British politicians were to be more preoccupied with maintaining British rule in Ireland than in upholding the position of Irish Protestants. If the consolidation of the Union implied some form of rapprochement with the Irish Roman Catholic Church and the emerging Catholic middle class, then British governments were willing to pursue this course. By contrast, Irish Conservatives believed that their essential role was to uphold 'the Protestant interest in Ireland' and that the Union itself had essentially been designed to achieve that end.[15] As time progressed, however, it became increasingly clear that these objectives were not, necessarily, compatible ones. Indeed, it was the tension between these two conflicting positions that led to the ambivalence that characterised the relationship between Irish Conservative politicians and the British government throughout the period covered by this book.

Throughout its existence, there were three central planks on which the Irish Conservative Party rested. The first of these was the defence of the Union with Britain, the second, the defence of the Church of Ireland, the Established Church, and the third, the defence of the interests of the Irish landed classes. The three were interlinked; one of the features of the debate on the disestablishment of the Church of Ireland was the priority which Irish Conservatives placed upon the effect this would have on existing property rights. Again, a frequent argument used against disestablishment was that the position of the Church of Ireland had been guaranteed by the Union. Any changes in the status of its property, the argument ran, would undermine the legitimacy of the Union itself. This argument related back to the Irish Conservative sense that the Union had been an agreement between sovereign nations, rather than one imposed on Ireland by the superior strength of Britain. The flaw inherent in this argument was the fact that Irish Conservatives ultimately relied upon the British government to uphold their position in Ireland. At moments of extreme disillusionment with the British government, as in the early 1830s after the passing of Catholic Emancipation and in the early 1870s after the disestablishment of the Irish Church, a minority of Irish Conservatives did flirt with the idea of a limited form of Home Rule. In both cases, however, this mood did not last long, as the reality of their position was that their political future was bound up with the continuance of British rule. Without the Union, they faced the prospect of becoming merely a minority party within Ireland.[16]

While the Union gave Irish Conservatives at least the illusion of being equal partners in the United Kingdom, the long-term problem for the party was that, outside the North of Ireland, its base was not broad enough to guarantee it a viable long-term future. A party so dependent on landlord influence could not fail to be affected by the decline in that influence in the second half of the nineteenth century. The introduction of the secret ballot in 1872 and the radical extension of the franchise in 1884 were serious blows to the Conservative Party. The falling off of their support outside the north is shown by the fact that they won only seven seats outside Ulster in the 1880 general election. In the North of Ireland, the party survived longer and was given fresh impetus in 1886 by Gladstone's adoption of Home Rule. After 1886, Ulster Conservatism blended with other pro-Union elements there to create the Unionist party. For the party in the south, however, the agricultural depression of the late 1870s and the long-term changes in landownership, initiated by the land purchase clauses in the 1885 Ashbourne Act and dramatically increased by the Wyndham Act of 1903, signalled the death knell. The party's identification with the Irish landlord class meant that it could not survive the decline of its influence in the latter half of the nineteenth century.

Whatever the position may have been for Conservatives elsewhere in Britain, the Irish party was increasingly dependent on a 'shrinking base',[17] one that ultimately it proved unable to expand. Unlike its British counterpart, the Conservative Party in Ireland was unable to reinvent itself as an 'alliance between the old landed property and the newer industrial and commercial wealth'. Furthermore, it could not draw on the support of the urban and suburban middle class in the way that Conservatism in Britain, especially under Lord Salisbury, was able to do.[18] The subsequent decline of the party should not, however, blind us to its strength and resilience in the years covered by this book. In the mid-nineteenth century, this strength and resilience had helped to mask the party's limitations, which could be seen as representing the reverse side of its strengths. Thus, for example, despite the efforts of moderate Conservative politicians like Donoughmore and Naas, the party's internal coherence rested on an exclusiveness and on a general lack of empathy with the Roman Catholic population which contributed to its eventual political extinction in the South of Ireland. Despite this, as the authentic mouthpiece of a powerful section of Irish society, the Irish Conservative Party had played a central but neglected role in mid-nineteenth century Irish history. The aim of this book has been to restore that role, too long neglected, to its proper significance.

NOTES

1   This can be compared with the case of the Scotland, where the Conservative Party suffered a series of severe political reverses in the 1850s. At the 1857 general election, for example, the party was reduced to fifteen seats, it worst result there since 1835. See Hutchinson, *Political History of Scotland*, p. 90.

2   As Jonathan Parry has pointed out, 'the Conservative Party was always a more coherent force [than the Liberal Party], more homogenous, less independently minded, and usually more amenable to central direction and organization'. Parry, *Rise and Fall of Liberal Government*, p. 1.

3   See Hoppen, *Elections, Politics and Society*, pp. 125–7.

4   See Hoppen, *Ireland since 1800*, p. 87.

5   *Hansard*, ClXXXII, 1045.

6   Whiteside to Derby, 8 January 1865, Derby papers, 154/6A.

7   *Hansard*, CLXXXII, 1912.

8   *Hansard*, CLXXV, 335.

9   *Daily Express*, 14 May 1852.

10 *Hansard*, CX, 1347.

11 Napier to Naas, n.d., Mayo papers, 11,020 (15).

12 *Daily Express*, 7 May 1853. For a discussion of the development of Irish 'Protestant Nationalism', see Boyce, *Nationalism in Ireland*, pp. 94–122.

13 From a speech by Napier at a banquet for the Dublin Conservative MPs, quoted in the *Daily Express*, 16 April 1857. In the same speech, Napier declared that Irish Conservatives 'wanted to realize [*sic*] the benefits of the Union'. They wanted every Irishman 'to feel that he is a citizen of the United Kingdom'. Irish people wanted 'the same laws' and 'the same dispensation of patronage' as applied in England. They also wanted 'equality in all respects' with their 'fellow-subjects in England'. In May 1859, Naas complained to Disraeli that Irish Conservatives had not been fairly treated in terms of Indian and colonial appointments. See Naas to Disraeli, 17 May 1859, Disraeli papers, B/XX/BO/10.

14 Malcolmson, *John Foster*, p. 448. Malcolmson also compared the relationship between the Ascendancy and the British government to 'a marriage of convenience' and a

'loveless' marriage. See Malcolmson, *John Foster*, p. xxi.

15   See Jackson, *Home Rule*, p. 22.

16   See Spence, *The Philosophy of Irish Toryism*, p. 60.

17   See Paul Smith, *Disraelian Conservatism and Social Reform* (London, 1967), p. 26.

18   Smith, *Disraelian Conservatism*, p. 316.

Bibliography

I. Private Papers

Public Record Office of Northern Ireland, Belfast
Abercorn papers
Tennent papers

Dublin Diocesan Archives, Dublin
Cullen papers

National Archives of Ireland, Dublin
Diary of Henry Bruen
W.W.F. Hume papers

National Library of Ireland, Dublin
Domville papers
Farnham papers
Inchiquin papers
Larcom papers
Mayo papers
George Henry Moore papers
William Smith O'Brien papers
O'Hara papers
Ormonde diary
Otway papers

Trinity College Archives Department, Dublin
Donoughmore papers

Scottish Record Office, Edinburgh [now held in the National Archives of Scotland, Edinburgh]
Eglinton papers

Hertfordshire Record Office, Hertford
Lytton papers

Liverpool Record Office, Liverpool
Derby papers

British Library, London
Carnarvon papers
Gladstone papers

House of Lords Record Office, London
Ashbourne papers

Public Record Office, London
Cairns papers
Carnarvon papers

Bodleian Library, Oxford
Disraeli papers
National Club papers

Rhodes House, Library, Oxford
Pope Hennessey papers

Somerset Record Office, Taunton
Jolliffe papers

Private possession
Holland papers (papers of Spencer Walpole in the possession of Mr D. Holland)
Lefroy papers (in the Possession of Mr J. Lefroy)

II. Parliamentary Debates and Papers

Hansard Parliamentary Debates, 3rd Series, 1852–68.

Report from the Select Committee on Outrages (Ireland): With Proceedings of the Committee, Minutes of Evidence, Appendix and Index, HC 1852 (438), xiv.
Report from the Select committee of the House of Lords Appointed to Inquire into the Practical Working of the System of National Education in Ireland, 2 pts, H.C. 1854 (525), xv.
Census of Ireland for the Year 1861, Report on Religion and Education, HC, 1863.
Report of Her Majesty's Commissioners on the Revenue and Condition of the Established Church in Ireland, HC 1867–68, xxiv.
Copy of Correspondence Relative to the Proposed Charter to a Roman Catholic

University in Ireland, HC 1867–68 (779, 791), liil.

Return of Owners of Land in Ireland, Showing with Respect to Each County, the Number of Owners Below an Acre, and in Classes up to 100,000 Acres and upwards, with the Aggregate Acreage and Valuation of Each Class, H.C. 1876 (422), lix.

III. Newspapers and Periodicals

College Elector and Gazette (1865)
Daily Express
Dublin Evening Mail
Dublin University Magazine
Morning Herald
The Nation
The National Magazine (1831)
The New Review (1863)
The Irish Law Times
The Irish Times
The Times
Quarterly Review
The Tablet (1852–59)
The Warder

IV. Reference Works

Ball, F.E., *The Judges in Ireland*, 2 vols (London, 1926).

Bateman, John, *The Great Landowners of Great Britain and Ireland* (New York, 1973 edn).

Burtchaell, G.D. and Sadleir, T.V., *Alumni Dublinenses: A Register of the Students, Graduates, Professors and Provosts of Trinity College, in the University of Dublin* (London, 1929).

Cannon, John (ed.), *The Oxford Companion to British History* (Oxford, 1997).

Connolly, Sean (ed.), *The Oxford Companion to Irish History* (Oxford, 1998).

De Burgh, U.H., *The Landowners of Ireland: An Alphabetical List of the Owners of Estates of 500 Acres or £500 Valuation and Upwards in Ireland* (Dublin, 1878).

Fleming, N.C and O'Day, Alan (eds), *The Longman Handbook of Modern Irish History since 1800* (Harlow, 2005).

Foster, Joseph, *Alumni Oxonienses: The Members of the University of Oxford 1715–1886: Their Parentage, Birthplace, and Years of Birth, with a Record of their Degrees*, 4 vols (London, 1888).

Matthews, H.C.G and Harrison, Brian (eds), *Oxford Dictionary of National Biography: From the Earliest Times to the Year 2000* (Oxford, 2004).

Stenton, Michael and Lees, Stephen (eds), *Who's Who of British Members of Parliament*, 4 vols (Hassocks, 1976 to 1981).

Thom's Directory and Official Almanac (Dublin, 1852–68).

Venn, J.A., *Alumni Cantabrigienses: A Biographical List of all Known Students, Graduates and Holders of Office at the University of Cambridge, from the Earliest Times to 1900*, Part. II, vols I–VI (Cambridge, 1927–54).

Walker, B.M. (ed.), *Parliamentary Election Results in Ireland, 1801–1922* (Dublin, 1978).

V. Books and Pamphlets by Contemporaries

'An Irish Catholic', *The Government of Lord Aberdeen and the Government of Lord Derby: A Contrast for the Calm Consideration of Intelligent Catholics* (Dublin, 1853).

Ball, J.T., *The Reformed Church of Ireland, 1537–1886* (London and Dublin, 1886).

Belmore, Earl of, *Parliamentary Memoirs of Fermanagh and Tyrone from 1613 to 1885* (Dublin, 1887).

Benson, A.C. and Esher, Viscount (eds), *The Letters of Queen Victoria: A Selection from Her Majesty's Correspondence Between the Years 1837 and 1861*, 3 vols (London, 1907).

Blackburne, Edward, *Life of the Right Hon. Francis Blackburne, Late Lord Chancellor of Ireland* (London, 1874).

Brooke, R.S., *Recollections of the Irish Church* (Dublin, 1878).

Bullen, Edward, *Modern Views of the Relations Between Landlord and Tenant, Tenant Right, and Compensation for Improvements* (London, 1853).

Burke, O.J., *The History of the Lord Chancellors of Ireland from AD 1186 to AD 1874* (Dublin, 1879).

Burke, O.J., *Anecdotes of the Connaught Circuit: From its Foundation in 1604 to Close upon the Present Time* (Dublin, 1885).

Butt, Isaac, *A Voice for Ireland: The Famine in the Land: What Has Been Done and What is to be Done* (Dublin, 1847).

Butt, Isaac, *National Education in Ireland: A Speech Delivered at a Meeting of the Church Education Society in Youghal on Monday, October 16 1854* (Dublin, 1854).

Butt, Isaac, *Land Tenure in Ireland: A Plea for the Celtic Race* (Dublin, 1866).

Church Congress, *Authorised Report of the Church Congress Held at Dublin on September 29, 30, October 1st, 2nd, 3rd 1868* (Dublin, 1868).

Church Education Society, *Sixteenth Report of the Church Education Society for Ireland, being for the Year 1855* (Dublin, 1856).

Clancarty, Earl of, *Ireland: Her Present Condition and What it Might Be*

(Dublin, 1864).

Cooke, A.B. and Malcolmson, A.P.W., *The Ashbourne Papers, 1869–1913: A Calendar of the Papers of Edward Gibson, 1st Lord Ashbourne* (Belfast, 1974).

Cooke, A.B. and Vincent, J.R. (eds), *Lord Carlingford's Journal: Reflections of a Cabinet Minister 1881* (Oxford, 1971).

Cross, R.A., *A Political History, 1868–1900* (privately printed, 1903).

Curran, J.A., *Reminiscences of John Adye Curran KC, Late County Judge and Chairman of Quarter Sessions* (London, 1915).

Davis, Richard (ed.), *'To Solitude Consigned': The Tasmanian Journal of William Smith O'Brien* (Sydney, 1995).

Dawson, R.P ['Feeva'], *A Psalter of Derry: Letter of 'Conservative-elector' on the Political Condition and Parliamentary Representation of the County* (Dublin, 1859).

Disraeli, Benjamin, *Lord George Bentinck* (London, 1881 edn).

Downey, Edward, *Charles Lever: His Life in his Letters* (London, 1906).

Dublin Protestant Association, *The Report of the Dublin Protestant Association, 1860* (Dublin, 1861), copy in the Cullen papers.

Duffy, Sir Charles Gavan, *The League of North and South: An Episode in Irish History, 1850–1854* (London, 1886).

Duffy, Sir Charles Gavan, *My Life in Two Hemispheres*, 2 vols (London, 1898).

'Eladrius', *Thoughts on the Late General Election in Ireland* (Dublin, 1853).

Ewald, A.C., *The Life of Sir Joseph Napier, Bart, ex-Lord Chancellor of Ireland from his Private Correspondence* (London, 1887), revised condensed edn (London, 1892).

Ferguson, Lady M., *Sir Samuel Ferguson in the Ireland of his Day*, 2 vols (London, 1896).

Ferguson, W.D., *Literary Appropriations and the Irish Land Bills of the Late Government* (Dublin, 1853).

Ferguson, W.D. and Vance, Andrew, *The Tenure and Improvement of Land in Ireland Considered with Reference to the Relation Between Landlord and Tenant and Tenant Right* (Dublin, 1851).

Fitzgerald, Percy, *Memoirs of an Author*, 2 vols (London, 1895).

Fitzgibbon, Gerald, *Ireland in 1868: The Battle-field for English Party Strife* (London, 1868).

Fitzpatrick, W.J., *The Life of Charles Lever*, 2 vols. (London, 1897).

Fraser, Sir William, *Disraeli and his Day* (London, 1891).

Gardiner, Grace (ed.), *The Lectures, Essays and Letters of the Right Hon. Sir Joseph Napier, Bart* (Dublin and London, 1888).

Gathorne-Hardy, A.E., *Gathorne Hardy, First Earl of Cranbrook, a Memoir, with Extracts from his Diary and Correspondence*, 2 vols (London, 1910).

Gladstone, W.E., *A Chapter of Autobiography* (London, 1868).

Gregory, Lady Augusta (ed.), *Sir William Gregory, K.C.M.G., formerly*

Member of Parliament and sometime Governor of Ceylon: An Autobiography (London, 1894).

Hamilton, Lord George, *Parliamentary Reminiscences and Reflections* (London, 1916).

Hancock, W.N., 'The present law of landlord and tenant, as exhibited in the recent decision of the master of the rolls in the case of O'Fay v Burke', *Journal of the Dublin Statistical Society*, 11, XV, January 1860, 345–49.

Hancock, W.N., *Two Reports for the Irish Administration on the History of the Landlord and Tenant Question in Ireland, with Suggestions for Legislation: First Report made in 1859; – Second in 1866* (Dublin, 1869).

Hawkins, Angus and Powell, John (eds), *The Journal of John Wodehouse, First Earl of Kimberley for 1862–1902* (London, 1997).

Head, Sir Francis, *A Fortnight in Ireland* (London, 1852).

Hennessey, Sir John Pope, *Lord Beaconsfield's Irish Policy: Two Essays on Ireland* (London, 1885).

Hewett, O.W., '. . . and Mr Fortescue': A Selection from the Diaries from 1851 to 1862 of Chichester Fortescue, Lord Carlingford K.P.* (London, 1958).

Hunter, W.W., *A Life of the Earl of Mayo; Fourth Viceroy of India* (London, 1875).

Irvine, Rev. Christopher, *The Present State of the Controversy Between the National Board and the Church Education Society* (2nd edn, Dublin, 1861).

Jenkins, T.A. (ed.), *The Parliamentary Diaries of Sir John Trelawney, 1858–1865* (London, 1990).

Jennings, Louis J. (ed.), *The Croker Papers: The Correspondence and Diaries of the Late Right Honourable John Wilson Croker LL.D, F.R.S.*, Vol. 3 (London, 1884).

Johnson, Nancy (ed.), *The Diary of Gathorne Hardy, Later Lord Cranbrook 1866–1892: Political Selections* (Oxford, 1981).

Kebbel, T.E., *Life of the Earl of Derby K.G.* (London, 1890).

Kebbel, T.E., *Lord Beaconsfield and Other Tory Memories* (London, 1907).

Kenealy, Arabella, *Memoirs of Edward Vaughan Kenealy L.L.D.* (London, 1903).

Laing, Andrew, *Life, Letters and Diaries of Sir Stafford Northcote, First Earl of Iddersleigh*, 2 vols (London, 1890).

Lambert Henry, *A Memoir of Ireland in 1850, by an ex-MP* (Dublin, 1851).

Lecky, Elizabeth, *A Memoir of the Right Hon. W.E. Hartpole Lecky* (London, 1909).

Le Fanu, Joseph Sheridan ['J. Figwood'], *The Prelude; Being a Contribution Towards a History of the Election for the University* (Dublin, 1865).

Le Fanu, William, 'Notebooks of Sheridan Le Fanu' in *Long Room*, 14 & 15 (Autumn 1976–Spring/Summer 1977), pp. 37–40.

Lever, Charles, *The Martins of Cro' Martin* (London, 1872).

Lever, Charles, *Sir Brook Fossbrooke* (London, 1895 edn).

Lever, Charles, *Lord Kilgobbin* (Belfast, 1995 edn).

Lucas, Edward, *The Life of Frederick Lucas MP*, 2 vols (London, 1886).

MacDonnell, J.C., *The Life and Correspondence of William Connor Magee, Archbishop of York, Bishop of Peterborough*, 2 vols, (London, 1896).

MacIvor, James, *A Letter to the Right Reverend the Lord Bishop of Derry and Raphoe, on the Present State of the Education Question* (Dublin, 1859).

MacKnight, Thomas, *Ulster as it is or Twenty-eight Years Experience as an Irish Editor* (London, 1896).

MacNeill, J.G. Swift, *What I have Seen and Heard* (London, 1925).

MacSuibhne, Peadar, *Paul Cullen and his Contemporaries with their Letters from 1820–1902*, 5 vols (Naas, 1961–77).

Madden, D.O., *Ireland and its Rulers since 1829*, 2 vols (London, 1843).

Madden, D.O., *The Voice of the Bar, No. 1, the Reign of Mediocrity* (Dublin, 1850).

Malmesbury, Earl of, *Memoirs of an Ex-minister*, 2 vols (London, 1884).

Marx, Karl and Engels, Frederick, *Ireland and the Irish Question* (Moscow, 1971).

Meekins, T.C. Mossom, *Report to the Attorney General for Ireland (the Right Hon. Joseph Napier, MP) on Compensation to the Tenants for Improvements* (London, 1852).

Morley, John, *The Life of William Ewart Gladstone*, 3 vols (London, 1903).

Morris, William O'Connor, *Memories and Thoughts of a Life* (London, 1895).

Napier, Joseph, *Address Delivered at the Dublin Oratorical and Literary Institute on the 5th of July 1847 by Joseph Napier, Esq., Q.C., President of the Society* (Dublin, 1847).

Napier, Joseph, *The Proposed Modification of the Non-Vested System; a Letter from Joseph Napier, Esq., MP to Rev. James MacIvor* (Dublin, 1850).

Napier, Joseph, *England or Rome, which shall govern Ireland?: A Reply to the Letter of Lord Monteagle* (2nd edn, Dublin, 1851).

Napier, Joseph, *Dublin Oratorical and Literary Institute: An Address Delivered to the Members of the Institute, on Friday evening, January 9th 1852, by Joseph Napier, LL.D, Q.C., MP* (Dublin, 1852).

Napier, Joseph, *The Landlord and Tenant Bills; Reply of the Right Hon. Joseph Napier to the Letter of the Earl of Donoughmore on the Landlord and Tenant Bills of the Last Session* (Dublin, 1853).

Napier, Joseph, *The Increase of Knowledge; A Lecture Delivered before the Young Men's Christian Association at The Rotundo, Dublin on December 20, 1853 by the Right Hon. Joseph Napier, MP* (Dublin, 1854).

Napier, Joseph, *The Education Question; Thoughts on the Present Crisis* (2nd edn, Dublin, 1860).

Napier, Joseph, 'Introduction' to J.N. Griffin, *Seven Answers to the Seven Essays and Reviews* (London, 1862), pp. i–viiii.

Napier, Joseph and Hamilton, G.A., *Case of the Achill Mission Estate;*

Proceedings for the New Scheme of Management and Reasons for the Resignation of their Office of Trustees (Dublin, 1864).

National Club, *National Club; A Report of Speeches Delivered at the Annual Meeting of the Members and Friends of the National Club held in the Club House, Whitehall, May 9, 1855* (London, 1855).

O'Brien, J.T., *Some Remarks on a Pamphlet Entitled 'The Education Question; thoughts on the Present Crisis'* (2nd edn, Dublin, 1860).

O'Brien, R.B., *The Parliamentary History of the Irish Land Question from 1829 to 1869 and the Origins and Results of the Ulster Custom* (London, 1880).

O'Flanagan, J.R., *The Lives of the Lord Chancellors and the Keepers of the Great Seal of Ireland from the Earliest Times to the Reign of Queen Victoria* (London, 1870).

O'Flanagan, J.R., 'The Late Right Hon. James Whiteside, Lord Chief Justice of the Queen's Bench, Ireland', *Law Magazine and Review*, 2, 224 (May 1877), 334–62.

Osborne, R.N., *The Landlord and Tenants Act of the Last Session with Introduction, Practical Observations, and Copious Index* (Dublin, 1860).

Ramm, Agatha (ed.), *The Political Correspondence of Mr Gladstone and Lord Granville, I, 1868–76* (London, 1952).

Reeve, Henry (ed.), *The Greville Memoirs: A Journal of the Reign of Queen Victoria* (Third Part): Vol. 1 (London, 1887).

Ross, Sir John, *The Years of my Pilgrimage: Random Reminiscences* (London, 1924).

Shee, Sir William, *Papers, Letters and Speeches in the House of Commons on the Irish Land Question, with a Summary of its Parliamentary History from 1852 to the Close of the Session of 1863* (London, 1863).

Smith, Paul (ed.), *Lord Salisbury on Politics: A Selection from his Articles in the Quarterly Review, 1860–1883* (Cambridge, 1972).

Swartz, H. M. and Swartz, M. (eds), *Disraeli's Reminiscences* (London, 1975).

Torrens, William McCullagh, *Twenty Years in Parliament* (London, 1893).

Urlin, M.E. Denny (ed.), *The Journal and Reminiscences of R. Denny Urlin* (Sussex, 1909).

Vincent, J.R. (ed.), *Disraeli, Derby and the Conservative Party: The Political Journals of Lord Stanley, 1849–1869* (Hassocks, 1978).

Warburton William, *The Results of Opposition to the National Education System in Reference to the Interest, Temporal and Eternal, of the Poorer Members of the Established Church* (Dublin, 1859).

Walling, R.A.J. (ed.), *The Diaries of John Bright* (London, 1930).

Ward, William, *The Life and Times of Cardinal Wiseman*, 2 vols (London, 1897).

Whately, E.J., *Life and Correspondence of Richard Whately, D.D., Late Archbishop of Dublin*, 2 vols (London, 1866).

White, William, *The Inner Life of the House of Commons*, 2 vols (London, 1897).

Whiteside, James, *The Speech of J. Whiteside, Q.C. (revised by himself) the Delivery of Which Occupied Two Days at the Late Irish State Trials* (Dublin, 1844).

Whiteside, James, *Whiteside's Defence of Mr Wm. S. O'Brien, Esq., MP, on his Trial for High Treason at Clonmel on Tuesday, 5th and 6th October, 1848* (Dublin, 1848).

Whiteside, James, *The Past and the Present: An Address Delivered at a Meeting of the Working Classes Association in the Music Hall [Belfast] on October 22nd, 1849* (London, 1849).

Whiteside, James, *Italy in the Nineteenth Century, Contrasted with its Past Condition*, 2 vols (London, 1848), revised one-vol. edn, (London, 1860).

Whiteside, James, [Edited by W.D. Ferguson] *Essays and Lectures, Historical and Literary* (Dublin, 1868).

Whiteside, James, *Early Sketches of Eminent Persons* (Dublin, 1870).

Whitty, E.M., *St Stephens in the Fifties: the Session, 1852–53, A Parliamentary Retrospect with an Introduction by Justin McCarthy and Notes by H.M.W.* (London, 1906).

Wiebe, M.G., Conacher, J.B. and Matthews, John. (eds), *Benjamin Disraeli: Letters,* Vol. 5 (Toronto, 1993).

VI. LATER WORKS

Acheson, Alan, *A History of the Church of Ireland, 1691–1990* (Dublin, 1997).

Akenson, D.H., *The Irish Education Experiment: the National System of Education in the Nineteenth Century* (London, 1970).

Akenson, D.H., *The Church of Ireland: Ecclesiastical Reform and Revolution, 1800–1885* (New Haven, CT, 1971).

Althoz, J.L., 'The political behaviour of the English Catholics, 1850–1867', *Journal of British Studies*, 4 (1964), 89–101.

Arnstein, W.L., *Protestant versus Catholic in mid-Victorian England: Mr Newdegate and the Nuns* (Columbia, 1982).

Atlay, J.B., *The Victorian Chancellors*, 2 vols (London, 1908).

Auchmuchty, J.J., 'Acton's Election as an Irish Member of Parliament', *English Historical Review*, 242 (1946), 394–405.

Bane, Liam, *The Bishop in Politics: Life and Career of John MacEvilly* (Westport, CT, 1993).

Bardon, Jonathan, *A History of Ulster* (Belfast, 1992).

Bartlett, Thomas, *The Fall and Rise of the Irish Nation: The Catholic Question, 1690–1830* (Dublin, 1992).

Bell, P.M.H., *Disestablishment in Ireland and Wales* (London, 1969).

Bence-Jones, Mark, *The Viceroys of India* (London, 1982).

Bence-Jones, Mark, *Twilight of the Ascendancy* (London, 1987).

Bernard, Toby, *A New Anatomy of Ireland: The Irish Protestants, 1649–1770* (New Haven, CT and London, 2003).

Bernstein, G.L., 'British Liberal politics and Irish Liberalism after O'Connell', in S.J. Brown and D.W. Miller (eds), *Piety and Power in Ireland: Essays in Honour of Emmet Larkin* (Belfast and Notre Dame, 2000), 43–64.

Best, G.F.A., 'The Protestant constitution and its supporters, 1800–1829', *Transactions of the Royal Historical Society*, 5th Series, 8 (1958), 105–27.

Bew, Paul, *Land and the National Question in Ireland, 1858–82* (Dublin, 1978).

Bew, Paul and Wright, Frank, 'The agrarian opposition in Ulster politics, 1848–87' in Samuel Clark and J.S. Donnelly (eds), *Irish Peasants: Violence and Political Unrest 1870–1914* (Manchester, 1983), 192–229.

Biggs-Davison, John and Chowdhary-Best, George, *The Cross of St Patrick: The Catholic Unionist Tradition in Ireland* (Abbotsbrook, 1984).

Blake, Robert, *Disraeli* (London, 1966).

Blake, Robert, *The Conservative Party from Peel to Thatcher* (London, 1985).

Bowen, Desmond, *The Protestant Crusade in Ireland 1800–70: A Study of Protestant–Catholic Relations Between the Act of Union and Disestablishment* (Dublin, 1978).

Bowen, Desmond, *Paul Cardinal Cullen and the Shaping of Modern Irish Catholicism* (Dublin, 1983).

Bowen, Desmond, *History and the Shaping of Irish Protestantism* (New York, 1995).

Boyce, D.G., *Nationalism in Ireland* (London, 1982 edn).

Boyce, D.G., *The Irish Question and British Politics, 1868–1986* (London, 1988).

Boyce, D.G., *Nineteenth Century Ireland: The Search for Stability* (Dublin, 1990).

Boyce, D.G., '"Trembling Solicitude": Irish Conservatism, nationality and public opinion', in D.G. Boyce, Robert Eccleshall and Vincent Geoghegan (eds), *Political Thought in Ireland Since the Seventeenth Century* (London, 1993), 124–41.

Boyce, D.G. and O'Day, Alan (eds), *Defenders of the Union: A Survey of British and Irish Unionism Since 1800* (London, 2001).

Bradley, Ian, *The Call to Seriousness: The Evangelical Impact on the Victorians* (London, 1976).

Brady, J.C., 'English law and Irish land in the nineteenth century', *Northern Ireland Legal Quarterly*, 23 (1972), 24–47.

Brady, J.C., 'Legal Developments, 1801–79', in W.E. Vaughan (ed.), *A New History of Ireland, Vol. 5, 1801–1870* (Oxford, 1980), 451–480.

Bromley, John, *The Man of Ten Talents: A Portrait of Richard Chenevix Trench, 1807–76: Philologist, Theologian, Archbishop* (London, 1959).

Brooke, Peter, *Ulster Presbyterianism: The Historical Perspective* (Dublin, 1987).

Brown, S.J., *The National Churches of England, Ireland and Scotland, 1801–1846* (Oxford, 2001).

Brynn, Edward, *The Church of Ireland in the Age of Catholic Emancipation* (New York, 1982).

Buckland, Patrick, *Irish Unionism, Vol. 1: The Anglo-Irish and the New Ireland, 1885–1922* (Dublin, 1972).

Budge, Ian and O'Leary, Cornelius, *Belfast, Approach to Crisis: A Study of Belfast Politics, 1613–1970* (London, 1973).

Bull, Philip, *Land, Politics and Nationalism: A Study of the Irish Land Question* (Dublin, 1996).

Bull, Philip, 'Isaac Butt, British Liberalism and an alternative nationalist tradition', in D.G. Boyce and Roger Swift (eds), *Problems and Perspectives in Irish History since 1800: Essays in Honour of Patrick Buckland* (Dublin, 2004), 147–63.

Butler, Perry, *Gladstone, Church, State and Tractarianism: A Study of his Religious Ideas and Attitudes, 1809–1859* (Oxford, 1982).

Cahill, G.A., 'Irish Catholicism and English Toryism', *Review of Politics*, 19 (1957), 62–76.

Callanan, Frank, *The Parnell Split, 1890–91* (Cork, 1992).

Cannadine, David, *The Decline and Fall of the British Aristocracy* (Oxford, 1996).

Chadwick, Owen, *The Victorian Church, Part 1: 1829–1859* (London, 1971).

Charmley, John, 'The view from Knowsley', *History Today*, 54 (2004), 47–53.

Comerford, R.V., *The Fenians in Context: Irish Politics and Society, 1848–82* (Dublin, 1985).

Comerford, R.V., 'Ireland 1850–57: Post-Famine and mid-Victorian', in W.E. Vaughan (ed.), *A New History of Ireland, Vol. 5, 1801–1870* (Oxford, 1980), 372–95.

Comerford, R.V., 'Churchmen, tenants and independent opposition, 1850–56', in W.E. Vaughan (ed.), *A New History of Ireland, Vol. 5, 1801–1870* (Oxford, 1980), 396–414.

Comerford, R.V., 'Conspiring brotherhoods and contending elites, 1857–63', in W.E. Vaughan (ed.), *A New History of Ireland, Vol. 5, 1801–1870* (Oxford, 1980), 415–30.

Comerford, R.V., 'Gladstone's first Irish enterprise, 1864–70', in W.E. Vaughan (ed.), *A New History of Ireland, Vol. 5, 1801–1870* (Oxford, 1980), 451–480.

Conacher, J.B., *The Aberdeen Coalition, 1852–1855: A Study in Mid-Nineteenth Century Party Politics* (Cambridge, 1968).

Conacher, J.B., *The Peelites and the Party System, 1846–52* (Newton Abbot, 1972).

Connolly, Sean, *Religion and Society in Nineteenth-century Ireland* (Dublin, 1985).

Connolly, Sean, *Religion, Law and Power: The Making of Protestant Ireland, 1660–1760* (Oxford, 1992).

Connolly, Sean, 'Reconsidering the Irish Act of Union', *Transactions of the Royal Historical Society*, Sixth Series, 10 (Cambridge, 2000), 399–408.

Conwell, J. J., *A Galway Landlord During the Great Famine: Ulick John De Burgh, First Marquis of Clanricarde* (Dublin, 2003).

Corish, Patrick, 'Catholic Ireland, 1864', *Irish Ecclesiastical Record*, 102 (1964), 196–205.

Corish, Patrick, 'Political problems, 1860–78', in Patrick Corish (ed.), *A History of Irish Catholicism*, Vol. 5, Fascicule 3 (Dublin, 1967).

Corish, Patrick, 'Cardinal Cullen and the National Association of Ireland', in Alan O'Day (ed.), *Reactions to Irish Nationalism, 1865–1914* (Dublin, 1987), 117–65.

Cowling, Maurice, 'Disraeli, Derby and fusion, October 1865 to July 1866, *Historical Journal*, 8 (1965), 31–71.

Cowling, Maurice, *1867: Disraeli, Gladstone and Revolution: The Passing of the Second Reform Bill* (Cambridge 1967).

Crossman, Virginia, *Politics, Law and Order in Nineteenth-century Ireland* (Dublin, 1996).

Cunningham, Rev. T.P., 'The Burrowes–Hughes by-election', *Breifne*, III (1967), 175–211.

Curtis, L.P., *Coercion and Conciliation in Ireland, 1880–1892: A Study in Conservative Unionism* (London, 1963).

Dagg, T.C., *College Historical Society: A History, 1770–1920* (Cork, 1969).

D'Alton, Ian, *Protestant Society and Politics in Cork, 1812–44* (Cork, 1980).

Davies, John, *A History of Wales* (London, 1994 edn).

Davis, Richard, *Revolutionary Imperialist: William Smith O'Brien* (Dublin and Sydney, 1998).

Delany, V.T.H., *Christopher Palles, Lord Chief Baron of His Majesty's Court of Exchequer in Ireland, 1874–1916: His Life and Times* (Dublin, 1960).

Devine, T.M., *The Scottish Nation, 1700–2000* (London, 1999).

Donnelly, James, *The Land and the People of Nineteenth-century Cork: The Rural Economy and the Land Question* (London, 1975).

Donnelly, James, *The Great Irish Potato Famine* (Stroud, 2001).

Dooley, Terence, *The Decline of the Big House in Ireland: A Study of Irish Landed Families* (Dublin, 2001).

Dowling, M.W., *Tenant Right and Agrarian Society in Ulster, 1600–1870* (Dublin, 1999).

Eccleshall, Robert, 'Anglican political thought in the century after the Revolution of 1688', in D.G. Boyce, Robert Eccleshall and Vincent Geoghegan (eds), *Political Thought in Ireland Since the Seventeenth Century*

(London, 1993), 36–72.

Faber, Richard, *Young England* (London, 1987).

Finlayson, Geoffrey, *The Seventh Earl of Shaftesbury, 1801–1885* (London, 1981).

Foster, R.F., *Lord Randolph Churchill: A Political Life* (Oxford, 1981).

Foster, R.F., *Modern Ireland, 1600–1972* (London, 1989).

Foster, R.F., 'To the Northern counties station: Lord Randolph Churchill and the Orange card', in *Paddy & Mr Punch: Connections in Irish and English History* (London, 1993), 233–61.

Foster, R.F., *The Irish Story: Telling Tales and Making It Up in Ireland* (London, 2001).

Gailey, Andrew, *Ireland and the Death of Kindness: The Experience of Constructive Unionism, 1890–1905* (Cork, 1987).

Gash, Norman, *Reaction and Reconstruction in English Politics, 1832–1852* (Oxford, 1965).

Gash, Norman, *Peel* (London, 1976 edn).

Gash, Norman, *Politics in the Age of Peel: A Study in the Technique of Parliamentary Representation, 1830–1850* (Hassocks, 1977 edn).

Gash, Norman, 'The organisation of the Conservative Party, 1832–46: part 1: the parliamentary organization', *Parliamentary History*, 1 (1982), 137–81.

Gash, Norman, 'The organisation of the Conservative Party, 1832–46: part 2: the electoral organization', *Parliamentary History*, 2 (1983), 131–52.

Ghosh, R.P., 'Disraelian Conservatism: a financial approach', *English Historical Review*, 99 (1984), 268–96.

Gibbon, Peter, *The Origins of Ulster Unionism: The Formation of Popular Protestant Politics and Ideology in Nineteenth Century Ireland* (Manchester, 1975).

Grant, James, 'The Great Famine and the Poor Law in Ulster: the rate-in-aid issue of 1849', *Irish Historical Studies*, 27 (1990), 30–47.

Gray, Peter, *Famine, Land and Politics: British Government and Irish Society, 1843–50* (Dublin, 1999).

Greenall, R.W., 'Popular Conservatism in Salford, 1868–1886', *Northern History: A Review of the History of the North of England*, 9 (1974), 123–38.

Greenlee, Graham, 'Land, religion and community: the Liberal Party in Ulster, 1868–85' in Eugenio Biagini (ed.), *Citizenship and Community: Liberals, Radicals and Collective Identity in the British Isles, 1865–1931* (Cambridge, 1996), 253–75.

Gurowich, P.M., 'The continuation of war by other means: party and politics, 1855–1865', *Historical Journal*, 27 (1984), 603–31.

Hanham, H.J., *Elections and Party Management: Politics in the Time of Disraeli and Gladstone* (London, 1959).

Hardinge, Sir A.H., *The LIfe of Henry Howard Molyneux Herbert, Fourth Earl of Carnarvon*, 3 vols (London 1925).

Hawkins, Angus, *Parliament, Party and the Art of Politics in Britain, 1855–59* (London, 1987).

Hawkins, Angus, 'Lord Derby and Victorian Conservatism: a reappraisal', *Parliamentary History*, 6 (1987), 280–301.

Hempton, David, 'Bickersteth, Bishop of Ripon: the episcopate of a mid-Victorian Evangelical', *Northern History, A Review of the History of the North of England*, 17 (1981), 183–202.

Hempton, David, *Religion and Political Culture in England and Ireland: From the Glorious Revolution to the Decline of the Empire* (Cambridge, 1996).

Hempton, David and Hill, Myrtle, *Evangelical Protestantism in Ulster society, 1740–1890* (London, 1992).

Heuston, R.V., 'Hugh McCalmont Cairns', *Northern Ireland Legal Quarterly*, 26 (1975), 269–290.

Hill, Jacqueline, 'The Protestant response to Repeal: the case of the Dublin working class' in F.S.L. Lyons and R.A.J. Hawkins (eds), *Ireland Under the Union, Varieties of Tension: Essays in Honour of T.W. Moody* (Oxford, 1980), 35–68.

Hill, Jacqueline, 'Artisans, sectarianism and politics in Dublin, 1829–48', *Saothar*, 7 (1981), 12–27.

Hill, Jacqueline, *From Patriots to Protestants: Dublin Civil Politics and Irish Protestant Patriotism, 1660–1840* (Oxford, 1997).

Hilton, Boyd., *The Age of Atonement: The Influence of Evangelicalism on Social and Economic Thought, 1783–1865* (Oxford, 1988).

Hogan, Daire, *The Legal Profession in Ireland, 1789–1922* (Naas, 1986).

Hogan, Daire, '"Vacancies for their friends": judicial appointments in Ireland, 1866–67' in Hogan, Daire and Onsborough, W.N. (eds), *Brehons, Serjeants and Attorneys* (Dublin, 1990), 211–29.

Holmes, R.F., *Henry Cooke* (Belfast, 1981).

Hoppen, K.T., 'Tories, Catholics and the general election of 1859', *Historical Journal*, 13 (1970), 48–67.

Hoppen, K.T., 'National politics and local realities in mid-nineteenth century Ireland', in A. Cosgrave and Donal McCartney (eds), *Studies in Irish History Presented to R. Dudley Edwards* (Dublin, 1974), 190–227.

Hoppen, K.T., 'Landlords, society and electoral politics in mid-nineteenth century Ireland', *Past & Present*, 75 (1977), 62–93.

Hoppen, K.T., *Elections, Politics and Society in Ireland, 1832–1885* (Oxford, 1984).

Hoppen, K.T., *Ireland since 1800: Conflict and Conformity* (London, 1989).

Hoppen, K.T., 'Priests at the hustings: ecclesiastical electioneering in nineteenth century Ireland' in Posada-Carbo, Eduardo (ed.), *Elections Before Democracy: The History of Elections in Europe and Latin America* (London, 1990).

Hoppen, K.T., *The Mid-Victorian Generation, 1846–1886* (Oxford, 1998).

Howell, P.A., *The Judicial Committee of the Privy Council, 1833–1876: Its Origins, Structure and Development* (Cambridge, 1979).

Hutchinson, I.G.C., *A Political History of Scotland, 1832–1914* (Edinburgh, 1986).

Jackson, Alvin, *The Ulster Party: Irish Unionists in the House of Commons, 1884–1911* (Oxford, 1989).

Jackson, Alvin, *Ireland, 1798–1998: Politics and War* (Oxford, 1999).

Jackson, Alvin, 'Irish Unionism, 1870–1922', in D.G. Boyce and Alan O'Day (eds), *Defenders of the Union: A Survey of British and Irish Unionism Since 1800* (London, 2001), 115–36.

Jackson, Alvin, *Home Rule: An Irish History, 1800–2000* (London, 2003).

Jackson, Alvin, 'Ireland, the Union and the Empire' in Kevin Kenny (ed.), *Ireland and the British Empire* (Oxford, 2004), 123–153.

Jenkins, Brian, *Sir William Gregory of Coole: A Biography* (Gerard's Cross, 1986).

Jenkins, T.A., 'Benjamin Disraeli and the spirit of England', *History Today*, 54 (2004), 9–15.

Jones, W.D., *Lord Derby and Victorian Conservatism* (Oxford, 1956).

Keenan, Desmond, *The Catholic Church in Nineteenth Century Ireland: A Sociological Study* (Dublin, 1983).

Kerr, D.A., *Peel, Priests and Politics: Sir Robert Peel's Administration and the Roman Catholic Church in Ireland, 1841–46* (Oxford, 1982).

Kerr, D.A., *A Nation of Beggars: Priests, People, and Politics in Famine Ireland 1846–52* (Oxford, 1994).

Knowlton, S.R., *Popular Politics and the Irish Catholic Church: The Rise and Fall of the Independent Irish Party, 1850–1859* (Stanford, CA, 1991).

Kriegel, A.D., 'The Irish policy of Lord Grey's government', *English Historical Review*, 86 (1971), 22–45.

Larkin, Emmet, 'The devotional revolution in Ireland', *American Historical Review*, 77, (1972), 625–652.

Larkin, Emmet, *The Making of the Roman Catholic Church in Ireland, 1850–1860* (Chapel Hill, NC, 1980).

Larkin, Emmet, The *Consolidation of the Roman Catholic Church in Ireland 1860–70* (Dublin, 1987).

Larkin, Emmet, *The Historical Dimensions of Irish Catholicism* (Dublin and Washington, 1997).

Lee, Joseph, *The Modernization of Irish Society, 1848–1918* (Dublin, 1973).

Lyons, F.S.L., *Ireland Since the Famine* (2nd edn, London, 1972).

Macatasney, Gerard, 'The educational views of [Archbishop] John McHale', *Cathair na Mairt: Journal of the Westport Historical Society*, 14 (1994), 39–64.

McCaffrey, L.J., 'Irish federalism in the 1870s, a study in Conservative Nationalism', *Transactions of the American Philosophical Society*, New Series,

52, Part 6 (1962).

McCormack, W.J., *Ascendancy and Tradition in Anglo-Irish Literary History from 1789 to 1839* (Oxford, 1985).

McCormack, W.J., *Sheridan Le Fanu and Victorian Ireland* (Dublin 1991 edn).

MacDonagh, Oliver, 'The politicization of the Irish Catholic bishops, 1800–1850', *Historical Journal*, 18 (1975), 37–53.

MacDonagh, Oliver, *Ireland: the Union and its Aftermath* (London, 1977).

MacDonagh, Oliver, *States of Mind: A Study of Anglo-Irish Conflict* (London, 1983).

MacDonagh, Oliver, *O'Connell: The Life of Daniel O'Connell* (London, 1991).

Mc Dowell, R.B., 'The Irish executive in the nineteenth century', *Irish Historical* Studies, 9 (1955), 264–80.

McDowell, R.B., *British Conservatism, 1832–1914* (London, 1959).

McDowell, R.B., *The Irish Administration, 1801–1914* (London and Toronto, 1964).

McDowell, R.B., *The Church of Ireland, 1869–1969* (London, 1975).

McDowell, R.B., *Land & Learning: Two Irish Clubs* (Dublin, 1993).

McEldowney, John, 'Lord O'Hagan (1812–1885): a study of his life and period as Lord Chancellor of Ireland (1868–74)', *The Irish Jurist*, 14 (1979), 360–77.

Machin, G.I.T., 'The Maynooth Grant, the dissenters and disestablishment, 1845–47', *English Historical Review*, 82 (1967), 61–85.

Machin, G.I.T., *Politics and the Churches in Great Britain, 1832 to 1868* (Oxford 1977).

Macintyre, Angus, *The Liberator: Daniel O'Connell and the Irish Party, 1830–1847* (New York, 1965).

Maguire, Martin, 'The organisation and activism of Dublin's Protestant working class, 1883–1935', *Irish Historical Studies*, 29 (1994), 65–87.

Malcolmson, A.P.W., *John Foster: The Politics of the Anglo-Irish Ascendancy* (Oxford, 1978).

Matthew, H.C.G., *Gladstone: 1809–1874* (Oxford, 1986).

Miller, D.W., *Queen's Rebels: Ulster Loyalism in Historical Perspective* (Dublin, 1978).

Monypenny, W.F. and Buckle, G.E., *The Life of Benjamin Disraeli, Earl of Beaconsfield*, 6 vols (London, 1910–20).

Moore, M.G., *An Irish Gentleman: George Henry Moore: His Travels, his Racing, his Politics* (London, 1913).

Napier, Sir Joseph, *An Account of the Napiers of Luton Hoo (1600–1797) and of the Descendants of the Branch which Settled in Woodstock, (1620–1700), Ireland (1700–1884) and Later Removed to England* (privately printed, n.d.).

Norman, E.R., *The Catholic Church and Ireland in the Age of Rebellion,*

1859–1873 (London, 1965).

Norman, E.R., *The Catholic Church and Irish Politics in the Eighteen Sixties* (Dundalk, 1965).

Nowlam, K.B, 'Disestablishment: 1800–1869' in Hurley, Michael (ed.), *Irish Anglicanism, 1869–1969* (Dublin, 1970), 1–22.

O'Farrell, Patrick, *Ireland's English Question: Anglo-Irish Relations, 1534–1970* (London, 1971).

O'Ferrall, Fergus, *Catholic Emancipation: Daniel O'Connell and the Birth of Irish Democracy* (Dublin, 1985).

O'Grada, Cormac, *Ireland Before and After the Famine: Explorations in Economic History, 1800–1925* (Manchester, 1993 edn).

O'Grada, Cormac, *Ireland: A New Economic History, 1780–1939* (Oxford, 1994).

O'Shea, James, *Priests, Politics, and Society in Post-Famine Ireland: A Study of County Tipperary, 1850–1891* (Dublin, 1983).

O'Shea, James, *Prince of Swindlers: John Sadleir, M.P., 1813–1856* (Dublin, 1999).

Parry, J.P., *The Rise and Fall of Liberal Government in Victorian Britain* (New Haven, CT and London, 1993).

Parry, J.P., 'Disraeli and England', *Historical Journal*, 43 (2000), 699–728.

Peatling, G. K., *British Opinion and Irish Self-Government: From Unionism to Liberal Commonwealth* (Dublin, 2002).

Pope-Hennessey, James, *Verandah: Some Episodes in the Crown Colonies, 1867–89* (London, 1964).

Pottinger, George, *Mayo: Disraeli's Viceroy* (Salisbury, 1990).

Ramsden, John, *An Appetite for Power: A History of the Conservative Party since 1830* (London, 1999 edn).

Ridley, Jane, *The Young Disraeli, 1804–1846* (London, 1995).

Ridley, Jasper, *Lord Palmerston* (London, 1972).

Royle, S.A., 'The Lisburn by-elections of 1863', *Irish Historical Studies*, 25 (1987), 277–292.

Savage, D.C., 'The Irish Unionists, 1867–1886', *Eire-Ireland*, 2 (1967), 86–101.

Shannon, Richard, *The Age of Disraeli 1868–1881: The Rise of Tory Democracy* (London, 1992).

Shannon, Richard, *Gladstone: Peel's Inheritor, 1809–1865* (London, 1999 edn).

Shannon, Richard, *Gladstone: Heroic Minister, 1865–98* (London, 1999).

Sheedy, Kieran, *The Clare Elections* (Dun Laoghaire, 1993).

Smith, Paul, *Disraelian Conservatism and Social Reform* (London, 1967).

Smyth, A.P., *Faith, Famine and Fatherland in the Irish Midlands: Perceptions of a Priest and Historian, Anthony Cogan, 1826–1872* (Dublin, 1992).

Southgate, Donald, *The Most English Minister: The Policies and Politics of*

Palmerston (London, 1960).

Southgate, Donald, *The Passing of the Whigs, 1832–1886* (London, 1962).

Spence, Joseph, 'Isaac Butt, nationality and Irish Toryism, 1833–1852', *Bullán*, 2 (1995), 45–60.

Spence, Joseph, 'Isaac Butt, Irish nationality and the conditional defence of the Union, 1833–70' in D.G. Boyce and Alan O'Day (eds), *Defenders of the Union: A Survey of British and Irish Unionism since 1800* (London, 2001), 65–89.

Steele, E.D., *Irish Land and British Politics: Tenant Right and Nationality, 1865–1870* (Cambridge, 1974).

Steele, E.D., *Palmerston and Liberalism, 1855–65* (Cambridge, 1991).

Stevenson, Lionel, *Dr Quicksilver: The Life of Charles Lever* (London, 1939).

Stewart, Robert, *The Politics of Protection: Lord Derby and the Protectionist Party, 1841–1852* (Cambridge, 1971).

Stewart, Robert, *The Foundation of the Conservative Party, 1830–1867* (London, 1978).

Stewart, Robert, 'The Conservative reaction': Lord Robert Cecil and party politics', in Robert Blake and H. Cecil, (eds), *Salisbury: The Man and His Policies* (Basingstoke, 1987), 90–115.

Stewart, Robert, *Party and Politics, 1830–1852* (London, 1989).

Thomas, J.A., *The House of Commons, 1832–1901: A Study of its Economic and Functional Character* (Cardiff, 1939).

Thompson, Frank, *The End of Liberal Ulster: Land Agitation and Land Reform* (Belfast, 2001).

Thornley, David, *Isaac Butt and Home Rule* (London, 1964).

Thornley, David, 'The Irish Conservatives and Home Rule, 1869–73', *Irish Historical Studies*, 11 (1959), 200–22.

Townshend, Charles, *Political Violence in Ireland: Government and Resistance Since 1848* (Oxford, 1983).

Turner, Michael, *After the Famine: Irish Agriculture, 1850–1914* (Cambridge, 1996).

Vaughan, W.E., 'An assessment of the economic performance of Irish landlords, 1851–81', in F.S.L. Lyons and R.A.J. Hawkins (eds), *Ireland Under the Union: Varieties of Tension* (Oxford, 1980), 173–99.

Vaughan, W.E., (ed.), *A New History of Ireland: Vol. 5: 1801–1870* (Oxford, 1980).

Vaughan, W.E. *Landlords and Tenants in Mid-Victorian Ireland* (Oxford, 1997).

Vincent, J.R., *The Formation of the British Liberal Party, 1857–1868* (Hassocks, 1976 edn).

Walker, B.M., 'Party organisation in Ulster, 1865–92: registration agents and their Activities', in P. Roebuck (ed.), *Plantation to Partition: Essays in Ulster History in Honour of J.L. McCracken* (Belfast, 1981), 191–209.

Walker, B.M., *Ulster Politics: The Formative Years, 1868–86* (Belfast, 1989).

Ward, J.T., *Sir James Graham* (London, 1967).

Warren, Alan, 'Disraeli, the Conservative Party and the government of Ireland, 1837–68', *Parliamentary History*, 18 (1999), 45–64.

Warren, Alan, 'Disraeli, the Conservative Party and the government of Ireland, 1868–81', *Parliamentary History*, 18 (1999), 145–67.

Warren, Alan, 'Disraeli, the Conservatives and the National Church, 1837–81', *Parliamentary History*, 19 (2000), 96–117.

Whibley, Charles, *Lord John Manners and His Friends*, 2 vols (London, 1925).

White, Terence De Vere, *The Road of Excess* (Dublin, 1947).

Whyte, J. H., *The Independent Irish Party, 1850–9* (Oxford, 1958).

Whyte, J. H., 'Landlord influence at elections in Ireland, 1760–1885', *English Historical Review*, 80 (1965), 740–60.

Whyte, J. H., *The Tenant League and Irish Politics in the Eighteen-fifties* (Dundalk, 1966).

Whyte, J. H., 'Political problems, 1850–60', in P. Corish (ed.), *A History of Irish Catholicism*, Vol. 5, Fascicule 3 (Dublin, 1967).

Wolffe, John, *The Protestant Crusade in Great Britain, 1829–1860* (Oxford, 1991).

Wright, Frank, *Two Lands on One Soil: Ulster Politics Before Home Rule* (Dublin, 1996).

Wylie, J. C., *Irish Landlord and Tenant Law* (Dublin, 1990).

Wynne, Maud, *An Irishman and His Family: Lord Morris and Killanin* (London, 1937).

VII. UNPUBLISHED THESES

Holmes, R. F., 'Henry Cooke, 1788–1868', University of Dublin, M.Litt. thesis, 1970.

McNiffe, Liam, 'The politicisation of Leitrim, Sligo and Mayo in the general election of 1852', St Patrick's College, Maynooth, MA thesis, 1979.

Melvin, Patrick, 'The landed gentry of Galway, 1820–1880', University of Dublin, Ph.D. thesis, 1991.

Spence, Joseph, 'The philosophy of Irish Toryism 1833–52: a study of reactions to liberal reformism in Ireland in the generation between the first reform act and the famine, with especial reference to expressions of national feeling among the Protestant ascendancy', Birkbeck College, University of London, Ph.D. thesis, 1990.

Index